LITERARY DISSENT IN
COMMUNIST CHINA

ORIGINALLY PUBLISHED BY HARVARD UNIVERSITY PRESS
IN THE HARVARD EAST ASIAN SERIES

Merle   Goldman

LITERARY

DISSENT
in
COMMUNIST

CHINA

E   70

ATHENEUM   *New York*   *1971*

Published by Atheneum
Reprinted by arrangement with Harvard University Press
Copyright © 1967 by the President and Fellows of Harvard College
All rights reserved
Library of Congress catalog card number 67-17311
Manufactured in the United States of America by
The Murray Printing Company
Forge Village, Massachusetts
Published in Canada by McClelland and Stewart Ltd.
First Atheneum Edition

TO MARSHALL

PREFACE

This book focuses on the conflict between the Chinese Communist party and China's writers in the 1940's and 1950's. The events of the 1960's and the Cultural Revolution are not included. Nevertheless, the story told here of unorthodox intellectuals, recalcitrant youth, and revisionist influences describes the milieu from which the Cultural Revolution has evolved. An understanding of this earlier period illuminates the dramatic happenings of the sixties — the subject, I hope, of my next endeavor.

Without the help and stimulation of various people, it is certain that this book would never have been written. My adviser, John K. Fairbank, professor of history at Harvard, has shown infinite patience, given constant encouragement, and provided invaluable counsel. Professor Benjamin Schwartz, also of Harvard, has asked provocative questions and offered thoughtful suggestions. Many of my colleagues deserve my thanks. I am especially grateful to Anne Clark, Edward Friedman, Winston Hsieh, Robert Irick, Priscilla Johnson, Donald Klein, Roy Hofheinz, C. T. Hsia, the late T. A. Hsia, John Israel, Mark Mancall, Harriet Mills, David Roy, and Lyman Van Slyke. Leo Ou-fan Lee has given me valuable assistance with the Chinese translations and has conscientiously rechecked my notes. Bonita Colburn has typed the manuscript with dedication, and Jan Pinkerton has offered editorial advice. The Radcliffe Institute for Independent Study has provided financial help, and the East Asian Research Center at Harvard has given me material and spiritual support. Portions of Chapter 2 are based upon an article published in *The China Quarterly* and are used with the permission of the editor, Roderick MacFarquhar.

Most important of all has been the assistance of my family — my parents, my in-laws, and my four children, Ethan, Avra, Karla, and Seth. They have all been understanding, forbearing, and good-humored throughout the long period that has finally brought forth this book. Above all, I must thank my husband, who has given his limited time to edit and act as "devil's advocate" for what is set forth here.

Cambridge, Massachusetts   MERLE GOLDMAN
October 1966

CONTENTS

Profiles of the Major Protagonists   xi

one   The Conflict Between the Party and Revolutionary Writers   1

two   Literary Opposition During the Yenan Period   18

three   Conflicts Between Left-Wing Writers in the KMT Area
and the CCP   51

four   Resumption of Thought Reform Drives in 1948   67

five   Re-emergence of Literary Factions, 1949–1952   87

six   The Relaxation of 1953 and the Campaign Against
Feng Hsüeh-feng in 1954   106

seven   The Hu Feng Campaign of 1955   129

eight   Writers Bloom in the Hundred Flowers Movement   158

nine   The Antirightist Drive Against the Writers, 1957–1958   203

ten   The Great Leap Forward and Ho Ch'i-fang   243

eleven   The Significance of Literary Dissent   272

Notes   281

Bibliography   307

Glossary   329

Index   331

PROFILES OF THE MAJOR
PROTAGONISTS

THE REVOLUTIONARY WRITERS

Ai Ch'ing, a poet famous for his epic poetry about the war, was born in Chekiang in 1910, the son of a landlord. Well-schooled in the Confucian classics, he also studied art in Paris. There he became interested in impressionist painting, French symbolist poetry, and the works of Byron, Pushkin, Whitman, and the Soviet poet, Mayakovsky. He also came in contact with leftist movements. On his return to China in 1932, he went to live in Shanghai, where, soon after, he was arrested for participating in a Marxist study group and was imprisoned for three years. After his release, he began to write poetry which vividly evoked the sufferings of the times through strong emotional force and powerful imagery. The robust quality of his poems won him a large audience in China and abroad. When the Sino-Japanese War broke out around Shanghai in 1937, he went to Yenan, where the Chinese Communist party had established its headquarters after the Long March. In the 1940's and the first half of the 1950's, he held several influential political and editorial posts, but was purged in the antirightist movement of 1957.

Feng Hsüeh-feng, an essayist and poet, was regarded as the closest confidant of China's most famous modern writer, Lu Hsün. Born in Chekiang around the turn of the century, he began his career as a poet. In the early 1920's, he wrote lyrical panegyrics to love and nature. Toward the end of the decade when he became a member of the Chinese Communist party, he directed his literary talents more to essays of a polemical nature than to poetry. He became active in the party's political and cultural subversion of the 1930's and participated in the Long March. Yet, his literary ideas stressed the spontaneity and individual emotions expressed in his earlier poems. During the Sino-Japanese War, he remained in the Kuomintang areas, but when the party took over the mainland, he was given several prominent positions, among them the editorship of Communist China's most important cultural journal, *Wen-i pao* (Literary gazette). Nevertheless, he was denounced in 1954 and again in 1957.

Ho Ch'i-fang, a lyrical poet, was born in 1911 in Szechwan and given a strict Confucian education. In 1931, he entered Peking University and soon after began to publish poetry. Unlike his fellow revolutionary writers, he did not participate in the left-wing movements in Shanghai of the 1930's, but remained in Peking among literary groups more concerned with literary standards than with political ideas. He was influenced by the English school of poetry and the French impressionist and symbolist poets. In 1936 he published several collections of poetry which marked him as a poet of stature. His poems, which expressed the subtleties of nature and the longings of his personal dreams, were written in beautifully controlled literary language. In the late 1930's, he went to Yenan, where he became a spokesman for the party's cultural policies. Nevertheless, his poems continued to reflect his own individual feelings and his concern with disciplined literary style. He clashed openly with the party's literary bureaucrats in 1959 and 1960.

Hsiao Chün was regarded as the most prominent modern writer from Manchuria. Born in 1908 of peasant stock, he held various jobs in his youth. For a while, he was a vagabond wandering through the northeast, and for a time he fought with the guerrillas in Manchuria. Though he had no systematic education, he studied Chinese classical poetry and a wide range of Western literature on his own. In 1934, he went to Shanghai, where he published, with the help of Lu Hsün, a novel, *Village in August*. It was an immediate success and a best seller for years. Though the style was clumsy, its description of conditions in Manchuria and its cry for all-out war with Japan gained for the party a large public receptive to its demands. Still, there were many aspects of the novel that did not conform to the current Comintern line. Hsiao depicted the people's resistance to the Japanese as a spontaneous movement rather than one led by the party, and he portrayed the masses not as heroes, but as ignorant and sometimes brutal, yet under certain circumstances capable of great deeds. He worked with the party for several years at its base in Yenan and returned to Manchuria when the party took it over in 1946. There he criticized certain aspects of the party's policies and subsequently was made the target of the rectification drive of 1948.

Hu Feng, a poet and literary theorist, urged Chinese writers to break away from the shackles of Chinese tradition and come under the influence of Western realism. Like Feng Hsüeh-feng, he also emphasized the emotional and individual quality of literary creation. He was born in 1903 into a poor family in Hupeh. The financial circumstances of his family improved enough to send him to Nanking for his education. There he became a member of the Communist Youth League for a short period in the mid-1920's and joined the May 30th strike of 1925. Like many other left-wing intellectuals after the Kuomintang-Chinese Communist party split of 1927, he went to Japan. There he was imprisoned for leftist activities. He returned to China in 1933 and became involved in the left-wing literary movement in Shanghai, where he gained a position of leadership and a coterie of young writers. In the late 1930's and throughout the 1940's, he wandered through the southern part of China, where in various cities he set up literary journals which protested against political control of creative activity. He was made the focus of a year-long, nationwide campaign in 1955.

Ting Ling, considered one of China's foremost novelists, was born in 1909 into a well-to-do family in Hunan. Her father died when she was young, and her mother — a militant feminist — joined the party in 1927. Influenced by her mother and by Communist youth groups at Shanghai University, which she attended in the late 1920's, she was active in several leftist and anarchist movements. At this time, she also began to read widely in Western literature, especially Gorki, Tolstoy, Flaubert, and de Maupassant, and to write short stories. Her early works were highly personal, focusing on the emotional crises of youth and students. Most of her heroines were like herself — young girls who rebelled against the patriarchal society in order to lead their own lives and win personal freedom. She articulated the exasperations of youth living in a society in transition. In 1931 she joined the party and was arrested in 1933 by the Kuomintang for her leftist activities. Upon her release in 1936, she went to Yenan, where she held several posts, the most important as literary editor of the party's official newspaper, *Chieh-fang jih-pao* (Liberation daily). In 1948 she published a novel on land reform, *Sun Over the Sangkan River*, which was the first Chinese novel to win the Stalin prize. With the establishment of the Communist government in 1949, she was given several positions of leadership in the intellectual realm and was regarded as a spokesman for women and particularly for young intellectuals. She maintained her prestige and influence among these groups until 1957 when the party launched an intensive campaign against her.

Wang Shih-wei, an old revolutionary, was known primarily as a translator of Marxist-Leninist works. In 1926 he joined the party, but a few years later became close to several Trotskyites, published in their journals, and translated some of Trotsky's works. He was in Moscow in the early 1930's, where he studied Communist ideology. When he returned to China in the later part of the decade, he had broken off his connections with his former Trotskyite associates. He went to Yenan, where he lectured in the party training school and was regarded as an authority on ideology. Nevertheless, he continued to express independent views on theoretical questions. When the party embarked on its first ideological remolding campaign in 1942, his heterodoxy was made the focus of attack.

THE LITERARY BUREAUCRATS

Ai Szu-ch'i, born in Yunnan, was one of the top theoreticians on Marxism-Leninism from the late 1930's until the mid-1950's. In the 1930's he lectured on dialectical materialism in Shanghai and worked actively to promote the policy of a United Front adopted by the party in 1935. In the late 1930's, he went to Yenan, where he was the editor of several party journals and was active in prosecuting the party's thought reform campaign of the early 1940's. When the party won control of the mainland in 1949, he became editor of

Hsüeh-hsi (Study), the party's most important theoretical journal until its dissolution in 1958. He tended to work behind the scenes in imposing ideological controls over the intellectuals.

Ch'en Po-ta, an ideologist and writer, is supposedly the ghost writer of a number of Mao Tse-tung's reports and speeches. He was born in Fukien around 1905 of poor peasant stock. Soon after receiving his secondary school training in Amoy, he joined the party and worked as a political activist during the Northern Expedition. With the 1927 split between the Chinese Communist party and Kuomintang, Ch'en fled to the Soviet Union, where he studied at Sun Yat-sen University, an ideological training center for Asian students. He returned to China in 1930, and expounded a Marxist-Leninist interpretation of history and philosophy at China University in Peking. About 1937, he went to Yenan, where he taught in the party training school, acted as personal secretary to Mao Tse-tung, and became the director of research of the Propaganda Department of the party, a post he maintained once the party took over the mainland. In 1945, he became a member of the Central Committee and in 1956 an alternate member of the Politburo. His most important positions are as editor of *Hung ch'i* (Red flag), which became the party's chief theoretical journal after the demise of *Hsüeh-hsi* and as a writer of editorials for *Jen-min jih-pao* (People's daily), the party's official newspaper. In 1966, he was identified as head of the Cultural Revolution. Since the Yenan days, he has steadily moved forward as one of Mao Tse-tung's spokesmen on ideology.

Chou Yang, from the early 1940's until the mid-1960's, was the Chinese Communist party's official mouthpiece and ideological watchdog in the literary and intellectual realm. He was in charge of the ideological orthodoxy of the higher intellectuals. Born in Hunan in 1908, Chou attended Ta Hsia, Great China University in Shanghai, and in 1928 went to study in Japan. Though he studied English literature, his main literary endeavors were translations of Russian literature, particularly Tolstoy's *Anna Karenina* and the works of the nineteenth-century populist writer Chernyshevski. He was arrested for participating in a leftist demonstration in Japan and returned to China in 1930. Soon after, he became a party member and an organizer of party activities in Shanghai. In 1937 he left for Yenan, where he was made director of education in the Communist-controlled Shen-si-Kansu-Ninghsia Border Region and head of Yenan University. When the party took over the mainland, he held several posts in literary organizations and became deputy-director of the Propaganda Department. He wielded much more power than his official positions connote. His chief function was his unofficial responsibility in evolving a pattern of ideological control not only in literature, but in every sphere of intellectual activity. Throughout the 1940's and 1950's, he organized ideological remolding campaigns which set the pattern for tightening ideological standards in the creative arts, the humanities, and the social sciences. His chief assistants throughout this period were the literary theorist Shao Ch'üan-lin, the ballad writer Yüan Shui-p'o, and the poet Lin Mo-han. In the summer of 1966, he was made the chief scapegoat of the Cultural Revolution.

Kuo Mo-jo has been a dynamic leader in Chinese culture for several decades. By general acclaim, he and the novelist Mao Tun have been regarded second only to Lu Hsün as China's leading writers. He was born in 1892 in Szechwan into a wealthy family. He left China for Japan in 1913 to study medicine. There he became interested in literature and was influenced by Heine, Goethe, Shelley, Tagore, and Walt Whitman. From the time he returned to China in 1921 until 1949, he wrote a voluminous collection of poems, short stories, and plays, several volumes of autobiography, studies of ancient Chinese oracle bones and bronze inscriptions, translations from Japanese, English, and German, and numerous essays. He introduced Western images and Western expressions into his poetry. He founded many journals, organized literary coteries, served in government, participated in revolutionary activities, and was forced into exile several times. The Creation Society, which he helped establish in 1921, reflected Kuo's own ideological development. Starting as a coterie dedicated to the quest for beauty, it became by the mid-1920's an organization instrumental in making proletarian-oriented literature the creed of Chinese literary circles. With the party take-over, his writing was reduced to public addresses, reports, a few plays, and occasional poetry, now written in the vocabulary of the folk song. He became vice-premier of the government from 1949 to

1954, vice-chairman of the Chinese People's Political Consultative Conference, chairman of the All-China Federation of Literary and Art Circles, and president of the Academy of Sciences. Nominally, he was in charge of research and creativity in Communist China, but in fact, he has been a front man for the party. He has carried out its bidding without any deviation. In contrast to Mao Tun, who has also conformed to the party's line, he has not revealed any of his previous concern with literary and humane values beneath his apparent orthodoxy.

LITERARY DISSENT IN
COMMUNIST CHINA

ABBREVIATIONS IN TEXT

ACFLAC	All-China Federation of Literary and Art Circles
CC	Central Committee
CCP	Chinese Communist party
CDL	Chinese Democratic League
CPPCC	Chinese People's Political Consultative Conference
GLF	The Great Leap Forward
JMJP	*Jen-min jih-pao*
KMJP	*Kuang-ming jih-pao*
KMT	Kuomintang
NPC	National People's Congress

chapter one

THE CONFLICT BETWEEN THE PARTY AND REVOLUTIONARY WRITERS

Throughout the history of China, every ruling group has sought to gain the allegiance of the intellectual class and to impose upon it an orthodox doctrine guiding all of its activities. The Chinese Communist regime is no exception. In the manner of past Chinese governments, the Communist leadership has sought to utilize the skills of the intellectuals and to indoctrinate them with an all-embracing ideology — the ideology being Marxism-Leninism rather than the traditional Confucianism. With modern technology and modern means of communication at its disposal, the party has been able to achieve its aim more comprehensively and more intensively than the rulers of old. From the early 1940's on, it has attempted to impose a form of internalized consensus through an unending series of ideological remolding campaigns directed toward the intellectuals.

Yet party policy toward the intellectuals has not been simply one of repression. Because the Communist regime is determined to build an industrialized society, it is on guard against producing an atmosphere which might permanently stifle the initiative and creativity of the intellectuals who are needed to modernize China. Therefore, the party has carried out a contradictory policy. On the one hand, it has compelled thinking individuals to a strict orthodoxy, and, on the other, it has tried to stimulate them to carry on creatively and productively with their work. This contradictory approach has resulted in a policy toward the intellectuals which has oscillated between pressure and relaxation. The party has pressed down on the intellectuals and then relaxed its pressure with varying degrees of intensity.

These shifts in policy have been determined in large part by internal economic and political factors and sometimes by international events. They have not necessarily been planned ahead of time by party leaders, but are a result of the circumstances in which the party finds itself. During periods of economic crisis, for example, the party has eased somewhat its pressures on the intellectuals in order to gain their cooperation in solving the problems it faces. Its oscillating approach toward the intellectuals has also been governed by an inner dialectic of its own, as it has sought to establish an equilibrium between the opposing forces of orthodoxy and creativity. The party has driven toward orthodoxy until the intellectuals appeared reluctant to produce and create; then it has relaxed until its political control appeared threatened. Though the main concentration has been on either pressure or relaxation at any one time, there have always been minor countercurrents present which could be revived when circumstances demanded a reversal.

In the brief intervals of relative relaxation, the party has fostered, or at least permitted, criticism of the party functionaries, called the cadres, by the intellectuals. It also has sought to enhance the position of the intellectuals and impress the population, particularly the cadres, with the crucial role the intellectuals have to play in China's development. Convinced that once the grip of the routinized, semiliterate cadres over the intellectuals is loosened intellectual activity will flourish, the party has used these techniques as its main instruments for encouraging intellectual ferment. By demonstrating to the cadres that there is another group, the intellectuals, who could carry out their functions, the party has also used these methods to keep the power of the cadres in check. At such times, the internal conflicts, pent-up ideological disputes, animosities, and intrigues disrupting the intellectual world have welled to the surface.

Invariably, the most vocal group to speak out in these intervals has been a small number of revolutionary, left-wing writers. The most prominent among them were the literary theorists Hu Feng and Feng Hsüeh-feng, the translator Wang Shih-wei, the novelists Ting Ling and Hsiao Chün, and the poets Ai Ch'ing and Ho Ch'i-fang. They were joined in the Hundred Flowers period by several younger writers, of whom the most outspoken were Ch'in Ch'ao-yang and Liu Shao-t'ang. They are called revolutionary because they criticized the regime in power, whether the KMT or the CCP. In the 1920's and 1930's, they were rebels against the established order.

They used their writings to attack the prevailing political system and to expose the social evils of the time. They considered their works powerful weapons in a heroic struggle against the forces of darkness and in behalf of the oppressed. This romantic view of their writing has some validity. Though these writers were not necessarily the most distinguished, they did exert widespread influence in Chinese society. In the final analysis, the Communist party in China came to power not only by championing the cause of the peasant, but also by winning the sympathy of the intellectuals, students, clerks, and journalists in the cities and towns. A pivotal force in arousing the sympathy of the educated class for the revolutionary cause was the works of these revolutionary writers.

Yet, once the party established a base of power, these writers were among the first to voice dissatisfaction with the inconsistency between Communist ideals and communism as a political reality run by party functionaries. They retained their faith in the utopian view of communism, but intermittently they continued the life of protest and criticism they had led under the KMT. What they protested against in the 1940's and 1950's, however, was quite different from what they had preached before the party came to power. No longer were they political and social reformers seeking to impose a new order. They were now critics of the very system they had worked to establish. However, as the party's authoritarian controls were imposed in one area after another, they found they were no longer able to hold dissident views and to preserve their intellectual integrity as they had under the ineffectual control of the KMT. Because of their inability to fit into the world for which they had fought, many of them resorted in time to conscious, though unorganized, opposition to certain features of party control. They expressed their opposition by setting forth a set of values different from the official ideology, yet they never questioned Marxist-Leninist doctrine nor the establishment of a Communist system for China.

The party's response to these critics was far out of proportion to the provocation. The works of these writers could have been banned and they could have been imprisoned or killed as was done with dissident writers under Stalin. But instead the CCP used them and their writings as the focus for its thought reform campaigns. Though the ebb and flow of these campaigns were dictated in large part by circumstance, once they were initiated the party molded them into very conscious, organized endeavors. The campaigns usually started from the capital and spread outward. Repeatedly, they reached their climax during the summers, when they would be less disruptive to work in the universities and offices. Most important, the party used the time-honored Soviet practice of making a point of general application by singling out an individual as a scapegoat and holding him up for censure. The revolutionary writers became the prime scapegoats of the party in its attempt to shape the thinking and outlook of China's intellectuals. The party would explain some program to be enacted or theory to be understood universally by demonstrating that one or more of these writers represented a certain pattern of thinking and behavior diametrically opposed to the party's current policy. Also, by condemning these individuals the regime sought to channel hostility for its mistakes onto them. Finally, this procedure served as a technique of governing designed to purge the intellectuals of heterodox ideas and disgruntled attitudes and to inculcate them with the party line.

The choice of the revolutionary writers as scapegoats was determined partly by ideological and partly by factional reasons. Though these writers were charged at various times in the 1940's and 1950's with every crime from Trotskyite deviationism to counterrevolutionary activity, their real crime was the advocacy of creative and intellectual freedom and the toleration of a variety of viewpoints. In the party's frame of reference, however, their demands contained the nucleus of potential political opposition. As long-standing left-wing figures with a wide audience among China's reading public, this small group of writers could establish alternate loyalties that would threaten the monolithic intellectual and political community through which the party maintained its control. Furthermore, their example could encourage others to demand that academic discipline and creative activity take precedence over devotion to the party. The infallibility of Marxism-Leninism as the universal "truth" applicable to all problems and the need of party leadership as the interpreter of this doctrine would then be called into question.

Equally important in explaining why these particular writers became the focal point of the thought reform campaigns was the struggle for power in the intellectual realm. Like Stalin, the CCP, as it consolidated its power, sought to replace the intellectual leadership of vague, humane, literary visionaries committed to Communist ideals with disciplined, obedient administrators committed to an organization. This latter group, led by the party overseer of the creative intellectuals, Chou Yang, managed the ideological remolding drives. Since they were in constant conflict with the revolutionary writers, Chou Yang and his associates used the campaigns to settle old scores, dislodge the competing group from positions of authority, and, most important, to enhance their own careers. Their part in organizing and maintaining these drives was closely related to their position and function in the party. Personal factors, as well as the larger ideological and political issues, therefore, are of real importance in understanding the nature of the campaigns.

The works and activities of the revolutionary writers will be discussed in this book as they react to these campaigns and clash with the party and its functionaries. Correspondingly, the policies of the party will be studied as they respond to these critics within the larger context of the prevailing political, economic, and ideological situation. These events will be discussed as they occurred in the 1940's and 1950's. The happenings of these two decades laid the basis for the developments of the 1960's, but a discussion of that period awaits another study. The views, contests, frustrations, and tragic fate of this critical-thinking minority in the forties and fifties warrant discussion not merely to understand the revolutionary writers and what they stood for, but also to gain insight into the kind of totalitarianism that has evolved in Communist China. The clash between the revolutionary writers and the party dramatizes the moral dilemmas of means versus ends, ideal versus reality, and conscience versus authority which have faced thinking men in all civilizations.

Ideological Background to the Conflict

Before tracing the conflict between the revolutionary writers and the party in the 1940's and 1950's, it is illuminating to sketch the background out of which these events occurred. Some of the common influences affecting these writers before they came under direct party control may help explain why they became and remained critical of any form of authoritarianism or doctrinaire thinking. One of the basic reasons can be found in the highly individualistic nature of their literary vocation. Even when a regime dictates the writer's subject matter and literary style, the actual creation must still be by the writer himself. Yet, China's revolutionary writers cannot be viewed within the same frames of reference we apply to American and European writers. They, like most Soviet writers, were unconcerned with the search into the subconscious and memory and the accompanying revolutionizing of language and form that have absorbed Western writers since Freud. Instead, they considered literature to be one of the principal battlegrounds of the political and ideological struggle. The artistic value of their work was fettered by this narrow concept of literature. Nevertheless, within this limited area, they did insist on certain artistic criteria and did attempt to present their own special view of man and of reality. Such an approach must allow for some degree of freedom if it is to be carried out.

Though relatively unaffected by the new trends of twentieth-century Western literature, these writers were profoundly influenced by nineteenth-century Western realism. They were attracted to French literature, particularly the works of Zola, Balzac, and Romain Rolland. By far the most meaningful stimuli for them came from the Russian writers — Tolstoy, Pushkin, Chekov, Turgenev, Dostoyevsky, and Gorki — and the Russian critics — Chernyshevski and Belinsky. Perhaps they were drawn to the Russian intelligentsia because, like them, the Chinese revolutionary writers were a distinct social group with a specific political role of their own. Moreover, they too were obsessed with large moral and social questions. It was mainly through these Russian writers that they became aware of Western ideas in literature. Even more important, they were impressed by the Russian writers' concern with humanitarian values and social idealism and by the Russian critics' assigning to writers the task of scrutinizing and criticizing the wrongs in their society. Like the Russian intelligentsia, they came to look on themselves as a group destined to lead the fight against autocratic government and to point the way toward the liberation of society.

Within their own environment there were also factors which made them question autocratic rule. The role of the writer as a social critic was not new in Chinese history. China's intellectuals had always been involved in the country's political life and in broad social and economic issues. For centuries the ethical and humanitarian traditions of Confucianism had taught scholars to speak out with courage against injustice in government and to concern themselves with the welfare of the people. There was a tradition of the scholar suffering death for the sake of a humanitarian cause. A different kind of influence which may have affected these wrtiers unconsciously came from Taoist and Buddhist thought. These systems of belief contain principles of freedom from the state and the right to a private and creative inner life.

The writers were also influenced by more contemporary happenings in their history. The events of the May Fourth Movement pointed to the role intellectuals could still play in China. On this date in 1919 students and professors rose in protest against the Chinese government's acquiescence to the Versailles Treaty's decision to cede the former German territory in Shantung to Japan. This episode demonstrated that the populace still looked to the intellectuals for leadership, and that, in moments of crisis, intellectuals could act as spokesmen for public opinion and exert political pressure on their government. Moreover, the iconoclastic attitude of the participants in the May Fourth Movement toward the traditional culture set an example for intellectuals in their approach toward the prevailing society. This general ideological background coupled with rebellious tendencies within their own personalities provided these writers with the mental and psychological proclivity to question authority and resist regimentation.

In addition to a skeptical, independent attitude toward the status quo, these writers held specific ideological viewpoints that were ultimately to lead them into direct conflict with the party. They were not a homogeneous group and had by no means formed any unified system of thought. However, they did come to similar conclusions on Marx and on the relation of art to politics that diverged from those of the party. Like many Chinese intellectuals, they were attracted to the Marxist view of society and history, but their attraction to Marxism was more emotional than intellectual. They were drawn to the party primarily because of its determination to resist Japan, its concern with the impoverished masses, and its professed idealism.

Therefore, while several were party members, they were not orthodox Communists. Almost all insisted on the right to define communism in their own way. They had a sincere commitment to the
humanitarian aspirations of Marxism and believed themselves true
to its basic ideals when they emphasized equality, democracy, and
intellectual freedom. When these principles were abandoned by the
party as impractical once it established its own base, these writers
refused to conform to the party's expediency. In the 1940's they
protested against the party's having forsaken its original principles
and sought to purify the revolution which they believed had become
contaminated by bureaucracy and opportunism. As scholars had
criticized their government in the past in the name of Confucian
ideals, these writers did so in the name of Marxist principles. Similarly, they did so without ever directly challenging the fundamental
truths of their ideology.

When in the 1950's they were denied the right to discuss directly
the crucial political and social issues of the day, they, like the Russian intelligentsia, expressed their views by expounding heretical
ideas on literature. Specifically, they set forth views that differed
from socialist realism, the Soviet aesthetic canon which the Chinese
Communist party adopted in the early 1930's. This doctrine proclaimed that literature could not merely reproduce life, it must
depict life as it should be or as the party says it should be. Events
and characters of literature should be idealized portrayals in order
to educate and indoctrinate the public in the party line at a given
moment. Though the revolutionary writers also claimed to believe
in socialist realism, their interpretation of this concept was closer
to the nineteenth-century European view of realism than the Soviet
concept. Like the party, they called for description of contemporary
life. However, it was to be based not on specific political and economic formulas, but on direct observation. Literature, by showing
society as it is and pointing to its evils as well as its virtues, was a
vehicle, they insisted, for expressing criticism, not merely praise. If
writers were to do only as the party demanded — depict a glorious
future where peasants and workers were heroes — they feared literature would be diverted from revealing the actual conditions of the
people.

The revolutionary writers called for attaching art to politics as did the party, but again their interpretation of politics differed from the party's. Like the Russian Marxist philosopher Plekhanov, whom several of them had read extensively, the writers believed that the masses of people had instinctively socialist demands. In their view, therefore, a writer displayed a political spirit by perceiving the grass-roots demands of the people and understanding the everyday realities of their lives. One of the revolutionary writers, Hu Feng, vividly described this process as the writer assimilating the objective world into his own consciousness and seizing the essence of political ideas as they pass through the pulse and nerves of people's lives.[1] If, as the party commanded, literature were forced to coincide with specific programs, it would in their view deteriorate into a maze of slogans and theories and would lack the artistic quality that distinguishes literature from party directives.

Background of the Factional Conflict

As important as the ideological outlook of these revolutionary writers in understanding their open clash with the party are the factional and personal rivalries which had their roots in the 1930's. The majority of China's outstanding writers at that time were living in Shanghai, the cultural center of prewar China. Among them were the literary critics Hu Feng and Feng Hsüeh-feng, the novelists Ting Ling and Hsiao Chün, and the poet Ai Ch'ing, all of whom were in the circle around Lu Hsün, China's most famous modern writer. Lu Hsün's vivid condemnation of China's traditional society and his fervent expression of the need for revolutionary change set an example for a whole generation of Chinese writers. But he had an even more direct impact upon these writers. To most of them, he was a personal friend and counselor.

They joined the League of Left-Wing Writers, which had been established with the support of Lu Hsün in March 1930. The League was a front organization for the party and an organ for cultural and ideological subversion. Nevertheless, because of its vigorous stand against imperialism and because of Lu Hsün's sponsorship, it was able to incorporate the majority of China's prominent writers. Ostensibly, Lu Hsün was the head of the League, but the actual policy-makers were party officials. From 1931 to 1933 Ch'ü Ch'iu-pai, former secretary of the party, exercised predominant power. After he left in January 1934 to become Education Minister in Kiangsi, the literary theorist Chou Yang became the real authority in the League.

However, because Shanghai was cut off from the Red areas and because Comintern control was weak in this period, the party's representatives in Shanghai did not have the power to establish strict ideological guidelines or impose direct controls over literary expression. Despite KMT censorship and the acceptance of the canon of socialist realism, this was still a period of relative relaxation for left-wing writers. They discussed and experimented with Western literary trends. In this atmosphere many writers, including the ones around Lu Hsün, gained an appreciation for artistic criteria and the need for some degree of freedom as prerequisites for creative work.

There were wide-open debates on various approaches to literature in which Lu Hsün and his colleagues, particularly Feng Hsüeh-feng and Hu Feng, figured conspicuously. In spite of increasing contact with the party, Lu Hsün and his followers sought to maintain an independent, nondoctrinaire attitude not only toward Marxism and literature, but also toward the party organization. Consequently, they conflicted with Ch'ü Ch'iu-pai and constantly clashed with Chou Yang who obediently followed the Comintern and party line. Not only was Lu Hsün's faction out of sympathy with the rigid orthodoxy of Chou Yang and his associates, but they were also angered at having their leadership gradually usurped by Chou Yang's aggressive administrative power. Chou had published nothing of distinction or of a creative nature. Yet, because of unusual organizational ability and unquestioning obedience to the party, he quickly gained a position over others more famous and talented than he. These two groups competed with each other in a fierce struggle for pre-eminence which was motivated as much by personal aims as by aesthetic and ideological considerations.

The first encounter between these two factions occurred in the early 1930's when two left-wing writers, Hu Ch'iu-yüan and Su Wen, rebelled against the pressures in the League to write only about the class struggle. They called for a "third kind of literature" that would be oriented neither to the right nor to the left and would reveal universal feelings not limited by class character. Lu Hsün and his group joined with Ch'ü Ch'iu-pai and Chou Yang in a blistering counter-attack on Hu Ch'iu-yüan and Su Wen. Yet Feng Hsüeh-feng, who was Lu Hsün's closest confidant, at the same time also censured Chou Yang and Ch'ü Ch'iu-pai, a clear indication of the developing disenchantment of Lu Hsün's group with the party's representatives in the League. Writing under the pen name Ho Tan-jen, Feng condemned them for their doctrinaire attitude toward others who did not agree with them. Although the advocates of a "third kind of literature" de-emphasized the class struggle, Feng, nevertheless, insisted that because they described the decadence of the landlords and the imperialists, they should be treated as allies not as enemies. He declared, "It cannot be denied that left-wing critics are often mechanical in theory and in sectarianism . . . We must rectify these traits shown by Ch'ü Ch'iu-pai and Chou Ch'i-ying [Chou Yang]." [2]

The next overt sign of growing antagonism between these two factions was revealed in a debate in 1935 between Hu Feng and Chou Yang over representative characters in literature.[3] Feng Hsüeh-feng left Shanghai in 1933 for Jiuchin, then the capital of the Red areas, and Hu Feng succeeded to Feng's close association with Lu Hsün. Here again, it is likely that Hu's stand was supported by Lu Hsün. In this debate Hu urged writers to describe their characters as representatives of certain groups and classes in society; Chou emphasized that characters should be drawn as individuals as well as types. Paradoxically, Chou appears to have taken the less doctrinaire position in this controversy. As the debate developed, however, it expanded beyond an ideological question into a struggle for power between the two groups. Hu's erudite reasoning on this subject and his belittlement of Chou's intellectual capacities were soon echoed by others. To halt the reverberations, Chou accused Hu of neglecting the real individuals who struggled against Japan in his overriding concern with artistic representative types. He asserted that Hu's lack of concern for creating characters that coincided with the opposing sides in the current Sino-Japanese War helped the enemy, and, therefore, made him a traitor. He also used unsubstantiated evidence to show that Hu was connected with the KMT. In an obvious act of desperation, Chou and other party officials, in the hope of winning Lu Hsün to their side, met with him in August 1935 to make their allegations personally against Hu. Lu Hsün rejected their charges and thereafter, along with Hu, was accused of traitorous acts in leftist magazines. [4]

The controversy over representative literary characters soon moved into another dispute that was far more acrimonious. Ostensibly, this dispute was over a new cultural policy for the period of the United Front, but again it was also a manifestation of the sectarian maneuvering of Communist and leftist writers for literary leadership. In December 1935 the party in Shanghai, following Comintern directives, called for a United Front. Chou Yang disbanded the League in the spring of 1936 without consulting Lu Hsün and replaced it with another organization of his own making, the United Association of Chinese Writers, which brandished the slogan "Literature for National Defense." Obedient to the policy of the United Front, Chou Yang welcomed writers with non-Marxist views. The only condition for writers who joined his organization was that they oppose Japan. Instead of confining its activities as the League had to a small left-wing circle within a limited geographical area, the new organization sought to unite writers of all political persuasions on a nationwide scale.

Fearing the dilution of the revolutionary spirit by the incorporation of nonleftist writers, Lu Hsün's group set up its own organization called the Chinese Literary Workers in opposition. It adopted a slogan more revolutionary than that of Chou Yang's group — "People's Literature of the National Revolutionary Struggle." It was not a formal, tightly-knit organization like Chou's, but included other famous names from the Shanghai literary world. In addition to Hu Feng and Feng Hsüeh-feng, who had returned to Shanghai, there were the translator Huang Yüan, the novelist Pa Chin, the playwright Tsao Yü, and the novelist Hsiao Chün.[5] The independent attitude of Lu Hsün's group and its refusal to fall into line gave rise to vehement polemics. Chou Yang and his associates, though proclaiming a more liberal platform, would not tolerate an alternative organization or an alternative slogan. Concomitantly, Lu Hsün and his associates supported, though somewhat reluctantly, the party's political policy of a United Front, but rebelled against its literary directives and literary leaders.

Although internal literary warfare commenced with an essay by Hu Feng published on March 9, 1936, in which the alternative slogan was first presented, it was Lu Hsün and Feng Hsüeh-feng who appear to have masterminded and spearheaded a policy of deliberate insubordination to the party's cultural directives. As a party member, Feng's actions were even more defiant than Lu Hsün's, who as a fellow traveler was not theoretically bound by party discipline. Feng's loyalty to his mentor's views above his allegiance to the party's amounted to virtual heresy.

The opposition of Lu Hsün's group took the form of public volleys against Chou Yang. Lu Hsün's attack was triggered by the actions of a close colleague, Hsü Mou-yung, who had been enticed by Chou Yang to write a letter to Lu Hsün insinuating that Hu Feng and his associates were working against the party. Lu Hsün replied by publishing Hsü's letter and attaching an angry retort in which he defended Hu Feng and accused Chou Yang of labeling people traitors merely to enhance his own position.[6] Feng Hsüeh-feng delivered an even more devastating blow against Chou and his cohorts in an article written under the pen name Lü K'e-yü, entitled "Opinions on Several Problems in the Literary Movement." In this essay Feng directly accused Chou and indirectly the party of suffocating creative and intellectual freedom. "Chou Yang's and his group's denial of the demands for creative freedom . . . proves again their lack of perception of writers' sentiments . . . We want freedom to create, to publish and to help all kinds of authors to write freely . . . (How can Chou Yang believe that if writers have freedom they will become traitors?)"[7] Feng also charged them with using the method of debate to impose forcibly their own ideas. The purpose of "a debate on theory should not be to call others counterrevolutionaries . . . or traitors . . . It should be to convince, not to oppress others with accusations."[8]

Feng questioned Chou's right or even the party's right to appoint themselves directors of literature. He accused Chou and his associates of compelling writers to adopt the party's interpretation of Marxism-Leninism so that they, encased in their orthodox armor, could assume leadership over the literary world. Emphasis on a correct world view, Feng alleged, "was only so Chou Yang could justify himself and elevate himself above others."[9] Not only did Feng censure Chou and his group for their dictatorial attitudes, he, as his friend Hu Feng did earlier, also challenged their intellectual qualifications.

In a vein reminiscent of the Western-oriented scholar Hu Shih, Feng declared, "We should talk less of absolute theories, talk more of concrete problems and study more concrete literary works . . . Our literature is of a poor quality . . . because our critics do not devote themselves to creative work . . . and often are not interested in studying literature . . ." [10] Feng suggested to Chou that instead of recklessly spouting theories, he try to learn something about literature and understand the complicated nature of art.

Though this article of Feng Hsüeh-feng and the published retort of Lu Hsün were far more vituperative in their assaults on party officials than the initial article in this debate by Hu, it was Hu and not they who was made the focus of attack by the party. Hu was charged, in leftist magazines, with everything from being a traitor to acting as a spy for the KMT. Most likely, Hu's opening shot and the memory of Hu's recent clash with him over literary types rankled in Chou. Moreover, Lu Hsün and Feng were too prominent and powerful in the mid-1930's to be criticized directly. Though not of comparable stature with Lu Hsün, Feng enjoyed a distinction at this time which his opponents could not rival. He had participated in the Long March and had just returned from the northwest where he had been in contact with top party leaders.

In fact, Feng's and Lu Hsün's charges issued in the fall of 1936 brought a feeble response. The contest subsided as the quarrel was ostensibly patched up. Shortly after, the Sino-Japanese War erupted around Shanghai. Chou and many of his allies left for Yenan. Lu Hsün had died, but his close associates had also been beckoned to Yenan. Ting Ling, Hsiao Chün, and Ai Ch'ing answered the call, but Hu Feng and Feng Hsüeh-feng remained in the KMT areas. Their choice may have been determined in large part by the dispute they had just had with the party's representatives.

In 1936 Feng withdrew from the party.[11] Perhaps the party had asked him to leave because of his opposition to their policies. However, in light of his own complaints during this period against the restrictions that the party's organizational discipline placed upon writers, and in view of his anger at the party's support for Chou, it is just as likely that Feng left of his own accord. He returned to his native province of Chekiang and led the life of a recluse. In fact, this became a pattern for Feng. Whenever he found himself in sharp conflict with party leaders, he suddenly dropped out of the battle. Hu Feng also withdrew from the factional squabbles. When he left Shanghai in 1937, he roamed from Hankow to Hong Kong to Kweilin and finally to Chungking. Yet, in his wanderings he kept a small coterie that had gathered around him in Shanghai at his side and set up a magazine, *Ch'i-yüeh* (July), to publish their literary works.[12] Until nearly the end of the 1930's, he confined his attention primarily to the affairs of his journal and to literary matters.

However, in 1939 the inner-party rift between Feng Hsüeh-feng and Hu Feng on the one hand and Chou Yang and his group on the other, broke out again. This time the conflict developed over the question of national forms in literature. National forms is the term used for the indigenous, semiliterary folk styles that have been enjoyed by the ordinary Chinese for hundreds of years. The origin of this quarrel dates back to the early 1930's. During this period of ineffectual party and Comintern control in Shanghai, Ch'ü Ch'iu-pai and his associates began to formulate their own cultural program in response to China's immediate needs. Ch'ü claimed that the literary revolution which followed the May Fourth Movement had not been completed. The *pai-hua* style of writing introduced at that time was filled with Western sentence structures and Westernized expressions that could be understood only by the middle class. A further revolution was necessary, he reasoned, to adapt literature to the tastes of the ordinary working people. He, therefore, urged writers to use national forms as their literary style so that their work could be appreciated by the less-educated and could produce more effective propaganda than literature based on Western models. Chou Yang seized on these ideas and became their most vocal proponent. The development of the political consciousness and creativity of the masses through this type of literature became an article of faith for him.

The spark that ignited Hu Feng's and Feng Hsüeh-feng's opposition to this type of literature was Mao Tse-tung's speech of October 1938 on "The Position of the Chinese Communist Party in the National War." In this speech Mao repeated Ch'ü Ch'iu-pai's and Chou Yang's advocacy of national forms. He urged Chinese writers to repudiate Western literary traditions and to create their own style by using indigenous literary forms. Though Mao merely restated earlier arguments, his speech was a clear indication that from this point on he intended to concern himself with the cultural direction of the nation. As soon as his views were published in the KMT areas and party functionaries began commending national forms with renewed vigor, Feng and Hu once again stepped forth to do battle — now not only with the party's cultural authorities but with the policies of Mao himself.

They scorned China's old literature and objected to turning back to the past for the style of modern Chinese literature. They did not accept the view of party theoreticians that there was a distinction in the old culture between the literature of the landlord class and that of the masses. To Feng and Hu all literature of the past was feudal in nature. In a booklet Hu compiled on the subject, "Questions on National Forms," and in meetings he organized specifically to discuss this question, he charged that the democratic and revolutionary elements which party ideologists found in the old folk literature were purely of their own fabrication. He warned that unless Chinese culture made a complete break with its past, it would become based on a largely unconscious folk culture. Both men also pleaded eloquently for the continued development of Chinese literature along the Western-oriented, realistic traditions that evolved from the May Fourth Movement and for the sustained infusion of Western culture into China. As Feng expressed it, "This is a time for the unification of the cultures of all nations and for the development of mutual relations, mutual influences, and mutual changes in order to form an internationalized culture." [13] He considered the internationalization of Chinese culture as a prerequisite for China's growth: "The more the road of a nation is of mankind, the greater the development of the nation." [14] Though neither Hu Feng nor Feng ever mentioned it, their scorn for China's old culture and their strong advocacy of Western literary forms coincided with the attitudes of Hu Shih.

Outwardly, this clash between Lu Hsün's former associates and the party's cultural leaders was an ideological issue. There appears to have been relatively little name-calling in contrast with the earlier encounters. However, from oblique references in Feng's and Hu's essays during this period, there were indications of a resumption of the earlier factional quarrels, but this time they were carried on behind the scenes. Though he did not mention any names, Hu Feng lamented, "We do not realize how much 'struggle' there is over self-importance in literary circles. There are rumors filled with evil and sectarian quarreling . . . This not only wastes valuable strength, it also harms proper theoretical criticism." [15] With obvious emotion, he complained of being called a "renegade" and "traitor" in leftist papers and of students receiving orders not to read his journals and books.[16] A hint of the bitterness of this dispute can be seen in the fact that in 1940 Feng Hsüeh-feng again withdrew from party activities and once more returned to his native province.

Nevertheless, in view of Hu's and Feng's open opposition to Mao's cultural policies, the party's response, as earlier, was mild. Because the party was preoccupied with military affairs and because their chief antagonist, Chou Yang, was far away in Yenan, there was only scattered criticism of their views on national forms. An open ideological and factional clash did not occur. This was to happen in the next decades when the party consolidated its position sufficiently to carry out thought reform campaigns on an organized basis.

chapter two

LITERARY OPPOSITION
DURING THE
YENAN PERIOD

When the Sino-Japanese War broke out around Shanghai and along the coast in the later part of the 1930's, not only party members but also many writers and large numbers of students and intellectuals made their way to Yenan, drawn there by the belief that the CCP was the only group capable of bringing China out of chaos. They arrived in the darkest, most difficult days of the war for the Communist regime. The Japanese had blockaded its garrison posts and sent large convoys of troops into the guerrilla areas. There was a series of natural disasters — famine, drought, and crop failure. The inhabitants were forced into virtually a self-sufficient economy; they made their paper of grass and their pots of earth. At the same time, the leadership cadres were losing some of their zeal for revolution and the spartan life. They were becoming more concerned with finding and maintaining their niches in the bureaucracy. The influx of intellectuals and writers became another disruptive factor. Many, accustomed to the unregimented life of the large cities, continued to think and behave in an undisciplined fashion.

Beset by so many difficulties, the party saw that in order to meet the challenge of the KMT and the Japanese and attain its tactical goals, its organization must be adaptable and its discipline strong. Its followers must be highly motivated so as to carry out the party's orders with a minimum of control. Very much in the traditional Confucian spirit, the party leadership believed that before one could change the world, one must first rectify one's own thought. Consequently, a movement began in the early 1940's [1] to develop a corps of devoted, disciplined cadres and intellectuals convinced of the rightness of the party's cause. It sought to change basic patterns of behavior and implant the strict party line. This kind of drive, called the cheng feng movement, literally the "rectification of (unorthodox) tendencies," was to emerge as one of the greatest efforts of human manipulation in history.

The Initial Stage of the Cheng Feng Movement

The methods used in this period revealed the rudiments of techniques which were to become more fully developed in the 1950's. Though the harshness, thoroughness, and sophistication of later thought remolding campaigns were not so apparent in the early 1940's, nonetheless, the procedures that would be used in future rectification drives were all present. Party members were compelled to undergo an intense psychological experience in which their sense of shame and guilt was employed by the party for its own purposes.[2] The actual reform process for each member was divided into three different stages, extended over several months and conducted in small groups.[3] These small groups were formed within party organs and schools. At first, their members studied and discussed prescribed speeches and articles of party leaders and resolutions of the party which were called the cheng feng documents. Among them were works of Lenin, Stalin, Mao Tse-tung, and Liu Shao-ch'i.[4] Since there was no freedom of silence, everyone was expected to express an opinion on these works.[5]

This was followed by a second stage of investigations of individual members of the group. Records of these investigations were kept as a source of reference.[6] The ideas and attitudes that the individual had previously held were subject to intense and prolonged criticism by others. This produced a profound emotional crisis within the individual. The incessant recitations of his failings, the constant exposure to indoctrination, and the steady heightening of tension eventually broke down his inner will. In this environment, he could find atonement for his "sins" and relief from these pressures only by surrendering to the party's authority and its sense of values.

The beginning of this process of submission started with the individual presenting a self-criticism to be approved by the group's leaders. Usually the initial confession was not accepted. Several self-criticisms were demanded, each one to be more corrosive than the last in its attack on one's own personality. Parroting Communist theory or the official line was insufficient; the individual had to give convincing evidence that his past behavior was totally wrong and that his surrender to the party's will was complete. The party did not demand merely passive acquiescence, but insisted upon positive conversion to its beliefs. Consequently, when the individual's final confession was approved and he was released from his sense of guilt, he felt rejuvenated and regarded himself, at least for a while, as a new person ready to carry out the party's orders with the "proper" zeal. A few held out and maintained their original attitudes even under these severe pressures. They were treated as enemies of the group and were ostracized, but not to the point where they could escape. Their fate will be part of the story that will be told in these pages. The fact that these methods of thought reform became progressively severe and efficient may be due in part to the resistance that these individuals, primarily the revolutionary writers, gave to the party's attempt to remold their thought.

At first, the party used these methods of ideological reform to do away with all forms of heterodoxy, whether on the left or right. The cheng feng movement initially spoke out against both dogmatism and liberalism with equal degrees of intensity. Therefore, while this movement indicated the determination of the party to assert Lenin's concept of strict centralized control and tight party discipline, there was also a parallel attack on the dictatorial attitudes and misuse of power by the bureaucracy. Liu Shao-ch'i began to speak on ideological training as early as August 7, 1939, in "On the Training of a Communist Party Member." In this speech he asserted that the interest of the individual should be subordinated unconditionally to the interests of the party. Yet, he also demanded that individual party members have the opportunity to use their own specialized talents.[7] Again, on July 2, 1941, Liu, in "On the Intra-Party Struggle," disparaged liberalism in the party as loosening party solidarity, but at the same time, he criticized discipline and bureaucratic methods that destroyed the initiative and creativity of party members.[8] Meetings were convened specifically to hear criticisms of the cadres from the public.[9]

In this confused atmosphere of contradictory policies, a group of revolutionary writers, convinced that the party was genuinely interested in a free exchange of ideas,[10] issued a barrage of critical essays. These essays appeared within a period of a month, from the middle of March until the middle of April 1942, when they were abruptly stopped. All of them were published in the literary page of the party's official organ, *Chieh-fang jih-pao*, edited by the woman novelist Ting Ling, with the assistance of the literary critic Ch'en Ch'i-hsia. Their authors, Ting Ling, Wang Shih-wei, Hsiao Chün, Lo Feng, Ai Ch'ing, and Ho Ch'i-fang, were party members or closely allied with the party. Several of them, particularly Ting Ling and Hsiao Chün, had been part of Lu Hsün's inner circle, though they had not participated actively in the debates of the 1930's. Like their former mentor and his associates, Hu Feng and Feng Hsüeh-feng, their faith in communism did not submerge their critical attitudes. Not having hesitated in the past to criticize persons or situations with which they disagreed, they did the same in Yenan. Their means of speaking out was through short essays, patterned after the type used by Lu Hsün in the 1930's, called *tsa wen*, which were short, biting pieces of criticism and satire. Instead of attacking the KMT, their literary "daggers" were now pointed toward the leadership cadres in Yenan. They etched the apathy, hypocrisy, and bureaucratism of the cadres with the same sharp pen they had used against KMT officials earlier.

This was the period before Mao Tse-tung's famous "Talks on Art and Literature," in which he set down the strict party line on all intellectual and cultural expression. The party's official doctrine had not yet become dogma. The essays of these writers were an effort to engage party officials in a debate on some fundamental ideological issues. Though each essay was on a different subject, all of them expressed the writer's disillusionment at finding that life in the revolutionary base did not measure up to their own cherished ideal. Through their criticisms, these writers sought to halt what they considered to be the distortion of Communist ideals in practice and the subordination of the humanitarian values of communism to short-term tactical goals. Their essays revealed a feeling of betrayal by a movement to which they had given themselves in misunderstanding.

Another common theme running through their essays was disagreement with the leadership over the role of the writer in a party-run society. To them, the writer's function was to criticize and speak out against what he thought was wrong in his environment, not to act as propagandist for the regime. To fulfill this role, the writers in their essays insisted on creative freedom and a certain degree of independence in thought and action. In addition, they looked upon writers, artists, and intellectuals in general as the molders and custodians of man's spirit. They separated the intellectuals' tasks from those of the party's. Whereas the party was to concern itself with man's material and physical needs, the writers and other intellectuals were to care for man's spiritual needs. This division of labor challenged the party's right to interfere with man's emotions and his intellectual endeavors which it was in the very process of doing through its cheng feng movement.

The Critics and Their Criticisms

Ting Ling

The first one to open the attack on the party's policies in Yenan was Ting Ling. After three years of imprisonment by the KMT in Nanking, she escaped in 1936 and reached Yenan in 1937, where she was personally greeted by Mao himself. Besides being from the same province as Mao, she had been a schoolmate of Mao's first wife. Well known for her work for women's emancipation, she, along with Chou En-lai's wife, was asked to establish a women's league in the northwest area, which was called the Women's National Salvation Association. She also helped organize the propaganda cadres for the 8th Army. She made an outstanding name for herself in Yenan, not so much for her creative work, which fell off considerably, but for her propaganda and organizational activities. Her words carried great weight in many circles and she was described by those who met her at this time as a person of natural command and leadership.[11]

Yet, while she was very active in carrying out the party's policies, she expressed dissatisfaction with some of them. An early hint of her dissatisfaction is seen in one of the few short stories she wrote in Yenan, "In the Hospital," published in 1941. In this story, she was concerned with a question which must have disturbed her personally at this time — the party member's internal conflict between following party discipline and yet remaining an independent person. The main character, a young girl from Shanghai, wanted to become a writer, but, because of the exigencies of war, her individual interests and talents were disregarded. She was trained as a nurse and was assigned to a new hospital. Ting Ling described the administration of the hospital as inefficient and inhumane. It was composed of old cadres who were depicted as incompetents, without any knowledge of running a hospital and indifferent to the problems of its patients or doctors. The heroine attempted to correct some of the abuses, but her actions only brought her censure. Finally, in frustration, she left the hospital.

It is likely that Ting Ling was using this description of the happenings in the hospital to symbolize the inflexibility of government and party organs in Yenan and the powerlessness of the individual to express himself within them. Also, she seemed to be protesting indirectly against politically reliable, but untrained officials directing professional and specialized cadres. In this work, as in the criticisms of the other revolutionary writers, there is an element of the traditional scholar's disdain for the untutored peasant who had fought his way up to a leadership position. Whatever Ting Ling implied, the story disturbed party authorities enough so that meetings were convened specifically to criticize it.[12] Afterwards, Ting Ling, apparently under pressure, revised the story so that it was suitable for publication in the Communist literary journal in Chungking, *Wen-i chen-ti* (The literary base). Most likely because of her compliance, her important posts were not as yet jeopardized.

Her most defiant act came in 1942, as the cheng feng drive gained momentum, with the publication of a *tsa wen* entitled "Thoughts on March 8," the date celebrating women's day.[13] This essay revealed the difficulties, bitterness, and disillusionment of women living in Yenan. The fate of women, supposedly emancipated but actually subjected to inequality and contempt, distressed her With emotion she described their plight. If women did not marry, they were ridiculed; if they did and had children, they were chastised for holding political posts rather than being at home with their families; if they remained at home for a number of years, they were slandered as backward. Whereas in the old society they were pitied, in the new one they were condemned for a predicament not of their own making.

Actually this article's description of Yenan as a place where certain groups had privileges over others was an attack on the social system established by the party. While admitting that the position of women in Yenan was better than elsewhere, Ting Ling claimed that it did not measure up to the theories the party had proclaimed about equal rights. She specifically blamed the top party leaders for empty promises and lack of action. Men in important positions, she declared, "should talk less of meaningless theories and talk more of actual problems. Theory and practice should not be separated." [14] Since the party had asked for the union of theory and practice, Ting Ling believed her exposure of their division in Yenan would help the party's rectification movement.

Lo Feng

After Ting Ling's opening shot, an onslaught of verbal bullets zipped across the literary page of *Chieh-fang jih-pao*. Following Ting Ling's lead, several revolutionary writers used the critical spirit of Lu Hsün as the symbol with which they fought against the injustices they saw in Yenan. As early as October 23, 1941, Ting Ling, in an editorial comment in *Chieh-fang jih-pao*, had urged writers to heed Lu Hsün's example. She wrote, "I think it will do us most good if we emulate his steadfastness in facing the truth, his courage to speak out for the sake of truth and his fearlessness. This age of ours still needs the *tsa wen*, a weapon that we should never lay down." [15]

This theme was developed further by Lo Feng, a short-story writer from Manchuria who was a member of the group around the novelist Hsiao Chün. In an article entitled "Still a Period of *Tsa wen*," he warned his comrades that "darkness" was overspreading Yenan. "Clouds not only cover Chungking, but frequently appear here too." [16] He defined this darkness as the return of the decadence that had existed in China for hundreds of years. On the surface, life in Yenan appeared quite different from that in the KMT regions. There was a unity of spirit and of organization, but underneath Lo Feng complained that comrades "were inflicting scars on one another." [17] These "scars" were inflicted by cadres who suppressed criticism and restricted the freedom to write.

Lo Feng chided his colleagues for their cowardice in the face of these thrusts and exhorted them to expose and attack the shortcomings in Yenan as Lu Hsün had done in Shanghai. Lu Hsün's "dagger [*tsa wen*] . . . has become buried in the ground and has rusted . . . We have used this weapon insufficiently . . . Ting Ling has attempted to make it live again . . . but hers is still too weak . . . I hope our literary page will henceforth become a sword which will shock people and at the same time make them rejoice." He begged his fellow writers to use their pens as "swords which would cut open the darkness." [18]

Wang Shih-wei

It was the translator and ideologist Wang Shih-wei who most penetratingly analyzed exactly what was this "darkness" that the revolutionary writers found in Yenan. Whereas Ting Ling and Lo Feng talked of its manifestations — social inequality and limitations on freedom of expression — Wang looked into its causes. In an essay, "The Wild Lily," he presented one of the most discerning critiques of the CCP made from within its ranks, and one of the most controversial articles to be published within the Chinese Communist camp. This essay, which appeared in the middle of March 1942, has caused repercussions that are still being felt in China today.

Like his colleagues, Wang was primarily concerned with the relationship between the leaders and the led in Yenan. In the manner of Djilas' condemnation of the Yugoslav Communist party several years later in his book *The New Class*, Wang upbraided the party for not eliminating class differences as it had promised. Instead it had created a new upper class composed of a closely-knit clique of party bosses fighting to preserve its own newly-won, special privileges. The one-time rebels against inequality had now become new bureaucrats in their own system of injustice. They suffered from the very same evils of corruption and indifference that they had tried to destroy. In fact, they were actually spreading them further. However, unlike Djilas, who saw the development of a new class as an outgrowth of communism itself, Wang considered it a carry-over from the old society. "Since our camp exists in the old, dark society, there is bound to be darkness here too." [19] In the belief that he upheld the orthodox view of Marxism, Wang insisted that he was acting as the conscience of the revolution by reminding the party leaders of their ideals and sacrifices. As the Confucian scholars had criticized their governments in order to prolong the life of the dynasty, Wang drew a negative picture of Yenan, in the hope that he could awaken its leaders in time to save the revolution.

Like Ting Ling, Wang chastised the party for propounding theories of equality and democracy, but not practicing them. He depicted the cleavages between the leadership and the community in concrete terms. The leadership wore better clothes and ate more lavishly than the rest of the population. Insisting that he himself was not an equalitarian, Wang nevertheless termed the practice of "dividing clothes into three different colors and food into five different grades was unnecessary and irrational." [20] Whenever officials did any work, they "built themselves high platforms from which to instruct the people." [21] They had assumed so many privileges that they considered themselves of a different species. Consequently, they had lost contact with their fellow comrades and had become indifferent to them. Likewise, the rank and file had drawn apart from their leaders. This was especially true of the youth. Many had accepted the Communist mystique unquestioningly and had come to Yenan "in search of beauty and warmth, but saw only ugliness and coldness." [22]

Also like Ting Ling, Wang granted that Yenan might be better than other places, but he too could not shut his eyes to its defects. Even if the leadership ignored certain shortcomings, Wang urged others, especially the young people, to work in their own way to eliminate them. "Youth are precious because they are simple, sensitive, enthusiastic, courageous, and full of the new strength of life. The evil which others have not perceived they perceive first, . . . the words others will not and dare not speak, they utter bravely." The party, for its part, instead of attacking these critics should see "their grumbling not as something to be suppressed, but as mirrors with which to look at itself." [23] Realistically, Wang acknowledged that "At present, it is impossible to destroy all darkness completely, but to reduce the darkness to the smallest degree is not only a possibility but a necessity." [24]

Probably because these views aroused support from some segments of the intellectuals and youth in Yenan,[25] Wang grew more daring. In another article entitled "Statesmen and Artists" written at this time, Wang presented his ideas on the role of the statesman and the writer in society. Wang was one of the first to theorize on the need to separate certain spheres from that of politics. Statesmen were the leaders of society, the directors of the revolution, and the formulizers of policies; artists reformed "man's spirit, mind, and ideas . . . and stimulated the moral strength of the revolution." [26] Thus, Wang gave the artist a task which the party had deemed to be its own. Actually, Wang was indirectly criticizing the cheng feng movement itself by challenging the party's right to enter an area in which he believed it did not belong.

Wang asserted that writers and intellectuals were better suited to worry about man's spirit than statesmen. Except for the very top political leaders, most of the leadership cadres used the revolutionary movement merely for their own benefit. Writers, on the contrary, approached their fellow men from a feeling of love and with an interest in all aspects of human nature. In this argument, Wang appears to have fallen back on the ideas expressed by the advocates of the "third kind of literature." Like them, Wang insisted that literature expand beyond descriptions of the class struggle to encompass the realm of universal emotions. According to Wang, writers should not only be interested in changing the world, they should be concerned with the universal traits in man's nature and personality.

In the same way that he had urged youth to speak out in "The Wild Lily," Wang now called on writers and artists "to raise the lid and boldly bring the darkness and filth out into the open." [27] It was more important that writers, as spiritual teachers, devote their time to observing reality and exposing its deficiencies than to praising its achievements. "With darkness vanquished, brightness will naturally increase." [28] He looked on this critical attitude toward one's own environment as the best way to reform the spirit of the men within it. With an emotional plea, he beckoned his fellow writers, "Let us take up the superb task of remaking the soul and let us first proceed with ourselves and with our own camp." [29]

Hsiao Chün

Another outspoken critic of the Communist regime at this time was the popular Manchurian novelist Hsiao Chün. Like his colleagues, he also arrived in Yenan in the late 1930's. Soon after, he was made a member of the legislative body in Yenan which was called the Shensi-Kansu-Ninghsia Border Region Government Assembly. He also surrounded himself with a coterie of refugee writers and youths from Manchuria and became intimate with Ting Ling and the group of writers around her. He frequently published stories and criticisms in the literary journals of Yenan. In the latter part of March 1942, he wrote several articles on various subjects. One of them was a *tsa wen* which echoed many of Ting Ling's sentiments on the position of women in Yenan.[30]

Hsiao Chün's most penetrating criticism appeared in an article entitled "On Love and Patience Among Comrades." This essay, like those of his friends, discussed the conflicts that had arisen among various levels of the party. Comrades, he claimed, were losing their respect and devotion for one another. "The wine of comradely love is becoming more and more diluted."[31] He did not blame the party per se, but only those cadres who sought positions for which they were unqualified. He compared them to "racers with no sportsmanship, who wearing nailed shoes run past their friends and newcomers by stamping on their faces."[32] Instead, he urged the cadres to have patience and love for their fellow comrades, especially intellectuals and youth who did not strictly follow party discipline.

Like his master Lu Hsün, Hsiao undertook to act as spokesman for the young intellectuals, especially for the ones who had difficulty conforming to the party's demands. He tried to make the party aware of some of their problems. "Some comrades have become dissatisfied with their environment — with the people around them . . . and with their work. They have even become weary of the revolution."[33] In the manner of Ting Ling's heroine, Hsiao explained that their dissatisfaction was due to the fact that they were forced at times to act against their own wishes. They found "revolution difficult, sometimes cruel and demanding great sacrifices."[34] Moreover, they had been physically weakened by the poor food in Yenan so that their endurance had been strained to the point that they made small mistakes in their jobs. Still, because they wanted to continue revolutionary work, Hsiao pleaded that their shortcomings be overlooked and that they be given another chance. They would work more effectively, Hsiao advised, if the party treated them with sympathy and understanding rather than with unrelenting indoctrination and strict discipline. Like Wang, he too was troubled by the cleavages he saw developing between the leaders and the led. Like the others, he looked on the cheng feng movement as widening instead of closing the gap between them.

Ai Ch'ing

Another famous author who spoke up at this time was the poet Ai Ch'ing. Partly through the encouragement of Chou En-lai, Ai Ch'ing came to Yenan in 1941. Because of his reputation, he too was immediately given important positions. He was made a member of the Shensi-Kansu-Ninghsia Border Region Government Assembly, a teacher at the Lu Hsün Academy of Art, and a member of the editorial board and head of the poetry section of *Ku yü* (Grain rain), the journal with the largest circulation in Yenan. He was also given facilities to set up his own journal, *Shih k'an* (Poetry). Around this time he became a member of the party. His many administrative duties and propaganda activities gave him little time to work on his poetry. The style of the few things he did write became more reportorial and less lyrical. He began to eulogize political leaders, as in his poem "Mao Tse-tung," and to affirm political policies.

Nevertheless, on March 11 in *Chieh-fang jih-pao* he reverted to a more critical stance and published "Understand and Respect Writers," in which he revealed views that were contrary to the ones expressed in some of his poetry at this time. He maintained that one of the functions of a writer was to compel his nation to scrutinize itself. A writer is "not a Mongolian Lark, nor is he a singer who sings solely to please others." [35] Like Wang Shih-wei, Ai Ch'ing believed another equally important function of a writer was to look after the spiritual health of mankind, and he defined more precisely than Wang what he meant. He considered writers the most sensitive members of the community and therefore "best able to perceive its problems." These problems went beyond the concerns of the material world. Some were of a metaphysical nature for which Marxism or the party had no answers. "Writers seek to answer the questions men wonder about in isolated moments when they silently ask why they live." For this reason, the party should give their writers more respect and understanding. To prove the great value of writers to their nation, Ai Ch'ing quoted an Englishman who observed that "The loss of Shakespeare would mean far more to England than the loss of India." [36]

A nation showed its appreciation of its writers, Ai Ch'ing declared, by acknowledging that the nature of creative work demands freedom to write. He explained that "one of the reasons why writers offered their lives to uphold democratic government was in the hope that this kind of government would guarantee the independent spirit of literary creation. Only when artistic creation is given independence can art help advance social reform." [37] Although Ai Ch'ing had learned about Marxism in the West, it is obvious he had also imbibed the view that freedom was a prerequisite for cultural development. In line with his colleagues, Ai Ch'ing's article was a protest against the intrusion of the party into an area where writers and other intellectuals should reign and a plea that this realm be left alone so that true feelings and objective criticism could still be presented.

Ho Ch'i-fang

This barrage of criticisms was concluded by the poet Ho Ch'i-fang. As opposed to his fellow poet Ai Ch'ing, Ho used the poetic rather than the essay form to express his dissatisfaction with the party's policies. When he arrived in Yenan in 1938, he admitted that he had little understanding of the class struggle or political doctrine. In a short time, however, he apparently had learned enough so that he was given important positions in the areas of publishing and education. With Ting Ling, Liu Pai-yü, and Chou Wen, the latter two confidants of Chou Yang, he edited *Ta-chung wen-i* (Mass literature). He was also on the editorial board of *Wen-i chen-ti*, of which Chou Yang was in charge. He became head of the literary department of the Lu Hsün Academy of Arts and was one of the leaders of the Yenan branch of the writers' association. In the literary debates of the early 1940's, he took the side of the orthodox group. For example, on the issue of national forms, he urged writers to bridge the gap between themselves and the masses by using their old literary forms.

Still, while Ho was rising in the cultural hierarchy and mouthing the official literary line, some of his own poems expressed personal emotions that were quite different from the prescribed sentiments.

In the early part of 1942 he published several poems intimating dissatisfaction with his environment. Most likely, the despair and suffering they reveal represent the innermost feelings of many intellectuals in Yenan as their sensitive, free-ranging minds were gradually
circumscribed. More poignantly than the essays, his poems expressed
these emotions. This is seen in his poem, "How Many Times I Have
Left My Everyday Life": [38]

> How many times I have left my everyday life
>   That narrow life of dirt and dust
>
> .   .   .
>
> And have gone to a place where there are no human faces
>   There I throw myself on the grass
> As if I return to the arms of my most generous, most
>   consoling mother
>
> .   .   .
>
>   There she tenderly bathes me
> With the sound of the river and sight of the sky and
>   clouds
> Until she completely cleanses all the troubles, heavi-
>   ness and distress from my mind

Though in the concluding section of this poem, Ho affirmed that he
should return to the "dust" and "dirt" and "struggle alongside his
comrades," it is obvious from this first part that the demands of the
party were in conflict with his own inner desire to escape from them.

Since these writers were highly acclaimed cultural leaders, anything they wrote was eagerly received by the reading public, especially by the youth. They were listened to more readily than any
other professional group or even party officials. When their articles
first appeared, many intellectuals and some of the top theorists in
the Central Research Institute, the highest school for training cadres
and an arm of the Propangada Bureau, had openly agreed with their
views and echoed them publicly without hesitation.[39] However,
after the first week of April 1942, these revolutionary writers apparently were prevented from publishing, because no more of their
tsa wen appeared. Subsequently, they showed their disagreement
with the regime by a type of passive resistance to certain aspects of
the cheng feng movement that were becoming increasingly important in the spring of 1942. They showed little interest in the study

of the prescribed documents and refused to participate fullheartedly in the self-criticism sessions. At a mobilization meeting in March at the Central Research Institute, Wang Shih-wei spoke out, but instead of publicly criticizing himself as was expected, he again attacked the leadership cadres.[40]

Apparently, this form of resistance to the cheng feng movement had gained sufficient support by the end of April so as to provoke several party leaders to upbraid publicly members of the cultural cadres for belittling and even actively opposing the cheng feng movement. A front-page editorial in *Chieh-fang jih-pao* on April 23, charged that "Certain groups of high-class cultural intellectuals . . . want to study these [cheng feng] documents with the kind of superficial, nonpenetrative method used in their school days." The next day another front-page article elaborated, "When the cheng feng movement began, some comrades did not cooperate . . . With their views of absolute egalitarianism and extreme democracy they opposed it . . . Therefore, there have been incorrect tendencies which have hindered the tasks of rectification, reform and consolidation of the cadres and the whole party." Evidently, as of April 1942 the party still had not been able to gain the full concurrence of party intellectuals to its rectification campaign and, in fact, had come up against a hard core of resistance.

The Response of the Party

The protests of the revolutionary writers and the amount of opposition they kindled in no way explain, however, the intensity and scope of the campaign subsequently directed against them. Their undisciplined actions could have been easily stopped by merely removing them from the scene, but the party had other plans. The drive against them can be understood within the framework of the cheng feng movement in progress at the time. These writers were singled out to dramatize particular patterns of thought which the party regarded as inimical to its current policies. Their disrespect for organization and discipline and indifference to party leadership and interpretation of ideology were just the traits the party wanted to use as examples in its campaign to remold the thinking and actions of its followers.

At the very time the revolutionary writers were publishing their *tsa wen*, the cheng feng movement shifted into high gear. In February and March of 1942, investigations of all schools and party organs were underway. By April 1942, the party announced that there would be three months of ideological study. Within this time virtually all work was to stop in party units while comrades examined documents and criticized one another. Organized attacks on these writers began in May and became the material with which the party brought the cheng feng movement to a climax.

Yet, while these writers were used as pawns in the cheng feng movement, the very nature of their criticisms of the party affected to some extent the specific course of the campaign. Their censure of the party leadership, most likely, was an important factor in the party's increasing concentration on the particular problems of the intellectuals, especially writers, in the spring of 1942. Though cadres were still being censured for their disregard of public opinion and their terrorizing of those with opposing views, less and less attention was given to the wrongdoings of the bureaucracy and more and more emphasis was put on remolding intellectuals and writers into loyal, disciplined, obedient functionaries.

Party members were now urged to air diverse points of view, not so much to learn the opinions of the rank and file, but to bring ideas out into the open so they could be criticized. When academic freedom was discussed, it was now meant primarily for natural scientists. Still, even in this field, though the party admitted that Marxism-Leninism did not have too much to contribute, it warned against overemphasis on technical training at the expense of political education and political goals.[41] In other fields, such as philosophy, literature, and the social sciences, the dialectic was to guide all academic research. Criticism of Hu Shih was presented to underline this approach to scholarship. Intimations of a later line of attack on Hu Shih can be seen in an article by the Marxist dialectician Ai Szu-ch'i, in which he opposed Hu Shih's pragmatic attitude toward research by asserting that "A concrete problem must be linked with a general theory." [42]

However, the major problem was not so much the influence of Hu Shih, who could easily be identified with the opposite side, but with left-wing intellectuals, who had reinterpreted Marxism in light of their own creative and academic disciplines. Demands for intel-

lectual independence originating from within the party were far
more subversive than those coming from outside it. Consequently,
the drive to enforce intellectual and literary orthodoxy had evolved
by May 1942 into a refutation of the views expressed by the revolutionary writers in their articles. Since these writers spoke for other
intellectuals and comrades, condemnation of their unorthodox attitudes was not merely aimed at them in particular, but at intellectuals and party cadres in general.

Mao himself ordered the convening of the literary meetings in
May 1942, where he delivered his famous "Talks on Art and Litera-
ture." These "Talks" laid the foundation for the party's policy
toward literature and scholarship. Though they were presented as
Mao's original doctrine, they were in reality a combination of the
Soviet theory of socialist realism and Ch'ü Ch'iu-pai's and Chou
Yang's views on national forms. In phrases that could have come
directly from the speeches of the Soviet literary czar, Andrei Zhdanov,
Mao called for optimistic heroic literature that served the cause
of the party. Also with words reminiscent of Ch'ü Ch'iu-pai's and
Chou Yang's a decade ago, Mao demanded that literature be produced for mass consumption and be written not in Western styles,
but in forms the masses understood. Mao added the peasants to Ch'ü's
and Chou's more general description of the masses as the working
class and soldiers. What was new in Mao's "Talks" was the fact that
these ideas which hitherto had been merely one among many in
left-wing circles now became the one and only doctrine of artistic
and cultural expression.

Mao's "Talks" had another purpose besides serving notice that
henceforth literature and all phases of intellectual activity were to
be dictated by party policy. Viewed within the context of the period,
they take on an added dimension. Delivered after several weeks of
criticism from the revolutionary writers, they were also meant as a
direct rebuttal to the criticisms of Wang Shih-wei, Ting Ling, and
their associates. They were an implicit attack on these writers who
had attempted to stay independent of the encompasing rule of the
party. By refuting their major arguments, Mao established his own
policy.

In his first speech, given on May 2, Mao claimed that the writers
in Yenan were Communists merely in organization but not in ideas.

Though he never mentioned them by name, he disparaged the various literary concepts brought up by the revolutionary writers as being examples of non-Marxist thought. He decried as lacking in class consciousness their demands that literature be motivated by love of mankind, be concerned with universal aspects of human nature, and be created under conditions of freedom. Obviously in reference to the resistance the writers were giving to the cheng feng movement, Mao declared that "The science of Marxism-Leninism is a required course for all revolutionaries, not excepting artists and writers." [43] He urged them to desist in their unwillingness to study the dialectic and in their reluctance to participate in remolding so that these unorthodox views could be eradicated.

In the interval between this speech and the next on May 23, many heated debates and high-pressure study sessions were conducted. Evidently, these writers still refused to retract their earlier statements, because Mao began his second talk by again berating intellectuals for maintaining their old ways of thinking. Clearly alluding to the revolutionary writers, he expressed particular annoyance with the stubbornness of those intellectuals who had worked in the Communist areas and in the Red Army for a number of years.

His talk then moved into a point-by-point criticism of the arguments presented by the writers in their articles, though again he never mentioned their names. On the question of the relation of art and politics, Mao rejected the contention of Wang Shih-wei, Hsiao Chün, and Ai Ch'ing that art be independent of politics. Anyone who believed such, Mao claimed, was using the Trotskyite formula "politics — Marxist, art — bourgeois." [44] This charge was not only aimed at Wang Shih-wei, who at one time was interested in Trotsky's thought, but generally at all those who had been influenced by Western culture — which, of course, included all of these writers. In opposition to their request for independence, Mao insisted that art be subordinated to the revolutionary tasks prescribed by the party at a given time. Though literature may be necessary for the revolutionary machine, he insisted that in comparison with the machine's other parts, it was less essential. Therefore, political criteria must be put before artistic criteria. Like Ai Ch'ing, Mao acknowledged that specialists and professionals should be respected, but, he added, only if they were spokesmen for the people, not for themselves. Showing his distrust of intellectuals, Mao admonished writers against thinking themselves too important.

Next, Mao refuted the concept of human nature that had been expressed by several left-wing writers since the 1930's, and, most recently, by Wang Shih-wei. To Mao, there was no abstract human nature nor universal human emotions, only a particular kind of human nature or a specific emotion belonging to a certain class. "The [concept of] human nature boosted by certain petty-bourgeois intellectuals is . . . opposed to that of the mass of the people; what they call human nature is nothing but bourgeois individualism." [45] Because of the existence of class societies, there could be no all-embracing love of mankind as Wang had suggested nor love for one's enemies as Hsiao Chün had sought. "We cannot love our enemies or social evils; our aim is to eliminate both. How can our artists and writers fail to understand this common sense view?" [46] Literature, Mao maintained, must mirror the distinctions in society, not talk about universal qualities.

Mao devoted a large portion of his talk to demolishing the belief held by the revolutionary writers that the function of literature was to reveal the dark side of society as impartially as the bright side. This approach, Mao contended, came in part from the left-wing writers' misinterpretation of Lu Hsün's style of writing. Mao then enunciated the official party analysis of Lu Hsün and his work. Though Lu Hsün was a great national hero, his satiric style, which was suited for writers living under the KMT, was no longer necessary in Communist areas, where everyone had freedom and democratic rights. Moreover, Mao asserted that Lu Hsün did not paint the masses in dark hues. In actual fact, Lu Hsün was just as critical of the apathy and backwardness of the peasants as he was of the corruption of reactionary leaders. Mao admitted that the masses may have some shortcomings, but "these were to be removed by means of criticism and self-criticism within the ranks of the people." [47] In other words, defects in society were to be exposed and handled by the party, not by writers or intellectuals. Therefore, the function of literature in the Communist areas was to be different from what it had been and what it was elsewhere. No longer were writers to criticize, but rather to portray and extol the masses and their party. No longer were their writings to reflect life as it was, but as the party saw it.

The Campaign Against Wang Shih-wei

Mao's "Talks" signaled an all-out campaign against the writers who had published critical articles about the party. Though all of them were censured, Wang Shih-wei was the only one who was used as a public example. In addition to the fact that he had been the most caustic of the group, there appear to be other reasons for his choice. In many ways, he was the most vulnerable. He was not so well known to the general public as his colleagues. Ting Ling, Ai Ch'ing, and Hsiao Chün, for instance, had all written literary works which had brought the adulation of large sections of the population. They had been acclaimed by Communist officials, and Mao himself had lauded Ting Ling.[48] It was much easier to discredit someone for whom the public had little personal attachment. Also, Wang's past connection with the Trotskyites had already laid him open to attack.

It appears that Wang's factional disputes with top officials in the Central Research Institute of which he was a member were another element in his selection. Ch'en Po-ta, who was reported to have been Mao's secretary at the time and an official in the Institute and in the party's Propaganda Department, was in constant conflict with Wang. The enmity between them began in the spring of 1941, when both engaged in a debate on the use of national forms in literature. At this time, Wang wrote an article, "On National Forms of Literature," which argued as Hu Feng and Feng Hsüeh-feng did in the KMT areas that national forms should not be accepted as the basis for literary style because the songs and fables of the masses could not measure up to any standards of culture. In one of Ch'en Po-ta's numerous denunciations of Wang, he revealed that when he sought to counter Wang openly in the press on this question, Wang had tried to prevent the publication of his article. Furthermore, he disclosed that while they were in the Institute together, Wang had criticized Ch'en and his colleagues for grabbing official positions.[49] Yet, Wang himself had not been above competing for high posts and demanding special privileges, such as eating in private and wearing cadre clothes.[50] It seems clear that there was a bitter struggle for power among party ideologists, with those closest to Mao and to the party's views winning the upper hand. Most likely, Ch'en's access to Mao and his dislike of Wang influenced the choice of Wang as the scapegoat.

The campaign against Wang began in the Central Research Institute and the Lu Hsün Academy of Arts. It was led by Ch'en Po-ta, Ai Szu-ch'i, and the historian Fan Wen-lan. A few mild criticisms of Wang's unorthodox views began to appear in *Chieh-fang jih-pao* in the middle of March. However, after Mao's second talk, attacks on Wang became more and more vociferous and appeared almost daily in the paper until the end of June. Beginning on May 27, a series of meetings took place for two weeks specifically to discredit Wang.[51] His articles were distributed to the participants, along with the cheng feng documents, to be used as the basis for study and criticism. Throughout this period, Wang was constantly visited by delegations and colleagues and was sent letters by party leaders urging him to renounce his views and study the party's documents, but he refused to do either. Under such pressure, Wang, on June 2, asked permission to withdraw from the party, but he would not admit any guilt. On the contrary, he declared that he withdrew because his own beliefs could no longer compromise with the spirit of utilitarianism that had overtaken the party. All he asked was to be left alone to work out his own problems without anyone's help.

His pleas went unheard. The campaign gave more and more attention to his past Trotskyite affiliations. Wall newspapers were seen in Yenan entitled "Wang Shih-wei, the Trotskyite." Unexpectedly, at the beginning of the second week of discussions, Wang suddenly appeared at the proceedings. He announced that he would discontinue his conflict with the party because "The love of several friends whom I respect has moved me." [52] He implied that they had suffered for his recalcitrance. However, he did not capitulate, declaring "I have read all the articles in the newspaper, but I still do not see my mistakes." [53] He specifically directed himself to refuting the charges of Trotskyism brought against him and accused party leaders of recklessness in their name-calling. He explained that when he first came to Yenan, he believed that people could hold different views, and so he had seen no reason to report his past. Besides, by that time he had already broken off his correspondence with the Trotskyite Ch'en Tu-hsiu and his connections with the Trotskyite movement. Wang affirmed his support of the United Front, although he admitted that he still had reservations about Stalin, particularly because of his purges in the 1930's. With his criticism of Stalin, Wang was quickly silenced, and he left the meeting. At that point, he disappeared from the scene.

Still, the meetings against him continued to grow in size and in intensity. On June 8, a thousand people attended a session for all the party organs and schools in the Yenan area. The condemnations of Wang now ran the gamut from denial of his literary beliefs to charges of Trotskyite subversion. Even his cohorts turned against him. Ting Ling and Ai Ch'ing, on June 9, attacked him mercilessly and renounced the very views they had propounded just a few months earlier. Most of his friends, unlike Wang, had been unable to hold out against the unrelenting pressures put upon them. His group had been split off one by one.

The speeches and articles of the party's theoreticians and cultural leaders [54] throughout this period indicated that the party used this campaign to set down the line on several issues that had disturbed it in its relations with the intellectuals: the position of the intellectual and writer in a party-run society, and the place of Communist ideals in party practice. By picturing Wang and his colleagues as holding views on these questions totally opposed to the party's, the intellectuals and cadres were to be educated in the "correct" ideas. In many cases, however, these contrasts contrived by the party were, in reality, only differences in degree rather than in substance.

Therefore, when the party sought to inculcate writers and intellectuals with the doctrine that the party was to lead all aspects of intellectual life, it did so by showing that Wang and his group advocated that the party withdraw from all areas of society. Furthermore, it accused Wang of trumpeting the slogan, "Politics follows art." This was a distortion of Wang's theories to highlight the reverse maxim, "Art follows politics," which thereafter became dogma in literary circles. In reality, Wang had granted that in certain realms the party should take command, but in others, such as the creative sphere, the party should protect the independence of this kind of activity. Similarly, party leaders enunciated the doctrine that literature concentrate on the revolution, the party, and the working masses by contrasting it with Wang's view that literature reveal the universal aspects of human nature. Wang's concept, the party ideologists insisted, was devoid of any consciousness of the class struggle. Again this was a misrepresentation of Wang's ideas. He had written that literature should disclose the universality of all men, but should also encompass the class struggle.

For holding these alleged literary theories, Wang was labeled a Trotskyite. Actually, Trotsky accepted the conventional Western, as opposed to the Communist, view of literature. He believed that art and science had their own special characteristics and methods which politics or Marxism-Leninism could not direct. However, in this period of China's alliance with the United States against Japan and of the United Front, the epithet of "Trotskyite," rather than a "running dog" of imperialism or Chiang Kai-shek, carried a more ominous meaning. Moreover, Stalin's purges of the Trotskyites in the 1930's and the conflict of the party with the Trotskyites in China were of recent memory. When the party accused Wang of a Trotskyite view of literature, it was, in reality, using a convenient term for attacking the influence of Western ideas on modern Chinese literature.

Even though Wang was termed a "Trotskyite" for his literary ideas, he was called a "petty-bourgeois idealist" for his political views. His belief that equality and democracy should be carried out in practice were dismissed by the party as the illusions of middle-class intellectuals. The fact that the party also had talked of these ideals appeared to have been forgotten by his accusers. On the contrary, party ideologists attempted to justify the need for certain distinctions in society and certain limitations on democracy. They declared that it was only logical that older revolutionaries with heavier responsibilities have special privileges and better living conditions than the average party member. Furthermore, if in these perilous times there was the extreme democracy which Wang desired, rather than democratic centralism, the nation would be without leadership to carry out the revolution.

The party maintained that Wang's exposure of the class distinctions and restrictions on freedom in Yenan undermined the party's authority. His insistence on the implementation of utopian ideals only provoked friction between the ordinary functionaries and the leadership, between young cadres and old revolutionaries, and between creative people and the organizational leaders. Actually, Wang too had acknowledged that it was impossible to run a society without certain groups in charge, but he believed that the unity of a party-governed society could be achieved by recognizing and trying to close the gaps between these various groups instead of ignoring them. Cohesion of the party could be attained more effectively by efforts of the leadership to understand the sentiments of those they led rather than by compelling them to conform outwardly to political policies.

Throughout this campaign, these views of Wang Shih-wei and the revolutionary writers were labeled as ideological subversion, but in reality, their crime was idealism. The fact that their criticisms of the regime appeared within a few weeks of each other and in the same paper would imply that they were planned. Nonetheless, there was no intrigue involved, but rather a lack of comprehension of the full implications of the cheng feng movement and the naïve belief that the party wanted to hear all shades of opinion. Still, this campaign of the early 1940's was not carried to the point where the victims were accused of antiparty plots or political conspiracy. As yet, the party did not conduct its drives with the fanatical zeal of later campaigns. The misdeeds of the revolutionary writers were not so serious that they could not be corrected with the proper education. Moreover, this campaign did not go beyond the reaches of the party itself. It was a restricted, but intensive, drive limited to party cadres and party intellectuals in the areas under party control.

Apparently the party had some difficulty at first in foisting their picture of Wang onto the intellectuals and cadres in the party. This may have been due to the fact that Wang's articles had aroused a positive response when they were first published. His criticisms had a profound impact on the youth and the intellectuals in Yenan, many of whom were similarly disillusioned with the party's policies. Wang's profession of humanistic values along with his use of leftist terms struck a familiar chord with those fellow-traveling intellectuals whose attachment to communism was more emotional than intellectual. Party leaders conceded that Wang had "gained the sympathy of those who believed in petty-bourgeois humanism." As a result, they had difficulty organizing discussions against him.[55] In fact, there seems to have been no spontaneous reaction against Wang's remarks.

Criticisms of Wang from the rank and file did not appear until the party had turned its full propaganda guns upon him. This may have been one of the reasons for the increasing intensity of the campaign.

Even when the campaign reached its climax at the end of May, several members of the Central Research Institute arose to speak on Wang's behalf, insinuating that the charges against him were false. Some criticized his ideas, but refused to attack him personally. There were others who accepted the party's denunciation of Wang, but disapproved of the severity of the campaign against him. Fan Wen-lan complained, "Some comrades still claim that the criticism of Wang Shih-wei has been too extreme." [56] Writers were particularly unwilling to participate fullheartedly in the drive. Yet, by the end of the meetings, even Wang's closest friends had rejected him and his ideas. Only Hsiao Chün apparently did not make a thorough enough disavowal of Wang so that it could be presented in public. Thus, by the middle of June, after several months of relentless pressure, the party's propaganda machine had at least externally imprinted the party's extreme image of Wang onto the cadres and intellectuals. With the exception of Wang, and possibly Hsiao Chün, even the most independent party members had ostensibly fallen into line.

The Effect of the Campaign on Wang's Colleagues

While the public attack on Wang was proceeding, an undercover drive against his associates was underway. Though all of them appeared at first to have resisted various kinds of coercion from the party, in the end they were forced to surrender. Subsequently, most of them lost their positions and were dispersed to the countryside. There, they supposedly reformed their thoughts through labor and acquaintance with the masses. The contacts of this group of writers with one another were severed. However, the seeds of their future rebelliousness can be seen in the course of the reform of each of them.

For weeks, Ting Ling was forced to attend meetings expressly devoted to a discussion of her thought. Apparently, she did not readily step into line, because on June 10 a criticism of her story, "In the Hospital," appeared in *Chieh-fang jih-pao*, in which she was accused of having the same traits as her heroine. Like her heroine, she was charged with showing little interest in the masses. She was also censured for using the old method of realism, which was defined as criticizing one's own group. "Ting Ling has forgotten that she is describing a Communist party member, not an ordinary person." [57] Her portrayals of the cadres were called false because they gave the impression that incompetence was general in party organs rather than unusual. Essentially, this book review was an indirect public criticism of Ting Ling herself.

The day after it was published, on June 11, Ting Ling confessed. It seems that the open criticism of her story may have been a factor in her confession, for she began her self-criticism by admitting, "I did not intend to speak, but events have compelled me to express an opinion." [58] Then she not only lashed out at Wang, but at her own article on women. Her initial remarks about that essay showed that the sentiments presented in it had meant a great deal to her, though in the end she renounced them. "Much as I have poured out my blood and tears in that article and infused it with the bitterness and fervent hopes which I have held for years, . . . my essay only brought out and viewed problems in a biased way." [59] Though the full text of this confession and later ones were not published, their general tenor can be seen from her conversation with the journalist Gunther Stein, who interviewed her in Yenan.[60] She admitted to him that her problem and that of some other women in Yenan was that they still had the same attitudes they had formed in the man-centered society of old China. In Yenan where there was equality between the sexes, she had not realized that her narrow feminism was outdated. Instead of improving cooperation between men and women and all social groups, she had caused disunity.

From this time until 1944, Ting Ling went through a series of thought reform experiences. She studied in party schools and spent time in villages and factories. She was removed from her post as literary editor of *Chieh-fang jih-pao*, which was taken over by one of her chief accusers, Ai Szu-ch'i. Her chief literary activity consisted in writing vivid newspaper accounts of the life of the masses. In her remaining years at Yenan, she appeared to have become outwardly docile in her relations with the party.

Still, her interviews with Western journalists who travled to Yenan revealed that she had not completely surrendered her artistic standards.[61] She acknowledged that before coming to Yenan her inspiration had come from her dissatisfaction with the oppressive atmosphere in which she lived. In the Communist areas she had to find her inspiration elsewhere, primarily from the workers, peasants, and soldiers, but she conceded that she and her colleagues had had some difficulty in doing this. Consequently, she could write little of a creative nature. She also resented having to use her literary talents only for propaganda purposes. To her such work had merely temporary significance. She wanted to engage in writing that would have a lasting quality. This undaunted desire to be involved in artistic expression that had more than purely utilitarian goals was a strain that ultimately was to lead to further conflict with the Communist regime.

Ai Ch'ing's thought reform followed a slightly different pattern from Ting Ling's. His pen did not lie idle during the intensive period of thought reform in the spring of 1942. After his criticism of the party was printed, he continued to publish poems which were primarily descriptions of nature that had little political connotation. Perhaps they were an indirect form of protest. Apparently, however, heavy pressure was put on him in the late spring. Chu Teh, second in command at Yenan, personally ordered him to reform. Thus, after Mao's first talk on literature, Ai Ch'ing was among the first to recant some of his past views.[62] In his initial public confession, he denied his earlier statements about the atmosphere of fear and oppression in Yenan, declaring that descriptions of "darkness" were exaggerations.

Yet, when he discussed the subject of artistic creativity, Ai Ch'ing, like Ting Ling, appears to have budged only slightly. He agreed with party leaders that literature should follow politics, but he qualified this by adding "in the struggle," implying that once the fighting was over, literature could follow its own course. Furthermore, he maintained that even when literature was mobilized for a cause, it could not merely be a "phonograph for politics," a phrase used by the advocates of the "third kind of literature." In Ai Ch'ing's view, writers should be loyal to reality, not to narrow political goals. His reality was complicated. It included all levels of society, which Ai Ch'ing described as "a limitlessly deep, rich and broad sea."[63] He also protested against cultural officials who did not read literature as "the worst kind of bureaucrats."[64] Intimating that they too should reform, he again urged them to try to understand the meaning of literature, its techniques, language, and emotional quality.

Evidently, this semiconfession, semiattack on the party reinvigorated the thought reform process against him. By June 16, when he confessed again, his recantation was far more abject and his assault on Wang more devastating than those of Wang's enemies. Thereafter, he became one of the most outspoken critics of Wang and his thinking. Now, when he described Yenan, he painted it as a pleasant place where there was freedom to speak and create. Moreover, he no longer termed the defects in Yenan the results of party misrule, but the "products of bourgeois sentiments . . . and shortcomings which cannot be avoided in the revolutionary process." [65] His confessions appeared in several party journals, even in the Communist newspaper in Chungking, *Hsin-hua jih-pao* (New China news).

Having conformed to the party's wishes, Ai Ch'ing was then sent to the countryside to reform through labor and to learn the folk songs of the people. Officially, his poems continued to be praised for their love of country, though the readers were warned that a certain pessimism, carried over from the old society, was unconsciously revealed in his writings. Ai Ch'ing, for his part, loudly proclaimed his allegiance to party doctrine, but quietly chafed under the restrictions put on his creative work. In an interview with the peripatetic writer Robert Payne,[66] he lamented that he had so little time in which to write anything worthwhile. While both the party and Ai Ch'ing seemed satisfied with each other, underneath they had serious reservations.

Outside of Wang, only Hsiao Chün and some of his followers consistently resisted the party's demands that they engage in thought reform. Meetings were convened in October 1942, several months after Wang had been silenced, specifically to criticize Hsiao Chün's ideas. His old friend Ting Ling was chairman. Nevertheless, Hsiao still refused to accept their criticisms or to reform himself. Public support from other writers,[67] the popularity of his patriotic works, and the fact that Wang had already served the party's purposes, most likely insulated Hsiao from the same kind of severe attack directed against Wang. He was merely sent to the countryside to reform through labor. Apparently, he must have made some accommodation with the regime, because his fate was no worse than that of his colleagues. Whatever form his accommodation took, however, it did not conform to the standards the party had set for the others. There was no confession nor criticism of Wang by Hsiao Chün in the party newspapers. Nor was there any report that he had denounced Wang at the struggle meetings as his colleagues had done.

In fact, the few articles that appeared by Hsiao Chün after Mao's "Talks on Art and Literature" still expressed independent views, though more subtly than previously. The first one appeared on May 14, twelve days after Mao gave his initial talk at the Yenan forum. He began by agreeing with Mao's basic premise that an author must write from a definite class stand. But then he injected another prerequisite: that literature focus on the liberation of the nation and mankind. This was to take precedence even over the class struggle. Concomitantly, he agreed with Mao that literary works should easily be understood and readily appreciated by the readers, but he did not specifically categorize readers as workers and peasants. Literature was to appeal to all groups, not just certain classes. Similarly, the material for literature was not to be taken merely from the workers, peasants, and soldiers, but "gathered everywhere, in villages, cities, the front lines and even around you." [68]

Hsiao Chün's sharpest divergence from Mao was in his insistence that a writer adopt an independent position. Like Mao, he believed that the writer should immerse himself deeply in his subject matter, but he warned that his involvement should not reach the point where he loses his objectivity. He cautioned, "A writer must go into the sea — the sea of life — in order to pick up the pearls, but still he should not be drowned by it." [69] He maintained that the writer should be fervently involved in the major issues of the day, yet be able to stand aside and judge them impartially. Connected with his desire for an independent view of reality was his reiteration of Wang Shih-wei's and Lo Feng's demand that literature depict the dark side as well as the bright side of society. He stated this belief with a succinct quote. "From the ugly, let us bring out the beautiful — and develop it; from the beautiful, let us bring out the ugly — and destroy it." [70] He reiterated his belief and that of his colleagues that it was the duty of the writer to expose the faults of society in order to improve society.

A month later, at the very height of the cheng feng campaign, Hsiao Chün published another article entitled "The 'Bulba' Spirit in Literary and Art Circles." In light of the circumstances of the time, it could be construed as a covert criticism of the whole procedure of thought reform. On the surface, it was a discussion of a portion of Nikolai Gogol's novella *Tarus Bulba*, but implicitly it was a protest against some of the inhumane practices being used by the party in its ideological remolding campaign. He described how Tarus Bulba welcomed his sons home with great joy. He showed his feelings by challenging the youths to a wrestling match. When he was knocked down by them, he did not express anger, but satisfaction at having engaged in the fray.

Hsiao Chün urged his fellow comrades, especially the writers, to emulate the spirit that existed between Tarus Bulba and his sons. Older and entrenched party officials and writers should participate in debate and in the competition of ideas with younger and newer members for their own enlightenment, not to demolish their opponents. We "should not be afraid to be knocked down by those who follow after us . . . and should enjoy the battle even when we lose." [71] Much more was to be learned, Hsiao advised, from a discussion between comrades predicated on the feeling of "love" for the other than on merely teaching others without an exchange of ideas. By couching his views in a talk on Tarus Bulba, Hsiao adopted the technique of the nineteenth-century Russian intelligentsia who disguised their complaints against the regime in literary discussions. Seemingly the pressures of thought reform had not deterred Hsiao Chün from asserting his role as a critic of his society.

When Mao enunciated his literary doctrine, Ho Ch'i-fang, the last writer to criticize, had been among the first to confess unreservedly. After he had completely refuted his past ideas and gone through a period of labor and study, he became a member of the party's literary hierarchy and performed his duties with fervor. His self-criticisms, more than those of any of the other writers, foreshadowed the tone of the next stage of the campaign. He demanded a totally new orientation of Chinese cultural life based on political goals and China's own literary tradition. His principal target was the high degree of Western influence prevailing at the Lu Hsün Academy of Arts, where he and the other revolutionary writers had taught at one time or another. He ranted particularly against those members of the Academy who were preoccupied with their own intimate experiences and with the perfection of literary techniques. Unsparingly, Ho castigated himself for these very same tendencies and for being more interested in artistic criteria than in political considerations. The internal conflict within Ho himself, between the requirements of art and politics, apparently, was covered over by his ideological reform. It remained quiescent for a long time, but was to haunt him again toward the end of the 1950's.

The Role of Chou Yang in the Second Stage of the Campaign

After the meetings against Wang Shih-wei were concluded in June 1942, the emphasis of the campaign shifted from stressing the "incorrect" to affirming the "correct." The tone of this aspect of the movement was affected by Chou Yang. When Chou left Shanghai in 1937, he immediately proceeded to Yenan where as he aptly described, "I put forth every effort to make myself an interpreter, propagandist, and practitioner of Mao Tse-tung's cultural ideas and policies." [72] In addition to his political orthodoxy, the fact that he was one of the first intellectuals to arrive in Yenan and was a native of Mao's own province aided his swift rise in the hierarchy. For several years he served concurrently as president of Yenan University and as dean of the Lu Hsün Academy of Arts. In 1939 he established the Chinese Writers' Resistance movement, another United Front organization of Chinese writers.

Most likely, some friction existed in Yenan between him and the former associates of Lu Hsün. Though those who were in Yenan had not clashed directly with him in the 1930's, several of them continued close relations with Hu Feng, one of Chou's chief antagonists. Even while living in Yenan, Hsiao Chün, Ting Ling, and Ai Ch'ing contributed to Hu Feng's journal, Ch'i yüeh (July). Ting Ling had openly expressed her support in the early 1940's for the position of Lu Hsün's group in the conflict with Chou over Literature for National Defense.[73] Still, Chou at first was not so conspicuous as his associates Ch'en Po-ta and Ai Szu-ch'i in attacking these writers and condemning their ideas. It was not until the second phase of the campaign that Chou took a leading role.

After Wang Shih-wei had been removed from the scene, his cultural values demolished, and his colleagues debilitated, the campaign assumed a new dimension. Its character became positive rather than negative and re-education rather than denunciation came increasingly to the fore. The cultural reorientation of writers and intellectuals in Yenan became an outgrowth of this campaign against Wang Shih-wei and an important component of the cheng feng movement. Unlike Stalin, the Chinese Communists did not do away with groups of intellectuals who refused to conform. There was a fundamental difference in approach. The Chinese used moral persuasion and indoctrination rather than violence against those who did not comply. The distinguishing feature of their type of purge was that it was more of an educational movement to remold the human psyche than a reign of terror to eliminate all wayward elements.

Though this phase of the drive was based on Mao's literary "Talks," its emphasis was colored by Chou's own particular interest in specific tenets of Mao's thought. He gave prominence to Mao's dictum that intellectuals should participate in the struggle of the masses, although in this he may have been affected as much by the Russian populist writer Chernyshevski, whom he had translated while in Yenan, as by Mao. Even more significant, Mao's affirmation of Ch'ü Ch'iu-pai's and Chou Yang's program to develop Chinese culture in its own national style was given an importance by Chou far out of proportion to Mao's other precepts. With this impetus from Mao, Chou intensified his efforts to mold Chinese literature into an expression of the life and feelings of the masses, cast in the traditional folk forms of the people.

Simultaneously, he led an assault on the influence of nineteenth-century Western literature, which he called the old-type critical realism. He cited Lu Hsün's writings as an example of this kind of literature. "Lu Hsün critically described the passive, gloomy, despairing aspects of the Chinese character." [74] This approach was no longer needed, Chou believed, for it only disunited the nation and made people lose faith in the revolution and communism. Instead, Chou asserted this was a time for "revolutionary [socialist] realism, which is not negative . . . It demands that the author write of brightness and of new things which are growing or will grow." [75] With these views on literature, Chou guided the re-education of writers in Communist China from 1942 on.

Because Chou was also the director of education of the Shensi-

Kansu-Ninghsia Border Region, his educational program for writers set the pattern in institutions of higher education in Yenan and foreshadowed Communist educational policies in the 1950's. Similar in spirit to his ideas on literature, Chou's approach to education was anti-intellectual and anti-Western. As they did in literature, Chou and the party leaders linked education inextricably with politics. They fashioned an education curriculum that played down intellectual accomplishments and specialization and stressed training in practical political tasks. A specific application of these views on literature and education can be seen in Chou's reform of the Lu Hsün Academy of Arts. Chou insisted that writers of the Academy had been incapable of creativity in literature because they "only emphasized accomplishments in techniques and knowledge from academic books." [76] Instead of concentrating on Western models and artistic techniques, they should look to their own native intelligence as the peasants did when they created their folk songs.[77] Consequently, Chou sent all the writers of the Academy to the villages, factories, and front lines. There they were to establish an organic relationship between their creative work and the customs, heritage, and practical work of the peasants.

Thus, toward the middle of the 1940's, the party had been able to enforce outward acceptance of their policies by using Wang Shih-wei's ideas and actions as examples of unorthodoxy, and by inculcating views and attitudes they claimed were diametrically opposed to those of Wang and his group. Nevertheless, the underlying conflicts between the party and its intellectuals remained. This wave of thought reform, limited primarily to the left-wing intellectuals in Yenan, was only the beginning of a systematic, continuing campaign to impose the party's standards on intellectual activity. In subsequent drives, Wang's colleagues were to be picked out as Wang had been to serve as symbols with which to remold the thought and activities of the Chinese intellectuals.

chapter three

CONFLICTS BETWEEN LEFT-WING WRITERS IN THE KMT AREA AND THE CCP

While one group of Lu Hsün's followers resisted the party's policies in Yenan, another, led by Lu Hsün's close companions Hu Feng and Feng Hsüeh-feng, carried on a similar struggle in Chungking. Several years before Mao's Yenan "Talks," these two writers, who were primarily literary theorists, had constructed a system of ideas on literature that diverged sharply from the one Mao was to set forth in 1942. Though there were some points of difference between them, in general, they had a similar approach to major ideological and literary questions, and they maintained it almost consistently throughout the twists and turns of the party line.

Literary and Ideological Beliefs

Their unique idea within the context of leftist literary theory was what they called the role of the "subjective spirit," a term describing emotional intensity and spontaneity. Their views, and even their phrasing, on this concept resembled one another's so closely that one could surmise that there had been collaboration between the two men. From their interpretation of the "subjective spirit," they derived their outlook on the whole artistic process. Hu wrote, "In entering the objective [reality], the writer's subjective consciousness must spontaneously welcome, select, or reject the object and must spontaneously use its truths to complete or change the writer's view . . . This leads to a profound self-struggle which is the source of artistic creation." [1] From this "spiritual clash" between the writer's consciousness and his environment, a unity finally evolves which they called art. Like the Soviet literary critic Lunacharsky, whom they both admired, they regarded the intensity of emotional feeling as the ultimate test of greatness in art.

They considered their theory on the subjective spirit to be in good Marxist tradition. Though there is no evidence that they had read the Hungarian theorist Lukacs, their interpretation of Marx was similar to his. Like Lukacs, they appear to have absorbed the view developed by Marx in his youth that the ultimate goal of human existence is the realization of self. They, too, assigned to consciousness an active role. Similarly, their concept of literature cannot be said to clash with Marx. Marx also believed that literature was a sphere of sensuous immediacy rather than general propositions and messages.[2]

Nevertheless, their interpretation of Marx did conflict with the party's. Their concept of creativity, which placed subjective cognition on a par and sometimes above objective reality, was in opposition to the party's literary theory, which viewed objective reality, specifically the political struggle, as the determining factor in literary practice. Also, Hu's and Feng's vision of literature as the product of the tension between the subjective and objective by its very nature made writers critical of their society. No matter how fervently a writer supported the regime politically, his literary works would never fully conform. Furthermore, the spontaneous intuition, intense individual emotions, and deep, soul-searching struggle which Hu and Feng asked writers to bring to reality lacked a definite political character and did not lend themselves to the depiction of an explicit doctrine. These were processes which the party could neither control nor direct. Finally, Hu and Feng appear to have presented their complex, almost mysterious concept of creativity in defiance of the party's simple, rationalistic explanations. Feng asserted, "The difficulty, anguish, and all that seems to be irrational, unorganized, and mystical in the spirit are attached to grasping this conflict and its unity . . . The joy of the victory of the artist cannot be understood by the ordinary person."[3] Such a view of creative practice stood in contrast to the party's interpretation of art as merely a description of reality expressed in Marxist-Leninist terms.

These views on the role of the "subjective spirit" led Hu and Feng to consider the incorporation of any specific teachings or doctrine into creative work as a hindrance to China's development. To them, the use of any theory or philosophy to interpret reality distorted its truths. Such an approach, they feared, would ultimately blind the party to the constantly changing happenings around them. Whereas the party asked writers to proceed from a priori assumptions, Hu and Feng urged them to proceed from the opposite direction, from reality to theory. Feng described this process when he revealed that one of the reasons he became a Marxist was that he had "arrived at similar conclusions in revolutionary activity and in his own analysis of real life." [4]

With this disdain for the imposition of any doctrine onto creativity, it was inevitable that Hu and Feng would resist thought reform by the party. They agreed that writers should change and reform their viewpoints, but under their own auspices, not the party's. They asserted that a writer, through experiencing life and creating literature, came closer to the "truth of life and a more healthy philosophy of life," [5] than he would through thought reform. Feng, in the early 1940's, wrote, "The creative process itself is a form of growth for the writer. As a writer completely grasps reality and goes deeply into it, he develops himself and at the same time his artistic ideas and content grow." [6]

Like Marx and Engels, Hu and Feng pointed to Balzac to show that reality could be depicted without the proper ideological training. In their view, good literature was not necessarily dependent on the writer's political bias, but on his careful mirroring of social history. They praised the works of Shakespeare, Tolstoy, and Lu Hsün for this quality. Here again, their approach to literature was in accord with Marx, but not with the party. Whereas the party regarded Lu Hsün's transformation into a revolutionary writer a result of his study of Marxism-Leninism and the influence of the party, Hu and Feng believed it was due much more to the fact that he was a realist than that he was a Marxist. In their terms, this meant that his ideas spontaneously coincided with Marxist ideology. Consequently, they believed that Lu Hsün's revolutionary spirit was strong not only in his later period, but also in his earlier period before he was affected by Marxism-Leninsm. Hu wrote, "Lu Hsün was not familiar with the classical Marxist writers nor did he participate in the official ideological reform. He changed his world view as he developed his own creative practice. His ideas came from his own self-reform." [7]

Hu and Feng used the example of Lu Hsün for a different purpose than did their fellow revolutionary writers in Yenan. They were not so concerned with his role as social critic as they were with proving that his acceptance of Marxist-Leninist precepts and his development of revolutionary literature came from his own experience and the very process of living fully rather than through ideological study and thought reform sessions.

Their rejection of compulsory study of ideology, emphasis on emotions, belief that artists and intellectuals should carry out their work in accordance with their own disciplines, stress on literary criteria and complexity, and desire as party followers to maintain literary independence were to undermine the party's ideological unity. As the party's ability to establish a uniform literary canon and stringent controls increased, they came into sharpening conflict with the party.

The Cheng Feng Movement in KMT Areas

By 1943, the cheng feng movement, having been thoroughly carried out in the Yenan area, was extended to left-wing intellectuals and party cadres in Chungking. Though ideological reform could not be conducted on the scale and with the intensity it had been carried out in the Communist areas, nevertheless, the same techniques of small study groups, discussions of prescribed documents, and criticism and self-criticism were used. Here, as in Yenan, Wang Shih-wei was used as the example with which the cheng feng movement was pushed forward, and the same party theoreticians, Ai Szu-ch'i, Ch'en Po-ta, and particularly Chou Yang, were the chief protagonists. Their articles and those of their colleagues in *Hsin-hua jih-pao* pointed out that the left-wing intellectuals in Chungking suffered from many of the same shortcomings as their counterparts in Yenan. However, the cheng feng movement outside the Communist areas had a slightly different emphasis than in Yenan. Because the intellectuals could be less effectively controlled, more attention was given to remolding their private lives than to incorporating them into party-run activities. Consequently, in addition to reading party documents and investigating their work, they were told "to revolutionize their personal habits, speak in revolutionary words, acquire revolutionary friends and follow Marxism-Leninism in their private lives." [8] Reluctance to change one's old way of life and thought or the desire to reform oneself through individual introspection rather than through prescribed party procedures were termed heretical acts comparable to those of Wang Shih-wei.[9]

About this time, Hu Feng and Feng Hsüeh-feng arrived in Chungking. Hu reached there after several years of wandering through the south of China, and Feng came after three years of imprisonment by the KMT. In Chungking, they joined with other left-wing writers to fight the party's battles through propaganda activities. Their previous disagreements with the party apparently did not deter them from satirizing the KMT and encouraging their readers to demand political and economic changes. While they had suffered at the hands of the party's literary bureaucrats, they had suffered much more from the KMT. Also, their faith in the ideals of communism had not wavered. Perhaps most important in explaining their continued support for the party was the fact that they were not fully aware of the implications of the party's cheng feng movement.

The initial response of Hu and his group to the thought reform procedures reveals their misunderstanding of the party's real purpose. Hu regarded them as formal rites which had to be performed, but which would not actually affect his thinking or his writing. In a letter to his colleague Shu Wu, he ridiculed the self-criticisms he was forced to write by calling them "eight-legged essays," a reference to the prescribed form for writing the old Confucian exams. Still, he advised his followers to join in the criticism and self-criticism sessions in the belief that having participated, they would then be left alone to continue their own writing. To his protégé, the short-story writer Lu Ling, he advised, "Insults are people's nourishment; suffer them for a while . . . and complete your own work." [10]

Yet, while Hu was urging the members of his coterie to participate in the cheng feng movement, it was obvious from his letters that he, himself, rebelled against it. In the beginning of 1944, Hu lamented, "Although I do not deserve to be called a wild animal, nevertheless, I still feel as if I am locked in a cage. Occasionally I roar, but the spectators are not concerned. Others consider my roar hateful and disagreeable and wish to put iron clamps on me so I cannot breathe." [11] The phrasing of this letter resembles that used by Lu Hsün in a similar letter he had written to Hu in the 1930's in which he expressed his distress about being mentally imprisoned by the orders and pressures of party officials.[12] Another letter of Hu's a few months later expressed the depression of one who obviously had been ostracized because of his reluctance to participate fully in the thought reform sessions. "My spirit has been low . . . I have the feeling of being in an environment . . . where I am considered a heretic. I am isolated from the rest of the world . . . We can expect nothing from the leftist writers and cultural workers in the KMT areas." [13] Although party representatives in Chungking had ostracized Hu, his small group of disciples remained loyally by his side.

When Mao's "Talks on Art and Literature" were published in *Hsin-hua jih-pao* in the later part of 1944, the rectification drive touched Hu and his followers more directly. As the party began to indoctrinate leftist writers with Mao's theory of literature and to interfere with the content and style of their works more directly, they actively resisted the infringement of their creative discipline. Like their counterparts in Yenan, they did not regard their resistance as out of line with party policy. While they now realized that the cheng feng movement sought ideological conformity, they took the party's simultaneous attack on "subjective dogmatism" to mean that criticism still could be expressed against party bureaucrats. They, too, assumed that one of the purposes in reading the cheng feng documents and in holding study sessions was to arouse genuine debate and criticism. Believing, therefore, that attacks on "subjective dogmatism" were sanctioned along with assaults on other unorthodoxies, Hu presumed he was in line with the goals of the cheng feng movement when he criticized the dogmatism of party officials.

With this reasoning, Hu and his followers established a journal, *Hsi wang* (Hope), whose main purpose was to attack the doctrinairism they felt was overcoming the party's cultural authorities. Since they did not live under direct party rule, they were not so concerned as their associates in Yenan with the party's social and political policies. They gave more attention to its cultural policies — that part of the party's program that touched them most directly. Another reason behind Hu and his followers' open attack on the party's increasing controls over culture may have been to defend themselves against the growing power of their old opponent Chou Yang. They were well aware that during the cheng feng movement, Chou had gained sufficient power to extend his influence to left-wing intellectuals in the non-Communist areas.

Whether the example of Wang Shih-wei's forthright opposition to the dogmatic thinking and sectarian activities of the bureaucracy in Yenan played any part in motivating Hu cannot be proved concretely. Certainly he must have seen the many articles on Wang in *Hsin-hua jih-pao*. A copy of a KMT interpretation of Wang's articles was found in Hu's home. Since he had maintained his relations with Ting Ling, Ai Ch'ing, and Hsiao Chün, it is likely their criticisms had influenced him. He was not the kind of person to be deterred by their lack of success or by the dire consequences they suffered for their efforts. Even before Hu's decision to publish *Hsi wang*, he had had a reputation as "one who would die for a righteous cause." [14] Though Hu ridiculed this description of himself, his letters in this period reveal that he was disposed to act as a martyr. In one to Shu Wu he announced, "At this time I think I must take the whole world as my responsibility . . . 'All things are a part of me.' " [15]

Preparing his weapon, *Hsi wang*, for the assault took many months of careful planning. Hu urged his followers to keep their plans quiet for fear that they would be stopped before they started. Members of his group prepared articles, stories, and poems which Hu guided with close attention and edited with care. The purpose of all their works was to stress man's subjective spirit and to criticize what they considered the "objectivism" and "materialism" of the party's literary tenets. For instance, in advice to Shu Wu, Hu counseled, "You say too little about individualism . . . you should have a chapter on the exultation and sublimation of the spirit . . . so as to see the power of ideals . . . The highest point of the essay should be a fatal blow to the merchants' materialism." [16] Hu frequently used the term "merchants' materialism" to express his disgust with the party's literary doctrine.

In January 1945, *Hsi wang* made its first appearance. One of the controversial works in this issue was the opening article by Hu Feng, "Placing Oneself in the Democratic Struggle," in which he eloquently reiterated his belief that the writer's feelings should be allowed full play, uninhibited by formal, ready-made concepts even when they were imposed by his own party. Also, he stated a theme very similar to the one expressed a few years earlier by Hsiao Chün in Yenan, that the writer should be involved in and at the same time critical of his society. "The writer, on the one hand, must have unyielding subjective strength with which to battle and criticize the objective world. On the other, he enters the objective world emotionally and therefore cannot easily separate himself from it and watch it coolly." [17] The essay in *Hsi wang*, however, that aroused the greatest storm and launched an ideological controversy that raged in cultural circles for ten years, was the concluding one, "On Subjectivism," by Hu's intimate associate Shu Wu. Since Hu had advised Shu closely in the writing of this article, there is every reason to believe that Hu played a role in the formulation of its ideas.

Shu Wu's "On Subjectivism" was as incisive as Wang Shih-wei's "The Wild Lily" in its indictment of party leaders for dogmatic, undemocratic attitudes and for their disregard of the true spirit of the revolution. Shu Wu charged that party revolutionaries had changed the Marxian dialectic into a dogma which made no allowance for new ideas nor for independent thinking. Shu, too, insisted on certain orthodox Marxist principles, but wanted to combine them with an individual interpretation of events and with a pragmatic approach to concrete problems. In Shu's view, these diverse approaches were complementary rather than contradictory. While Shu granted that the class struggle was the motive force of history and of the universe, he also stated that the most creative element in man's development was his individual struggle with reality which he called "the expansion of his subjective spirit in objective reality." [18] To Shu, history was propelled not only by the class struggle, but also by man's individual actions. Consequently, he concluded that man's struggle to preserve and develop his own existence was also a central force in history. This aspect of Shu's thought resembled Sun Yat-sen's doctrine of "The People's Livelihood," in which Sun presented man's search for livelihood as a determining factor in history and society. Whereas to Sun this doctrine replaced the principle of class struggle, to Shu, the doctrine of "The People's Livelihood" and the class struggle were coexistent.

Revolutionaries, Shu asserted, initially approached reality unhampered by dogmatic teachings. Their actual struggle with the objective world had given them "active principles and theories with which to direct the battle." Gradually, however, as they stopped acquiring their beliefs from real life, "their subjective spirits withered." They accepted ready-made formulas and "took on life-long careers as 'progressive representatives.'" When this happened, "If anyone brought up a new idea from his own practical experience or research, they questioned it and labeled it a distortion." [19] Worse still, in Shu's opinion, was the fact that these "progressive representatives" mechanically analyzed other people's class character. "Determining a person's class is not as simple as giving military rank . . . No one's thinking can be analyzed exactly as it is in theory." [20] Similarly, Shu held that a nation's culture cannot be understood entirely in terms of its class structure. "Since spiritual culture is the furthest and highest level from the class base, it is sometimes difficult to determine its correspondence to class." [21] Shu feared that the mechanical application of theories on class and society would hinder the party's effort to come to grips with the realities of China.

Like the revolutionary writers in Yenan, Shu Wu and Hu Feng did not see the "mechanical dogmatism" of party leaders as a result of forces within the party itself, but as a remnant from the old society. Their belief in communism remained undaunted. Also, similar to the views of Wang Shih-wei was their warning that "unless these impurities are taken out, harm will come to the progressive camp in the future." Their fear was that this increasing dogmatism would lead officials "to use their positions to control others." [22] Probably in reference to Chou Yang's vendetta with their group, Shu warned that "The greatest danger is that small groups will fight each other over little things and forget the broad world outside." [23] Though their concern was more with the artistic realm and that of their counterparts in Yenan more with the political realm, in essence, they expressed similar criticisms and demands. They criticized party officials for losing sight of the goals of the revolution and communism in their desire for position and power and advocated freer discussions within the party and greater tolerance of differing viewpoints.

Publication of the first issue of *Hsi wang* aroused much greater controversy than Hu had anticipated. Meetings were immediately called in Chungking literary circles to discuss Hu's journal. *Hsin-*

hua jih-pao and the Communist magazine *Wen-i chen-ti* led the counterattack. Hu's letters to his colleagues at this time acknowledged that they had unrealistically evaluated their chances for generating any changes in the thinking of the literary hierarchy. "For many years, my method of fighting has been a hand grenade . . . but some of my friends do not understand this and consider it a thousand-ton bomb. Actually, it is a small puff against their heavy tanks." [24] Hu realized that the attack being mobilized against them was not merely due to ideological disagreement, but also stemmed from Hu's factional disputes in the past. He wrote, "I have accumulated too many hatreds . . . my opponents have organized a gigantic campaign." [25]

Hu appears to have been impelled by an "internal gyroscope" which was aware of but unresponsive to outside pressures. While he clearly saw the power arrayed against him, he still continued to publish *Hsi wang* and to encourage his followers to stand by their own views. He urged them on with words like these: "We cannot be disappointed and must not lose strength. We must maintain a frontal attack for a long time." [26] However, by April party officials had attempted to halt the publication of *Hsi wang* completely. Their actions only pushed Hu to greater efforts. At this time, he declared, "We still must have more light and strength to beat down the opposition." [27] A few months later as the facilities for publishing *Hsi wang* were being denied to him, he warned, "We have suffered great difficulties and abuse for our journal . . . If we compromise, *Hsi wang* will be published, but if we compromise then why must we publish at all?" [28]

As his journal was being suppressed, Hu was also under constant pressure from party officials who, as Hu described, "always come to investigate." [29] Those investigating him were officials from Yenan — Hu Ch'iao-mu, party historian and trainer of party cadres, and Ho Ch'i-fang, now one of Chou Yang's right-hand men. Yet, amid increasing obstacles, Hu continued to publish *Hsi wang* irregularly until October 1946. Insight into the motivation for Hu's defiant actions and unflagging perseverance, even when he was well aware that he was doomed to defeat, can be seen in the introduction to the May 1946 issue of *Hsi wang* in which he quoted the sculptor Rodin: "Even when one discovers that his feelings are opposite to what is popular at the time, he should not hesitate to express himself. At first, he may not be understood, but his isolation will pass . . . because what is genuinely true to one person will become definitely true to millions." [30]

The criticisms and meetings on the ideas and attitudes of Hu's group continued intermittently for about a year and a half. Yet, in all the public denunciations at this time, Hu was not made the ostensible object of attack. Most likely, he was still shielded by the mantle of Lu Hsün and by his reputation as a sophisticated critic. Rather, Hu Feng's disciples, Shu Wu and Lu Ling, were made the targets. Shu Wu was criticized for his article "On Subjectivism," and Lu Ling for his novels and short stories. Literary critics have compared Lu Ling's writing with Emile Zola's and praised his psychological insights,[31] but party officials termed his work too obscure and too complex to be understood by the masses.

Though the chief critics against Hu's group were Kuo Mo-jo and Mao Tun, China's leading literary figures, a broad campaign comparable to the one against Wang Shih-wei did not develop. In addition to its inability to carry out such a drive in the KMT areas, the party appears to have been more tolerant of heterodoxy in their ranks in Chungking than in Yenan. The advantages of the left-wing writers "opposition spirit" as applied to the KMT evidently outweighed the disadvantages of their unorthodoxy and factionalism. Furthermore, because a certain degree of creative freedom did exist outside the Communist areas in 1945, Hu was not completely silenced. Though many channels of communication were gradually being closed to him, he was still able to speak out freely at meetings and publish his own journal. Consequently, he was able to defend himself and his colleagues and answer the charges against them. Probably, Hu's strong defense of his views and of his followers plus the fact that the party did not act decisively against him explain why he and his group still held a wide and enthusiastic audience in left-wing circles.

At these meetings to denounce Hu's disciples Feng Hsüeh-feng reappeared in his role as critic of the party. After Feng had been released from prison in the summer of 1943 and settled in Chungking, he devoted himself to writing. He did not engage actively at first either in party activities or ideological debates. Since he had been

friendly with Hu in Shanghai, most likely he renewed his acquaintance with him. However, various references to Feng in Hu's letters,
which often placed Feng in the same category as the other literary
authorities, would indicate that their relationship was not so close
as it had been in the 1930's.

Nevertheless, some of Feng's essays published around this time
expressed in a subdued fashion the views Hu was proclaiming vociferously in his journal, *Hsi wang*. Like Hu, he remained loyal to his
literary friends, even when the party directed otherwise. He, more
than Hu, who was occupied with the affairs of his own coterie, stood
by his colleagues in Yenan, particularly Ting Ling. Several of his
essays were devoted to praising her and appear to have been written,
albeit subtly, to defend her against the party's charges. For instance,
in *K'ua ti jih-tzu* (Days of transition), a collection of essays written
in the years 1945 and 1946, where Feng devoted most of his pages to
spouting the standard Communist line on the evils of imperialism
and reactionism, there is a small section on literature in which the
major portion was a panegyric to Ting Ling. He expressed admira-
tion for her ability to participate actively in revolutionary activities
and "still remain an artist of genuine accomplishments." [32] Besides
his support for his friends, Feng also reiterated some of the arguments
he had made in the previous debate on national forms in literature.
He particularly concerned himself with this subject in a collection
of essays, *Hsiang-feng yü shih-feng* (Spirit of country and city), in
which he once again stressed the need for China to assimilate the
culture of the West.

Feng's most controversial work at this time was "On the Literary
Movement of the Democratic Revolution." This long essay, divided
into four parts, was derived from talks Feng gave at cheng feng
meetings in 1945. Actually, Feng had already toward the end of his
earlier collection, *Hsiang-feng yü shih-feng*, begun to show appre-
hension over the position of intellectuals, particularly writers, in a
party-run society. He had argued there that intellectuals should be
allowed to carry on their work in their own way, unfettered by con-
straints from their class or party. Intellectuals, Feng declared, were
related to other classes in society, but "since they establish their
life in truth, they must use their intelligence to serve all social levels
which rely on them . . . These levels cannot restrict or influence
them in their search for truth." [33]

In "On the Literary Movement of the Democratic Revolution," Feng addressed himself further to this problem. Like Hu, Feng too appeared to be deeply disturbed by what he called "leftist mechanicalism," "vulgar materialism," and "objectivism," the same terms that Hu used to describe the dogmatism which he believed was seeping into left-wing circles. Though Feng also insisted that he was similarly troubled by pragmatism and right-wing individualism, his discussion of these flaws was negligible in contrast to his disputation on dogmatism. To Feng, dogmatism manifested itself in the literary theories of the party bureaucrats and most glaringly in the sectarianism pervading cultural circles. As he had done in the controversy over a "third kind of literature," Feng urged the party to listen to fellow travelers and liberals whose goals were the same as its own, even though their methods were more roundabout. He asserted that it was a mistake to regard nonrevolutionary writers in the same way as reactionaries. "We have insufficiently evaluated the non-Communist writers' discontent and dissatisfaction with the dark forces in society." Though they are less direct, "they too respond to the people and revolution and hate the ruling classes." [34] Feng begged the party not to reject their support in the revolutionary movement. He directed this advice particularly to those party members who insisted, he said, on ideological conformity merely to elevate themselves and hide "the emptiness and weakness of their own literary works." [35] Though he never mentioned Chou Yang by name, the charge of sectarianism was obviously in reference to him and his cohorts.

Like the other revolutionary writers, Feng too considered traces of the old class attitudes as a cause of this dogmatism. He also added another factor which up to this point none of his colleagues had noted: the evils that came from being in a position of leadership.[36] Among leftist intellectuals, he appears to be one of the first to recognize the consequences that could arise when the party became the governing power. Still, Feng gave only passing reference to this idea. He placed the major blame for dogmatism on the leadership's lack of appreciation for the power of the emotions in creative work, an old theme of Feng's.

Though Feng did not come out openly in support of Hu, he appears to have defended him indirectly by expressing similar ideas and using identical phrases, such as "subjective force," "fervent demands," "spiritual clash," and "search for the spontaneous, natural forces." Moreover, in the section of his essay which specifically discussed Hu's group, Feng wrote, "Some consider them dangerous, but they can only be regarded as people engaged in . . . lofty efforts to liberate culture and the individual and work for . . . the artistic ideals of the future." [37] Feng also devoted several pages to denouncing the detractors of Hu Feng's protégé, Lu Ling, although again not mentioning them by name. While he had reservations about Lu Ling's expressed desire to depict primitive feelings, nevertheless, he commended him for opening up a new area of literature and reprimanded literary officials who rejected his work unthinkingly. Feng's defense of Lu Ling against the attacks of the literary bureaucrats also revealed his reluctance to accept Mao's "Talks on Art and Literature" as literary canon. Feng asserted that many questions still existed in literary theory, and we "cannot say they have been solved correctly." [38]

This essay appeared about the time that Feng was asked to be one of the principal speakers at the meetings called in 1945 to denounce Hu's group. Although Feng had remained politically inactive and had obviously not conformed to the party's cultural policies in his writing, most likely he was selected because of his past relationship with Lu Hsün and because of his known friendship with Hu. Even mild condemnation of Hu by Feng would carry more weight than vociferous invective from Hu's known antagonists. Feng's talk at one of these meetings appeared at the outset as a criticism of Hu's ideas. He began with the standard, negative comments about Hu's concept of subjectivism, but then he proceeded to present views similar to those in his essay "On the Literary Movement of the Democratic Revolution," the very ideas that the meeting had been called to criticize.[39] Still, Feng never referred to the fact that these views were shared by Hu.

Soon after, on January 23, 1946, in the literary supplement of *Hsinhua jih-pao*, Feng, under the pen name Hua Shih, published another ideological attack on Mao's literary ideas in an article entitled "Irrelevant Words." Though Feng never alluded to Mao's "Talks," the substance of his essay opposed one of its major tenets, that political standards must be put before artistic standards in literature. He called the use of the terms "political standards" and "artistic standards" empty phrases, and declared that "Art is complicated. One cannot merely have an artistic or political approach." [40] In Feng's view, art and politics were intrinsically bound together in a literary work as unified, not separate, entities.

Consequently, Feng's position in this Hu Feng episode of 1945 was ambivalent. He spoke under the auspices of the party and announced his support for the party's policies, yet he showed himself clearly in agreement with some of Hu's ideas, though not with Hu himself. He criticized Hu's group for "petty-bourgeois sentiments," yet he praised Lu Ling's stories at the very time that meetings were called to attack them. Even more inconsistent with Feng's attempt to ally himself with the party writers was his evident opposition to the fundamental principles of Mao's literary doctrine. It appears that Feng desired a position in the party structure, but would not relinquish his views on the meaning of art and literature.

This compromise which Feng sought could not be accepted within the party. Feng, like Hu, was reprimanded by party officials for his critical attitude. However, because Feng's opposition was not so noisy and, even more important, because he had attempted to win his way back into the good graces of party officials, the criticism meted out to him was far less abusive. The two different approaches toward Hu and Feng can be seen in an article by Ho Ch'i-fang,[41] in which he censured both men. Whereas Hu was not even designated as being a member of the same camp, Feng was always referred to as a colleague. While Hu's ideas were shown to have little in common with those of the party, Ho pointed out the areas where Feng's views coincided.

The debate subsided in 1946 because the major antagonists again dispersed to other areas. Hu and Feng went to Shanghai; most of the party's cultural authorities went to Hong Kong, which became a postwar center for uninhibited Communist propaganda. Criticisms of Hu and his group became no more than sporadic. An isolated thrust at Hu's circle came in the spring of 1947, from Kuo Mo-jo, who wrote a critical article against them, but it aroused little more than indignation from Hu's followers. One of them declared that Kuo Mo-jo "acts and commands as if he were the emperor of literary circles." [42] They were willing to withdraw from the controversy for a while and devote themselves to their writing. Furthermore, the party's literary officials did not move in at this time to back up Kuo Mo-jo's challenge.

Throughout this whole period of conflict between Feng and Hu on the one hand and the party on the other, the party's counter-attacks do not appear to have been part of a planned drive. The party's response was haphazard and spontaneous. Moreover, the most outspoken critics of Feng and Hu were well-known writers such as Kuo Mo-jo and Mao Tun, not the party's cultural functionaries. Also, the criticism sessions were more free-ranging debates than directed discussions. Consequently, the attacks on Feng and Hu in the mid-1940's appear to have been an aspect of the cheng feng movement and a carry-over of the Wang Shih-wei campaign into the KMT areas rather than a specific drive against these particular individuals. Nevertheless, they mark the beginning of Hu's and Feng's deliberate opposition to the party's literary policies and literary bureaucrats.

chapter four

RESUMPTION OF THOUGHT
REFORM DRIVES IN 1948

After the extension of the cheng feng movement into Chungking in 1945 and its completion in the early part of 1946, the party had little time to concern itself with the intellectuals as the struggle with the KMT moved into its final stage. Yet, in the spring of 1948, it suddenly embarked on drives reminiscent of the one it carried out against Wang Shih-wei and his colleagues in the early 1940's. The party launched well-organized, systematic campaigns against Hu Feng's group and particularly against Hsiao Chün, one of the writers who had criticized the party in Yenan in 1942.

Why did the party resurrect a cheng feng campaign at this time? Perhaps the reasons can be found in the party's over-all program in 1948. This was the period just before the complete take-over of the mainland. There was widespread disillusionment with the KMT within nearly all segments of China's population, especially the intellectuals. Though China's non-Communist intellectuals were largely Western-educated and influenced by Western political democracy and scientific learning, in the later half of the 1940's they were ready to welcome the rule of the Chinese Communists. Along with the rest of the population, they suffered from economic chaos, runaway inflation, and general frustration. In addition, they were specifically embittered by the KMT's virtual disregard of their capabilities and accomplishments. Consequently, a sizeable number of China's intellectuals expressed approval of the party in a degree varying from sympathy to a willingness to cooperate. Simultaneously, party leaders, in contrast to the KMT, courted these scholars and scientists, who they realized would be necessary in their drive to industrialize China. The intellectuals were assured that their services and leadership would be respected and appreciated in the new regime.

However, while the party was ingratiating itself with the non-Communist intellectuals, it was attempting to regiment and control the intellectuals within its own ranks. As the party began to occupy more and more cities from 1945 to 1948, it incorporated a large number of intellectuals, unaccustomed to obeying strict orders and unfamiliar with the requirements of the party. Such an influx was bound to shake the party's organizational and doctrinal foundations, just when the party apparatus needed tightening up. In preparation for the end of the fighting, the party sought to mold a well-disciplined, unified core of administrators that could undertake the tasks of rehabilitation and handle the increasingly complex problems of social and political control. Therefore, along with its program of land reform in 1948, the party conducted a concomitant drive of "rectification" among enclaves of cadres and left-wing intellectuals in large party centers, particularly Shanghai, Hong Kong, and Harbin. The examples of Hu Feng and especially Hsiao Chün were used to further this part of its program.[1]

The Drive Against Hu Feng's Group

The party used the heterodoxies of Hu's group expressed in *Hsi wang* in 1945 as symbols of "incorrect" thinking to be thoroughly criticized in 1948. At this time, the major critics were not Kuo Mo-jo and Mao Tun. In fact, these men appear to have played a minor role in the 1948 drive against Hu Feng's group. This campaign was instigated and managed by the hard-core organizers of the party's propaganda activities and by Chou Yang's associates, the literary critic Shao Ch'üan-lin, the poet Lin Mo-han, and the party ideologists Hu Ch'iao-mu and Hu Sheng.

The attack was set off in the pages of a journal called *Ta-chung wen-i ts'ung-k'an* (Digest of mass literature),[2] which was run by Chou Yang's assistants. Its main purpose seems to have been to attack the thinking of Hu's group, in the same manner that *Hsi wang* was published for the reverse purpose a few years before. The journal came out in the spring of 1948 in Hong Kong. Most of the articles redirected the previous discussion on the ideas of Shu Wu and Lu Ling along stricter party lines. Though the criticisms of Hu's colleagues were meant for Hu, he was still not exposed publicly as the main target. Furthermore, Feng Hsüeh-feng was not assailed openly, but because his views paralleled Hu's so closely, the censure of Hu's group could be considered an oblique attack on him.

Chou's associates principally condemned the stress of Hu's group on the expression of individual, subjective feelings rather than on the portrayal of the collective thinking of the working classes or party. Accusing Shu Wu in "On Subjectivism" of turning the process of consciousness upside down, Shao Ch'üan-lin asserted that "It is not from emotions that we reach ideas, but from rational consciousness that we move to emotions." [3] By rational consciousness, Shao, of course, meant Marxism-Leninism-Maoism. Justifiably, the party feared that literary characters motivated by individual, spontaneous emotions would not make their readers amenable to collective action directed by the party. Actually, Hu and his followers did not put feelings on a higher plane than ideas. To them, feelings and ideas were inextricably combined in the writer's consciousness. Nevertheless, they devoted more attention to the role of the emotions primarily because this facet of the human personality had been neglected by the literary officials.

Hu's group was also used to illustrate another characteristic of China's modern intellectuals, their critical attitude, which the party was anxious to eliminate. Party leaders welcomed this attitude when it was applied to the KMT, but not when applied to itself. Since the political situation had now moved in its favor, the party declared that there was no longer any need "to doubt everything and oppose everything." [4] Hu's group was specifically reproached for its critical attitude toward the backward, apathetic spirit of the masses. Such an approach, party propagandists asserted, opposed Mao's precept that the petty bourgeoisie must surrender unconditionally to the workers and the party. They did not add that Hu Feng, too, had asked writers to unite with the working people. Similarly, they exaggerated the concern of Hu's friends for the special characteristics of art into the charge that they "worshipped artistic creation to the point of mysticism." [5] Again, the party advanced this misrepresentation in order to contrast it with their own politically-oriented concept of art.

In view of the rectification movement that party officials were conducting at the time, more disturbing to them than the unorthodox beliefs of Hu's group was the steadfast resistance of its members both in words and deeds to the procedures of thought reform. In addition to the publication of several articles condemning the reluctance of Hu's group to participate in study sessions, various kinds of pressures were applied to Hu privately. Some indication of their form can be seen in his letters at this time. A letter of his to Shu Wu in the fall of 1948 described the types of coercion used against him. "On the one hand, they use various base devices like propaganda to oppose us and counterattack. On the other, they exert great effort to compel us to talk and make an advantageous truce." [6] Also, he found it increasingly difficult to publish his works in Shanghai and held party officials to blame. He complained, "A petty party bureaucrat is now in authority here. He bears grudges and instigates editors against me." [7] Simultaneously, the party's cultural leaders were again trying to cajole Hu to go to Hong Kong, where they could more easily engage him in thought reform. Apparently, Hu did not obey their orders because he did not go.

Despite his insubordination, Hu was not read out of party ranks completely. In the areas not yet under its control, the party still needed the help of left-wing intellectuals, even nonconforming ones like Hu and his circle, against the KMT. Therefore, even while he and his group were mercilessly criticized, they were credited with serving an important function because they had called attention to the evils of dogmatism and helped the party reach out to a larger number of people. In the very same article in which Shao Ch'üanlin assailed Hu's followers, he added, "Still, the theories of the subjectivists further the attack on dogmatism in literature. This is beneficial at this time and has a function in the dark areas." [8] At this juncture, the party suffered Hu's and Feng Hsüeh-feng's reluctance to undergo reform and to revise their own concepts of art, an action it was to find intolerable once it gained control of the mainland and sought to maintain the status quo. Moreover, Hu and his group were a sidelight, not the focus, of the rectification campaign of 1948. The spotlight was reserved for Hsiao Chün.

The Drive Against Hsiao Chün

Hsiao Chün in 1948

A drive far more intensive and unrelenting than the one carried out against Hu Feng in the south of China was concurrently conducted against Hsiao Chün in Manchuria, where the party by 1948 was virtually in complete control. Hsiao, like Wang Shih-wei in 1942, became the main example of unorthodoxy that the party utilized in its 1948 drive to re-educate China's left-wing intellectuals.

After the termination of the Sino-Japanese war, the party sent Hsiao back to his home region of Manchuria. He returned with the Red Army in 1946 to help the party solidify its position in this area. Although he had been severely reprimanded in 1942 for his criticism of the party and special meetings had been held specifically to denounce him, the party was apparently willing to overlook his "mistakes." Hsiao could still be used in its effort to win popular support for its cause. Furthermore, in left-wing circles Hsiao had an influential position because of his intimate relationship with Lu Hsün and because his *Village in August* was one of the first books on the Sino-Japanese war. He was held in particular esteem in Manchuria, where he was regarded as the region's foremost author and was praised for his ability to express the feelings and thoughts of the ordinary Manchurian peasant. Consequently, the party hoped to use his name and reputation to help promote its program there.

In line with party expectations, Hsiao, shortly after his arrival, became the main speaker for all cultural and literary activities in Harbin. The party helped him set up a journal, *Wen-hua pao* (Cultural news), which first appeared in May 1947 and was published weekly. Hsiao was chief editor and virtually ran the paper single-handed. With the party's support, Hsiao also set up his own publishing company and bookstore, both named for Lu Hsün. The bookstore became a meeting place for intellectuals and students in Harbin and Hsiao acted as their leader.

However, Hsiao soon became the first one among the Yenan critics to renew the attack on party practices with which he disagreed. Signs of his divergence from the party appeared as early as issue No. 5 of *Wen-hua pao*. In an article, "Talk on Government and Education," Hsiao advocated the separation of the duties of government officials from the activities of intellectuals, similar to the way in which Wang Shih-wei had attempted to separate the functions of the party and of the writers in Yenan. This separation that Hsiao desired produced his basic conflict with the party. In Hsiao's view, both government and education had the same objectives — the liberation of mankind — but they approach their goal in different ways. Intellectuals were "to educate with reason or truth, teach with feeling, and master a skill." Officials were "to govern with orders, administer through laws, and cause prosperity." [9] Connected with this distinction between the two fields was Hsiao's belief that a person concerned with scholarship "must speak out the words in his heart, without any restrictions or fears about expressing his feelings." [10] In contrast, Mao's Yenan "Talks" clearly enunciated that the intellectual realm was not to be separate, but definitely subservient to the political.

Within his view of the intellectual, Hsiao assigned an even more important role to the writer. He had the same kind of romantic vision of the writer as Feng Hsüeh-feng and Hu Feng. To Hsiao, a revolutionary writer was a heroic spirit who constantly battled in all places and at all times for what he considered right. Lu Hsün, Gorki, and the French writer Romain Rolland were regarded by Hsiao as the best examples of heroic spirits. He quoted Romain Rolland's view of a writer as one with which he was in full sympathy. The life of a writer is "one of constant struggle that is often bitter without greatness or fortune and fought alone in obscurity." [11] Hsiao, too, believed that an author must continually fight against overwhelming obstacles because, and again he quoted Rolland, "not to struggle is to die." [12]

Most important, he saw writers as agents of social change. In his view, revolutionary change was not merely dependent upon the proletariat or even the party, but also upon intellectuals who direct the forces of change. Hsiao repeatedly emphasized that the articulation of the ideas, psychology, and consciousness of the people were factors as important in social change as the circumstances of their material conditions. He wrote, "The development of revolution is this: first people are dissatisfied with life, the system, the rulers, and the ruling class. This dissatisfaction becomes the psychology of society . . . Then a person or group expresses, explains, and clarifies the discontent about life . . . in phrases, words, and art. This group grasps the echo of mankind." [13] Consequently, Hsiao looked upon himself and other left-wing intellectuals as responsible for expressing the underlying demands and dissatisfactions of society.

There were several other strains that played a significant part in Hsiao's thinking. One was a strong sense of nationalism. Hsiao's close association with the party and left-wing groups had stemmed primarily from his belief that the party could save China from destruction and had not stemmed from any genuine ideological conversion to Marxism-Leninism. Hsiao was more of a nationalist than a Marxist. His whole outlook was colored deeply by his feeling for China and his special loyalty to Manchuria. Another abiding element in his thinking was an intense desire for freedom of thought and action. Having grown up in a period when his homeland was devastated by war, he had spent most of his youth wandering from place to place. His life of constant movement appears to have produced in him an almost innate resistance to any form of control even when it emanated from his own party. Hsiao's passion for freedom appears to have been re-enforced by his belief in some of the more democratic strains in Chinese tradition and Western thought. He believed that there were concepts in Taoism and Buddhism and ideals from Western humanitarianism that should continue to be valued in China.

As Hsiao witnessed the growth of party power in Manchuria in the second half of the 1940's, his disillusionment with the party became even more profound than it had been in Yenan. He saw that the society the party was establishing in Manchuria diverged sharply from his ideal. In the belief that Manchuria's own interests and demands for freedom were being ignored by party officials, he sought through *Wen-hua pao* to act as spokesman for the outrage felt by his countrymen.

His most dramatic protest was made against the party's alliance with the Soviet Union. In left-wing circles, his journal seems to have been a single voice shouting out against sole dependence on the Soviet Union. Today such a protest would be welcomed, but at that time it was in direct opposition to the party's reliance upon the Soviet Union as its chief ally, its ideological big brother and main source of assistance. What were the reasons for Hsiao's attack? Hsiao shared the prejudice of his fellow Manchurians in his intense dislike for the Russians, a consequence, most likely, of Russia's repeated occupations and economic plunder of Manchuria. This bias is clearly seen in the third chapter of his novel, *Village in August*. When speaking of the Manchurian guerrillas, he wrote that they not only regarded the Japanese as utterly worthless, they "sometimes even sneered at the Russians. Old people would say that the Russians were defeated by the Japanese because in those days they were un-disciplined drunkards." [14]

Articles in *Wen-hua pao* in 1948 revealed that Hsiao was deeply disturbed by the Russians' dismantling of Manchuria's industrial bases at the conclusion of the Second World War and by their sack-ing of its resources. Like many Manchurians, he resented the rough manner of the Soviet soldiers and their continued presence on Chi-nese soil. There was a widespread feeling among the local popula-tion that Soviet assistance was motivated more by a desire to control China as a source of power and food than by concern for interna-tional solidarity.[15] These underlying sentiments were succinctly ex-pressed by Hsiao in an article entitled "Different Shades of Im-perialism," published in *Wen-hua pao* on August 15, 1948, the day of the third anniversary of the Soviet liberation of Manchuria from Japan. He began his essay by warning American imperialists to with-draw their "bloody paws from Chinese soil," but he soon turned to Russian imperialism, which he declared, should be hated in the same way as American imperialism.[16] He made no effort to distin-guish between the actions of Imperial Russia and the Soviet Union. A few issues later, Hsiao wrote, "It does not matter what foreign nation it is, we should be treated with equality and respect. If it be Russians, they should be even more respectful . . . We should point this out and give criticism in the spirit of international friendship and criticism and self-criticism. Friendship without prin-ciples is irrational." [17]

Apparently, the party reacted sharply to the articles in *Wen-hua pao* on Russia and applied various kinds of pressures, because sev-eral issues later Hsiao backtracked a bit from the previous criticism. In No. 59 he asserted that when his journal spoke of "Russians," it had been referring to the White Russians in Harbin, not the Soviet Russians. He wrote, "The Russians in Harbin are not completely Soviet . . . Those Russians who act badly should not be put in the same category as the Soviets . . ." [18] However, this modification must not have been too convincing. At that time, it is unlikely that there were enough White Russians left in Harbin to make them appear as an imperialist power.

An equally bold criticism of party policy and another expression of Hsiao's fervent nationalism was his plea that the party discontinue its contest with the KMT for control of China and cooperate with other parties to build a strong democratic China. He regarded China's civil war as a senseless tragedy. As opposed to the sudden outburst against the Soviet Union, Hsiao led up to his request for conciliation with the KMT gradually. In No. 2 of *Wen-hua pao*, he wrote, "Philosophers have said that the difference between men and animals is that we can make tools, we have a high degree of organizational capacity . . . and that we help and cooperate with one another." [19] Much more in the spirit of Sun Yat-sen than Marx, this statement reveals that Hsiao considered man's progress as a development of his ability to cooperate and organize with others rather than as a product of the class struggle.

Some time later, in issue No. 37 of *Wen-hua pao*, Hsiao spoke out against the party for taking too precipitous action against people who were not of the same group or class. He did not mention the KMT or any other political parties directly, but he urged the party to adopt a more conciliatory attitude toward outside groups and modify its drive for supreme power. "Those who have thoughts of dictatorship must be more patient . . . Even if it is a dictatorship, it is a dictatorship of a class, not of a party . . . we will certainly not kill all those who do not belong to the proletariat . . . This kind of petty thinking in the mold of the first Emperor of the Ch'in is not acceptable." [20] Hsiao indicated a belief in a multiparty system and challenged the party's right of autocratic rule. Finally, in No. 53 of *Wen-hua pao*, the same issue in which he criticized the Russians, Hsiao directly implored the party to end its war with the KMT. He asked, "Isn't it true that on either side in the war, the highest portion of those who die belong to the worker and peasant masses? . . . Do not the enemy have peasant masses? . . . Are not they our brothers?" He even included Chiang Kai-shek in this category when he again asked, "Do we have any evidence that Chiang is not Chinese?" [21]

Hsiao was not only critical of the party's measures toward groups outside the party, he also was disturbed by its policies within its own ranks. A hint of this dissatisfaction can be seen in one of the early issues of *Wen-hua pao*, No. 17, in which he asserted that he found as much confusion in party-controlled areas as in the KMT areas.[22] He showed his dissatisfaction with the party's program in Manchuria by expressing a feeling of alienation from the society the party was building there and by admitting an inability to find a place for himself within that society. In No. 45 of *Wen-hua pao*, he wrote, "While I was living in Shanghai I sometimes felt very depressed . . . This was because people were strangers in Shanghai and could not find roots . . . When I finally returned to my own countryside, I hoped that I would not have this feeling of desolation, but it still exists and is even worse. It seems that I have not found my roots." [23]

A few issues later, Hsiao metaphorically described what troubled him and provided some explanation for his feeling of alienation. As in Yenan, Hsiao, in Manchuria, was acutely aware of the broadening gulf between the party leaders and the rank and file. In an article called "Talk on Clowns" in No. 51 of *Wen-hua pao*, he compared the rule of party officials in Manchuria to the actions of clowns on a stage. He criticized party officials by comparing their approach to their subjects with clowns' treatment of their audiences. In Hsiao's view, clowns treat their audiences as objects of laughter and derision, which frightens and at the same time hypnotizes them. "When clowns have power, living people are talked about, ridiculed, and humiliated. The people beneath the stage look at them and clap loudly . . . but increasingly lose touch with reality and increasingly harden their sensibilities." [24]

Hsiao was particularly disturbed by two specific programs of these "clowns," land reform and thought reform. In No. 8 of *Wen-hua pao*, he published a New Year's greeting in which he sharply criticized the land reform drive being carried out by the party in Manchuria. He was not against land reform in itself, but against the bloodshed and abrupt changes that were accompanying it. Here again, he appears to have been expressing the latent dissatisfaction of the local population. While there was virtually unanimous support for the land reform program, the landlord executions and class struggle in the countryside aroused misgivings, particularly among the younger party workers and intellectuals.[25] In a very strong statement, Hsiao asserted that "land is repeatedly divided, wealth distributed, and provisions taken away till a point is reached where people are destitute . . . why should the Communists be so unkind and heartless?" Even the policies of the Japanese and Manchus, he claimed, were not so tyrannous as those enforced by the party.[26] This appears to have been Hsiao's only outright attack on the party's land reform policies. One could surmise that he had been severely rebuked by the leadership and had not chosen to speak out again on this subject.

When it came to the party's thought reform movement, however, Hsiao appears to have been undeterred by party strictures. He wrote several criticisms of the party's methods of ideological rectification in the spring of 1947 and was still attacking them a year later. To describe the party's techniques of enforced study of Marxism-Leninism-Maoism and enforced self-criticism, Hsiao used such terms as "mechanical form of unification" and making "everyone of one color." [27] In one of the articles referred to earlier, "Talk on Government and Education," Hsiao alluded to what he considered a similar kind of ideological conformity in China's past which he asserted "disrespected and even crushed the positive character and creativity of the people." [28] He implied that similar consequences would follow in present-day China, unless the creative strength of the people were allowed to develop freely. Moreover, he was not only concerned with liberating the talents of the mass of people, he also wanted the knowledge and abilities of the upper- and middle-class intellectuals to be utilized. He feared that the wisdom and learning that came from the old society would be destroyed by the party's methods of thought reform. Intellectual endeavor, in his view, should be respected no matter from which class it came. For instance, he believed that one of the factors that made Gorki a great writer was his retention of some of the knowledge and craftsmanship which had been a part of the culture of the old Russian aristocracy and middle class.

Consequently, Hsiao saw no need for Chinese intellectuals to become "proletarianized" through thought reform. In fact, his opposition to the rectification movement appears to have been based partly on his reluctance to accept the party's anti-intellectual approach to scholarship. In addition to its practical benefit, Hsiao valued intellectual endeavor for its own sake. In issue No. 37, he wrote, "In primitive society, they worshipped force, . . . in bourgeois society, they worship money, . . . but in the future society, I know what we will worship — we will put talent and wisdom into first position." [29]

The Party's Program in Manchuria in 1948

The party did not react in any systematic fashion to Hsiao's criticism and nonconformity until the late summer of 1948. Then, it suddenly chose Hsiao as an instrument to implement its rectification movement among party cadres and intellectuals in Manchuria. Actually, the drive in Manchuria had begun about eight months earlier in January 1948, but there were only fragmentary criticisms of Hsiao at that time. It appears that at first the party had not planned to use a specific example to push forth its program. In the spring of 1948, several rectification meetings were convened by the Northeast Propaganda Bureau of the party directed at two main targets which the party considered potentially disruptive. One target was the landlords and rich peasants who had recently come into the party and peasant organizations, and the other was the intellectuals who had allied themselves with the party. Even among the faithful, there was always the possibility of the resurgence of middle-class attitudes deep in the subconscious. Much attention was given especially to remolding writers' views so that they coincided with the party's and to establishing control over all cultural groups in Manchuria.

Party leaders admitted that these early meetings were more a series of free-ranging discussions than directed debates based on clear-cut ideological principles. A considerable number of unorthodox ideas and sentiments were expressed which the party confessed it "had not been able to liquidate." [30] Although the number of criticisms of Hsiao increased at this time, he was still not specifically singled out for attack. Then, in June 1948, the CC of the party issued instructions to its local units to redouble its efforts to enforce "a unity of ideas, action, and discipline" [31] upon its followers. This directive, plus the ideological confusion found among Manchuria's intellectuals and cadres, apparently led the party to its decision to impose ideological conformity by use of an example.

Hsiao was chosen for many of the same reasons Hu Feng had been selected. One of the common elements underlying the campaigns against Hsiao and Hu Feng was that both writers had sharply attacked certain party policies prior to the party's launching of its rectification campaign. In the case of the party's drive against Hsiao, the elements in this formula were mixed together in a much more combustible compound. Whereas some time had elapsed between Hu's criticism of the party's cultural programs and the start of the rectification drive in Shanghai and Hong Kong, Hsiao's opposition, like Wang Shih-wei's earlier, coincided with the movement in Manchuria and was in part brought on by it. Even more important, Hu had been primarily concerned with the party's attitude toward its writers and intellectuals. But Hsiao hit directly at the party's current and most crucial political policies, its alliance with the Soviet Union, the civil war with the KMT, land reform, and thought reform. His words reached out beyond the circle of students and intellectuals to a much broader group of people. He touched upon the national sensibilities of the ordinary Manchurian citizen. Since Hsiao had written under the official auspices of the party, was a well-known disciple of Lu Hsün, and had praised some aspects of the party's program, many accepted some of his heretical teachings in the belief that they were sanctioned by the party.[32] Most people in Harbin, even among left-wing adherents, were as yet unfamiliar with the party's insistence on ideological conformity. Consequently, Hsiao's articles fostered confusion and misunderstanding about the party's ideology and political requirements among the literate population in Harbin.[33]

As for the party, its drives were more intensified in Manchuria than they were elsewhere in 1948. Since the party was fairly well in control of Manchuria, it was able to carry out its program of land reform and thought reform there on a much larger scale and much more thoroughly than elsewhere in this period. The fact that by the spring of 1950 Manchuria had already gone through the process of land reform and distribution indicates the high degree of pressure the party must have used in carrying out its programs in this area. The need, therefore, to eliminate any distracting influence in Manchuria during this period was perhaps even more imperative than it was elsewhere. Though Hsiao was certainly more representative of the intellectuals and fellow travelers than of the rich peasants, he was used to symbolize all of these elements in Manchurian society. Because this was still the stage of the New Democracy when the party was supposedly allied with the petty bourgeoisie and because the main thrust at this time was against the landlords, Hsiao was condemned more often for being the "concentrated expression of the decadent, reactionary ideas of the backward intellectuals of the semi-feudal, semi-colonial society" [34] than for being a product of "petty-bourgeois" liberalism.

In addition to his unorthodoxy, there is evidence that there were factional reasons for his selection as the scapegoat. Though the CC of the party had initiated the rectification drive, it was too busy with military affairs at this time to direct the actual campaign itself. Its implementation was left to the party's propaganda leaders in Manchuria, chiefly the vice-director, Liu Chih-ming, and the party ideologist, Chang Ju-hsin. Both men had been active in the earlier attack on Hsiao Chün and his colleagues in 1942, and both were close associates of Chou Yang. Another one of Hsiao's accusers was Hsü Mou-yung, the writer whom Chou Yang had inveigled into denouncing Lu Hsün and his followers in the 1930's. When the rectification drive focused on Hsiao directly, his journal, *Wen-hau pao*, reprinted [35] Lu Hsün's reply to Hsü Mou-yung in 1936 in which he lambasted the sectarian feuds in left-wing circles. Apparently, Hsiao wished to point out that he was a victim of the same kind of personal vindictiveness as Lu Hsün had been earlier. Hsiao also intimated that Hsü Mou-yung was being used by others as he had been in the 1930's. Furthermore, there appears to have been a fierce competition between Hsiao's journal, *Wen-hua pao*, and another party paper, *Sheng-huo pao* (Life gazette). The editors of *Sheng-huo pao* were part of the investigating teams that interrogated Hsiao personally and were active in attacking him publicly.

The drive against Hsiao was conducted through a barrage of articles in *Shen-huo pao* from late August through October of 1948, the very time that criticism against Hu Feng was in full swing in Hong Kong. These articles initiated a more intensive stage of ideological struggle in Manchuria. Full-scale meetings were held in schools, factories, and party organs in the Harbin area, specifically to criticize Hsiao's ideas. The procedures of the previous cheng feng movement in Yenan, small group discussions and criticism and self-criticism sessions, were also used. Their principal purpose was to redirect the nationalistic enthusiasm, which had motivated all classes of Chinese society against Japan, to the class struggle that was now underway against the KMT. Since Liu Chih-ming was the chief organizer of this movement, an analysis of his criticism shows how the party used Hsiao for this end. Throughout his criticism, Liu portrayed Hsiao as an example of an individual who had given too much attention to national goals and too little to class interest. Actually, in the past the party had been willing to overlook Hsiao's disinterest in the class struggle because his patriotic works had had a positive function against Japan, but now that the war was over, this attribute of Hsiao's was no longer so important to the party as the rejection of his "negative" qualities.

Liu went back to Hsiao's activities in the 1930's to demonstrate that Hsiao had never based his beliefs on Marxism-Leninism but purely on nationalistic and individualistic interests. As his evidence, he used Hsiao's famous novel, *Village in August*, which hitherto, even during the 1942 cheng feng movement, had been almost universally praised in left-wing circles. Now the party, through Liu Chih-ming, reinterpreted *Village in August* [36] to fit in with its current drive of emphasizing class character. Liu suddenly discovered that Hsiao had shown, as was proper, that the struggle against Japan had been propelled by the fury and drive of the ordinary Chinese peasant, but he had not demonstrated, Liu declared, that this mass power had been evoked by the party and the proletariat. Nor had Hsiao made any mention of the class character of the enemy. The most blatant example Liu found of Hsiao's lack of class consciousness and proof of "petty-bourgeois sentiments" was the pity that the hero had shown for the landlord when he died. Liu chastised Hsiao for "not looking on this incident politically, but humanistically." [37] Actually, Hsiao's work was not completely devoid of interest in the class struggle. Even though his novel had been written at the time of the United Front, when the party had directed its followers to underplay class distinctions, Hsiao's heroes had cried out for the revolution of the proletariat. Obviously, the party chose to disregard their shouts.

Not only did Liu criticize the content of Hsiao's novel, he also considered himself a judge of its literary style. Liu granted that when Hsiao portrayed the resistance his writing was powerful, but when he talked of the landlords and workers, his style, Liu declared, became feeble. Furthermore, Liu chided him for describing the spirit of the masses through the depiction of individual cases of heroism. Instead, Liu advised Hsiao to paint the heroism of the masses through the presentation of collective groups with the party at its head. Liu was even more oblivious to literature as a form for the expression of individual character than Chou Yang, who saw at least some value in such depiction. Through his criticism of Hsiao's work, Liu crudely directed literature toward propaganda tracts.

Hsiao's recently expressed desire to end the civil war with the KMT was singled out as another manifestation of his lack of appreciation for the class struggle. The party ideologist Chang Ju-hsin interpreted his plea for the suspension of the civil war to mean that Hsiao "wants us to forget our hatreds and make friends with our enemies." [38] Actually, Hsiao had not asked the party to become friends with Chiang Kai-shek; he merely suggested that a "modus vivendi" be established between China's warring factions. At this point, however, the party insisted that this was not even a time to modify differences. Party followers should develop "strong likes and dislikes." [39] This advice was reminiscent of the reply given by party leaders to Hsiao when in 1942 he had urged them to have a more tolerant and conciliatory attitude toward others who did not think exactly as they did. The party also pointed to Hsiao's conciliatory approach toward the KMT as an example of neutralism, another attitude among the intellectuals it was trying to eliminate. *Sheng-huo pao* declared, "At present, there are two camps — the revolutionary and anti-revolutionary, there is no third one. To be above these two camps is to aid the enemy." [40] Such an approach was equated with the concept of "the third kind of literature," the viewpoint party representatives had condemned strongly in the early 1930's.

Hsiao's rejection of the class struggle combined with a "narrow nationalism" was also blamed for his antagonism toward the Soviet Union. This aspect of his thinking was given the most attention, probably because it reflected an attitude among Manchurians the party found most difficult to dispel. *Sheng-huo pao* frankly admitted that "Because the Manchurians at present harbor some doubts and prejudices [against the Soviet Union] . . . we must educate, persuade, and reform them." [41] The party sought to overcome this hostility by distinguishing the Soviet Union of the present from Russian imperialism of the past. Hsiao's "error," like that of his fellow Manchurians, was, as *Sheng-huo pao* stated, "He thinks that the mistakes committed by the old Russian imperialism of the Nerchinsk period extend into the present." [42]

Moreover, Hsiao was accused of an inability to differentiate the Soviet Union from Western imperialist nations. A country like the Soviet Union that was established on Marxist-Leninist principles and that helped weak nations, Liu Chih-ming wrote, "could not become an oppressor nation over other oppressed nations." [43] Though Hsiao's journal had expressed merely distrust of Russia, Liu interpreted its articles on Russia as a reflection of anti-Soviet, anti-Communist, and anti-people feelings. These unsubstantiated conclusions of Liu were among the chief charges against Hsiao. In contrast to Hsiao's questioning of Russia's intentions toward China, Liu Chih-ming at that time called for an unconditional alliance with the Soviet Union.[44]

Another major criticism of Hsiao was his resistance to the imposition of an orthodox interpretation of Marxism-Leninism. Party leaders complained that even though Hsiao had been personally trained in ideology in Yenan, he continued to spout his own individual interpretations. This line of criticism was similar to the one being used simultaneously against Hu Feng. Even the phraseology was the same, demonstrating again that the movement against Hsiao was to enforce the goals of the rectification movement rather than to criticize his ideas with any degree of accuracy. In fact, several of the criticisms were more suitable for Hu Feng than for Hsiao. Unlike Hu Feng, Hsiao was not interested in the role of the "subjective spirit," yet Chang Ju-hsin used the exact same phrases and terms against Hsiao that Shao Ch'üan-lin had used against Hu. Chang wrote, "Marxism-Leninism believes that the objective determines the subjective . . . but Hsiao has completely turned this question upside down — he advocates that the subjective determines the objective and that social consciousness determines social existence." [45] Chang also reprimanded Hsiao for advocating "a theory of human nature above class," [46] a charge the party had used against Wang Shih-wei in the first cheng feng movement in Yenan. Like the "subjective spirit," a theory on human nature was another topic with which Hsiao was slightly concerned. These charges became stock phrases which were used against nonconformists in the party's rectification drives no matter whether or not they fitted the individual concerned.

The party sought to culminate its campaign against Hsiao by evoking a public self-criticism from him. Besides the fact that this was regular procedure in a cheng feng movement, the party apparently considered it all the more urgent in this case because there were still some intellectuals, especially among the young, who, as *Shenghuo pao* complained, "disagreed with the criticism of Hsiao's ideas and claimed that accusing him of an anti-Soviet, anti-people stand was too extreme." [47] Paradoxically, the party's onslaught against Hsiao had rendered him to many a sympathetic rather than a condemned figure. Therefore, the fervor aroused in party cadres by the effort to compel Hsiao to confess, the example of Hsiao's self-criticism, and the proof it would provide of the validity of the party's arguments were considered invaluable in indoctrinating others. Various pressures were imposed on Hsiao to achieve this end. The party discontinued its support of his journal, *Wen-hua pao*. Consequently, he was left without any financial backing or publishing facilities with which to put out his journal. This meant that he was not only stripped of his means of livelihood, he was deprived of a platform from which to answer the charges against him. Hu Feng had also been denied all assistance from the party, but since he had not been living in an area directly controlled by the party, he could turn to other sources to help him continue his publication.

Perhaps the most severe form of pressure on Hsiao came from his "comrades" and colleagues who implored him to prepare a self-criticism. Even his old friend, Ting Ling, had voiced such a plea. Actually, her censure of Hsiao was an indirect criticism of herself. She attacked those people in Yenan, of whom she had been one, who had applauded Hsiao's work and thereby given him the feeling that he had support.[48] Another explanation she gave for Hsiao's unwillingness to make a public confession was that "he was too taken up with his own fame," [49] a complaint that had also been made against her. She concluded her denunciation with a warning to Hsiao that unless he were willing "to correct his mistakes, study the workers, peasants, and soldiers, and follow the party, . . . he would have no future," [50] a fact of Communist life of which Ting Ling herself had been made well aware. Finally, she offered her services to help Hsiao reform. Almost all the criticisms of Hsiao ended with similar offers. Even Liu Chih-ming ended his attacks with the remark that all would be well for Hsiao if only he would confess. He, too, offered to aid Hsiao in this endeavor.

Yet, with all these chastisements and entreaties, Hsiao still refused to undergo ideological remolding. Initially, he made some effort to acknowledge his "errors," but apparently he had not debased himself sufficiently because no public confession of his appeared in the press. In fact, there were reports that Hsiao responded to later demands for a self-criticism by charging party officials with "trying to make Harbin and the emancipated areas into a place without sounds" and by insisting on his freedom to speak and criticize.[51] The party retorted that since Hsiao's views were not even those of the petty bourgeoisie, but represented the intellectuals of the landlord and capitalist classes and were in opposition to the masses, his right to speak and criticize must be taken away.[52] Thus, through its case against Hsiao, the party was also able to demonstrate that the right of free speech and criticism in a party-governed society was determined by the party's judgment of one's class and of whether one spoke in the interest of the people.

For his refusal to present an acceptable public confession, Hsiao was sentenced to hard labor at the Fushun coal mines in Manchuria. Though he had disappeared from the scene, the campaign against him persisted until the spring of 1949, serving as the focus of the discussion sessions of party members and intellectuals in Manchuria and the northern part of China.

While it is true that a large portion of China's intellectuals initially welcomed the Communist government and were willing to work for it, nevertheless, the party's campaign against Hsiao would suggest that there was not unquestioning support from the intellectuals within its own ranks. Moveover the party felt the need to anticipate possible deviation. Therefore, on the eve of its complete takeover of the mainland, the party sought through this campaign to warn its followers of what could happen to them if they veered from the path it had laid out. The left-wing intellectuals in particular were made well aware of the fact, as seen in Ting Ling's injunctions to Hsiao, that unless they were willing to participate in the study of Marxism-Leninism-Maoism and engage in self-criticism, they would find no place for themselves in the new regime. By setting limits on how far intellectuals could go in their criticisms and by reindoctrinating them with the party dictum, this campaign helped keep the more vocal elements of the population in line as the party prepared to set up a new government.

The greater intensity of this rectification movement, as opposed to the earlier one in Yenan and to the one going on simultaneously outside the Communist areas against Hu Feng, can be seen in the fact that Hsiao's mistakes were no longer discussed on purely an ideological or literary level. The main emphasis was on the political nature of Hsiao's disagreement with the party. Hsiao was shown to be not merely a critic of the party's cultural program nor even just a heretic within the party; he was charged with actually opposing the government, the Soviet Union, and the masses. Though Hsiao was essentially a writer, Liu Chih-ming and his assistants gave only passing comment to Hsiao's literary views, which they rejected with the very same arguments used against him in 1942. This may have been due in part to the fact that Hsiao was more directly concerned with political issues. But, more important in explaining the political nature of the accusations against him was the fact that toward the end of 1948 the party was in control of Manchuria and was about to wield power over the whole of China. Any criticism within its ranks was now regarded as a form of political subversion. Treatment of ideological differences as political opposition became standard practice thereafter. The Hsiao Chün campaign was also extended beyond left-wing intellectuals and party cadres to a number of people and groups outside the party, another indication of the future course of the cheng feng movement.

chapter five

RE-EMERGENCE OF LITERARY
FACTIONS, 1949–1952

With the defeat of the Kuomintang and the establishment of the Chinese Communist party as the government of China, party leaders at first relaxed their drive to enforce ideological control over China's left-wing intellectuals. Faced with the immediate task of setting up a new government for all of China, they needed these trained intellectuals to fill important positions within the administration and handle the multiplying and complex duties confronting the new regime. The party could not afford to alienate or divert them from the urgent work of consolidating the party's rule.

Party Policy Toward the Intellectuals, 1949–1952

Very early in the regime, however, there were indications that this conciliatory policy toward the intellectuals would be short-lived. The party, in its "Common Program" presented in September 1949, declared that all intellectuals would be given a political education in Marxist ideology. A "learn from the Soviet Union and oppose America movement" was launched in December 1949. It was a continuation of the drive begun in Manchuria a year earlier and was intensified by the Korean War. Nevertheless, the intellectuals did not immediately realize nor feel the full implications of these measures. Most of them considered the introduction of ideological courses to be consistent with Chinese educational tradition. Though they were being mobilized to participate in several campaigns, such as land reform and "Resist America — Aid Korea," these drives affected them indirectly and were not specifically conducted against them.

Gradually, the party began to impose its doctrine on the intellectuals more directly. In the second half of 1950, it embarked on a broad, loose movement of ideological remolding, which touched all groups and which, like the initial stage of the cheng feng movement in Yenan, was against both the "liberalism" of the intellectuals and the "bureaucratism" of the officials. In June 1950, at the second conference of the National Committee of the CPPCC, an advisory body made up largely of leading non-Communist citizens, Mao instructed people from all walks of life to start a campaign of self-education and self-reform through criticism and self-criticism. Soon, the focus concentrated more and more on the intellectuals. At the third conference of the National Committee of the CPPCC, October 1951, Mao this time emphasized that thought reform was particularly for intellectuals. He declared that "Ideological remolding, especially the ideological remolding of all types of intellectuals, is one of the important conditions for realizing industrialization and democratic reform." [1]

Hence, in the summer of 1951, a concentrated campaign of thought reform began among university professors in the northeast and soon spread out to the rest of the country. Scholars in the social sciences and the humanities were among the first groups to be condemned in the new regime. Their major crime was that their scholarship had been influenced by Western learning. Using many of the same phrases that had been applied to Hsiao Chün a few years earlier, party leaders accused these professors of "ambiguous thought which failed to distinguish between the enemy and ourselves." [2] Many professors were compelled to acknowledge that their reluctance to accept Soviet scholarship was based on "narrow nationalism." [3] The main object of their re-education was to orient them away from the West and toward the Soviet Union, eliminate their Western democratic and liberal values, and indoctrinate them in Marxist-Leninist ideology.

As in 1942, the party attacked the thought of Hu Shih. His belief that scholarship should be pursued unimpeded by ideological or political considerations was an intellectual approach the party sought to purge from Communist China. In the latter part of 1951, he was attacked in the press and denounced in meetings at the universities. Totally ignoring Hu Shih's efforts in education and his appeals for democratic government, party leaders argued that "When China was without food and clothing, Hu Shih was exclusively engrossed in textual criticism." [4] Through this characterization, the party sought to shame Chinese scholars into committing their intellects to the regime's economic and political programs.

With the inauguration of the three-anti movement which was against bureaucrats held over from the Kuomintang government and the five-anti movement which was against private industry and commerce, the thought reform drive in the early part of 1952 was intensified and broadened. By this time, the party had achieved secure control over the country, so that it could devote more attention to manipulating intellectuals for its own specific purposes. Scientists, who hitherto were subject to less political control than the social scientists and writers, were now ordered to learn from the Soviet Union and were warned against approaching their subjects from a purely technical view. Also, another drive to re-educate leftist writers was launched. Thus, by 1952 thought reform drives were carried out against both Communist and non-Communist intellectuals. That this process was to become a regular institution of Communist China is seen in a declaration of the CPPCC on June 6, 1952, which informed all intellectuals that, henceforth, ideological remolding would be implemented once a year for a period of two months, at which time all regular work was to stop in order to concentrate on pertinent documents and to practice criticism and self-criticism.

Chou Yang and the Wu Hsün Campaign

The CCP was able to move with far more alacrity and deftness than the Soviets in imposing political controls on scholarship and arts in the early years of its reign. The Soviet Communist party, partially because of lack of experience and partially because of an inability to do so, made comparatively modest efforts in this direction in the first decade of its rule. By contrast, when the CCP assumed power, it not only had the example of Stalin's effort to imprison the creative and intellectual spirit of the Russian intellectuals, it also had officials and cadres trained in the cheng feng movements in Yenan, Chungking, and Harbin. The organizers of the earlier campaigns, Chou Yang, Ch'en Po-ta, Hu Ch'iao-mu, Ai Szu-ch'i, and Shao Ch'üan-lin, were a hard core of functionaries delegated to enforce and maintain ideological orthodoxy among the intellectuals.

Within this group, Chou Yang gradually achieved pre-eminence in this endeavor. His official positions in no way signified this. Nevertheless, his active and supervisory role in the ideological remolding movements resulted in his eventual management of most areas of intellectual thought in Communist China. Moreover, he held pivotal posts on several important committees. Chou, in the late 1940's, had been vice-president of North China's Associated Universities, actually cadres training centers, and the head of the Propaganda Department of the party in North China. When the party established its regime, Chou was appointed a deputy-director of the Propaganda Department of the CC along with his colleagues Hü Ch'iao-mu and Ch'en Po-ta. This organization, under the chairmanship of Lu Ting-i, was the ultimate source of ideological orthodoxy in Communist China. Another organ that exercised direct authority over intellectuals in the early 1950's was the Committee of Cultural and Educational Affairs in which both Chou and his associates mentioned above held important posts.

Other channels of ideological control were the Ministry of Culture, in which Chou was a vice-minister under Mao Tun and secretary of its party committee, and the ACFLAC, in which he was again vice-chairman under Kuo Mo-jo. This latter body was one of the first organizations to be formed under the new regime. Chou had played a signal role in setting it up even before the party takeover. It was a device for combining all factions and all the intellectuals in the creative arts into one body over which the party could exercise direct supervision. Further, the ACFLAC was one of the most influential organs for communicating party policies to the reading public. It was the parent group to numerous specialized groups. One of them, the Association of Literary Workers, was another organization in which Chou was a vice-chairman under the chairmanship of Mao Tun. Though he ranked officially below such famous writers as Kuo Mo-jo and Mao Tun, Chou wielded the real power in these organizations and operated decisively behind the scenes. This reliance on organization men to direct scholarly and professional endeavors was characteristic of the party's method of exercising control. As in the past, he continued to apply a nationalistic, nonprofessional approach to all cultural endeavor.

The extent of Chou's authority was revealed in his direction of the major thought reform drive of the early 1950's, the campaign against the film, "The Story of Wu Hsün." This was the most extensive ideological movement since Yenan. The drive concerned the interpretation of the nineteenth-century educator, Wu Hsün. The film had portrayed him as a poor peasant who had been turned down by the village teachers. Realizing the difficulties faced by anyone who sought to improve himself through education, Wu Hsün determined to earn enough money in order to set up schools for the poor. He began as a beggar, then became a moneylender, and finally a landlord. After thirty years of saving his proceeds, he was able to establish his first school in 1888. He opened several other schools until he finally received the help of the Manchu officials in his endeavor. The film depicting his story, directed by the American-trained student, Sun Yü, and produced by a private studio, K'un Lun, had its premiere in December 1950. Subsequently, there were over forty articles in the newspapers and journals of Peking, Shanghai, and Tientsin praising the film. It was particularly lauded in such newspapers as *Kuang-ming jih-pao*, *Wen-hui pao*, and *Ta-kung pao*, which were not controlled directly by the party. At first, there was little negative criticism. The film appeared to be a big success and ran for several months throughout China.

However, at the time the picture was being shown, the party decided to accelerate the cheng feng movement then underway against university professors. Apparently, the self-criticism sessions were not proving as effective as the party had hoped. Hence, in the spring of 1951, the film suddenly became a weapon in the party's effort to indoctrinate Western-educated intellectuals in the party's political requirements. The articles and speeches of Chou Yang and his associates portrayed Wu Hsün as exemplifying the qualities of thought which the party was determined to eradicate. Wu Hsün was depicted as a muddle-headed idealist who sought to change China through education and reform rather than through the class struggle and revolution. Chou Yang pointed out that many intellectuals like Wu Hsün believe that "it is not necessary to have a revolutionary struggle of the people to overthrow the old system and establish a new one, it is only necessary to give people education and reform." [5] To counteract this "nonproletarian" thinking, the party sought to inculcate intellectuals with the doctrine that scholarship must be combined with political goals. Chou Yang asserted that "Although we should emphasize education, we should not consider it above class and politics." [6] Furthermore, he served notice that there was no room in this society for independence or withdrawal from the political realm. One of his colleagues, the writer Chou Wen, declared that "A person's ideas at present are either progressive or reactionary — there is no third way." [7]

The discussion on Wu Hsün filled Communist Chinese newspapers and journals from May 20 until the middle of July. For two months, the daily newspapers devoted a quarter of their space to defining Wu Hsün's "objectionable" traits. *Hsüeh-hsi*, edited by Chou Yang's old colleague Ai Szu-ch'i, and *Wen-i pao* came out with special issues on Wu Hsün. Denunciations, investigations, and confessions were the substance of the articles. Nearly all prominent intellectuals expressed an opinion. The writer Kuo Mo-jo, the historian Fan Wen-lan, and even the party ideologist and friend of Chou Yang's, Hu Sheng, all of whom had at one time or another praised Wu Hsün, now publicly presented self-criticisms. The film was withdrawn from circulation, and its writer-director, Sun Yü, published a public confession in *JMJP* on June 10, 1952. The K'un Lun studio was taken over by the state. This move was another way of symbolizing the party's current program to bring all independent enterprises under party control. Finally, on August 8, 1951, the campaign subsided with the appearance of a 15,000-word article on Wu Hsün by Chou Yang in *JMJP*. He presented the definitive interpretation of Wu Hsün and formally brought the drive to a close.

Chou Yang emerged from this campaign with more power than when it began. His active role enhanced his authority not only in the creative arts, but in all cultural and scholarly endeavors. The fact that Kuo Mo-jo had to present an abject confession in which he chastised himself for "petty-bourgeois sentiments" and "blind ignorance" [8] underlined still further that while well-known intellectuals like Kuo Mo-jo might hold positions above Chou in the hierarchy of various organs, it was Chou and not they who wielded the power. With such phrases as "Chou Yang correctly pointed out my mistakes," [9] Sun Yü in his public confession praised Chou's guidance in helping him clarify his ideas. Outside of Mao himself, Sun Yü considered only Chou responsible for putting him on the "right" path. The view that most intellectuals and party cadres held of Chou's role in the party structure can be seen from various letters written at this time to the party journals. A typical one published in *Wen-i pao* stated, "When I saw 'The Story of Wu Hsün,' I decided to write to Chou Yang and ask him to oppose having it shown." [10] Apparently, Chou Yang was generally regarded as the foremost fighter for ideological purity and party orthodoxy in culture.

Ting Ling and the Literary Cheng Feng Movement, 1951–1952

The only one who exerted authority comparable to Chou Yang's in the literary and art realm was Ting Ling. Like Chou, Ting Ling, too, appears to have been favored with special treatment from Mao Tsetung. Even when she had fallen out of favor with the party in 1942 for her editorship of the literary page of *Chieh-fang jih-pao* and for her provocative article on women, Mao still maintained his friendship with her. The story is told that at the meeting when Mao gave his famous "Talks on Art and Literature," which were in part to criticize Ting Ling and her friends, Mao was reported to have given up his seat in the middle of the front row to Ting Ling with the remark, "Let our woman comrade take the middle seat. We don't like to be rebuked again on March 8." [11] This date was in reference to Woman's Day, the day Ting Ling had written her criticism of the party's treatment of women.

Shortly after these meetings, Ting Ling was sent to party training schools from 1942 to 1944. Subsequently, under the direction of Chou's associate Hu Ch'iao-mu, she started to write again and gradually began to regain her former position in party circles. She became a member of the Shensi-Kansu-Ninghsia Border Region Government Assembly and the party's literary associations. On the basis of her exemplary conduct after her re-education, Mao not only commended her work in sessions of the Assembly and in cadre meetings, but he also re-established personal relations with her. [12] Ting Ling interpreted Mao's attentions as his way of encouraging her to follow along the path he had laid out. Few of her colleagues had the close personal contact with Mao that Ting Ling enjoyed.

In the second half of the 1940's, besides taking on an increasing number of administrative duties, Ting Ling wrote a highly-acclaimed novel, *Sun Over the Sangkan River*, the first large work to reflect the complex picture of land reform going on in the Chinese countryside. Through her depiction of representative types of landlords, rich peasants, poor peasants, and cadres, she described the class relationships in the village, the peasant struggle against the landlords, and the redistribution of land. The novel was widely read throughout the Communist world and was considered one of the best literary works of Communist China by Communist and non-Communist critics. In 1951 it won the Second Stalin prize and became the first Chinese novel to receive such an honor.

Ting Ling, unlike Chou Yang, held a pre-eminent place among China's intellectuals. Yet, like Chou Yang, she also was a power in the party's cultural hierarchy. She usually ranked just behind Kuo Mo-jo and Mao Tun in official listings,[13] but similar to Chou, it was she and not they who exercised the real authority. Furthermore, she held many posts comparable to Chou's. She, too, was on the powerful Committee of Cultural and Educational Affairs and was a vice-chairman of the Association of Literary Workers. Along with Chou, she was instrumental in the establishment of the ACFLAC. The Ministry of Culture and the ACFLAC jointly set up the Central Literary Institute in 1950, a training school for Communist writers of which Ting Ling became the head. She was also in charge of the literary bureau of the Propaganda Department and was sent to international conferences all over the world — Budapest, Moscow, and Paris. Perhaps the most influential position she held was as editor of *Wen-i pao*, the journal of the ACFLAC and the principal organ for relaying the party's cultural policy. Her assistant editor was again Ch'en Ch'i-hsia, who had assisted her in Yenan in the literary supplement of *Chieh-fang jih-pao*.

None of her old colleagues in any way came close to her in authority. Unlike Ting Ling, many of them had not been fully pardoned for their rebellious pasts. Feng Hsüeh-feng, though still regarded as a foremost literary critic and interpreter of Lu Hsün, initially was merely made chairman of the Shanghai unit of the Association of Literary Workers. Still, he was in close contact with Ting Ling and apparently hoped to rise to a more important position through her efforts. Ai Ch'ing was given some significant posts, most important of which was assistant editor of *Jen-min wen-hsüeh*, the journal of the Association of Literary Workers and the second most influential literary journal after *Wen-i pao*. Still, in 1952 he was accused of a "freedomistic" attitude toward the leadership and was sent with a group of writers to reform himself by studying life in the villages. Hsiao Chün was still lingering away in the coal mines of Fushun. Consequently, while all these men may have wished to resist Chou Yang's domination, only Ting Ling was in a position to do so with any hope of success.

Apparently, this is what she attempted to do through circuitous means from the first days of the party's takeover. She did not, at first, contend with Chou Yang by opposing his literary and ideological views. In fact, to a large degree, she ostensibly accepted them. It was only later, in the middle of 1952, after she had won a fairly secure position for herself in the party hierarchy, that hints of ideas other than those of the party began to appear in her works. In the early days of the regime, however, she played with Chou and his followers at their own game — mouthing the correct party line and fervently enforcing the indoctrination of intellectuals. Her advice to writers, like Chou Yang's own admonitions, constantly stressed the need for reform. "If we create, we must first have correct, rich enthusiastic feelings; nourishment of these feelings demands a long period of reform in order to have truly proletarian, Communist ideas." [14] Her literary criteria were merely restatements of the standard Soviet platitudes on literature. Since Communist China sought to imitate the Soviets in all matters intellectual and cultural at this time, her words re-echoed the decrees of the Soviet cultural commissar, Andrei Zhdanov, who was in his heyday at the end of the 1940's. Like the Soviet commissar, she demanded stylized images of revolutionary heroes in order to inspire the masses. She was even willing to accept national folk forms as a literary style and expressed regret that she had not appreciated them earlier.

More significant was the role she played in the ideological remolding movements of the early 1950's. She actually competed with Chou in her efforts to reform writers. Her eager enforcement of thought reform was not only motivated by her rivalry with Chou Yang, but also by the desire for a prominent place in the party's cultural hierarchy. Such a position could be won by demonstrating positive proof of loyalty. The surest way was to impugn the loyalty of others. Also, like many other Chinese intellectuals, she initially carried out the party's bidding because of faith in the party's ability to solve China's problems.

It was Ting Ling's journal *Wen-i pao* that first focused attention on the film of Wu Hsün. Almost a month before *JMJP* published its editorial against "The Story of Wu Hsün" and before Chou Yang denounced it, *Wen-i pao* had published several articles against the film.[15] Nevertheless, Ting Ling was not so active in the Wu Hsün campaign as Chou Yang. The principal targets of this campaign were the non-Communist intellectuals, and they were the virtual monopoly of Chou Yang. It was among left-wing writers and artists that Ting Ling made her mark as a crusader for orthodoxy. When the ACFLAC had conducted its first ideological remolding sessions in 1949, Ting Ling was one of the directors. Her school, the Central Literary Institute, was highly praised for reforming the heterodox views of its members.

Most important, she, along with her friend Feng Hsüeh-feng, played a leading role in the literary cheng feng movement launched in November 1951. This movement, which dovetailed the Wu Hsün campaign, had a slightly different emphasis. Before 1949, about one-third of China's writers had already been re-educated. Many more participated in criticism and self-criticism sessions organized by the ACFLAC as early as August 1949. Apparently, however, the impact of these ideological remolding efforts was temporary. Chou Yang explained that "Many of our comrades in the new environment have become numbed in their thinking and politics. They have lost the sharpness of thought which party members should possess and the ability to distinguish and criticize opposing and erroneous ideas." [16] Therefore, the literary cheng feng was to reinvigorate and reindoctrinate writers who had already been exposed to Marxism-Leninism-Maoism. It was a resumption of the drives of 1942 and 1948. Writers were given the unique privilege of a rectification campaign specifically devoted to them. *Wen-i pao* told them that "To reform and then retreat is far worse than to begin to reform or not yet to have reformed." [17]

Even before the campaign was officially started, Ting Ling had almost singlehandedly in the summer of 1951 laid the groundwork. She did this by sending off a barrage of criticism against a story by the left-wing writer Hsiao Yeh-mu, entitled "Between Husband and Wife." As criticism of Wu Hsün became the mechanism that impelled the ideological remolding movement against non-Communist intellectuals, condemnation of this story became the vehicle that pushed the rectification of left-wing writers. Ting Ling was at the controls of this latter drive. In brief, "Between Husband and Wife" is the story of an intellectual from the city and his peasant wife who had lived happily together in the Communist areas. When the party took over the mainland, they moved to Peking. In the environment of the city, their relationship became strained. The husband's quick assumption of the urban way of life conflicted with his wife's crude country manners and her zeal in denouncing the "evils" of city life. Her attitude was soon condemned by the party cadres. After she criticized herself, her husband once again felt the love he previously had had for her.[18]

Jen-min wen-hsüeh had published this story in January 1951, with an editorial comment praising its freshness and realism. Like the film about Wu Hsün, this story, when it first appeared, was praised and welcomed, particularly by cadres and youth in Peking, Tientsin, and Shanghai. It was given no more critical attention than other literary works published at the time. Not until July, six months later, did party leaders suddenly discover that it was subversive to the party's interests. The decision to criticize this work as a symbol of "petty-bourgeois" thinking probably was taken in line with the party's preparations for the literary cheng feng that was about to unfold. This incident illustrates the feeling of insecurity with which most writers lived. A shift in ideological climate was enough to reverse the official evaluation of a work overnight.

Again, Ting Ling, through her journal *Wen-i pao*, played a signal role in directing public attention to Hsiao Yeh-mu's story and establishing the "correct" party interpretation. She wrote an open letter to Hsiao Yeh-mu in the July issue of *Wen-i pao* in which she expressed the party's dismay with left-wing intellectuals. Using the hero of his story as representative of a typical intellectual, she condemned him because he had gone through thought reform without genuinely acquiring the proletarian viewpoint. She asked Hsiao, "How is it possible for you to point to him as an example for present-day intellectual youth?" [19] She was even more disturbed by Hsiao's portrayal of the wife as an ignorant, clumsy peasant. Again she asked, "If you do not love this untutored peasant type . . . why do you write of her?" [20] In effect, Ting Ling criticized Hsiao's handling of his characters because he showed them with their faults and weaknesses as well as their virtues. Instead, she demanded that Hsiao obey the party's dictum that literary characters symbolize party doctrine. She also chastised him for writing about the private, ordinary feelings of individuals, once the subject matter of her own works. She directed him to focus instead on the party's enterprises and collectivized activities. Through her condemnation of this story, she informed writers that the first prerequisite of art in Communist China was the thorough, continuous reform of the writer.

Following Ting Ling's open letter, criticisms of Hsiao's story immediately appeared in the party's theoretical and cultural journals. Ting Ling spoke before various groups in the large cities elaborating on the ideas in her letter. By October 25, 1951, Hsiao published a confession which acknowledged the "truth" of Ting Ling's accusations. As she had ordered, he repudiated the characters of his story because they "never studied nor worked, but spent all their time with trifling affairs." [21] In addition to the usual party documents such as Mao's Yenan "Talks" and Stalin's discussions of literature, criticism of Hsiao Yeh-mu plus his confession became the study material for the literary cheng feng.

Since Hsiao had already confessed before the campaign was formally launched, the drive did not have the crusading zeal that propelled the earlier cheng feng movements against the unrepentant Wang Shih-wei and Hsiao Chün. This drive was built more on quiet, directed discussions of a piece of literature than on emotional frenzy directed against a particular individual. Another effect of the pre-campaign criticism against Hsiao was to enhance Ting Ling's position before the onset of the actual drive. As Sun Yü had credited Chou Yang for the "invaluable education" he had given him, Hsiao Yeh-mu in his numerous self-criticisms repeatedly credited Ting Ling with similar enlightenment. Hence, by the time the literary cheng feng officially began, Ting Ling was in a natural position to lead it.

Chou Yang was also active in the drive to re-educate the writers. Nevertheless, his role in this 1951 rectification of the literary realm appears to have been subservient to Ting Ling's. As chairman of the Peking Study Committee on Literature and Art, she directed the investigations of writers and arranged the criticism and self-criticism sessions. She was also in charge of sending writers to factories and villages. The extent of her activity can be seen in her management of the reform of the party's cultural and literary journals. There had been some criticism and self-criticism by editors in the spring of 1950. Ting Ling was responsible for accelerating and intensifying this process in the fall of 1951. In an address to the editorial boards, she declared, "You publish material based not on political demands, but on your own individual tastes and interests." [22] She accused them of lacking a clear political and ideological direction. Though she also criticized her own journal, *Wen-i pao*, and herself as an editor, the fact that she confessed publicly in no way means that she was relinquishing any of her authority. Perfunctory self-criticisms, not too critical in nature, were presented at this time by other members of the literary hierarchy, including Chou Yang. They appear to have been offered as examples to the rank and file rather than as confessions of any guilt.

The main force of her attack was reserved for *Jen-min wen-hsüeh* and two of its editors, Mao Tun and Ai Ch'ing, both of them close friends of hers. Since the authority of these two writers did not challenge hers and since in the past she had been willing to share power with her friends, it appears that she assailed them more to demonstrate her crusading spirit than to dispose of two rivals. She admitted that hitherto she "had been afraid to accuse friends," and "considered my friends more important than the masses." [23] Apparently, she was successful in suppressing her feelings of personal loyalties, for she now attacked them sharply for having a nonproletarian outlook.

Following her numerous and incisive criticisms of the publishing world, a stream of public confessions poured forth. Many of them began with a reference to Ting Ling's political guidance. The literary editor of *KMJP* acknowledged that "Ting Ling's remarks were appropriate to me." [24] The editors' expressions of gratitude to Ting

Ling for setting them on the "correct" path resembled the obsequiousness which people involved in the Wu Hsün episode had paid to Chou Yang.

Ting Ling's Heterodoxy

Ting Ling had a schizophrenic-like character in this period. Her actions in the early days of the regime resembled those of the writer Ilya Ehrenburg in the Soviet Union. Both were moved by a mixture of political opportunism and genuine enthusiasm for the party to implement its dictates vigorously. Yet, both tried at the same time to hold onto their own beliefs. Despite Ting Ling's orthodox statements and activist role in the party's thought reform drives, there were still certain abiding elements in her thinking which had conflicted with the party's policies in Yenan and remained beneath her fervent orthodoxy. Though she wrote, "Even at present, whenever I think of [Yenan], I'm very ashamed," [25] beneath her "correct" exterior, signs of her previous heterodoxy can be detected. Some of them can be found even in her highly acclaimed novel, *Sun Over the Sangkan River*. The overriding purpose of this novel was obviously to tell the party "truth" about land reform. Nevertheless, there were episodes where Ting Ling, through her characters, uttered "truths" other than those of the party. Though she portrays several reactionary, selfish landlords, she does not make them merely one-dimensional. When they lose their authority in the village, she shows them to be as fearful of persecution as their peasant counterparts once were. In fact, she paints this feeling of fear as pervading all classes of the village at the beginning of land reform.

Although it is clear throughout the novel that Ting Ling has little sympathy with the landlords or with the village teacher, she has them express criticisms of the party which she does not refute and which she allows to stand on their own merits. One of the criticisms is reminiscent of Wang Shih-wei's accusation against the party in 1942 for establishing a new ruling class. A landlord asserted that "the Communists always say they are working for the poor . . . but that is just so much fine talk . . . In Kalgan who lives in the best houses? Who rides in cars? Who are always coming in and out of fine restaurants? Aren't they the ones who have grown fat?" His companion replies, "A new dynasty needs new ministers." [26]

Ting Ling also has the village school teacher voice the resentment she had expressed in her story "In the Hospital" against untutored party cadres directing professionals and specialists. The schoolteacher, referring to the party functionaries, exclaimed, "Look, we teachers have to be guided by the so-called commissioners of popular education . . . This commissioner is that fellow Li Chang. The bastard knows a few easy characters, but he's a fool. Yet without any sense of shame, he keeps coming to issue orders for this, that and the other." [27]

Actually, this question of professional standards versus party standards had continually troubled her in the 1940's and was still disturbing her now. Throughout the early 1950's, while she was constantly urging intellectuals and writers to carry out the party's orders, she herself was wishing again for the time when she could be her own free agent and give full attention to her own creative work. Impatience with her official duties was indicated in the postscript to a collection of her essays, *K'ua-tao hsin ti shih-tai lai* (Leap into the new period), published at this time. She belittled the literary works she had written while in an official capacity. "This is all demand writing in which the subject is determined by others." [28] As opposed to the views of others in the cultural bureaucracy, creative work to Ting Ling was not something that could be turned out during one's vacation or after a few months' stay in a village. It had to be worked at constantly by writers freed from the responsibility of administrative tasks. Creativity, she declared, "is work which should be carried out regularly and unceasingly through writing and studying; . . . it develops like other kinds of work step by step and cannot be done in one jump." [29]

Her desire to increase professional and literary standards preoccupied her more and more in the early years of the regime. At the conclusion of her speech before the Association of Literary Workers in June 1953, she announced, "I continue to have the ambition that I will still write a good book." [30] By the Second National Congress of Writers and Artists in September 1953, this was her main concern. She urged writers to strive for the same standard she set for herself. She advised them to use the eighteenth-century classic, *Hung lou meng* (The dream of the red chamber) and the works of Lu Hsün as their criteria of good writing. She begged them to write books that would find their place among the masterpieces of all time, "To 'write a good book' should be our objective . . . The book must have high ideas and artistry; it should be enjoyed not only by oneself or a few friends, but be loved by tens of thousands of readers, . . . be forever imprinted on people's minds and be a book which people enjoy quoting. Its influence will not only last for a time, but will continue on into later periods." [31]

Another area of potential clash between Ting Ling and the party was in the difficulty she had resolving the conflict between loyalty to her friends and obedience to the party. In her attack on Wang Shih-wei in 1942 and again in her denunciation of Mao Tun and Ai Ch'ing, she obviously followed party orders rather than her own conscience. Nevertheless, her constant castigation of herself for devotion to her friends and colleagues reveals that this was a sentiment she found hard to discard. She repeatedly admitted her reluctance to criticize her friends for fear of giving them a bad name. She frequently denounced intellectuals who went to live among the masses but could only communicate with one another. This was a form of indirect criticism of herself. She insisted that "You always think of past friends, . . . and imagine how nice it would be if one of them came to talk to you." [32] She also had other "incorrect" personality traits which she singled out for censure. They were characteristics which would tend to clash with the anti-intellectual, anti-internationalist attitudes of the party leaders. For example, she admitted that she "likes to hear people tell her she is highly cultured." Moreover, she confessed that in her own conversation she "loves to talk of foreign places, use difficult phrases and quote famous people." [33]

Potentially, the most controversial facet of Ting Ling's thinking vis-à-vis the party was her view of the nature of creative work. Her concepts on art had some similarities to the ideas of Hu Feng and Feng Hsüeh-feng, though she was not concerned with "the subjective spirit." Her divergencies from the party were revealed in her speech commemorating the Tenth Anniversary of Mao's "Talks on Art and Literature." Like Hu Feng and Feng Hsüeh-feng, she advocated a pragmatic, individualistic approach to writing and an end to the imposition of specific political doctrines. In words that could almost have been written by them, she declared that "Scientific theories [Marxism-Leninism] . . . can help writers understand life and formalize a theme clearly . . . , but the writer himself must genuinely grasp his subject through his life practice and must rely on his own self to perceive rich emotions and consciousness." Furthermore, she added, a writer must also be able "to make new discoveries." [34]

Though Ting Ling was at this very moment a crusader for thought reform, in this speech she urged writers to find their creative inspiration from their own feelings rather than from those imposed by others. "Authors must understand the importance of the correct themes, but they must do so by going deep into life, by engaging in the mass struggle, and by struggling within their own selves." [35] She then applied these ideas to the creation of types in literature, a view which clashed with her simultaneous demand for the creation of positive heroes. She contended that literary characters derived from a theory lacked life. A true type can come alive for the reader only when "he has strong individuality." [36] This can happen, she believed, when the writer himself experienced a full, rich life. Finally, Ting Ling was concerned with a question that had disturbed her mentor Lu Hsün and his followers in the 1930's — the increasing tendency of party leaders to turn literature into propaganda tracts. She agreed with the party that "Literature's basic responsibility was to . . . educate the people and propound the revolutionary ideas of the working class to the people." But, she added, "Literature is not equal to general propaganda and text books . . . , though we have people who now think so." [37]

She had opened this commemorative speech by asserting that "Mao's Talks . . . must be used by all writers, especially those in leadership positions and with influence among the masses, as a compass for everyday work." [38] However, if writers were to follow the interpretation she forthwith presented, the results would have been contrary to Mao's intention that creative work correspond strictly with the party line.

Ting Ling's view of the party's role in the process of literary creation was contradictory. At one point, she praised party officials for their generous help in assisting writers to analyze the world about them. Yet, at another, she asked for the diminution of the party's control over writers. She maintained that creativity was purely an individual experience that should not be interfered with by organizational authority and discipline. "I am not against our present creative work being organized, but . . . a writer is not like a child who cannot leave his mother, he must be independent." [39] In fact, she, like Hu Feng, asked that writers because of the nature of their work, be freed from the controls placed on other members of society. "We must have all kinds of social controls, but we should not adopt parental authority. A writer is not the kind of person that can be nurtured; he must develop by himself among the masses." [40]

Though these unorthodox ideas were spotted in several of Ting Ling's speeches and essays in the early 1950's, not much attention was given to them at this time. There was some criticism of her for not completely eliminating her middle-class values. Also, there were a few criticisms of *Sun Over the Sangkan River* mixed in the predominantly laudatory comments. On the whole, however, there appears to have been very little public discussion of Ting Ling and her work that was of a negative nature. In fact, the party portrayed her as an exemplary party leader and seemed to have forgotten her rebellious actions in Yenan. When *Chinese Literature*, the party's English language journal, published *Sun Over the Sangkan River* in 1953, its editors introduced Ting Ling and her work with the statement, "She has never swerved an inch from the path taken by the Party." [41]

In addition to Ting Ling's own ability to command an important position for herself in the new regime and to her pre-eminence among creative writers, tolerance of her contradictory views may also have been due to the party's own mood at this time. The campaigns of the early 1950's against Wu Hsün, Hsiao Yeh-mu, and the editorial boards of cultural journals were conducted in a more subdued manner than the previous drives against Wang Shih-wei and Hsiao Chün. They were drives that were focused more on anticipating potential subversion than on stamping out any public expression of criticism. Moreover, since the party was at this moment fully occupied with agrarian reform and consolidating its political rule, ideological purity was of secondary importance. Finally, although the party subjected intellectuals to reform, its approach was still wary for fear that harsh measures would alienate them. It was not yet ready to push ideological conformity with zealousness. Therefore, it was apparently willing to overlook Ting Ling's subtle unorthodoxies and contradictory statements as long as it could utilize her effectiveness as an administrator and her reputation as a writer for its own purposes.

Therefore, the year 1953 saw Chou Yang and Ting Ling both in prominent and powerful positions in the party's cultural hierarchy because of their abilities to play leading roles in the party's ideological reform movements. During these drives, they had both drawn to themselves loyal supporters from the Communist literary and intellectual world. While Chou may have been in closer contact with the very top leadership of the party and apparently in charge of the reform of the non-Communist intellectuals, he was by no means fully in control of all the party's cultural organs. Ting Ling shifted in 1952 to *Jen-min wen-hsüeh* to become one of its chief editors. In her place as editor of *Wen-i pao*, she was able to have appointed her close friend Feng Hsüeh-feng and to have remain as assistant editor her old colleague Ch'en Ch'i-hsia. She controlled two of Communist China's most influential journals. Thus, in the early years of the regime it would appear that Ting Ling and her associates, who represented the relatively more professional, more independent approach to creativity and intellectual activity, clearly rivaled Chou Yang and his group, who represented the more bureaucratic, orthodox approach.

Obviously, the party's efforts to unite all the writers under one rule was not wholly successful. As in the past, distinct literary camps quickly re-emerged. Their conflict, which manifested itself in veiled ideological differences and competition to dominate influential journals and strategic organizations, was to become increasingly intense.

chapter six

THE RELAXATION OF 1953
AND THE CAMPAIGN AGAINST
FENG HSÜEH-FENG IN 1954

By the end of 1952, the party had restored China's productive facilities and stabilized the economy. It proclaimed an end to the period of reconstruction and the beginning of the period of economic development and transition to a socialist economy. Inauguration of the first Five-Year Plan was officially announced at the start of 1953, but it encountered immediate problems. In the first eight months of 1953, only one-half of the annual goal for capital construction was fulfilled. One of the chief difficulties was inefficient and overambitious planning by individual enterprises. As a result, China's drive toward industrialization was temporarily halted in order to study and remedy defects evidenced in the first year of the plan. The interval of 1953 and the first half of 1954 was more a period of exploration and preparation than a time when the party actively put its plans into effect.

Slight Relaxation Toward Intellectuals, 1953–1954

Just as the party's economic program vacillated at this time, so too did its approach toward the intellectuals. The party's policies toward the intellectuals were contradictory and had somewhat the same exploratory quality displayed in the economic sphere. Conflicting directives were issued to cadres in the academic realm. They were told to tighten the party's organizational controls at the same time they were urged to allow intellectuals and scholars more leeway in using their individual talents. Party leaders simultaneously attempted to regiment and cajole the intellectuals. They believed these diametrically opposed approaches would win the voluntary cooperation of the intellectuals and their active participation in the party's program.

The party's control over the intellectuals was intensified through diverse methods. Politically, most intellectuals after the campaigns of 1951 and 1952 accepted party doctrine and used Marxist-Leninist frames of reference, but intellectually, they still tried to work as they had in the past, divorced from party supervision and utilizing methods learned from the West. Therefore, the party launched a Marxist-Leninist study movement in the spring of 1953 among university professors and students. This movement differed from the previous ideological remolding campaigns in that it was carried out with less pressure and was conducted more in the manner of study sessions than of confessionals. Local branches of the Chinese Democratic League, one of the supposedly "independent" political groups composed of Western-educated intellectuals, convened small study groups in the universities under the direction of party officials. The purpose of these meetings was to make intellectuals understand that "Marxism-Leninsm is the foundation of scientific research and must be studied by all sciences." [1] The party's demand that intellectuals learn from the Soviet Union became increasingly louder. It was stimulated by an influx of Soviet specialists in 1953 and the large-scale translation of Soviet textbooks. Besides trying to turn the intellectuals away from the West, the party's emphasis on the Soviet Union was tied in with its plans to impose ideological and political direction on academic work. It pointed out as stated in a *KMJP* editorial of July 1, 1953, that "the success of Soviet science was inseparable from the mastery and practice of Marxism-Leninism and dialectical materialism." [2]

An example of the party's increased control is seen in the literary field. In the spring of 1953, special committees in the large cities organized writers into groups based on their literary medium — novels, plays, poetry, and cinema. These committees formulated work programs for each author, supervised his writing, and helped him study the political and artistic views of Marxism-Leninism. At the fall 1953 Second National Congress of Writers and Artists the content and style of literary work were more specifically prescribed than earlier. The vice-chairman for Economic Affairs told writers to present their "heroes" at work "in the socialist reform of capitalist industry and commerce during the transition to socialism." [3] As for style, Chou Yang ordered writers "to assimilate the heritage of Chinese classical literature and art which stands at one with realism, artistic skill and closeness to the people." [4] Though Chou had been prescribing national art forms for many years, his prescription now had the organizational apparatus to enforce it.

Yet, while the party was intensifying its over-all supervision and direction of intellectuals, it attempted to ease the cadres' grip over individual academic and artistic endeavors. In order to move ahead with its first Five-Year Plan, the party offered the intellectuals a modicum of relaxation in the expectation that they would reciprocate by carrying on more productively and creatively with their work. Since China was still following the Soviet pattern, this modification of policy may have been due also to the fact that the Soviet Union, in this period immediately after Stalin's death, permitted some relaxation in the academic and artistic realm in an effort to gain more popular backing and support. Finally, the party's more flexible approach appears to have been a product of the earlier ideological remolding movements, particularly the Wu Hsün drive and the literary cheng feng. In the belief that the campaigns of 1951 and 1952 had gone too far, the party attempted to backtrack a bit. Henceforth, movements to pull back and relax somewhat after a big push forward in ideological reform increasingly characterized the party's treatment of the intellectuals.

The party now frankly admitted that the earlier drives had silenced large sections of the intellectuals. *JMJP* acknowledged on October 8, 1953, that "There is a lack of enthusiasm in the arts and, as a result, many artistic workers have neglected their work." [5] Of even greater concern to the party was the fact that increased tension had developed between the intellectuals and the party cadres in charge of the educational and academic sectors. The party was obviously concerned that the hasty actions of the cadres would alienate the intellectuals. This is seen in a communication of the party to the cadres in an engineering school: "Some Party cadres do too much in too short a time and are preoccupied with the grandiose. The number of students and teachers who support them is very small." [6]

Party leaders did not hold their repressive policies responsible for the paucity of intellectual achievement and the widening gap between the party and the intellectuals. Since the party and Mao must remain infallible, the blame was placed on middle- and lower-level cadres who were charged with distorting the party's policies in practice. They were accused of mismanaging academic work and underestimating the value of scholars trained before the party came to power. The party now professed great concern for the intellectuals. It called previous neglect of them in favor of nurturing new party-educated intellectuals a result of errors by the cadres. A flood of articles poured forth from China's most influential newspapers and journals accusing the cadres of many of the same charges leveled against them by the revolutionary writers in 1942 — ignorance, putschism, and bureaucratism. Over and over again the cadres were ridiculed for their oversimplified, unlearned attitudes which prevented them from comprehending the complexity of intellectual work. The cadres in the universities particularly were criticized because they "do not understand that the nature of educational work is different from the nature of production and they seek to apply production methods mechanically to teaching. They do not comprehend that . . . the knowledge of teachers and students cannot be judged by mechanical standards." [7]

In contrast to its previous policy of downgrading intellectual achievement, the party now sought to enhance the prestige of the intellectuals. It informed all groups of the population, particularly the cadres, of the crucial role the intellectuals played in the party's program for China. Articles in *JMJP* now stressed that the intellectuals, because of their knowledge, teaching, experience, and research abilities were of great value to the regime. [8] In an even greater change from its previous approach, the party advised cadres that furthering of intellectual endeavor rather than ideological orthodoxy should be the basis for their actions. A *JMJP* editorial commented that "Some comrades fail to see the value of the old teachers to national construction because they take the ability to grasp Marxism-Leninism as the sole criterion on which to base their judgments . . . We should first see whether the old teachers are capable of working honestly and of knowing their work." [9]

Top party officials even went so far as to suggest that intellectuals may be better suited to lead academic work than party cadres. Some articles compared the abilities of the cadres unfavorably with those of the intellectuals. *KMJP* maintained that, in contrast with the new party-trained intellectuals, "some of the old teachers may hesitate in their work, but their academic foundation is more profound." [10] For a brief period, instead of the cadres taking the lead, the party urged the cadres to follow the intellectuals. Similar in tone to the party's exhortations during the later Hundred Flowers period, party directives on the one hand encouraged intellectuals to criticize the cadres and on the other instructed the cadres "to listen humbly to their criticism and opinions and learn from them." [11] Therefore, a rectification drive was underway against the cadres at the very time they were ordered to tighten the party's organizational controls over the intellectuals.

Apparently, the intellectuals did not readily come forth with the criticism the party had requested. Again the party blamed their silence on the dictatorial practices of the cadres. Addressing the cadres, the party's theoretical journal *Hsüeh-hsi* declared, "Some . . . suppress people who hold different views with crude methods and do not allow them to say what they wish." [12] Repeatedly, party leaders implored the cadres "to cooperate with them [the intellectuals] in earnest and encourage them to criticize party members." [13]

Nevertheless, the relaxation of 1953–1954 differed from the later Hundred Flowers episode when the party was genuinely interested in a freer intellectual climate. Perhaps, the party sought to provoke a more stimulating atmosphere in the natural and applied sciences, but in all other academic fields, its encouragement of diverse ideas was to produce ultimately a unified, politically-oriented view of scholarship. In return for its concern, the party expected the intellectuals not only to work more effectively, but also to be more willing to accept ideological remolding and follow the party line. This was the aim behind the party's call for the expression of differing viewpoints. *Hsüeh-hsi* clearly stated the party's purposes: "We must change from confused, incorrect consciousness into clear, correct understanding . . . Unless we have fervent discussions, many questions on ideology cannot be thoroughly solved." [14] Party leaders did not seem to be disturbed by the inconsistencies in their approach. Contradictory orders were issued over and over again to the cadres in charge of the intellectuals.

As in other fields, the party's relaxed grip in the literary realm took the form of blaming the cadres for the poor quality and small quantity of output. The bureaucratic methods and suppressive measures of the literary cadres were indicted more often throughout 1953 and the first half of 1954 than the writers' undisciplined habits and confused ideology. The cadres' bureaucratic attitude took many forms, one of them being undue interference in literature and art. A *JMJP* editorial of October 8, 1953, charged that the cadres "rigidly specify topics, form, and time limits and they subject writing to indiscriminate alterations and rejections." [15] They were even attacked for being overly harsh in their criticism. "We oppose the view of certain writers who want no part of criticism and are hostile to it in principle. But we also oppose critics who have no respect for the experience of writers." [16] In effect, the party blamed the cadres for the very things it sought to accomplish through the tightening up of its cultural organizations and literary controls.

Several nonorthodox views on literature which hitherto had been muffled were now allowed clear, public expression. Among them was the demand that literature be permitted to break out of the narrow confines of politically-dictated material and prescribed forms. Mao Tun in his address to the Second National Congress of Writers and Artists in September 1953 urged writers "to cast wide their nets in selecting themes and styles to satisfy the diversified needs of the people." [17] Again there was a parallel with happenings on the Society literary scene in this period. Though Chinese writers talked less than the Soviet writers of using satire, they voiced similar demands for a fuller presentation of reality that drew from a wider range of subject matter and a greater variety of literary styles.

Another demand heard clearly at this time in China as well as in the Soviet Union was for more professional standards in the creative arts. Writers asserted that literary work took much more than a little bit of talent and the "correct" ideology. It, like other professions, required time and care to acquire a skill. Mao Tun, in the same speech in which he asked writers to broaden their scope, also begged them to pay attention to their craft. He implored them to do away with the monotony and crudity in their literary styles by perfecting their language and structure. Echoing the words of Ting Ling in this period, he bemoaned the fact that writers had become political functionaries without sufficient time to pursue their craft. "After liberation, many literary workers took up administrative duties in the government and other organs; this weakened their creative efforts." [18]

This new emphasis on the intrinsic characteristics of art and on professionalism not only came from genuine writers like Mao Tun and Ting Ling, but from the very top leadership as well. Stress on artistic standards was not merely tolerated, it was actively promoted by the party itself. For example, the Association of Literary Workers was renamed the Chinese Writers Union. The change from *kung-tso-che* (literary workers) to *tso-chia* (writers) raised writers from the status of workers to that of a profession. The best proof, however, can be seen in the speech of Chou Yang given at the same series of meetings where Mao Tun expressed his views. Chou reprimanded his fellow officials, including himself, when he admitted, "We often disregard the principles of literature and art," and display "a crude attitude in the leadership of literary activity." [19] He denounced these attitudes, for which he himself was guilty, in somewhat the same terms that Ting Ling had used. The leadership of literature and art, he asserted, "does not pay attention to the different life experiences and writing abilities of writers. Party officials arbitrarily treat them like elementary school children to whom one gives an assignment. They determine when the assignment will be completed and even the form it should take . . . When the work is completed, they often simply and carelessly veto it." [20] Chou admitted that this treatment had filled writers with bitterness and with the feeling of being oppressed.

Though Ting Ling and Chou Yang recognized the same problem, their solutions were quite different. Whereas Ting Ling suggested that writers be allowed to follow their own literary instincts, Chou offered the same kind of contradictory solution the party recommended. He, too, asked that the writer be given a little more freedom, but within the same speech he also insisted that the writer's creativity be developed by the use of thought reform methods, "study, discussion, . . . mutual observation and self-criticism." [21] The unworkability of the party's cultural directives at this time can be seen further in Chou's specific pronouncements on literary practice. On the one hand, he declared that "there is room for utmost diversity in the literary and art forms of creativity." But on the other, he asserted that "We aim at socialist realism as the criterion of great works and literary criticism." [22] The first directive in the spirit of the later Hundred Flowers period was canceled out by the second, in line with the party's drive for ideological uniformity.

Throughout this period, as we have seen, writers were asked to combine two approaches which offset each other. Faced with contradictory directives, they apparently did nothing. The party's slight relaxation did not bring the results the party had intended. Writers had not willingly moved closer to the party's ideology, nor had they written more and better literary works. In fact, if anything, the party's policy of simultaneously letting go and tightening up had frustrated and confused writers still more. Intellectuals in other fields responded similarly. Consequently, by the middle of 1954, the party looked to other methods for developing productive yet obedient intellectuals.

The Re-emergence of Ideological Remolding Campaigns

The Causes

In the later part of 1954, the party's measures to regiment the intellectuals eclipsed its efforts to cajole them. In addition to the failure of its more conciliatory approach, there were several other reasons. One of them derives from the ebb and flow of the party's remolding campaigns. The party's effort to redress some of the excesses of the cadres and to pay special attention to the intellectuals had undermined the cadres. In a few cases, the powers of the cadres were somewhat curtailed. Some intellectuals and specialists had been given a larger voice in directing the work of their institutions and professions.[23] Hence, the party now found it necessary to check this trend and rally the cadres.

The most significant reason, however, can be found in the party's economic plans at this time. In the latter half of 1954, the party was completing its plans for a nationwide collectivization and industrialization program that was to burst forth in 1955. The population had to be made ready for these great changes and for the speed with which the party hoped to carry them out. The intellectuals, in particular, had to be prepared, because it was with their technical know-how and ability to educate the people that the party expected to implement these changes. In anticipation of the acceleration of industrialization and collectivization, the party had even less room for compromise in executing its plans. Since nothing could be allowed to divert energy from the straight and narrow course leading to the completion of its program, tighter control over the intellectuals became even more urgent toward the end of 1954.

Thus, once again the party turned to the thought reform campaign and to the use of an individual example with which to push forth its program. And once more the party chose its scapegoats from the literary realm and from among the old foes of Chou Yang. The movement began gradually, first with a relatively muted attack on the scholar Yü P'ing-po, who had been influenced by Hu Shih and was a representative of Western-oriented thinking. Then it quickly expanded from non-Communist intellectuals to an incisive drive against the left-wing intellectuals represented by Feng Hsüeh-feng. It finally reached its climax in a campaign against Hu Feng. With each successive victim, the campaign increased in intensity and broadened its scope. From the way each wave followed with increasing force, it appears that this procedure for nationwide indoctrination was carefully planned ahead of time. The final drive against Hu Feng affected the whole population from the peasant in Sinkiang to the professor at Peking University. All classes of people were aroused to a state of emotional frenzy and subjected to some form of thought reform — conditions the party considered necessary for the carrying out of its Five-Year Plan.

The reasons Yü P'ing-po, Feng Hsüeh-feng, and Hu Feng had been specifically selected as object lessons cannot fully be explained by the fact that they held ideas inimicable to the party's maintenance of monolithic control. It is true that these three men sought in diverse ways to separate scholarship and literature from the party's direction. Moreover, they advocated a degree of intellectual freedom and scholarly achievement that were part of the heritage the party was now determined to destroy. Yet, there were others in Communist China at this time who took similar stands. For example, the famous philosopher, Liang Sou-ming, continued to express his own and not the party's interpretation of Confucianism, Western philosophy, and Indian religion. He rejected the party's concept that Chinese society had been feudal and insisted that feudalism had ceased after the Han. Furthermore, he declared that class consciousness was alien to China. Finally, he had refused to participate in many of the party's drives, even when personally requested to do so by Mao.[24] Yü P'ing-po's and Feng Hsüeh-feng's resistance to certain party views were not so forthright nor so provocative as Liang Sou-ming's. There were several other intellectuals, such as the educator Ch'en Ho-ch'in, and the editor Ch'in Mu, who showed similar courage.[25] There were sporadic criticisms and meetings against these men. Nevertheless, the attack on them could not compare with the scale and intensity of the organized drives against Yü P'ing-po, Feng Hsüeh-feng, and Hu Feng. The story of these three writers reveals that they were selected not only because of their unorthodox views, but also because they had personally incurred the wrath of those in charge of ideological remolding, particularly Chou Yang and his associates.

Yü P'ing-po and Hung lou meng

The drive against Yü P'ing-po centered on his interpretation of the great eighteenth-century Chinese novel, *Hung lou meng* (The dream of the red chamber), the literary work with the largest circulation in China. Typical of many intellectuals before the Communist takeover, but unlike the revolutionary writers whose fate he was to share, Yü was a dispassionate scholar who remained aloof from the political conflicts of the time. Though he had written some poetry and philosophical essays, his chief work had been the study of *Hung lou meng* under the guidance of Hu Shih. He first published his research on *Hung lou meng* in 1923. With the party takeover in 1949, he remained in his position as a professor at Peking University, but was forced to participate in ideological remolding sessions and daily political meetings. When there was a flurry of criticism of Hu Shih's thinking in 1951, Yü was pressured into denouncing his former teacher.

In 1953, literary critics were ordered to reinterpret China's classics in Marxist-Leninist terms. Yü was set to work on this project. However, when the Writers' Publishing House, which had been specifically established to republish China's old works, came out with a new edition of *Hung lou meng*, Yü was aroused to opposition. On

March 1, 1953, Yü, in *KMJP*, criticized this new edition for not
using the same language as the original. His assistant, Wang Pei-
chang, with even more directness, declared in another article that
the new publication of *Hung lou meng* had no understanding of old
literature and harmed the original text by its arbitrary revisions.

The act which most antagonized the authorities was the publication by Yü of an article on *Hung lou meng* in 1954 which presented
essentially the same interpretation he had worked out in the early
1920's. He had been unwilling to disregard his thirty years of research and insisted on remaining loyal to its results. This was proof
again that an intellectual like Yü might be converted to Marxism in
his political thinking but not in his own work. He continued to regard *Hung lou meng* as an autobiographical novel of its author,
Ts'ao Hsüeh-ch'in. The party, on the contrary, did not look at the
decline of the Chia family, described in *Hung lou meng*, as an individual incident, but as representative of the decay of the whole
society. It claimed that through this one family, the author depicted
the conflicts in China's feudal society and criticized the entire social
structure.[26]

Yü came in conflict with the party over this article not merely because he had refused to accept the party's interpretation. Actually,
he had expressed many of the same views earlier, in 1952, without
any recriminations, when his original study on *Hung lou meng* was
reissued. The clash occurred this time because Yü had been insub-
ordinate to Chou Yang's close associate Hu Ch'iao-mu, who was a
deputy-director of the Propaganda Department and an editor of
JMJP. Initially, Yü's 1954 article on *Hung lou meng* had been com-
missioned for the magazine *People's China*. When he had completed
it, he had sent a draft to Hu Ch'iao-mu for approval. Hu Ch'iao-mu
made some suggestions and asked Yü to rewrite it. Instead of revising
it as Hu Ch'iao-mu had directed, Yü on his own initiative had sent
this article to the journal *Hsin chien-shen* (New construction) and it
was published in March 1954.

It was not until six months later, in September 1954, that the
accusations against Yü began. Most likely, the party in the spring
and summer of 1954 was not yet prepared to force intellectuals to
accept party doctrine. It was still trying to win them over through
conciliatory measures. But by the fall of 1954 the party appears to

have decided on a concentrated thought reform movement. Since Hu Ch'iao-mu was one of the major officials in charge, it can be surmised that Yü was chosen largely because of his refusal to heed Hu Ch'iao-mu's instructions. Though the campaign began with an obscure article written by two young students, Li Hsi-fan and Lan Ling, it was obvious from the first that this drive was well planned by the party's Propaganda Department. Their article, first published in a journal at Shantung University, *Literature, Philosophy, and History*, was reprinted in *Literary Heritage*, the supplement of *KMJP*, on October 10, 1954, and in *JMJP* on October 23, 1954. Subsequently, an avalanche of articles and editorials attacked Yü with unanimity on all questions.

From the substance of these articles, it can be seen that the purpose of this campaign went far beyond the establishment of the party's reinterpretation of *Hung lou meng*. Actually, as early as 1950, the party had already described *Hung lou meng* as a reflection of the decay of the feudal society. By far the overriding purpose of this campaign against Yü was to discredit his kind of scholarship and to use his case as an object lesson in re-educating China's intellectuals to a political view of scholarship.

The drive against Yü marked a shift of emphasis by the party from intellectual endeavor and professionalism to political orthodoxy and nonspecialization. Criticism of Yü sought to prove that the ideological militancy of party-trained students represented by Li Hsi-fan and Lan Ling was of greater value to the party than the scholarship and academic discipline represented by Yü. Party leaders praised their two products for their ability to produce a much better piece of research than scholars like Yü, who had been schooled in the Western tradition and who had devoted many years to their subject. Kuo Mo-jo declared, "This incident proves, on the one hand, that as long as one's thoughts and methods are based on Marxism-Leninism, one can come to the core of the problem studied in a short time, . . . on the other hand, Yü is an example [of the fact] that in spite of thirty years of research, the more he studies, the more he is confused." [27] Chou Yang expressed the contrast in this way: "Yü is accepted as the authority on *Hung lou meng*, but Li Hsi-fan and Lan Ling do not believe in authority blindly and have faith in truth and in the scientific theory of Marxism-Leninism." [28]

The party summoned party-trained intellectuals in other fields to follow a similar example by ousting the accepted authorities and imposing their own, that is, the party's view on scholarship.

These two students were not only contrasted with Yü because of their orthodoxy but also because of their youth. A great push was made at this time to dislodge older intellectuals from their honored positions in Chinese society and institutions and replace them with party-indoctrinated youth. Here is an example of the party's effort to do away with China's traditional emphasis on age and learning. To this avail Chou Yang asserted that "Li Hsi-fan and Lan Ling . . . expressed something lacking in many of us older people . . . namely, the necessary sharp fighting spirit." [29] Large numbers of students were mobilized to accuse Yü of leading them astray through his kind of research. Many of them, because of their active role in this drive, were able to move up the hierarchical ladder. These campaigns served as a source of mobility. As a result of the removal of the politically vulnerable, new openings were available. Those who played a key role in the exposure and criticism were promoted. In this case, Li Hsi-fan and Lan Ling, after their attack on Yü, immediately became research fellows at the People's University and members of the Chinese Writers' Union. Li Hsi-fan quickly rose to the position of ideological watchdog over young writers and intellectuals.

Criticism of Yü's political approach to literary research broadened into a general attack on the influence of Western scholarship in the social sciences and the humanities. As in the 1951 campaign against professors, these disciplines were the first to be affected. The natural sciences in the latter part of 1954 still remained relatively exempt. Hu Shih's pragmatic methods — an empirical treatment of all knowledge and the avoidance of preconceptions — became the main target for this aspect of the movement. As mentioned earlier, criticism of Hu Shih had been part of thought reform drives since 1942, but this time his ideas were made the focus for a concentrated attack. The article by Li Hsi-fan and Lan Ling was called "The first shot against the bourgeois methods and standards of Hu Shih." [30] In the party's view, Hu Shih symbolized "study for the sake of study, research for the sake of research . . . and search for truth for its own sake. [To Hu Shih] academic research is to satisfy one's own interests, not the needs of the country and people." [31] The party through its attack on Hu Shih sought to reverse this process. The attention given to Hu Shih's thinking was proof that his empirical method still exerted considerable influence in Communist China and undermined the party's demand that all material data be related to Marxist-Leninist theories and the party line.

Although the criticism of Yü's work had extended to Hu Shih and to other academic disciplines besides literature, censure of Yü himself showed a marked restraint. Chou Yang's speech that concluded the sessions against Yü was almost conciliatory in tone. "In criticizing Yü, we only criticize his literary views; we do not overthrow him as an individual. He supports communism." [32] Party officials made a special effort to show that even though Yü's scholarship was at fault, he still remained loyal politically. Ho Ch'i-fang stressed that "Yü P'ing-po and Hu Shih differed in their political views." [33] At the final series of meetings against Yü, which were called from October 31 to December 8, a conspicuous reserve was displayed in the denunciations of Yü. In light of the subsequent heightening of tension, this constrained attitude appears as an effort to hold back and keep the drive under firm control in order to build up to a climax later on. In fact, there was not much discussion of Yü and *Hung lou meng* at these meetings. Most of the speakers hardly mentioned them at all. These meetings had been convened for other purposes. One of them was to attack Feng Hsüeh-feng and his editorship of *Wen-i pao*. Again, to quote one of Chou Yang's concluding statements, "The present discussion of *Hung lou meng* is the start of an ideological struggle in academic circles against the bourgeois class." [34] Yü was only a small beginning.

Feng Hsüeh-feng, 1949–1954

It was now Feng's turn to serve as a target in the party's drive to impose political standards on scholars. With Feng, the party's effort expanded further. Since Feng was a party member as well as an intellectual, the campaign was extended into the ranks of party intellectuals. As the party worked to displace older, respected intellectuals from high positions in the academic world, it sought to do so in party organs. Also, since the campaign against the domineering leadership of the cadres no longer suited their purposes, party leaders redirected this drive toward the less obedient intellectuals in positions of authority in the party. Feng, therefore, was accused of the very same traits which hitherto had been attributed to the party cadres.

Before the party had decided to embark on a concentrated thought reform movement in the later part of 1954, Feng's star had been rising. This had not been true at the very outset of the regime. When party officials were cracking their whips over the left-wing intellectuals prior to the party's takeover, Feng had felt their lashes. He wrote to Shao Ch'üan-lin at that time: "Originally, I was a piece of stone for building the road, but now I have become a pebble that has been kicked to the side." [35] His early jobs in the regime, as head of the Shanghai branch of the Association of Literary Workers and as a film writer, in no way measured up to his previous positions in the party and to the respect shown to him as Lu Hsün's closest associate. Except for a short work, "Reminiscences of Lu Hsün," he did little writing.

In the few essays he did write around this time, he appears to have turned his back on his previous ideas on art. He no longer advocated the existence of independent literary groups as he did earlier.[36] Even when he wrote articles calling for more *tsa wen*, he no longer defined them as he had in the 1930's as sharp jabs at the existing social and political system. Instead, he adhered faithfully to Mao's interpretation of *tsa wen* as satire to be used against the enemies of the people and the party. Like his friend Ting Ling in this period immediately after the party takeover, he stressed ideological reform and the portrayal of new heroic characters. His despair at being pushed aside by party leaders evidently prompted him to produce works that would return him to the good graces of the authorities. His desire to gain a voice and position in the new system gave him no other choice.

Probably because of his professed orthodoxy and the machinations of his friend Ting Ling, he became chief editor of *Wen-i pao* in 1952. From then on his power increased steadily. He began to be mentioned in official listings just after Chou Yang's top guard.[37] Along with Ting Ling, he was elected to the Creative Work Committee, which planned work programs for all writers and artists. At the same time, he was put in charge of investigating literary publications. He was a frequent lecturer at political study sessions for writers and artists. Moreover, he was honored as the chief interpreter of Lu Hsün at a commemoration celebration for Lu Hsün in October 1953. Most important, he and Ting Ling were elected vice-chairmen of the Writers' Union. Other vice-chairmen, in addition to the writers Lao She and Pa Chin, were Chou Yang and Shao Ch'üan-lin. Thus, the presidium of the Chinese Writers' Union, under Mao Tun, had a fairly balanced representation from the two factions. Toward the end of 1953, Ting Ling's name figured less prominently in party events. She appears to have withdrawn somewhat from active party organizational work. Feng seems to have taken her place as the chief spokesman for the more professional, more independent writers.

Although *Wen-i pao* under Feng's editorship continued to publish the usual prescribed works, there was a sprinkling of less doctrinaire writings. *Wen-i pao* carried two attacks on Hu Feng by Ho Ch'i-fang and Yüan Shui-p'o, but it also published works of Hu Feng's group and even gave Lu Ling relatively favorable reviews.[38] Feng's writing, like his editorship, also showed some divergencies within a fairly orthodox framework. Politically, several of his essays loudly echoed the party's denunciations of American aggression and Western imperialism. Yet, as his position began to improve, his writings began to show hints of some of the views he had formulated in the 1930's. He once again talked of true feelings and criticism of society as inherent parts of literary work, though in a more roundabout way.

The subject on which Feng spoke out most forthrightly at this time was the party's lowering of literary and professional standards. Most likely, Feng and his colleague Ting Ling believed they could talk more freely on this issue that did not appear directly to undermine the party's control than they could on the need for more social criticism and more truthful characterization, which obviously did. Feng, like Ting Ling, insisted that literary works had to be much more than propaganda. They should be great works of art. Feng hoped that China was "gradually approaching the time when we will produce our own Dante." [39] These high literary standards are apparent in Feng's literary criticism. In a review of "Defend Yenan," a novel almost unanimously acclaimed by party leaders,

Feng praised some aspects of the work, but in his conclusion, he wrote, "In its methods of artistic technique and of expression, it does not achieve the level of a classical masterpiece." [40] Naturally, with such criteria, Feng insisted that writing literary works involved much more than merely the right political sentiments and facility with words. In opposition to the party's loosening of professional standards, Feng sought to tighten them. He urged writers to use more care in writing, develop stricter structure, and employ more precise language. He considered these the qualities that made for good writing.

In the relatively relaxed period of 1953 and the first half of 1954, Feng became more daring. At various meetings, he denounced China's current literature because it falsified reality. He held the party's cultural policies responsible. Such criticism was also being voiced in the Soviet Union at this time. Later attacks on Feng revealed drafts of speeches he had written which had been rejected by party authorities. He was reported to have stated that "Because the writer is commanded to write and commanded to experience life, his ability, struggling power, and independent ideas have been stripped from him and he is no longer an engineer of the soul." [41] He was also quoted as having said, "There is a backward psychology that often directs us; . . . our only fear is that a writer would commit a mistake politically. Mistakes in life and art become mistakes in politics . . . We appear like pitiful old ladies who worship the Buddha." [42] Feng was concerned that this fear so pervaded the literary world that writers were afraid to discuss serious issues and point out injustices.

Thus, the beginning of 1954 found Feng in charge of one of the most influential journals in Communist China and expounding views that were at variance with the party's.

The Party Attacks Feng Hsüeh-feng for His Editorship of Wen-i Pao

Suddenly, in the fall of 1954, the party switched from feeble strikes against Yü P'ing-po to virulent blows against Feng Hsüeh-feng. Feng was ostensibly attacked because of his praise of Yü P'ing-po's study of *Hung lou meng* and his refusal at first to publish Li Hsi-fan's and

Lan Ling's criticism of Yü in *Wen-i pao*. Actually, however the campaign against Feng was another manifestation of the clash between political and professional standards and a demonstration of the factional struggle in the literary realm.

When Yü P'ing-po's study of *Hung lou meng* was republished in 1952, it was praised in *Wen-i pao*. A book review of Yü's study stated that "The author has worked carefully at detailed textual criticism and collation; thus sweeping away many nonessential interpretations in the past studies of *Hung lou meng*. This is a very great accomplishment . . . Yü P'ing-po's research is a great help in our understanding." [43] This comment implied that the principles of Marxism need not necessarily enter into the methods and conclusions of research. The respect that *Wen-i pao* accorded Yü's scholarship enhanced his prestige in literary circles.

Before Li Hsi-fan and Lan Ling published their criticism of Yü's study in the Shantung University journal, they had first submitted it to *Wen-i pao*, but it was rejected. When their views were subsequently sanctioned by the classical literature division of the Chinese Writers' Union and apparently by the party itself, the editors of *Wen-i pao* attempted to recoup their "mistake." They reprinted the article on September 30, 1954. However, appended to it was a deprecating editorial remark which stated that "The views of these writers are not thorough enough nor complete enough in certain areas." [44] This apparently was one of the few negative comments the editors of *Wen-i pao* had ever attached to any of the articles they published.

These two actions, praise of Yü P'ing-po and initial rejection of Li Hsi-fan's and Lan Ling's article, were only slightly rebellious acts. Yet, because of them the party charged Feng with revolting against Marxism-Leninism, disobeying the party's orders, treating *Wen-i pao* as his own private property, surrendering to bourgeois ideas, and repressing new forces. The party's picking on these small acts was only an excuse to launch an attack that had other underlying purposes. After all, there had been many others who had openly expressed respect for Yü's scholarship and disapproval of the crude theorizing of Li Hsi-fan and Lan Ling. At the very meeting that had been convened specifically to criticize Yü, the writer Wu Tsu-hsiang expressed views similar to Feng's. He stressed that Yü's study had some good points and questioned the reasoning and propriety of the criticism of the two students. Moreover, the literary supplement of *KMJP* had also attached a deprecating comment when it had reprinted Li Hsi-fan's and Lan Ling's criticism. Yet, Wu Tsu-hsiang and the editors of *KMJP* were not attacked for their remarks. The drive against Feng was not only to instruct party as well as nonparty intellectuals on the need to subject their thinking and actions to the strict command of the party bureaucrats. It was an attempt by Chou Yang and his followers to displace Feng and his associates from their positions of power in Chinese cultural circles and install their own men.

Actually, the roots of the drive against Feng were laid many months before when the party embarked on a campaign to obliterate all independent elements within the party. This drive may have been connected with the ouster at this time of Kao Kang, Politburo member and secretary of the northeast bureau. Liu Shao-ch'i, in February 1954 at the fourth plenum of the CC, called for the elimination of "independent kingdoms" of party officials in politics, the military, and literature. An editorial in *JMJP* of April 13 declared that "Some . . . propagate the ideology of personal worship, refuse supervision and the investigation of party organizations, are hostile to criticism and form small groups." [45] Throughout the spring and summer of 1954, there were articles in *JMJP* of a similar nature. Among the accusations against those who built "independent kingdoms" in the arts and scholarship was the charge that they suppressed free discussion. Chou Yang asserted that "In the last few years, the atmosphere of discussion in academic circles has been greatly lacking and has profoundly affected the development of academic study and ideological uplift." [46] This atmosphere of repression had been blamed in 1953 on the crudity, dogmatism, and ignorance of the party cadres, but in the summer of 1954, nonparty and party intellectuals with influential voices in party organizations were held responsible. What the party now meant by its demand for open and free discussion was that the party's view on academic questions was to replace the Western-oriented views which hitherto predominated.

The campaign appears to have been planned at the very top of the party hierarchy. It evolved smoothly out of the criticism of Yü P'ing-po. Three days before a "struggle" meeting against Yü P'ing-po was to take place Yüan Shui-p'o, one of Chu Yang's closest followers and the editor of the literary section of *JMJP*, published an article entitled "An Inquiry of the Editors of *Wen-i pao*." He labeled Feng Hsüeh-feng's praise of Yü P'ing-po a surrender to the "bourgeois" school of scholarship. His rejection of Li Hsi-fan and Lan Ling, Yüan claimed, showed a lack of appreciation for the value of scholarship based on Marxism-Leninism. He called Feng's concern over scholarly standards an "aristocratic attitude." [47] At the meetings which began three days later, on October 31, and continued until December 8, 1954, it was Feng and not Yü who was made a target for attack.

In line with the party's program at this time, the speeches and articles censured Feng because he managed *Wen-i pao* according to his own principles instead of the party's. The party claimed that literary and art circles and the general public had been critical of *Wen-i pao* for some time, but that its editors, Feng and Ch'en Ch'i-hsia, had paid little attention to the criticism. "The editors regard *Wen-i pao* as their personal achievement, have become vain, and have indulged in decadent, authoritarian thought." [48] Employing the same epithets used a few months earlier against the party cadres, Feng and Ch'en Ch'i-hsia were assailed for their use of "dogmatic, over-simple formulas to criticize others" and for their "intolerance of countercriticism." [49] A few speeches complained about the complicated content of *Wen-i pao* and mentioned the difficulty the public had in reading Feng's essays. They asked that *Wen-i pao* be made more accessible to the nonspecialized, ordinary reader.

In contrast to the "dictatorial sway" that Feng and people like him supposedly held over cultural circles, party officials, reversing their 1953 stand, now pictured the cadres and new intellectuals as an oppressed minority. Feng and his ilk were charged with creating an atmosphere which stifled free debate, thereby preventing this "minority" from expressing its views. Specifically, Feng was charged with suppressing Marxist-Leninist interpretations of literary questions and criticism of Western literature. In addition, he was attacked for writing unenthusiastic reviews of popular literary works that were appreciated by the masses. The essays of his assistant, Ch'en Ch'i-hsia, were also denounced because they "satirized and criticized in an uncomradely fashion." [50] As usual, Chou Yang made the concluding remarks at the final meeting. He summed up the arguments against the editors of *Wen-i pao*: "Individual authority, friendship, and the power of their journal were more important to them than the interests of the people and the country." [51]

To eliminate the "repressive atmosphere" purportedly created by Feng, Yü P'ing-po, and their kind, party leaders and all the speakers at these gatherings advocated in high-sounding, democratic phrases free debate and the expression of different views. Kuo Mo-jo, on the opening day of the meetings, asserted that "the principle of making the minority yield to the majority in academic discussions cannot be followed. The minority must be listened to and be permitted to uphold its own proposals." [52] The "minority" Kuo was defending, of course, was only those intellectuals and writers who based their scholarship on Marxism-Leninism and political principles. In a later speech, Kuo Mo-jo showed that his and the other speakers' demand for free speech was merely a euphemism for the commencement of another round of intensive criticism and self-criticism. "The results of these debates have shown that the expression of diverse viewpoints will lead to common ideas and correct conclusions." [53] Furthermore, he declared that "In order to distinguish between what is right and wrong, we must rely on Marxism-Leninism as our criteria." [54] Thus, the call for open debate was, in effect, a means to intensify the process of ideological remolding.

In addition to discouraging party and nonparty intellectuals from making independent judgments, the campaign against Feng was also an instrument used by Chou Yang to settle old feuds. As with the attack on Hu Feng, this one stemmed from Feng's previous clashes with Chou and his group. To Chou, *Wen-i pao* must have been an uncomfortable reminder that his authority was not supreme and that his old adversaries still had one of the party's most influential journals at their command. Almost every other important cultural journal was under the control of one of Chou's followers. Ting Ling, who reached the height of her power in the party hierarchy in the early 1950's, left her position as an editor of *Jen-min wen-hsüeh* in the summer of 1953. Into her place on *Jen-min wen-hsüeh* stepped one of Chou's closest followers, Shao Ch'üan-lin. The principal theater journal, *Chü-pen* (Theater book), was edited by Chou's associate T'ien Han. Only *Wen-i pao* remained under a management that would not strictly obey Chou's orders. Because of his past disagreements with Chou and because of his disrespect for Chou's intellectual abilities, Feng obviously did not submit readily to Chou's directions. This was clearly indicated in the recurrent accusations against Feng for ignoring the opinions of the editorial board and his superiors. As in the other campaigns, Chou's right-hand men pointed the charges and shouted the accusations. Then, at the conclusion of the "struggle" meetings, Chou stepped in to make the final summation of the "evils" the party wished to remove and the "virtues" it wished to instill.

Before the meetings to censure Feng had begun, pressure apparently been put on him, because at the very first session he confessed. Characteristically, Feng, when attacked directly, immediately withdrew from the battle. As opposed to his response in the 1930's, when he left the scene and returned to his home province, the only way he could escape under the party regime was to present a self-criticism. In compliance with the party's order, he pleaded guilty to all the party's charges and promised to reform. His confession revealed the difficulty that an intellectual, even one who was a party member, had in adjusting his intellectual values to the party's political values. Feng stated, "I regarded Yü P'ing-po's work only as research. This definitely proves that I have lost my sensitivity to the erroneous ideas of the bourgeoisie . . . In fact, I have become a prisoner of bourgois ideas." [55] This last statement was an acknowledgement of the party's tenet that if one did not totally reject non-Communist thinking, he had surrendered to it.

After Feng's confession was published on October 30, 1954, *Wen-i pao* went through a month of reorganization. In December, the Chinese Writers' Union and the ACFLAC announced that the principle of collective leadership had been restored to the management of *Wen-i pao*. An editorial committee was established of which three of its members, K'ang Cho, Hou Chin-ching, and Ch'in Ch'ao-yang, all protégés of Chou Yang, were put in charge. Feng was demoted to a position on the editorial board, but, in fact, was stripped of almost all his power. Chou was now in command of Communist China's chief cultural journals and had dethroned and silenced some of his old rivals. Another result of the drive against Feng was the further enhancement of the power of Chou and his associates.

As the sessions against Feng concluded, there were indications that the charges against him were to be extended further than the circle of writers, artists, and journalists he represented to intellectuals in all academic fields. This was intimated by Kuo Mo-jo when he declared that the discussions on *Wen-i pao* and *Hung lou meng* "are a struggle between proletariat and bourgeois thought . . . Not only literature, but also history, philosophy, economics, art, language, education and even the natural sciences — all these fields should develop . . . an ideological struggle." [56]

Thus, by the close of 1954, the party had already set in motion widespread waves of ideological remolding. The initial waves had rolled ahead with Yü P'ing-po, the followers of Hu Shih, and Feng Hsüeh-feng. Each one was larger and more penetrating than the last. This movement had moved from scholars in classical literature to professors influenced by Western scholarship to intellectuals from left-wing circles. The party was now ready to roll out the largest and deepest wave which was to spread to all areas of China and to all groups of the population.

chapter seven

THE HU FENG CAMPAIGN
OF 1955

The main target of the meetings called against Yü P'ing-po and Feng Hsüeh-feng was not these two men, but the writer Hu Feng. The attack on Hu Feng triggered an intensive, nationwide ideological remolding campaign on a scale unprecedented in Communist China. Hu was chosen for several reasons. He was in sharp personal conflict with those in charge of the thought reform campaigns, particularly Chou Yang. Perhaps more important, he, unlike Yü P'ing-po and Feng Hsüeh-feng, had directly and unequivocally opposed the party's policies in the cultural sphere.

Hu Feng, 1949–1952

Hu and his followers greeted the party's takeover from the KMT with enthusiasm. Nevertheless, from the very outset of the regime, they remained as determined as in the past to resist the party's literary dictates. In a collection of essays written from 1949 to the end of 1950, *Ts'ung yüan-t'ou tao hung-liu* (From the source to the flood), Hu expressed sympathy with the political aims of the party, yet he did not refrain from presenting his own individual views on literature. The majority of the essays were devoted to political rather than literary matters. By any standards other than those applied by Communist critics in this period, these articles, written in simplified clichés, are among his weakest works. In general, Hu went along with the party's current line. He called for the destruction of feudalism, imperialism, and bureaucratic capitalism and for strong ties with the Soviet Union. He constantly reiterated that Marxism-Leninism, by means of proletarian leadership, would make possible the emancipation of mankind. Throughout, he pointed to Mao Tse-tung as the infallible political leader. He declared that "Under the enlightened leadership of Mao, the progress and reform of our nation . . . will provide us with the basic road to everlasting peace." [1]

Some of his remarks on literature also complied with the party's literary directives. He echoed the party's demand that writers grasp Marxist-Leninist and Maoist ideological guidance in order to understand reality. Yet, there were other statements in his book which contradicted this view and reaffirmed his basic belief that a writer should use no external "isms" to view life. As in the 1930's and 1940's, he continued to urge writers to use their own subjective impressions when describing people's lives and feelings. [2] In fact, in the concluding section he once again emphasized that the road literature must travel is quite different from that of politics, though the two roads may reach the same destination. [3] Perhaps such contradictory aesthetic standards are inevitable when a writer acquiesces only in part to the dictates of a totalitarian government. Hu's display of proper political sentiments, which at this time overbalanced his remarks on literature, seemed to say that Hu, the citizen, could accept political dictation, although Hu, the artist, could not wholeheartedly accept literary dictation.

Besides his unwillingness to dispense with his individual interpretation of literary standards, he also could not end the relentless battle with his foes simply because they were now in power. This was seen in his response to the regime's ideological remolding movements. If Hu had not fully appreciated the significance of these movements before 1949, his awareness of their meaning came quickly afterwards. As the party in the early 1950's began to subject intellectuals to increasing controls, Hu's free-ranging mind rebelled. However, his response was not rebellion against the party itself. Essentially, he did not blame the political leadership, whose authority he accepted, but rather the group in charge of the literary realm and thought reform, his old antagonists Chou Yang and his associates.

He believed they had distorted the leadership's directives. These sentiments were expressed in Hu's correspondence at this time. In one of the most revealing of his letters, Hu said of Mao's "Talks on Art and Literature," "People have made a totem of this small booklet; this is the most difficult problem at present." [4] Actually, Hu was not too disturbed by the content of the "Talks" and, in fact, praised certain aspects, such as Mao's stress on observation, personal experience, and analysis. What troubled him was that the literary officials used their interpretation of these "Talks" to enhance their own authority. He complained that "They have achieved a confused kind of mechanicalism as well as an overbearing attitude that suffocates the life of realism . . . While these critics are in power, other people cannot even grunt disapproval. And demands arising from reality will be suppressed. In this way, how can culture not wither?" [5]

Several of Hu's disciples, however, were not so anxious to distinguish between Mao and his subordinates. They held Mao as well as his underlings responsible for the withering of Chinese culture. One of them, Chang Chung-hsiao, wrote Hu, "Because I wanted to write, I read Mao's 'Talks.' But after reading them, I do not wish to write any more." [6] Referring to Mao's command that writers praise proletarian and party heroes, Chang said, "This is a completely formalistic, mechanistic way of looking at things . . . I believe we should write of suffering, happiness, searching and imagining." Chang concluded, "These 'Talks' probably were useful in Yenan but will not do now. In the present situation, they can destroy the spirit." [7]

The "mechanicalism" which Hu blamed primarily on a few officials was considered by some of his followers to be a product of the whole system of party control. Again Chang in a letter to Hu declared, "I am unusually suspicious of organizing life. What it demands is that everyone thinks the same way. I fear the training methods are not much different from Hitler's . . . I think some of the words in that book of Andre Gide's are appropriate now." [8] The book Chang was referring to was Gide's *Return from the USSR*, in which he expressed disillusionment with the Soviet system. Another of Hu's followers, Hsieh Tao, who taught at the People's University, wrote to Hu soon after the party takeover: "The new teaching methods utterly exhaust people. Originally, a teacher worked with his brains, now it has changed so that he almost completely cannot use his brains." [9]

Though Hu was not so prone to hold the whole Communist system responsible, he too was deeply concerned by the suffocating of artistic and intellectual creativity in China. Hence, he decided very early in the regime to stem the spread of what he called a "cultural desert." [10] He wrote to Chang Chung-hsiao: "According to my way of thinking, we should begin to act in the whole ideological realm . . . otherwise mechanicalism will have full control. Even if great works are produced, people will have lost the power of feeling." [11] At one point, Hu was so overwrought by this "mechanicalism" that he spoke in the spirit of the Confucian censors of old who were willing to risk death for their beliefs. He wrote to one of his colleagues, "I am now sharpening my sword for the attack and watching the trend of events. When I have finally set my eyes on the target, I will cut off my head and throw it at the filthy iron wall in order to destroy it." [12] However, this characterization of himself as a martyr appears infrequently at this time.

Instead Hu sought to express his opposition by working through the existing system. He believed that if he could break the control of his old enemies and win party sanction for his own views, Chinese culture would again bloom. He realized that the system would not allow the kind of wide-open warfare he had waged with his magazine *Hsi wang* in the 1940's. Furthermore, he knew that he and his group in no way wielded power comparable to that of the opposing faction. Though he was famous among literary circles and still praised for his revolutionary activities and anti-KMT stand, he was given no important posts when the party first took over. Nonetheless, he seemed confident that his methods of literary warfare would become effective with time and that at an opportune moment he would push through to victory.

His strategy initially was to comply with the requirements of the literary officials in order to build up his position and that of his followers so that they could later break down these requirements. He called this technique, "The monkey's trick of crawling into the belly." [13] This quote referred to the monkey in the sixteenth-century Chinese novel, *Pilgrimage to the West*, who used supernatural powers to turn himself into an insect in order to slip inside his opponent. Hu warned his colleagues that since they were dealing with officials they could no longer be on the offensive. He counseled one of them to revise an article he had written because "a sudden frontal attack will not be accepted any longer . . . The ones you are dealing with now are not 'enemies,' they are leaders." [14] Nevertheless, Hu constantly reminded his followers that compromise with the authorities was not to become an end in itself. It was not to be carried to the point of inconsistency with their own fundamental beliefs. He advised Lu Ling to ask the literary officials to judge the political merit of his work, but cautioned him, "You should refuse unreasonable corrections of your views." [15] To Chang Chung-hsiao, he wrote, "Of course, you must avoid things which are too sharp, you must consider making a living, but naturally, you must not speak empty words." [16]

His major preoccupation in these early years was to find positions and opportunities to publish for himself and his followers. Because of their past insubordination, particularly to the party representatives formerly in Hong Kong in 1948, his group had difficulty publishing their work. *Wen-i pao* would not print their material. Book shops refused to sell their writings. In a letter to his friend Shu Wu, the author of "On Subjectivism," he complained that "Because of the Hong Kong clique, when shops see your name, they shake their heads." [17] His letters to his colleagues in the early 1950's were filled with practical suggestions, editorial advice, and constant encouragement. In one to Chang Chung-hsiao about this time, he wrote, "Although at present it is difficult to publish in their journals, nevertheless do not stop work. I consider this most important . . . Go out, endure insults, one does not have any other way." [18]

Yet, though Hu persistently prodded his followers to write, he, after a short period, adopted a policy of silence. His silence, most likely, was induced by the constant rebuffs that his various efforts had met. At the very beginning of the party regime, he attempted to set up his own publication, *Ch'i tien* (Starting point), and his own publishing house, Ni-t'u she (Earth society), but as the party took over control of all publications, these enterprises quickly folded. Also, he had written a poem entitled, "Time Begun," celebrating the party's liberation of China and lauding Mao in super-human terms:

> Mao stands like an idol
> Speaks to the whole world
> Gives order to time [19]

When this poem first came out, Hu wrote to his friend Lü Yüan that "In Tientsin, it had set them afire." [20] The poem had received some praise from the literary historian Wang Yao. Yet, despite its glorification of Mao, the authorities found it lacking in orthodoxy. By the summer of 1950, *Wen-i pao* had published a sharp criticism of it which was followed by similar attacks in other journals. Hu then directed his cohorts to send letters and articles to the editors protesting the criticism. He advised them to write under several different names so that there would be more likelihood of their letters being printed. Moreover, the volume of letters would indicate that a large number opposed *Wen-i pao's* policy. However, very few of their letters were published.

Actually, in these early years of the regime, Hu appears to have been constantly fighting windmills. At the end of 1949 and beginning of 1950, when party leaders strived to win the cooperation of most party and nonparty intellectuals, Hu and his group, on the contrary, were subjected to blistering attacks. Ho Ch'i-fang shot the first volleys in the introduction to a collection of his essays, *On Realism*, published in late 1949. He reiterated the old cries against Hu of a year earlier. Once again he chastised Hu's group for its concept of an abstract "subjective fighting spirit" and for its reluctance to undergo reform and study Marxism-Leninism.

Even before the thought reform campaign of 1951 began, one of Hu's closest associates, the poet and essayist A Lung,[21] was subjected to special sessions in ideological remolding. He had published two essays in the literary supplement of *JMJP* which expressed views similar to Hu Feng's. The correspondence of Hu Feng's group reveals that it held Chou Yang personally responsible for instigating the attack.[22] Though Hu Feng's name was not mentioned in the criticisms at this time, several of his followers feared that Hu's already tenuous position had been further jeopardized by this affair. One reported that because of the A Lung incident many had begun to question Hu's literary concepts. What particularly disturbed them was that A Lung had no way of publicly answering the charges against him. Yüan Shui-p'o, the editor of the literary section of *JMJP*, had refused to publish A Lung's rebuttal to his critics.

This was only the first thrust against Hu Feng's group. Many more followed with the launching of the thought reform movement against professors in 1951 and the literary remolding campaign at the end of that year. Initially, the literary authorities used divisive tactics against Hu's colleagues, apparently with the intent of first splitting his ranks and then proceeding to Hu himself. Hence, when the campaign began, Hu's most vocal followers were among the prime targets. One of the first to be hit was Lü Ying, who was head of the Literature Department at Shantung University. *Wen-i pao* used Lü Ying as an example of a professor engaged in non-Marxist teachings and scholarship. As in the case of other professors accused in this movement, Lü Ying's students led the attack on him. The most vocal was Li Hsi-fan, who later opened the campaign against Yü P'ing-po. Apparently, at this early date, Li had already made contact with Chou Yang. Li blamed Lü Ying's emphasis on abstract literary values for distracting him from political activity. When the whole nation was engaged in the Wu Hsün movement, Li complained, "I locked myself in the library to study and buried myself in my books." [23] Criticism from other students of Lü Ying followed this pattern. Yet, despite all these public denunciations, Lü Ying did not disavow his literary ideas. He was willing to admit only that his lectures may have been too profound to have been understood by his students, but he balked at investigating his own thought as the party had directed.

After Lü Ying, the next disciple of Hu Feng to be hit was the short-story writer Lu Ling, who had been attacked in 1945 during the cheng feng movement in Chungking. The offensive against him began to gain momentum in the early part of 1952. In line with Ting Ling's campaign against unorthodoxy at this time, her journal *Wen-i pao* condemned Lu Ling's nonidealistic portrayal of the working class. One of its articles complained that "The proletariat under his pen are petty, wild, barbarous, cruel, disorganized, undisciplined and irrational. Almost all of his working people have such a backward ideology . . . that they stand in opposition to their own class." [24] In addition, Lu Ling was accused of the same approach that Ting Ling was criticized for in 1942. He writes of the old cadres "as lacking in knowledge and ability and as having lost their [revolutionary] stance." [25] Lu Ling's error, like that of his associates A Lung and Lü Ying, was that he had not reformed his middle-class views. This article concluded that "Lu Ling and those with similar mistakes must thoroughly reform their own subjective ideology." [26] This last statement, most likely, was meant for Hu Feng.

As a result of these criticisms, Lu Ling found it increasingly difficult to publish his work. Hu Feng had sent one of Lu Ling's stories
to a journal under a different name, but it was returned with the
note that "the characters . . . suffered from the evil influence of
Lu Ling's style of writing." [27] In commenting on this, Hu wrote,
"Obviously, these mandarins do not forget . . . From this, we can
see the depth of their hatred." [28] Besides the embargo on his works,
several "struggle" meetings were held against Lu Ling. He was also
paid repeated visits by party officials. Hu counseled him specifically
about his encounters with Chou Yang. "You should meet him with
a good, soft attitude which encases toughness. Be practical and careful, don't attack at random." [29]

As Lu Ling came under full seige in the spring of 1952, Hu's
followers sensed that a direct strike was being readied against their
master. There had been some intimations. The "Internal Correspondence" of *Wen-i pao*, which was a circular sent to a selected list
of writers, directed its correspondents to publish letters assailing
Hu's literary views. Apparently, this "Internal Correspondence" was
not directly managed by the editor of *Wen-i pao*, but by Chou Yang's
associates, particularly Yüan Shui-p'o. Referring to this in one of
his letters, Hu wrote, "This criticism is not a small affair, it has been
fermenting for three years." [30] In an effort to halt these undercover
moves, Hu's disciples pleaded with him to take the offensive. One
of them, Lu Tien, urged Hu Feng to inform Chou En-lai of these
moves and present his own ideas for invigorating the cultural scene.
He advised, "We must take the initiative. Don't wait for them to
bring out your problem. You must go first to the authorities and
bring out your ideas on the literary movement." [31] Such counsel
demonstrates the naïve, unrealistic attitude of Hu's group toward
political affairs. At this juncture, Hu was not influenced by their
emotional pleas. He realized that from his present unfavorable position such an approach would be futile.[32]

The literary officials finally hit their target on June 8, 1952. Hu's
friend, Shu Wu published a self-criticism in *JMJP* entitled, "Thoroughly Study 'Talks at the Yenan Forum on Art and Literature.'"
It was more of an attack on Hu and his group than a public confession. He denounced the group to which he had belonged and
urged its members, especially Lu Ling, to give up their individual,

nonpolitical literary ideas and learn from Mao. Though Shu Wu did not mention Hu directly, Yüan Shui-p'o, the literary editor of *JMJP*, editorialized that the group Shu referred to was Hu Feng's, which was known for its bourgeois literary concepts.[33] It would appear that Chou Yang was again instrumental in engineering this attack. He was in a position of direct command over Yüan Shui-p'o. Moreover, Hu, in a letter on June 26, apropos of this incident, advised Lu Ling that in view of the hard facts, they must conciliate Chou Yang, though, he added, "We must not allow him to take advantage of us."[34]

Pressure mounted quickly. Following Shu Wu's self-criticism, several articles appeared directly critical of Hu himself. Then, on September 11, Shu Wu published an open letter in *Wen-i pao* addressed to Lu Ling, in which he begged him to acknowledge his "mistakes." He told Lu Ling, "I have only written to you, . . . but what I say pertains to all of my former friends."[35] This time he mentioned Hu explicitly. Soon intensive discussions extending over a period of several months were held for the sole purpose of reforming Hu's thought. Shu Wu was one of the main participants. Hu was also frequently visited by Chou Yang.

Apparently, Hu failed to benefit from all the official attention given to him. The authorities were exasperated by his self-criticisms. He refused to repudiate his literary beliefs; on the contrary, he insisted they were correct. He confessed only to mistakes in literary style, such as vagueness of expression. Ho Ch'i-fang complained that "Hu has prepared for two months and has been given advice by many comrades. If he had seriously considered the advice, he should have written a much better criticism."[36]

Such obstinacy led to a move to compel Hu to reform through public criticism. In January 1953 Lin Mo-han published an essay on Hu's anti-Marxist ideas, and in February Ho Ch'i-fang published an earlier speech against Hu's concept of realism. Their charges are significant because they enunciate many of the arguments which were later used against Hu in the campaign of 1955 and set forth the party's view on the "correct" relationship between art and politics in a Communist state.

Ho Ch'i-fang and Lin Mo-han attacked Hu's interpretation of art because it was based on his own rather than the party's standards.

Ho declared that "The seriousness of Hu Feng's mistakes are that
. . . he did not use Mao's directions to examine and change his own
ideas and that he used his own ideas to oppose the tendencies in
revolutionary literature." [37] The basis of Hu's views, Lin wrote, is
"an abstract subjective fighting spirit which is above class." [38] These
two critics, therefore, contended that Hu's view of literature was devoid of a class basis or of political consciousness. They accused him
of considering art more important than Marxism-Leninism. Furthermore, since Hu confined the writer's life to creative activity, they
claimed that he did not realize that a writer must also engage in ideological study and practical activities.

Actually, it is true that Hu minimized the need for Marxism-
Leninism in creative work. Nevertheless, he repeatedly insisted that
practice was the main source of creativity. In Hu's view, however,
"practice" meant the full experiencing of life, wherever it was; in
the party's view, the term meant experience in factories, fields, and
party organizations. Herein lies another point of the party's conflict with Hu. He claimed that any living material has meaning,
not just that pertaining to workers, peasants, and party members.
As Ho correctly pointed out, "Hu believes that the value of literary
work is not completely in the material, but in the standpoint of the
writer and his artistic approach." [39] Another clash between Hu and
the authorities was over Hu's rejection of native folk styles in literature. Lin accused Hu of "Westernizing" Chinese culture.[40] Ho
charged that "Hu does not know that revolutionary realism must
serve the masses and that, therefore, the literary form must be
easily understood by them." [41]

Finally, these two critics delineated the great gulf between the
literary theories of Hu and those of Mao Tse-tung by showing that
Mao emphasized objective reality, which is the class struggle, as
the basis of art, whereas Hu emphasized the writer's subjective view,
which is above class. Actually, these two men again misrepresented
Hu's views in their effort to contrast them with Mao's. Hu believed
that the subjective view and objective reality must be combined as
equal parts in the creative process. Nevertheless, the critics were correct in saying that he differed from Mao. An individual interpretation
of literature, even if based on Marxian premises, cannot be counte-
nanced by the party because it denies the subordination of literature

to politics and to the guidance of the party. This series of attacks against Hu and his group ended with the conclusion of the literary remolding campaign. The movement officially terminated in the autumn of 1952, although the two articles written specifically to persuade Hu to reform did not appear until early in 1953.

In both of these articles Hu was still spoken of as a revolutionary fighter who upheld an anti-imperialist, anti-feudal, anti-KMT stand. Furthermore, his critics granted that "His literary ideas had been influenced by Marx's literary theory." [42] His errors originated from the fact that he had not changed from a bourgeois to a proletarian view. Therefore, Hu was not condemned beyond reprieve and could still aspire to salvation if he reformed his ideas. Criticism of Hu in this period differed from the criticism of the later campaign, as it had no other purpose than to incorporate him into the literary remolding drive and avenge personal grudges. Also, the assaults were isolated, not a continuing attack in which Hu's ideas were made the focal point. The principal connection with the later campaign was that the forces that directed the criticisms were the same, Chou Yang and his associates.

Hu's Report to the Central Committee

Although Hu and his colleagues had not come forth with satisfactory self-criticisms, nevertheless, with the temporary lessening of the party's crusading zeal in 1953 and the first half of 1954, the position of Hu and his followers improved. In this period of comparative relaxation, Hu's associates had the opportunity to engage more actively in cultural activities. Even Lu Ling, while he continued to receive some negative reviews, was able to publish stories in *Jen-min wen-hsüeh* in 1953. Several in Hu's group began to receive important posts in local Writers' Unions, in propaganda bureaus, and in publishing houses. One of them, P'eng Po-shan was Deputy-Director of East China's Cultural Department and Chief of the Propaganda Bureau at Shanghai. Another, Liu Hsüeh-wei, became head of the New Literary and Art Publishing House in Shanghai and employed under him several of Hu Feng's followers. Lu Tien was Secretary-General of the Tientsin Writers Union. Nevertheless, the main base of Hu's followers remained in Shanghai. Most important, the party seems to have been more willing to accommodate itself to Hu's independent stand and tried to win his cooperation. In 1953, he was made a representative in the NPC, was appointed to the editorial board of *Jen-min wen-hsüeh*, and became a member of the executive board of the Chinese Writers' Union. He published a few poems and articles in *Jen-min wen-hsüeh*.

With his sudden rise in the literary hierarchy and with the party's more tolerant attitude, Hu jumped to the conclusion that his own position had advanced to the point where an open struggle might bring victory. He believed it was the proper moment to step forth and state his views as his followers had been urging. His plan was to present a report to the CC in which he would criticize the present literary movement and blame its failures on the thinking of his two critics, Ho Ch'i-fang and Lin Mo-han, as representatives of Chou Yang's group. While he was preparing his report, he directed his followers to show themselves as "correct" comrades. He wrote, "Now we must obey organizational principles . . . in order to secure the fight." [43] One of Hu's colleagues advised Hu to apply at this time for membership in the party.[44] Hu also directed his disciples to find suitable quotations from Soviet leaders and Mao to bolster his arguments, the usual practice in intra-party debates. His letters to his followers persistently urged them on. "Naturally, it is a troublesome affair, but the best thing is to do it." [45]

The prime purpose of the report Hu finally presented to the CC in July 1954 [46] was to overthrow the literary authorities and their polices and avenge the personal grievances of his group. It was not to disrupt the existing political system. Hu argued that cultural and intellectual activity in China since 1949 had not been led by the principles of the party and Mao, but by the dogmatic, sectarian ideas of a few literary authorities. Like the critics in classical times, he sought to prove that the country's good and wise leaders had been deceived by unscrupulous advisers. In the process of refuting the views of these advisers, he presented his own interpretation of Marxism and literature.

He opposed the arbitrary imposition on writers of a predetermined Communist world view. As in previous essays, he offered an empirical, as opposed to theoretical, approach to communism. To him, communism was not a set ideology, but a flexible system of ideas that expressed the constantly changing needs of the people. He asserted that "In practice, there is no abstract Party stand . . . The policies of the Party are the summation and crystallization of the life demands of the masses." [47] In regard to literature, he feared that "If we go as far as to use Marxism as a substitute for realism, then we will block artistic endeavor and will destroy art itself." To support his argument, Hu quoted Mao: "Marxism can only be a part of realism, it cannot be a substitute for it." [48] From this, he concluded that the literary officials had disobeyed Mao's dictates.

In opposition to these officials, Hu offered his own view of socialist realism. Though he claimed his interpretation derived from the Soviet theory, in actuality, it was much closer to the Western view of realism. In fact, he defined socialist realism in terms of nineteenth-century humanism. He declared that its fundamental spirit "is concern with man, . . . emancipation of man, . . . and the spirit of humanism. If we turn away from this spirit, we cannot depict man realistically." [49] This approach, Hu believed, would ultimately lead to the realization of the ideals of communism. Moreover, he claimed that "Socialist realism . . . made realism a high law and treated writing as a function to be carried out according to its own special quality and basic rules." [50] His belief that creative work has its own rules denies the party dictum that politics is the absolute directing spirit over literature. In other words, Hu negated the party's unitary concept toward all aspects of life.

Hu reprimanded officials like Lin Mo-han and Ho Ch'i-fang because they had imposed their own "narrow system of vulgar mechanicalism" onto socialist realism. In his opinion, their system, "which abandons reality, makes their world view totally dead and abstract and denies the complicated content of the writer's vision." [51] As a result, Hu claimed they had a crude understanding of great Western literature. "They believe that because realist writers of the past were inhibited by the limitations of their class and world view, they cannot reflect the struggle of the working class." [52] He pointed out that the strength of Balzac's realistic method made it possible for him to rise above the limitations of his class and politics and achieve a high degree of truth. Also he pointed out that though Tolstoy was a landlord with reactionary ideas, he still could "powerfully describe the oppressed masses and peasants and angrily criticize the bour-geoisie." [53] In Hu's terms, literature was great not because the writer had a "correct" proletarian stand, but because he was able to search deeply into the lives of the people around him. "Having felt the people's difficulties and hopes, great realistic writers are great humani-tarians." [54] In this attempt to shatter the party's narrow political approach, one can see Hu's steadfast concern for the humanitarian ideals of communism, for aesthetic literary standards, and for the incorporation of Western literary values into Chinese culture.

He also opposed the idea that the writer must immerse himself solely in the lives of the peasants, workers, and soldiers. Having to write about the lives of these groups specifically, Hu believed, caused the writer to overlook the significance of everyday life around him, which likewise communicates struggle and class conflict. This time, he used the examples of Lu Hsün's *Ah Q* and Pushkin's *Eugene Onegin* to show that the writer's ability to sympathize with the masses was not determined by what class he portrayed, but by how accurately and artistically he described his own environment.

Likewise, he opposed the party's dictum that "bright things" be emphasized and elements of backwardness and darkness be de-empha-sized. Such restrictions inhibited the writer, Hu asserted, because to write only of brightness generally meant writing what is false. Of even greater concern to him was that the preoccupation with brightness diverted writers and eventually the leadership from better-ing the lot of the masses. "If everybody wrote of the bright side, then the struggle for further improvement of life would become impossible." [55] Furthermore, the depiction of brightness negated the function of writers, which Hu declared was "to be at one with the sufferings of the people." [56] Hu again objected to the literary authorities' stress on the popular literary forms of the past as the national art form for the present. Consistent with his opposition to substituting formulas for practice, he declared that literary style, like ideology, was constantly developing. "National forms are not a fixed concept, but change along with the changes in content and the demands of history." [57]

This unorthodox approach to ideology and literature naturally led him to oppose any organized form of thought reform for writers. Hu believed it was neither necessary nor desirable for a writer to be equipped with a specific doctrine because it prevented him from assimilating reality as it exists and keeping pace with practical conditions. The result would be cultural sterility. Hu proposed instead that writers reform themselves according to their own needs and through the very act of writing.

In addition to liberating writers from dogmatism, Hu's ideological and literary pronouncements, as in the past, were also meant to break the control of his old foes, the literary bureaucrats. He depicted them as a dictatorial clique who treated all who disagreed with them as enemies. This clique suppressed those who did not belong by subjecting them to continuous thought reform, preventing the publications of their works, and labeling them reactionaries. He pointed directly to Chou Yang as exemplifying the arbitrariness of this group. He quoted Chou as saying that "Even if what you say is 99 per cent right, if one thing is wrong on one crucial point then everything is . . . totally wrong." [58]

He offered concrete proposals to undercut the control of this group and at the same time promote diversity and creativity in China's cultural life. Instead of a few official publications, he advocated the establishment of seven or eight independent writers' organizations which would edit their own publications. The editor would be approved by the CC and one-third of the publication's writers might be Communist members, but the authority of the editor would be absolute, subject to no inspection or supervision. This procedure, Hu hoped, would lead to free competition in creative work. Differing literary criteria would be resolved in the competitive process. Hu's proposal would not only have led to a variety of viewpoints; it also implied that the domain of art could be led only indirectly by the party. Essentially, Hu did not oppose the leadership of Communist authorities in literary work, but he had a different concept of their role. He believed that the party should establish a system to protect and help the writer, but not to command him.

In Hu's opinion, his report only demanded a greater degree of freedom for writers to develop their individual talents within the present Communist system. However, if Hu's view of the independent nature of artistic creation were put into effect, forceful party intervention in the creative arts would cease. Not only would the party's direction of the literary movement and of writers be weakened, but the whole system of controls on which the party maintained itself would have been undermined. The reading public would no longer see life solely through the eyes of the party.

The Campaign of 1955

Causes

Clearly, it could only be a matter of time before the party took some action against Hu. Yet, even the provocation of Hu's report to the CC in no way explains the drastic measures taken against him nor the intensity and nationwide proportions of the attack. To understand this phenomenon, we must examine the party's internal policy in 1955. Having completed its detailed long-range plan, the party launched a nationwide program of agricultural cooperatives and socialization of industry and commerce. Lu Ting-i announced that "Our Five-Year Plan cannot be brought into realization in a calm, placid way. It demands a class struggle, and acute, complicated struggle." [59] Hu Feng became the symbol against which this struggle was waged. He not only claimed more autonomy than the regime was willing to sanction, he had also shown outright intransigence. He, therefore, provided an excellent example with which to do battle and with which to instill the doctrine that the first and only duty of an individual was to serve the state. As in the preceding campaigns, Hu's old foes, Chou Yang, Ho Ch'i-fang, Yüan Shui-p'o, Lin Mo-han, and Shao Ch'üan-lin, were in command.

There is a noticeable difference between the 1955 campaign against Hu and the previous attacks upon him. The content before had been primarily ideological and personal; this campaign, as it advanced, became political. Its purposes were also different. The aim of the earlier attacks had been to compel Hu to reform; the aim now was to liquidate Hu's heterodox ideas and all heterodox tendencies, ideological or political. At the same time, it was meant to educate the intellectuals and then the people as a whole in the correct doctrinal approach.

The Campaign

The first formal move in the campaign occurred during the series of meetings between October 31 and December 8, 1954, called to criticize Yü P'ing-po and Feng Hsüeh-feng. Hu had been invited to speak. Before the meetings began, he was under the impression that the CC was going to take this occasion to introduce reforms in the literary realm. There were several reasons for optimism. It had been four months since he had sent his report to the CC, and he had received no negative response. In fact, he had heard that the report was to be published. He was buoyed by the prospect because he believed that the CC was publishing it in an effort to do away with dogmatism in cultural circles. In a letter to Chang Chung-hsiao, just three days before the start of the meetings, Hu wrote, "If it is true, it means the leaders have already decided to study the problem thoroughly." [60] In addition, the opening speech by Kuo Mo-jo demanded more freedom of discussion, and other speeches criticized the suppression of minority views in the literary and editorial field. Hence, Hu concluded, "The gentlemen probably want to use this occasion to reform the situation." [61] He believed that the moment had finally arrived to air publicly the disagreements and grievances which since 1949 he had expressed primarily in his letters.

Therefore, in the belief that he would receive a favorable response, Hu, in his speech at these meetings, extended the attack on Feng Hsüeh-feng, Yü P'ing-po, and Hu Shih to the literary hierarchy, Chou Yang, Yüan Shui-p'o, Lin Mo-han, and Ho Ch'i-fang. He almost disregarded Feng Hsüeh-feng in his effort to find these men guilty of the same acts that had been charged against Feng — surrendering to the bourgeoisie, wielding dictatorial power, and suppressing the emergence of new and vital forces. Though he insisted that these mistakes were not of a few individuals, but of everyone, he held these officials responsible.

He specifically indicted Chou Yang. He accused him of "crude sociology" which he defined as a way of thinking that "was not based on reality and does not use the instruction of certain principles to understand reality, but uses the principles themselves to represent reality . . . It also uses Marxism and political-policy phrases to judge works of art . . . This weapon is frightening, because it can stifle the real feelings of creativity and art." [62] Hu then returned to a theme his one-time colleague Shu Wu presented in his article "On Subjectivism." He charged the literary officials with using this "crude sociology" to maintain themselves in power. "With their crude sociology, critics begin to exaggerate their own importance and do not treat writers as fighting friends and working comrades. Sometimes they show their faces as political instructors and sometimes as technical instructors; of course, the worst is when they show themselves as judges who set down the deciding word. Generally they . . . have an extremely cold attitude toward the creative process." [63]

Another major charge Hu made against the literary authorities was "scholasticizing Marx." With this accusation, he went beyond the realm of literature and intellectual endeavor. He touched on the party's over-all method of ideological control. To Hu, "scholasticizing Marx" meant that "Only a small number of qualified, authoritative people can understand and apply Marx — only this group and no other . . . Their scholasticizing and mystifying of Marxism makes it the monopoly of a few." [64] Here Hu, like his predecessor Wang Shih-wei, was protesting the elimination of democratic practices in interpreting Marxist ideology. He pointed to the experience of his colleague A Lung to prove this argument. The party's cultural authorities "put the hat of 'falsifying Marxism-Leninism' on him . . . This frightening hat not only frightens ordinary people away from independently searching into Marx on their own, . . . but in practice it cuts them off from Marx and makes Marxism a monopoly." [65]

Hu also cited the "Internal Correspondence" of *Wen-i pao* as another illustration of the authoritarian control of a small number. "When they desire to attack certain persons, they print directions in their 'Internal Correspondence' and then ask the correspondents to send letters, convene discussion meetings, and write articles in order to give the impression it is reflecting mass public opinion . . . Apparently, the reading public is not to be trusted; instead, two or three hundred trustworthy individuals are selected to whom orders and directions are given." [66] With the "Internal Correspondence" as one of their weapons, Hu accused this small group of establishing their own "kingly domain." Finally, Hu, as in his report to the CC, presented his own individual interpretation of Marxism. Once again, he urged each person, through his own life experiences rather than through the prescribed study of ideology, to become aware of the social and political theories of Marx. If each person were allowed to search independently into life, Hu believed, the monopoly of a small group could not be maintained.

Besides his desire to realize some of the ideals of communism, it is evident from his recurring reference to the "small ruling clique of literary authorities" that part of Hu's speech, as was true of his report to the CC, was motivated by personal animosity and the desire for party support of his own approach. Obviously, in light of the party's over-all policy at this time and of the ascendant position of his more orthodox opponents, his attempt was ill-timed. He had played directly into the hands of his enemies by providing the very material that was needed for an onslaught against such thinking.

After Hu had spoken, Yüan Shui-p'o delivered the first blow. A quick change in attitude from that expressed in previous attacks was noticeable, an indication that a definite assault against Hu had already been decided upon. Hu was no longer referred to as "comrade" and was thereby eliminated from progressive ranks. Yüan insisted that since the literary authorities Hu had criticized worked under party leadership, their actions could not be separated from those of the party. Hence, he charged that Hu's accusations were actually not against private individuals, but against the party itself. At the final meeting of the series, Chou Yang gave the concluding speech in which he, like Yüan, defined Hu's views as diametrically opposed to those of the party. He was particularly intent on drawing the line between Hu's interpretation of Marxism and "our" interpretation. By the end of the meetings, Hu was pictured as an individual who had attacked the party and its policies.

There is every indication that Hu had been invited to participate in the meetings on *Wen-i pao* expressly to furnish a pretext for the campaign against him. After Hu's report had been submitted to the CC, it was turned over to the heads of the Chinese Writers' Union and the ACFLAC, in which Hu's opponents held the top positions. Therefore, they were well aware of his antagonism toward them. It seems unlikely that they would ask an outspoken opponent to speak at a public meeting unless they had an ulterior motive which was sanctioned by the CC. Given Hu's past actions, they could easily have expected him to use this opportunity to express his heterodox views and personal antagonisms against various officials. The rapidity with which the emphasis of the meeting suddenly switched from criticism of *Wen-i pao* to an attack on Hu, and the fact that Chou's concluding speech devoted one-half of its text to Hu, when the meeting had been called for other purposes, further substantiates this conclusion. Although some mention was made of the "errors" of the literary authorities during the course of the meetings, by their end these "errors" were blamed on only a few editors of *Wen-i pao*. It therefore appears that the CC had had little intention of blaming the mediocrity of literature on the narrow practices of the literary bureaucracy, as Hu had anticipated.

On December 10, Hu's speech was unexpectedly published along with Chou Yang's criticism of it. In a letter written a few days later to one of his friends, Hu acknowledged that "I was blinded by an optimistic strategy and proceeded adventurously." [67] At this time, Chou led a group to Moscow to join the Second Meeting of the Soviet Union's Writers Association. After his return, on December 25, the full campaign against Hu began. This would indicate that Chou took a major part in its direction. But where previously Hu's assailants had been his old enemies, they now included such top figures in the CCP as Chou En-lai. Though the new campaign was not activated by official pronouncements, the speed with which China's vast cultural machine was mobilized — through exposés in the press, through unanimous participation by high-ranking officials — leaves no doubt that it was sanctioned by the party. The party remained behind the scenes, exercising its influence through its cultural authorities.

Beginning in January, *JMJP* published essays and letters criticizing Hu along lines similar to the criticisms of Yüan Shui-p'o and Chou Yang. Enlarged meetings of the council of the Chinese Writers' Union from February 5 to 7 resolved upon all-out criticism of Hu's anti-Marxist ideology. China's most famous writers — Pa Chin, Lao She, Ai Ch'ing, Mao Tun, Kuo Mo-jo — attacked Hu. Only Ting Ling was not so active in this campaign as she had been in the previous ones. *Jen-min wen-hsüeh* and *Wen-i pao* criticized themselves for insufficiently attacking Hu's group and for publishing their works. *Jen-min wen-hsüeh* was particularly abject because it had put Lu Ling's work on the front pages of its journal. As the Hu Shih campaign was swept up in the Hu Feng movement, Hu Shih and Hu Feng were bracketed together because of their pragmatic approach to China's problems and because of their rejection of China's old literature. By the end of February, the Hu Feng campaign spread to other intellectual groups. Famous scholars and professional people criticized Hu's theories and organized discussion groups.

Unable to withstand the organized onslaught and in the hope of saving his colleagues and himself, Hu composed a confession in January of 1955. His personal letters at that time reveal that he took the initiative not because he had undergone any psychological change, but because he hoped to close the case or at least to divert the attack away from his followers. He felt responsible for what had happened and feared the repercussions it would have on his disciples. As soon as the meetings called against Yü P'ing-po and Feng Hsüeh-feng had turned to him, Hu wrote to his friend Fang Jan, "The responsibility is with me . . . I am ashamed for my fellow fighters." [68] After he had completed his self-criticism, he explained, "I have written my self-criticism . . . If it can be published, this then is the first step in relieving my responsibilities." [69]

The party, however, delayed in publishing Hu's self-criticism until May. It was finally published along with the first of three groups of Hu's letters which had been confiscated from his colleagues. His correspondence was presented as the main evidence against him. The notes which interpreted these letters to the readers were reported to have been written by Mao himself.[70] Perhaps the delay in printing Hu's confession was to give time to create an atmosphere in which his confession would be unacceptable. In his self-criticism, Hu had described himself as ideologically guilty. He admitted that he had minimized the value of Marxist principles and looked at life with an individual, aesthetic view.[71] However, by the spring of 1955, Hu's ideas were being represented as not only ideologically subversive, but as politically subversive. This is seen in Kuo Mo-jo's statement in *JMJP* on April 1, "Hu not only wants to grasp literary leadership, he wants to reform the whole nation according to his own method." [72] His self-criticism, therefore, was rejected as false. Of course, since Hu Feng's case was political ammunition in the current war against heterodoxy and in the continued re-education of the people, it is unlikely that his confession would have been approved, however abject.

With the heightened tempo of economic development in the late spring and summer of 1955, the campaign broadened still further. On May 26, a meeting of the ACFLAC and the Chinese Writers'

Union expelled Hu and resolved to expand the campaign to liquidate all Hu Feng elements throughout the country. By June, *JMJP* no longer talked of Hu as an ideological deviationist; he was now a leader of the imperialist and KMT secret service and commander of an anti-Communist, anti-masses underground. When the second and third batches of Hu's letters were published in the beginning of June, the editorial comments no longer called Hu antiparty, as it had done with the first batch, but counterrevolutionary. The New China News Agency declared that Hu's "Secret letters and other evidence prove that the clique was intriguing and acting as part of an over-all plot to overthrow the people's state and restore imperialism and KMT rule in China." [73] Various regional and occupational groups throughout the nation held special meetings to resolve to destroy the Hu Feng counterrevolutionaries. Hu Feng elements were ferreted out not only in educational and cultural organizations, but in trade movements, mass organizations, and the armed forces.

Then, in July, the movement shifted again. Hitherto, the "educational" aspects of the campaign had been applied primarily to the furtherance of Marxist-Leninist study among intellectuals. Now, an editorial in *JMJP* declared: "Our present task is to use the case of Hu Feng to push forward a universal and thorough educational process." [74] The drive against Hu Feng turned to re-educating the masses. The first stage of this process was to organize meetings among all segments of society — workers, peasants, soldiers, minority peoples, youth, "democratic" circles, women, and religious groups — to demand the punishment of Hu Feng. Finally, on July 18, it was reported that in conformity with "popular opinion," Hu had been arrested. The date of his trial was not given.[75] Since one of his colleagues confessed to having visited him as late as April, it would appear that he had not been arrested until he was charged with counterrevolutionary activity.

Hu had been eliminated, but the campaign did not end. On the contrary, it became noisier and more unyielding, proving further that the Hu Feng campaign had a function beyond the mere destruction of a disturbing influence. The party's enormous propaganda machine was set in motion to inform even the humblest peasant in the remotest area about the "facts" of the case and to encourage the whole population to uncover any latent "Hu Fengism" within themselves. The party continued to use his case in a general campaign to liquidate all unorthodox thinking, hunt out counterrevolutionaries, and, most important, to purify political consciousness in accordance with the needs of the First Five-Year Plan.

In the summer of 1955, this campaign hit the scientists, who hitherto had been relatively exempt. Kuo Mo-jo had declared earlier that "Scientists should join in the struggle against Hu Feng. The weakness of scientists is that they devote themselves to their own work and take no interest in political work. Therefore, they can easily be made use of by the Hu Feng group." [76] Evidently, the scientists were very slow in denouncing the Hu Feng elements in their ranks, because from July through October of 1955 they were persistently goaded on to greater vigilance. Radio broadcasts announced that "The attitude among the natural scientists toward the Hu Feng case was one of 'It's none of my business.' This proves that their vigilance in the revolutionary cause is low." [77] Again in September, *K'o-hsüeh t'ung-pao* (The journal of sciences) asserted that "Among scientists, there still exists the harmful ideology that counterrevolution may be found in other ranks, but not in the natural sciences." [78] In contrast to the immunity scientists had during the drive against Yü P'ing-po, the party now insisted that they were contaminated with the same counterrevolutionary germs as other professions.

Ideological Charges

The party asserted that Hu's theory of spontaneous struggle would not lead a writer to Marxism, but in other directions away from the orthodoxy laid out by the party. A *JMJP* editorial of July 12, 1955, claimed that Hu's emphasis on emotionalism and subjectivism separated artistic comprehension of the world from rational, scientific understanding, by which they meant Marxism-Leninism. Consequently, Hu was accused of eliminating politics altogether. In reality, Hu's concept of art did include politics. His empirical approach to Marxism demanded that writers experience life deeply. In so doing, they would inevitably learn of socio-economic relations which Hu believed were true to Marxist analysis. Therefore, in fact, Hu did claim to arrive at a Marxist political ideology, but through experience rather than through ideological study.

The party charged that Hu's advocacy of looking for literary material in one's own environment enclosed the writer in an ivory tower away from the people and from politics. Only after a writer immerses himself in the lives of the peasants, workers, and soldiers, the party insisted, can he reflect life and find the source of creativity. In fact, however, Hu's views repudiated this criticism. He maintained that a writer cannot create without experiencing the life of the people, but when he talked of "the people" he, like Hsiao Chün, did not refer to special categories. The party's emphasis on theory as necessary to understanding life was more conducive to an ivory-tower attitude than Hu's pragmatic approach. The party further charged Hu with fostering "art for art's sake." In reality, however, Hu, like his critics, urged the writer to discuss the most significant events of the moment. But he further insisted that the writer's perception was equally important.

The party accused Hu of insulting Chinese culture and destroying the people's self-confidence because of his rejection of Chinese literature written before the May Fourth Movement and his reluctance to see class content in the literature of the past. It claimed that he worshipped bourgeois culture and its literary style. Again, this was an exaggeration of Hu's ideas. He did not express disrespect for China's cultural inheritance, he merely opposed the application of its literary folk styles to the content of the present. He also did not worship bourgeois culture, he merely asked that the literary experience of other nations be drawn upon. Here Hu's ideas conflicted with the Communist drive to depict the Chinese laboring people as the creators not only of all material wealth but also of all spiritual wealth.

In reply to Hu's argument that a writer reform his thought through his own creative work, the party demanded that the cadres guide his reform. In the party's view, if the writer did not study Marxism-Leninism under party tutelage, then no matter how fervently he may try, he cannot change his own class thinking. Hu was represented as repudiating any form of thought reform, but the actual division between Hu and the authorities lay in Hu's advocating thought reform on an individual basis instead of under party direction. Here again, Hu's method was rejected because it did not ensure that the writer would reform himself strictly in accordance with the party's dictates.

Charges of Sectarianism

Although Hu was constantly referred to as a direct, ideological descendant of Wang Shih-wei and Hsiao Chün, he was considered far more dangerous because his "crimes" went beyond the ideological realm. He was accused of trying to usurp the leadership of the literary sphere from Mao and the party. It is true that Hu fought other factions for supremacy and was motivated by personal animosity. Nevertheless, he was also motivated by a sincere belief that his ideas on literature would invigorate what he considered to be a stagnant culture. He looked upon this battle as a responsibility he bore to his party and nation. Furthermore, though he was dissatisfied with the views of the leadership in literary circles, he did not consciously oppose the policies of the party. His disagreement with the literary hierarchy, however, was extended to mean disagreement with the political hierarchy. Since a few of Hu's followers disagreed with Mao's literary tenets, some of their remarks, such as Chang Chung-hsiao's, "Mao's theories had use in Yenan but not now," were put in Hu's mouth.

The party countered Hu's proposal that literature be less strictly directed by insisting that organization and discipline "do not fetter the free development of the personality, on the contrary, they are prerequisites for such development." [79] They charged that Hu sought to divorce himself from party control and discipline. In fact, however, Hu had been referring to the literary sphere, not necessarily the political sphere. Moreover, he did not reject the party's organization of the literary field, he only desired more freedom within the organization.

Charges of Counterrevolution

Accusations of counterrevolutionary activity and conspiracy with KMT agents were based on flimsy evidence. Hu had no formal organization or political program. His group of from twenty to thirty writers, journalists, and teachers were held together merely by the charisma of a strong leader and by some common ideas on literature. They could be called nothing more than a small literary group. Yet, the party accused its members of infiltrating party organizations, building up bases, and enlisting mass support to carry out counterrevolutionary activities. According to the party, Hu's letters provided the proof. The party interpreted statements in these letters that referred to literary affairs as applying to political matters. For example, in January 1950, Hu wrote, "Victory can be ours, but the way to success is not easy . . . it will take five years." [80] In the context of this letter Hu was referring to the overthrow of the literary authorities, not of the political regime. Hu's phrase, "using the tactics of the monkey to crawl inside the belly," was interpreted as carrying on counterrevolutionary acts. What Hu had meant was working for a position in literary organizations. Also, such phrases as "fighting with hand grenades" [81] were used by Hu as a metaphor not, as the party claimed, a description of the actual weapons at his command.

Charges of alliance with the KMT were based purely on guilt by association. Hu was accused of connivance with the KMT secret service because in the 1940's he asked one of his colleagues to intervene with a Nationalist police chief on behalf of a friend who had been wrongly arrested. In an article in the Taiwan *Central Daily News,* a KMT official claimed to have respected Hu's "cynical personality" when he had known him in Wuhan.[82] Because one of Hu's followers supposedly listened to broadcasts from Taiwan and because he had said it would not be easy to attack Taiwan, he was charged with wanting to restore Chiang Kai-shek and giving publicity to the United States's Seventh Fleet.[83] Such instances were offered as proof as Hu's close association with the KMT.

The accusations against Hu were only partly correct. It is true that Hu disagreed with some of the literary ideas of the literary hierarchy, but that does not mean his views were based on anti-Marxist bourgeois ideas, as the party also asserted. Similarly, it is obvious that Hu opposed some of the literary authorities, but that does not mean he also opposed the political authorities. As for the charge of counterrevolution, it seems to have no substantial proof whatsoever. However, since party leaders at this time indiscriminately lumped together all views diverging from the current orthodoxy as anti-Marxist bourgeois ideology, in their terms these charges were valid. Moreover, since erroneous thinking was considered the source of erroneous action, it was only a short step to linking this kind of thinking with counterrevolutionary activity.

Results

Initially, the Hu Feng campaign does not appear to have been as effective as anticipated. In the drive against Hu Shih, no one had challenged the party or defended Hu Shih. Hu Feng, on the contrary, was defended by several of his fellow writers. His Shanghai colleagues stood by him at meetings held to refute his ideas. At one of them, his friend, Wang Jung, asserted that "Hu Feng . . . had directly followed the party's great revolutionary enterprise for over twenty years." [84] Similar declarations were made by other colleagues. Another one, Chuang Yung, forthrightly explained, "This case is not a problem of literary theory, but of the personal relationship between Hu Feng and Chou Yang." [85] Still another in his self-criticism wrote, "If Lu Hsün were alive today, the same would have happened to him." [86] Several wrote to party officials, protesting the action against Hu.

The resistance of his friends apparently aroused the party to further repression. This was indicated in Hu's letters written during the campaign. Hu begged his more excitable followers to make a strategic retreat for their own welfare as well as his. He urged them not to act in his behalf. To Chang Chung-hsiao he wrote, "I don't want you to write any more letters or essays. Now is not the time to speak out." [87] Instead he encouraged them to criticize him and disassociate themselves from him. He implored Chang Chung-hsiao that "In future meetings, you must not be obstinate [with the authorities] and must speak of my mistakes." [88] Evidently at Hu's request, Chang subsequently sent the following instructions to Hu's friends: "First . . . it is imperative that you disconnect your own problems from the old master's [Hu Feng]. Second, when you are forced to speak, you can criticize the old master. Third, you can confess and investigate the weaknesses in your own work." [89]

Even though Hu begged his supporters to conform to the party's wishes, he continually urged them to continue their own work. Thus, to the end, he maintained his emphasis on the overriding importance of creative activity. This advice was also motivated by his hope that such work might help his disciples achieve their aims at some future time. This can be seen in another letter to Chang Chung-hsiao: "You must be extremely calm. There are still very many things we must endure. Only in endurance will we find rebirth. All of you are to continue with your work in order that you will have a better future." [90]

Still, despite his entreaties and the intense pressures from party officials, opposition to the attack on their old master died hard among Hu's disciples. Even as late as May 25, 1955, Lu Ying, the former head of the Literature Department at Shantung University, supported him at the meetings of the Chinese Writers' Union called to expel Hu. In fact, it appears that the party had difficulty in foisting their picture of Hu not only on some of the fellow writers, but also on other segments of the intellectual community. Perhaps one of the reasons for the increasing intensity and broadening scope of the campaign against him was because his stand found more of a response than the party had expected. For example, after Hu had delivered his speech at the meetings against Yü P'ing-po and Feng Hsüeh-feng, he wrote to one of his friends that many people "had secretly acknowledged that there was sectarianism in Chinese cultural circles." [91]

When the party by June 1955 began to portray Hu as a counter-revolutionary, its extreme portrayal was not fully accepted at first by the general public. *JMJP*, on June 10, admitted that even after Hu's letters had been published, there were people who protested that his group only had ambition in literary circles and did not necessarily have reactionary political backgrounds.[92] Lu Ting-i declared, "Some still believe that Hu Feng cannot be classified as a counterrevolutionary, because he was unarmed." [93] As late as July 16, *Chung-kuo ch'ing-nien* (China youth) stated that there were people who continue to say that Hu and his group produced some fine work in the past and insist that "their merit must not be erased with a single stroke." [94] Probably, the feebleness of the evidence made it difficult to discredit Hu and his group wholly in the eyes of the literate population.

Nevertheless, in the long run, compliance seems to have been achieved. By the end of August 1955, there were no longer articles criticizing people who still held Hu to be innocent on some points. The unrelenting pressure of the party's propaganda machine had, at least, externally imprinted on the public mind the party's extreme image of Hu. The party had achieved its main objective.

It also achieved results it had not expected. As the drive picked up speed and became much more intensive, it developed a momentum of its own that went far beyond the scope the regime had intended. The campaign evolved from an orderly instrument of the party into a reign of terror, particularly among the intellectuals. One of the informants in Robert Guillain's *Six Hundred Million Chinese* told him that at the height of the Hu Feng campaign "the pressure was so great . . . that many people's nerves gave way; suicides were frequent in cultural organizations." [95] Another reported that certain intellectuals and well-known professors "Were in a terrible state. I've seen them tremble like leaves. They lived in terror of the compulsory sessions." [96] This was particularly true in Shanghai, which had been Hu Feng's city. Obviously, the ideological remolding campaigns could have consequences which even the party could not control. Ironically, one of the results of this drive against Hu was to intensify the very problem that Hu had attempted to resolve — the increasing estrangement between the Chinese intellectuals and the party.

chapter eight

WRITERS BLOOM IN THE
HUNDRED FLOWERS MOVEMENT

The end of 1955 and the beginning of 1956 was a critical period for the party. As the party speeded up its conversion of peasant households into semisocialist collectives and quickened the tempo of industrialization, it encountered some grave economic problems. Because of irrational planning, dislocations occurred, shortages developed, and resources were wasted. Consequently, the party decided to put more trust in technical advice and professional skills. *KMJP* as early as December 3, 1955, stated that "a new situation has arisen in which intellectuals, particularly those of high standing in learning and technical accomplishment, must make greater contributions to society." [1]

However, by the end of 1955, because of the previous ideological remolding movements and the unprecedented ferocity of the Hu Feng campaign, a large segment of China's intellectuals was virtually demoralized. The impact of the Hu Feng campaign, as we have seen, went far beyond the creative arts and social sciences. Its crusading zeal had even alienated some of the much-favored scientists. The ever-present threat of liquidation as a consequence of deviation produced an intellectual environment where not only writers but thinking people in all fields avoided work, innovation, and research.

First Phase of the Hundred Flowers Movement,
January–December 1956

General Policy

Confronted with a passive intellectual community and in urgent need of its services, the party had to devise new ways and new methods to induce intellectuals to give wholehearted support. Toward the end of 1955, it decided to permit a controlled degree of intellectual freedom restricted to the academic sphere. The party's new moderation toward the intellectual reflected a general policy of relaxation in other areas. In 1956, its drive toward collectivization was eased, more emphasis was given to light industry, and the free agricultural market was expanded.

Chou En-lai, on January 14, 1956, set the stage for this new approach to the intellectuals with a report to the CC. He referred to a survey conducted by the party at the close of 1955 which revealed that the abilities of the intellectuals were being used irrationally. They were employed in administrative spheres where their knowledge was irrelevant. Chou insisted that the intellectuals were now ready for more responsible posts because they had been ideologically transformed. They must be given authority, their views must be respected, and the results of their professional research valued. Moreover, they should be rewarded with greater monetary benefits, improved work facilities, and a more rational system of promotion. In addition, a large number should be brought into the party so that within seven years one-third of the higher intellectuals would be party members.[2] Though Chou still called for ideological remolding, he said a distinction should be made between political counterrevolutionaries and those with erroneous intellectual views. The latter should be reformed with less violent, more subtle methods. All of these measures, Chou believed, would stimulate the intellectuals to apply their energies more productively to the party's enterprises.

As in 1953 and the first half of 1954, the party also attempted to rectify the bureaucratic attitudes of the cadres in the academic and literary realm. It believed that unreasonable treatment of the intellectuals by the cadres hindered their effective functioning and stifled China's cultural development. About the time Chou gave this speech to the CC, *JMJP* published several articles criticizing the interference of the cadres in areas with which they were unfamiliar. An eminent engineer wrote that "There is no denying that some Party members still do not fully comprehend the Party's policy toward the intellectuals and do not understand the part played by the intellectuals in national construction . . . Some party members do not trust technical persons." [3] *Hsüeh-hsi* further explained that "The rude attitude toward the intellectuals . . . was not due to any mistakes in party policy, but to the defects and mistakes of party members in individual organs in implementing the policy." [4] Hence, lower and middle cadres were used again as the scapegoats for the injustices the intellectual had suffered at the hands of the regime. The party's policy of ideological remolding, the underlying factor, was not mentioned.

In the first four months of 1956, the party's measures to win over the intellectuals were slow in getting underway. Although technicians received higher pay and honors were given for outstanding research, there was a reluctance in party ranks to go along with the new policy. It was not until Mao's speech of May 2, 1956, in which he brought up the slogans of "A hundred schools contend; a hundred flowers bloom," and Lu Ting-i's subsequent explanation of these slogans on May 26, 1956, that some of the party's new policies were implemented. Both men acknowledged that the party's recent efforts to win the confidence of the intellectuals by improving their material lot were inadequate. They expressed concern over the nondevelopment of China's sciences and the stagnation of her arts. Both gave further emphasis to the need for encouraging independent thought, debate, and criticism within the academic realm. Lu Ting-i asserted that "Although art, literature, and scientific research in a class society are still weapons of the class struggle, they are not the same as politics." [5] In these fields, Lu insisted on the right of the intellectuals to maintain independent ideas and individual opinions. Essentially, the party now sought to enact Hu Feng's demand of a year earlier, that the intellectual and political spheres be separated. Although debate was not permitted in politics, it was encouraged in scholarship and the arts.

Both Mao and Lu Ting-i reiterated that the ideological struggle was to continue but with new methods. Instead of being carried out through administrative orders, it was to be conducted through discussion. As in the slight relaxation of 1953 and the first half of 1954, intellectuals were encouraged to express different ideas so that errors could be pointed out. Unity was to be achieved through voluntary agreement instead of pressure. Though the party still sought ideological unity, yet, in contrast to 1953, it tried this time to produce also a genuine, free exchange of ideas in the academic realm. This is seen in the following policy statement in *Hsüeh-hsi*: "The aim of promoting independent thinking and free discussion in theoretical [ideological] studies is not the same aim as in scientific research;

scientific research is aimed at the creative development of different branches of science on the basis of earnest scientific research; independent thinking and free discussion in theoretical work is aimed at learning Marxist-Leninism." [6]

Party Policy Toward the Writers

The party was disturbed by the paucity of the literary output. Referring to literary criticism, *Wen-i pao* declared that "In the last two years, our critics have become fewer and fewer. Some comrades have stopped writing; those who write are mostly young critics whose ideological level and cultural level are low . . . We should certainly request those who stopped writing to take up their pens again." [7] Yet, changes in the literary field were slow in coming. The party was not willing to give as much leeway in literature as, for example, in the sciences. Thinkers whose output was ideas and words were more subversive to the regime than those who worked with such apolitical tools as equations, machines, and models. Whereas the sciences were usually the last area to be incorporated in the ideological remolding movements and the first to receive the benefits of relaxation, the opposite was true in literature. Since writers as a group had a more direct connection with ideology, included a large number of party members, and had been the most critical of the party, the call of party leaders for free debate in the literary realm was more to bring writers to a voluntary appreciation of Marxism-Leninism than to produce new flowers in literature.

The party's more conservative attitude toward writers than toward other intellectual groups was apparent even in Chou En-lai's speech announcing the new policy. Though he acknowledged that the benefits of socialism could be described through a variety of ways, he still insisted that socialist realism was the best method. Moreover, he prescribed that literature continue to criticize the old system and praise the new one. Finally, he inveighed against "bourgeois" ideas in literature and called once more for criticism of "the enemy, Hu Feng." His words served as a warning that any writer with views different from the leadership could still be labeled a Hu Feng supporter.

Consequently, when the Chinese Writers Union held an enlarged series of meetings from February 27 to March 6, 1956, they appear to have been only slightly affected by the new policy. The first part of Chou Yang's speech at these meetings was devoted to another denunciation of Hu Feng. The second half showed some appreciation for the burgeoning spirit of the Hundred Flowers movement. The monotony and drabness of Chinese literature, Chou claimed, was due to limited subject matter and stereotyped characters. He complained that writers "instead of depicting life in keeping with its varied complex nature, write according to a set formula." [8] But he, himself, strengthened the set formula by reiterating his belief that literature's "most important task is to elevate political consciousness." [9]

Moreover, Chou Yang, in his attacks on other writers at this time, implied that there could be no diminution of the party's controls over literature. He pointed to Feng Hsüeh-feng and Ch'en Ch'i-hsia as examples of "Those who attempted . . . to reject the party's and people's supervision over their work and adopted an exclusive, noncooperative attitude toward the party and nonparty orthodox writers." [10] He also accused his former enemy from Yenan, Ai Ch'ing, of not complying with party directives. Having attacked his old antagonists and having re-emphasized the need to follow the party's injunctions, Chou Yang then asked, "Why is it that the surging feelings which some writers displayed in their works at the stage of the Democratic Revolution have abated on the eve of the Socialist Revolution?" [11] Chou could have found the answer in his own speech.

In contrast to other fields where intellectual stagnation was now being blamed on the middle- and low-level cadres, the literary bureaucrats still held the writers themselves responsible. Instead of party controls being relaxed, a new organ was established in the literary sphere to strengthen them. At the conclusion of these meetings, a secretariat was set up in the Writers' Union under the direction of Chou Yang's right-hand man, Shao Chüan-lin. It was to supervise the daily work of writers. Hence, these meetings merely gave lip service to ending the rule of "formulism."

However, after Mao Tse-tung and Lu Ting-i voiced support for the Hundred Flowers movement in May 1956, members of the literary hierarchy gradually looked more favorably on the new policy.

Literary journals coaxed writers to express themselves more freely. The editors of *Wen-i pao* decried the reluctance of writers to step forth. "Free discussion of literary questions has not progressed . . . Divergent opinions on important questions still have not been debated publicly." [12] There was a turning away from imitation of official Soviet policy by the leadership as well as the intellectuals. Nevertheless, intellectuals were urged to emulate the questioning attitude of their Soviet counterparts. *Wen-i pao* praised the attack on "formulistic and mechanistic creativity currently carried on in the Soviet Union." [13]

Another series of meetings of the Writers' Union held in July 1956 focused this time primarily on the policy of the Hundred Flowers. In an effort to catch up with the new movement, writers were urged to use literary styles other than socialist realism, though they still had to present the party's interpretation of events. Also, these meetings finally shifted the blame for China's cultural stagnation from the writers' own ideological shortcomings onto the crude, bureaucratic attitudes of party functionaries. Mao Tun had already announced the transfer of this guilt a month earlier when in the vein of Hu Feng, he asserted that literary criticism based on "vulgar sociology" had "harmed the free, lively creative forces. Writers have not dared to search for new forms and new spirit." [14] Continuing this theme, the cultural leadership at these meetings, including Chou Yang's clique, now admitted that dogmatic methods had been used in implementing Mao's policy.

There was also an attempt to redress the excesses of the Hu Feng campaign. While all insisted that it was still necessary to continue steps against the Hu Feng elements, they conceded that everything he represented need not be negated. An article in *Wen-i pao* pleaded that, "Though it is necessary that we have measures against the Hu Feng clique, nevertheless in literary and artistic creativity and in study, we should advance independent ideas and encourage different schools and different styles." [15] Mao Tun, echoing Hu Feng of two years earlier, advocated that these different schools "engage in free debate and mutual competition so that their survival value may be tested." [16] Many of the suggestions presented at these meetings, in fact, resembled those made by Hu Feng in his report to the CC: The scope of material should be expanded, writers should establish their own rules, more respect should be given to writers and artists, and as much attention should be given to artistic technique as to content.[17]

The excesses of the Hu Feng campaign were also redressed by easing the party's rigid controls over writers and intellectuals. *Chungkuo ch'ing-nien pao* acknowledged that because of the Hu Feng case, there had been unreasonable interference in legitimate private contacts of individuals. "Some leaders mistakenly believe that people must not only have common aims and abide by party discipline, but also must have a unified set of living habits and literary tastes." [18] Independent literary groups were no longer labeled politically subversive. The party now appeared willing to allow writers a little more freedom in their private lives.

Finally, Chou Yang in September 1956 at the Eighth National Congress of the party, not only fully endorsed Mao's policy of a hundred flowers bloom in literature, but interpreted it in even broader terms than had Lu Ting-i. Since Lu Ting-i's advocacy of the Hundred Flowers movement, Chou Yang had championed a variety of literary styles, but now he suggested that the content of literature could also reflect more variety. Since Chou was Mao's faithful spokesman, it can be surmised that the party not only sanctioned a wider range of literary styles, but also of subject matter. He declared that "Contradictions, difficulties and defects in actual life are slurred over. Some writers have even lost their courage to criticize backward things. Whitewashing and oversimplification in the portrayal of real life have robbed literary works of their truthfulness and readers have lost faith in such works." [19]

The party backed up its relatively liberal words with concrete acts. Writers in administrative and editorial capacities were given two or three months off for creative writing.[20] Even more significant, Hu Feng's advocacy of competition among journals apparently had had some effect. At the meetings of the Writers' Union on editorial work at the end of November 1956, editors were given more responsibility in running their journals. Each journal was to acquire its own special flavor and gather together a group of writers with similar literary bents.

Nevertheless, these official measures to provide a certain degree of freedom in the literary world were erected on a tenuous base. The superficiality of this relative degree of relaxation can be seen in the contradictory statements peppered throughout the party's pronouncements. Lu Ting-i, at ceremonies on October 19, 1956, commemorating the death of Lu Hsün, praised Lu Hsün for advocating different methods in art, but ended his talk with the remark, "We need criticism, but it should be made for the sake of unity and nothing else . . . Different creative methods should coexist and compete; still writers . . . of the school of socialist realism should form a nucleus of unity for uniting others." [21] Even in the speech of Chou Yang that broadened the limits of the writer's material, the emphasis was nevertheless on the supreme control of the party over literary creation. In the concluding section he declared, "It is wrong to stress the special nature of literature and art as . . . an entirely spontaneous process which must not be placed under the leadership of the Communist party." [22] Evidently, the purpose of the debate in literary theory and even the competition in literary styles was to continue to prove the superiority of Marxism-Leninism and of socialist realism, although in a more roundabout fashion.

Response of the Writers to the First Phase

The writers, the group expected to be among the first to welcome a relaxation of control, were hesitant about entering into the spirit of the Hundred Flowers movement. Most likely, because of the initial reluctance of the literary leadership to support the new policy and because of the fate that had befallen several of their colleagues, writers were more hesitant at first than other groups to expound the party's new line. In the literary field, especially, we have seen that the shifts in party policy had succeeded each other so fast that the fear of being trapped in one of these changes apparently plagued writers more than other intellectuals. Consequently, though scientists and engineers soon after Chou En-lai's speech began to question the competence of party cadres to lead technical and scientific enterprises, writers remained relatively quiet.

It was not until the second half of 1956, when the literary hierarchy finally began to echo Mao's words, that a few daring writers spoke out. Those who blossomed most blatantly had certain common characteristics. They came mainly from the leadership group and were either party members or closely allied with the party. Several of them had been under Chou Yang's patronage. Among them were older revolutionaries and young writers who had received most of their education from the party. They not only used the literary form of *tsa wen*, which writers used in the past to express their opposition, they also spoke out through short stories and allegories. Many were affected by the intellectual ferment going on in literary circles in the Soviet Union.[23] Also like the revolutionary writers in the past, they did not oppose the party itself, but attempted to show where it had deviated from the humanitarian ideals of Marxism. With the exception of Ai Ch'ing, however, none of the older writers from Yenan and Chungking who had been so critical of the party in the past expressed themselves publicly to any great extent.

Criticisms heard from writers in the summer and fall of 1956 were fundamental to the very nature of party control over art. Like other intellectuals, the writers attacked the dogmatism of the party cadres and blamed the stagnation of the creative mind on the privileged position of the party. Yet, unlike some other intellectuals, they did not believe the situation could be remedied merely by the withdrawal of the party from intellectual endeavor. They asserted that some of the party's basic policies, such as thought reform and the disregard for human and cultural values, would also have to be changed. They expressed these views by attacking socialist realism.

Other academic fields also had significant debates — in biology, on heredity; in history, on periodization; and in philosophy, on the role of Marxism-Leninism — but perhaps no discussion hit more directly at the party's over-all policies than the discussion on socialist realism. Questioning of the principle of socialist realism paralleled a similar movement going on among writers in the Soviet Union. Whereas, intellectuals in other fields attacked the dominance of Soviet techniques and academic approach in China's intellectual life, the writers sought to follow the example of their Soviet colleagues. Since Stalin's death in 1953, the Soviet writers, encouraged by their fellow East European writers, had called for an end to the false, hypocritical portrayal of Soviet life produced in the name of socialist realism. Now, several Chinese writers similarly accused the party of using socialist realism to divert people from their own immediate difficulties. They implied that the party neglected the real problems of society. In effect, their attack on socialist realism was an attempt to introduce a new humanism into Chinese society and challenge the party's lack of concern for human values. Outstanding in this endeavor were three writers, high in the party hierarchy and representative of different segments of Chinese society. They were Huang Ch'iu-yün, Ch'in Ch'ao-yang, and Ch'en Yung.

Huang Ch'iu-yün was an old, leftist writer and translator of Romain Rolland into Chinese. His translation of *Jean Christophe* was widely read. Though he was criticized in the rectification movement of 1948 for his "bourgeois humanitarian ideas," he had been active in the Hu Feng campaign. However, Khruschev's denunciation of Stalin at the Twentieth Party Congress had given him a violent shock and made him question more closely the Communist system being established in China. His most important article in the first phase of the Hundred Flowers movement entitled, "We Must Not Close Our Eyes to the Hardships Among the People," was a reflection of this questioning.

Without the standard circumlocutions, Huang stated forthrightly that the socialism which existed in China and the socialism he imagined would come into being were quite different. "Nobody knows whether or not we will have any grief or tears twelve years from now, but at least at present, this kind of 'heaven' is only an illusion." [24] He urged writers to make this "heaven" a reality instead of an illusion by not averting their gaze from the real conditions before them.

While Huang feared "sick pessimism," he asserted that he was equally fearful of "cheap optimism," which he defined as the essence of socialist realism. Instead, he pleaded that the substance of literature be the depiction of life as the writer sees it. He then described the conditions of life as he saw them. "No one can deny that in our country at present, there are still floods and droughts, still famine and unemployment, still infectious diseases and the oppression of bureaucracy plus other unpleasant and unjustifiable phenomena." [25] Very much in the spirit of Wang Shih-wei in "Statesmen and Artists," Huang declared that, "A writer in possession of an upright conscience and a clear head ought not to shut his eyes complacently and remain silent in the face of real life and the sufferings of the people. If a writer does not have the courage to reveal the dark diseases of society, does not have the courage to participate positively in solving the crucial problems of people's lives, and does not have the courage to attack all the deformed, sick, black things, then can he be called a writer?" [26]

In place of socialist realism, Huang called for a form of realism in the tradition of nineteenth-century Western literature. "Realistic literature cannot defame life, but it also cannot avoid the truth or decorate life." [27] In essence, he wanted writers to resume the role they had in the 1930's as critics of their society. They should reveal the injustices and distress in man's immediate environment rather than paint glorious, utopian societies peopled by heroes. "The reason why all the ugly things which make people unhappy must be expressed in realistic literature is because they actually exist in our lives." [28] He concluded by sounding a clarion call in the tones of Hu Feng. "The cowardice of avoiding reality must be overcome and be replaced by a spirit fighting for truth." [29]

Ch'in Ch'ao-yang provided the theoretical framework for Huang Ch'iu-yün's contention that literature be used to criticize China's existing realities. There was nothing in Ch'in's history to destine him for the leader of China's "angry young men." In fact, quite the contrary, he was generally regarded as one of Chou Yang's protégés. Though originally an artist, he was one of the young talents Chou Yang had discovered in the 1940's and had educated into a writer fully committed to Mao's view of literature. His works virtually filled Chou Yang's prescriptions for literature. They were almost wholly concerned with peasants who either were enlightened by the party or who enlightened others with their wholesome, peasant wisdom. For example, in one series of short pieces called "Village Vignettes," he described an ignorant peasant wife who was taught to read by the cadres; in another he portrayed an old shepherd who taught to the cadres ancient agricultural techniques.[30] He followed the prescribed course so literally that even his mentor Chou Yang criticized him for "turning away from life." [31] Chou said of Ch'in, "Though he writes beautifully, he often prettifies life, deliberately giving it a pastoral air." [32]

Still more significant, Ch'in was one of Chou Yang's trusted trouble shooters in the various campaigns against the revolutionary writers.

After Feng Hsüeh-feng had been removed from the editorship of *Wen-i pao*, Ch'in became one of the three editors who took over its management. During the Hu Feng campaign which followed, Ch'in's attacks on Hu Feng appeared in all the major journals. He fervently upheld socialist realism, emphasized the need for ideologically-correct literature, and rejected Hu Feng's injunction to "write the truth." Most likely, in reward for his active role in the campaign, in the spring of 1956 he was moved over to the influential position of editor in charge of political affairs for *Jen-min wen-hsüeh*. In a short time, he took over the actual management of the whole journal.

Yet, just a few months later, at the age of thirty-six, standing in the next level of leadership below Chou Yang, he reversed himself and advocated the very things he had criticized in Hu Feng. Now his criteria for literature was its degree of realism, not its ideological correctness. He expressed himself through various forms, essays, *tsa wen*, and short stories, and through his editorship of *Jen-min wen-hsüeh*. It was in *Jen-min wen-hsüeh* that some of the most biting criticism of the party appeared.

A systematic presentation of his views in this period was presented in a long essay, "Realism — The Broad Road," published in the same issue as Huang Ch'iu-yün's article and written under the pen name, Ho Chih. Many of the ideas in this essay appear to have been culled from Hu Feng's report to the CC. Perhaps his recent study of Hu's writings had affected him. Though Ch'in never mentioned Mao Tse-tung directly, nevertheless, his essay repudiated Mao's principles on literature which had fashioned the creative and intellectual activity of Communist China since 1942. Ch'in perfunctorily presented the party line on the need for political ideology, class stand, and thought reform, but even at the very beginning of his essay, he asserted that "Later generations are not satisfied to take principles and theories which have already been determined." [33] In the manner of the young Soviet writers' challenge to the older generation at this time, he demanded that his contemporaries be allowed to develop ideas in tune with their own times.

Ch'in considered that the existence of principles to which everyone must turn for ready-made answers restrained people from using their own minds and eventually stifled all thought. Now Ch'in, like Hu Feng earlier, wanted to do away with all theoretical or ideological frameworks within which writers should work. He believed they interfered with the writer's perception of life around him. "No one can make the most complete, best interpretation [of reality]; usually, the interpretation which yesterday was claimed to be very correct is overturned today." [34] Instead, Ch'in, as did Hu Feng, suggested that the writer's ideological beliefs should develop in the very act of writing. "The Marxist world view functions organically, naturally, and vigorously in the process of the creation of realistic art and in the process of acknowledging life and forming images." [35]

Ch'in also criticized the simplified depiction of characters inherent in socialist realism. To Ch'in, this practice had denied people their individual personalities. "Every member of the working class is a common man. As writers, however, we must not only see his common side, but also find in him and his life the things which are not noticed by the average person, things which are deeper and which, therefore, seem somewhat uncommon." [36] A corollary to this was that writers should present members of the proletariat as whole people with their weaknesses as well as virtues. Otherwise, Ch'in wrote, "they will lose the luster of their internal spirit, individuality and life." [37] When the writer grasped the uniqueness of the individual, Ch'in believed, he became a true artist. "To present things which are not understood and not observed, this is an important method which expresses the writer's independent creativity and is a capability which every realist should search for." [38] In conclusion, Ch'in pleaded, "We are in a country which has a deep realistic tradition. How many masters of realism have emerged in our history! They all . . . broke through outdated rules and clichés. Let us follow their example." [39]

In the course of his discussion, Ch'in coined the phrase "realism of the socialist period." This slogan carried with it the ideas of this essay and became the clarion call that aroused many young writers to attack Mao's "Talks on Art and Literature" and the party itself. Ch'in suddenly appeared as the leader of a group of rebellious young writers.

As part of the attack on socialist realism, several writers underlined the special quality of literary creativity. They turned to Lu Hsün as their authority and quoted his famous lines: "Revolutionary writers bridle at the mere mention of technique. To my mind, however, though all literature is propaganda, not all propaganda is literature." [40] One of the loudest advocates of artistic standards was the literary critic Ch'en Yung. Paradoxically, he, like Ch'in, had previously denounced these very same values. He, too, had been active in the party's literary movement since the 1940's. Arriving in Yenan at the age of nineteen, he was quickly indoctrinated in the party's teachings. He was particularly vocal against Hu Feng's group in the late 1940's. After the party came to power, he initiated the first attack on one of its members, A Lung. He quickly became a part of the literary hierarchy, a member of the Institute of Literary Research at the Academy of Sciences, and an editor of *Wen-i pao* in 1955. Around this time, he began a study of Lu Hsün's stories. Perhaps this study had a profound impact on him. In any event, at the height of the Hu Feng movement, when he himself was defaming Hu and his followers with great zeal, he wrote a somewhat favorable review of Lu Ling's story, "The Children of a Rich Man." He condemned the content of the story, but praised certain aspects of Lu Ling's literary style. In addition to acknowledging the author's talent, he lauded his ability to capture the inner psychology of his characters. Shortly after that, Ch'en was criticized for this review, and he was charged with believing that art was above class. Most likely, in response to this rebuke, Ch'en, when given the opportunity six months later to express himself more freely, used the occasion to defend his concern with artistic style.

He bloomed before most of the other writers had shown their colors. In the spring of 1956, Ch'en, in an article in *Wen-i pao*, stated that "Although Hu Feng was condemned for his mystification of literature, we cannot on account of this, deny that literature has certain special characteristics . . . These special characteristics demand much serious study, but for the past six years since the establishment of the People's Republic, we have not had any professional monographs on this subject, not even valuable articles." [41] Ch'en defined "the special characteristics of literature" as concern with aesthetics and the emotions as opposed to political and economic matters. Using the same phrase as Hu Feng, Ch'en called the party's disregard for artistic qualities "vulgar sociology." To Ch'en, this meant that "Some people demand of literature and art what they demand of general propaganda and education . . . They do not see that the aesthetic quality of literature and art has a function more everlasting and profound." [42]

In his view, art was distinct from other intellectual fields because it did not have to serve the current needs of the state. He contrasted the writer's methods of encountering his world with those of the scientist and social scientist. "As opposed to the scientist, the material of the writer is primarily man — his thoughts, feelings, morality, psychology . . . They can be grasped through the writer's logical thought, but also through his sensitivity." [43] Though he rejected Hu Feng as a person, he admitted that he was expressing many of the same ideas on art that Hu Feng had emphasized.[44] Like Hu Feng, he now stressed that authors should write from their own feelings rather than from theory. He went even a step further to express an interest in aesthetics for its own sake. "Literature and art not only have the special characteristic of the emotions, but they also should have the special quality of arousing the feeling for beauty in people." [45]

Many of Ch'en's views had been formulated in a debate on aesthetics which occupied the literary world at this time. This discussion was specifically on whether beauty is real or imagined; that is, does man's aesthetic sense determine beauty or does beauty determine man's aesthetic sense? The orthodox Communist view on this issue had always been that beauty was real and inherent in the object itself. At a conference held on this subject in September 1956, however, not only Ch'en Yung, but several other members of the party's literary hierarchy stated that art was essentially the expression of subjective feelings and individual images. This approach was in distinct contrast to their previously stated views and came close to that of the Western-educated aesthetician Chu Kuang-ch'ien, who had repeatedly been denounced for his beliefs. A literary critic who was even more outspoken than Ch'en Yung in this discussion was Huang Yao-mien, one of the sharpest critics of Feng Hsüeh-feng in the second half of the 1940's and among those appointed to the new editorial board of *Wen-i pao* after Feng Hsüeh-feng's dismissal. He also held important posts in the CDL. In this debate, however, Huang, like Chu Kuang-ch'ien, asserted that beauty is the unification of the subjective and objective worlds and that the individual's aesthetic sense determined beauty. Though this debate concerned aesthetics, essentially these writers were protesting against having to express the party's impression of things rather than their own.

In addition to the debate on socialist realism, writers also challenged the party by attacking its leadership of literature. As in other fields, their attacks represented the protest of professional talent against political interference. In general, their major targets were the officials of the Writers' Union. They asserted that though they themselves may be appointed chairmen of certain organs, their positions were nominal. They were denied responsibility, because the leadership was in the hands of a few party cadres. In their view, this kind of leadership, armed with its politically-oriented literary theory, placed literature on the same level as any other government enterprise. These writers, as was true with Hu Feng, still respected the party's CC, but wanted to diminish the power of the literary bureaucrats.

Opposition to this bureaucratic control came from some of the writers who had borne the brunt of the party's ideological remolding movements in the first half of the 1950's. Among the first to speak out was Hsiao Yeh-mu, the writer who had been the focal point of the attack by Ting Ling in the literary remolding movement of 1952. Hsiao vividly described the humiliation he suffered because of the accusations made against him. "Though there was no official order, my works were no longer published, sold in bookstores, and charged out in libraries." Apparently, he had been removed from the Writers' Union. Until the spring of 1956, "I could not participate in any activities of the literary circles." Though he did not mention it directly, such punishment denied him almost any means of livelihood. He merely wrote, "In the atmosphere created by this kind of criticism which stifles a writer and makes it difficult for him to conduct himself as a man, one cannot carry on creative work." Then Hsiao spoke out against the criticisms of party officials and editorial boards. "We must have criticism . . . but we cannot carelessly change literary criticism into personal attacks and political criticism . . . The objective of criticism is to make an author write good works not to make him lay down his pen." [46]

Chu Kuang-ch'ien, the aesthetician, also related bitterly the intellectual suffocation he had endured at the hands of the party cadres. He wrote that before the Hundred Flowers movement, "I did not write one single scholarly article nor read a fairly good book nor seriously do some thinking on questions of aesthetics. It was not because I did not want to, it was because I did not dare . . . Beneath an attack from the masses, I gradually accumulated a deepening sense of guilt. I did not raise my head nor say a word . . . I thought there was no use thinking, reading, or studying." [47]

The only sounds to be heard clearly from the rebellious writers of the Yenan days came from the poet, Ai Ch'ing. When the party came to power in 1949, it took advantage of Ai Ch'ing's talents despite his unorthodox past. He became a teacher at People's University, and was on the council of the Chinese Writers Union. His most important position was as assistant editor to *Jen-min wen-hsüeh*. Although Mao Tun was the chief editor, Ai Ch'ing had the real power. Still, like his close friends Ting Ling and Feng Hsüeh-feng, he had never been able to adjust completely to the administrative duties assigned him. As mentioned earlier, he was constantly accused of being unresponsive to the party's wishes. For this, he was sent several times to the countryside and to the Korean front to reform himself through contacts with the masses.

At the very start of the regime, when it was still possible to express some individual concerns, a few of his essays revealed dismay at the debasement of artistic standards, particularly in poetry. Speaking of the new writing of young poets, Ai Ch'ing complained that "All lack knowledge of poetry . . . They believe that to write poetry is merely a matter of wielding a big brush on a momentary impulse. Whatever they think, they write; if they can rhyme, they rhyme; if they cannot rhyme, they do not rhyme." [48] In his advice to poets, he showed little concern for ideology and was primarily interested in poetic techniques.

Still, in the Hu Feng campaign, Ai Ch'ing loudly and repeatedly denounced Hu Feng and his associates, many of whom he had been close to in the past. Yet, at the meetings of the Writers' Union in February and March 1956, in addition to Chou Yang's criticism several other members of the literary hierarchy accused Ai Ch'ing of lacking the enthusiasm he had had for the regime in the period of the New Democracy. The attacks against him at the very time the party was purportedly relaxing its grip reached such a point that he was forced to present a public self-criticism. In it he declared that "Though it is not easy, the most important task of the poet above everything else is ideological remolding." [49] Apparently, he had not remolded himself thoroughly enough, because articles continued to appear accusing him of insincerity in his self-criticism.

Even though the attacks on him did not cease, Ai Ch'ing, aware of the tendency towards relaxation in the spring of 1956, took advantage of the new atmosphere to shift the blame for his poor poetic output away from himself and onto the party. In one of his articles, he explained that he had written better poetry before liberation because, "In the resistance, I did not have many duties; therefore, I wrote a good deal everyday and could do it with complete concentration . . . Now, having to carry on political work, I have written little of the national struggle and my images and ideas have decreased." [50] Suddenly, in the middle of 1956, Ai Ch'ing poured forth a flood of poems. Most of them were concerned with the beauties of nature, a small tree or a winding stream. They paid little attention to the working people and the great construction projects of the party.

The works that dramatized Ai Ch'ing's grievances with the party's bureaucratic control most vividly were a series of allegories that appeared in various literary journals for several months running. They, more than Ai Ch'ing's other writings, reflected eloquently views that Ai Ch'ing was reported to have expressed hitherto only in private. The allegory had been another literary form used by Lu Hsün, when it had been impossible to speak out directly against corrupt rule. Ai Ch'ing now resurrected the form. Among the most biting were "The Yellow Bird" and "The Dream of a Gardener."

"The Yellow Bird" was originally written in 1953, most likely during the slight breathing space before the attack on Yü P'ing-po. It was finally published in August 1956 in *Peiching jih-pao* (Peking news). It tells of a yellow bird, representing the writer, who stood on a tree singing. His sounds, however, make the magpie, representing the party's literary and cultural officials, very angry. They pick a fight with him, eventually forcing him to fly away. The magpie, then, takes over the branch of the tree on which the yellow bird formerly stood. Shortly, little birds fly to the side of the magpie who tells them, "The yellow bird just sings and sings, but we have doctrines and theories; the little birds chirp 'correct, correct.' " [51] For a long time, no sounds are heard, but then a light breeze, symbolizing the spirit of the Hundred Flowers movement, comes and once again, the yellow bird is heard to sing.

Another allegory, "The Dream of a Gardener," was written in July 1956, but was published the next February in *Wen-i yüeh-pao* (Literary art monthly). This allegory satirized not only the past attitude of the party bureaucrats, but also their present attitude during the Hundred Flowers movement. The gardener, representing the party officials in the Writers Union, had several hundred flowers in his garden, but he threw out all the different varieties so that he would have just one kind. Though the remaining flowers were of different colors and blossomed in different months, they were all the same shape and made his garden dull. Here, Ai Ch'ing apparently was satirizing the party's policy of urging other literary styles, but insisting that the style of socialist realism remain paramount. He was saying that this policy had not led to the varied, diversified literary styles and content that the party had asked for.

Then one night the gardener had a dream. He dreamt that all kinds of unusual flowers were begging to be included in his garden. A noble, lonely flower, the white orchid, pleaded, "You should try to appreciate my beauty." A cactus said, "Those obedient, submissive ones have weak natures, but we have spirit that cannot be bent." The gardener suddenly saw that he had been mistaken in planting only one kind of flower in his garden. He realized he had been too narrow in his choice. Through the gardener's dream, Ai Ch'ing apparently sought to show that party officials had not carried out the party's policy of relaxation correctly and had, in effect, rejected it. He hoped that the party cadres would understand, as did the gardener in his dream, that "to live more wisely, all kinds of flowers must bloom in the garden." [52]

Actually, the most active fighter against the party bureaucracy was the same Ch'in Chao-yang who had supplied the theoretical attack on socialist realism. His offensive was carried out primarily in his role as editor of *Jen-min wen-hsüeh*. Given a little more freedom, he gathered around him writers of his own choosing and tried to run his journal according to his own dictates. He fostered and published works which represented his idea of realism — that is, works which pictured the Chinese scene as it existed in fact rather than as the party portrayed it. These works depicted the incompetence and apathy of the party bureaucrats.

Before describing these works some mention should be made of Ch'in's own literary efforts along these lines. One of them was a *tsa wen*, "On the Spirit of Sharpness," in which he once again wrote under the pen name, Ho Chih. It condemned the party cadres who labeled as "bourgeois" individuals who did not conform to their ideas. In Ch'in's view, people who do this "frighten themselves and create confusion within their own camp." [53] In another short piece, again under the pen name, Ho Chih, entitled on "The Lack of Time," Ch'in ridicules the incompetence and inertia of some officials and complains of their interminable, pointless meetings. "If we are to have a meeting at eight o'clock, they do not come until nine and make the others wait. When they give a speech, they give a very long introduction . . . If reasonable suggestions are made by others, which should be carried out immediately, they will procrastinate so as to try the organization's spirit and discipline. They call many unnecessary meetings and establish troublesome systems and regulations. They also give reports without content and mimeograph typewritten documents which have no value. These are their talents of organization." [54]

Ch'in also expressed his cynicism about the bureaucracy in a short story, "Silence," written under the pen name, Ho Yu-hua.[55] He tells the story of a wagon train coming back to the agricultural cooperative after a trip to the village to deliver its quota of produce. As the wagons return, the first one moves very slowly, but the ones in the back want to go faster. The episode apparently was to show that the leadership was not reacting to the wishes of its followers. The mistress of the top official of the local district urges an old man at the back to rush out ahead, and when he does, all the rest follow him. In the next scene, the director of the party cadres criticizes the old farmer for defying the officials in charge. Then the head of the cooperative appears and talks to the director, and immediately the director apologizes to the old man. However, he apologizes to him not because he realizes he was wrong, but because he feared reprisal from the mistress of the high official. Manipulation and opportunism were shown to be the main concerns of the party cadres rather than any regard for the wishes of the people or getting the job done.

The title "Silence" evidently refers to the silence of the members of the cooperative as the old man was chastised. They were passive or suffered their anger in silence. Most likely, Ch'in meant this as a comment on the effect of the party's controls on the population. Through the forms of essay, satire, and short story, Ch'in spoke out against what he called the "evils in the party bureaucracy."

Yet, his greatest blow to the bureaucracy came through his publication of two stories by two young writers whom he had encouraged. These stories presented in greater detail and with even more pungency than Ch'in's short pieces, an indictment of the party functionaries. The first one to appear was "Our Paper's Inside News" [56] by Liu Pin-yen, a member of the editorial board of *Chung-kuo ch'ing-nien* and a party member. In some ways, Liu's story resembles Ting Ling's "In the Hospital." Like the heroine in Ting Ling's work, the heroine in "Our Paper's Inside News" carries on a relentless struggle for honesty and humaneness in the face of the indifference and corruption of the party bureaucrats. As a reporter for a newspaper that merely reiterates the party line, the heroine attempts to make the paper reflect more realistically some of the miseries and inequities in Chinese Communist society. She urges the editors to run an exposé on the exhausting work schedule and poor working conditions of the miners. Nevertheless, because she believes in the ideals of the party, she applies for party membership. Like Ting Ling's heroine, the reforming zeal and idealism of this young lady lead only to personal frustration. Though she is able to impress some members of the newspaper staff, the paper continues to publish only what the party approves. Also, because of her unwillingness to confess to faults for which she believes herself not guilty, she is refused membership in the party.

Ch'in regarded Liu's writings as heralding a new phase in Chinese literature. After the story was published, he encouraged Liu to continue to write more along the same lines. In a letter to Liu in August 1956, Ch'in wrote, "I feel your work will at least open a new way for our creative work and will make writers pay attention not only to the workers and peasants, but also to describing the spiritual depth of the people who live around us . . . You are opening your own road of realism and setting an example for others. This is so important." [57] Whereas in the Western literary context, to "open a new way" might mean experimentation in literary techniques and styles, in Communist China it means courage in exposing the shortcomings in the existing system.

The second long story that Ch'in published in *Jen-min wen-hsüeh* on the party bureaucrats caused an even greater sensation. This story, called "A Young Newcomer in the Organization Department," [58] was written by a twenty-two year old writer and party member, Wang Meng, and appeared in September 1956. Reportedly, Ch'in had advised its author and had a large hand in revising it. "A Young Newcomer in the Organization Department" portrays the conflict of an idealistic young man with the bureaucratic and routinized methods of the older party members in a district party office.

The hero, Lin Chen, is a former primary school teacher who enters the party organization filled with high ideals and with great respect for party officials but soon becomes disillusioned. He discovers that the party officials in his organization do not live up to the criteria of a party member that he had been taught to expect. Wang Meng portrays these various types of officials in variegated colors. There is Liu Shih-wu, head of the whole department, an enthusiastic revolutionary in his youth who now is cynical. Another is Han Chang-hsin, head of the factory section of the organization; he is ostensibly efficient, but actually irresponsible and indifferent to the problems under his command. The factory manager, Wang Ch'ing-ch'uan, is shown to be interested only in his own prestige. Though he undergoes criticism and self-criticism, his reform is merely superficial. After one month, he returns to his old, bureaucratic habits.

On encountering this factory manager, Lin Chen becomes disturbed and reports back to his department heads, but they refuse to hear his full story and pretend there are no problems in the factory. Lin, holding onto his ideals of how a party member should act, still continues to criticize the factory manager. The head of the factory section, Han Chang-hsin, instead of investigating Wang's mismanagement as Lin had asked, merely writes a report, claiming that everything at the factory runs smoothly. Seeing Han's unwillingness to make any reforms, Lin then goes directly to Liu, the department head. Liu tells him that Wang could not be attacked because he holds an important post in the party. He advises Lin merely to wait. Finally, however, Lin gets the assistance of the head of the party cell in the factory, who writes a public letter criticizing Wang which is published in *JMJP*. A mass meeting is held to criticize Wang and demand his dismissal from the party and the factory. The whole district is ordered to discuss the affair. However, Lin protests that Wang is not the only one at fault. Since Wang's superiors, Liu and Han, had been reluctant to act and refused to take care of their problems at the proper time, they too should be punished. Lin held them as responsible as their underling, Wang. No one, however, agreed with Lin, and Liu and Han remained in their old jobs. Sadly, Lin realizes that he cannot continue his fight because he is powerless against such highly-placed bureaucrats.

Wang Meng went beyond the party's limits at this time by his condemnation of high officials as well as their subordinates for inertia and distinterest. He also depicted, in the manner of Liu Pin-yen and Ting Ling, the frustrations and disillusionments of the young individual with high ideals who attempts to realize his ideals in practice. Though Lin solved a specific problem temporarily, he was powerless to work out any fundamental change in the bureaucratic system. As opposed to the optimism of Wang Shih-wei, who in 1942 believed it was still possible for idealistic youth to break down the vested interests of the party bureaucrats, Wang Meng in 1956 painted a rather bleak prospect.

Reaction of the Party Cadres

General Response

Though Mao, Chou En-lai, and Lu Ting-i talked of relaxation, the grip of the party cadres was released ever so slowly. As a result, in the summer and fall of 1956, newspapers not only blamed the cadres' distrust of the intellectuals for stifling the development of China's intellectual and cultural life, they further charged them with obstructing the implementation of the party's new policy. These criticisms revealed that the cadres regarded the relaxation as a threat to political and ideological unity. A *JMJP* editorial of October 9, 1956, complained that "Some are afraid argument and debate will cause disunity in inner-Party thinking." [59]

Even more important, the party cadres considered relaxation a challenge to their own entrenched positions in the ruling system. The demand of intellectuals for a more independent voice in affairs by virtue of their ability clashed head on with the resolve of the party cadres to defend the positions they had attained because of their political reliability. *KMJP* on August 17, 1956, observed that the preferential treatment of the intellectuals had made the cadres "afraid that it would lead to the emergence of a privileged class with an undesirable sense of superiority. This manifestation of egalitarianism in their thinking should be guarded against." [60] The resistance of the cadres to the new policy had led Mao at the Eighth National Congress of the party in September 1956 to call for the rectification of bureaucratic cadres and lower-echelon party members. In various parts of the country, party organs launched small-scale rectification campaigns at local levels.

Not only the middle and lower cadres held back the policy of the Hundred Flowers movement; there appear to have been some persons at the very center of power who were not in full agreement with Mao's policy. After the uprisings in Eastern Europe in October and November 1956, they became more vocal and more open. Their resistance reached such a point that the deputy-director of the Propaganda Department of the People's Liberation Army, Ch'en Ch'i-t'ung, along with three other cohorts, were able to publish an article in *JMJP* on January 7, 1957, actually opposing Mao's policy. The fact that such an article could be published in the official mouthpiece of the CC would suggest that they had the support of someone in the very top leadership. Apparently, Mao's policy of relaxation had met opposition within the party's inner circle. At the time this article appeared, Chou En-lai, an outspoken advocate of the Hundred Flowers movement, was in Europe.

In effect, the January 7 article implied that "the contending and blooming" had produced too many weeds and advocated that the policy be halted, or at least limited. Of all the intellectual fields, the authors feared that "blooming" in the literary realm had caused the greatest damage. As in the past, writers became the first targets of the counterdrive against liberalization. The article seemed aimed specifically at Ch'in Ch'ao-yang and the writers around him. Ch'en Ch'i-t'ung and his backers asserted that "The number of essays describing socialism have become less and less and the number of satiric articles which voice dissatisfaction and disappointment are increasing." They feared that, "If we do not take action against this, we will have the end of politics and will fall into the trap of limiting ourselves to the description of the trivial affairs of individuals and of personal sentiments." What disturbed this group most was the undermining of political requirements. "We must not think that formalization and generalization can be avoided by indulging less in politics." [61]

Subsequently, through the rest of January and into February, the Hundred Flowers campaign was in a state of suspension. Within this period, the campaign which hitherto had been almost exclusively against dogmatism and bureaucratism now began to speak out also against rightist revisionism. The Minister of Education on January 22, 1957, stated that, "The tendency to relax ideological and political indoctrination, to practice democracy in the extreme, to emphasize individualism one-sidedly, and to neglect collectivist acts and discipline should be rectified." [62]

Response in the Literary Field

The brakes on blooming in literature had been applied even before Ch'en Ch'i-t'ung's article appeared. Curbs had been imposed not only by the cadres in actual practice, but by the top leadership. *Wen-i hsüeh-hsi* (Literary study), the official literary organ of the Communist Youth League in December of 1956, and *JMJP* in the following months, opened a formal debate on Wang Meng's novel. This novel became the focal point of the drive to reverse the relaxation in literature, and subsequently, in other intellectual areas. The December issue of *Wen-i hsüeh-hsi* launched the offensive. The principal charges were that the story attacked the leadership cadres, had a hero who was not a member of the proletariat, and caused friction between the youth and the party organization.

After the publication of Ch'en Ch'i-t'ung's article in January 1957, a nationwide controversy raged over "The Young Newcomer in the Organization Department." Forty articles on the subject appeared in *Wen-i hsüeh-hsi* alone from December through February, most of them condemnatory. Wang Meng's description of the bureaucracy was now interpreted as a political indictment of the whole Communist system. In February, the onslaught grew heavier. *Wen-i hsüeh-hsi* reported that it had already collected eight hundred manuscripts on the subject.[63] In addition to the line of argument outlined above, a few more were added that were even more damaging to the spirit of the Hundred Flowers movement. Writers were now told, as they had been prior to 1956, to portray the bright aspects of Communist society and the heroes of the party. The attack on Wang Meng resembled the one simultaneously going on in the Soviet Union against Dudinstev for his *Not by Bread Alone*, a novel on a similar theme, the conflict between an idealistic young man and the entrenched Soviet bureaucrats. Both writers were accused of misrepresenting reality.

Among the most vocal of Wang Meng's critics was Li Hsi-fan, the accuser of Yü P'ing-po in the *Hung lou meng* episode. He was quoted in *Hsüeh-hsi* as saying that Wang Meng "wrote of party work and the party's internal struggle . . . in a way that went beyond the realm of criticism to the point of exaggeration and distortion." [64] As Li Hsi-fan's remarks reveal, several in the literary leadership sought through their attack on Wang Meng to discourage attacks on the bureaucracy. Along with the defense of the bureaucracy, there was a return to emphasis on political reliability and to downgrading cultural and academic achievement. Hence, by the end of 1956 and the beginning of 1957, the spirit of "blooming and contending" appears to have been stifled, and in some areas, especially the creative arts, the intellectual atmosphere again resembled the one that prevailed before 1956. Huang Ch'iu-yün claimed that "a cold wave of doctrinairism and factionalism spread over all the country." [65]

A few young writers protested against this interruption of the liberalizing trend. They sought to protect the beginnings of intellectual ferment that had bubbled forth in the spring and fall of 1956 by defending Wang Meng against the attacks of the more orthodox cadres. Their championship of a fellow writer and of his ideas was carried out in somewhat the same manner as Yevtushenko's defense of his colleagues against the old-line literary bureaucrats in Moscow at that time.

The leader of this protest was a twenty-two-year-old writer, Liu Shao-t'ang. He supported Wang Meng at meetings and in debates. Some of his arguments were summarized in an article he wrote at this time with another writer, Ts'ung Wei-hsi, entitled "Write the Truth — The Living Core of Socialist Realism." They first described the impact of Wang Meng's story on the Chinese reading public. "Because he sharply and genuinely was loyal to life, Wang Meng's story aroused a great response among a broad number of readers, including literary circles." They called the literary bureaucrats who criticized this story "the public opinion of vulgar sociology," an expression that had been used by Hu Feng. In answer to the "vulgar sociologists," Liu and Ts'ung insisted that Wang Meng had not in the least bit distorted the happenings in a party organization. "Literature which dares to participate in struggle and be faithful to life and truth does not lie." [66]

Their defense rested on the premise that Wang Meng's portrayal of officialdom had coincided with the party's Hundred Flower policy. They insisted that this policy demanded that writers describe life as they saw it. "We cannot demand that Wang Meng depict this Party organization according to our complete concept of the party, because that would be a formula. Only truth gives literature life and feeling." [67] Finally, they objected to others recklessly besmirching Wang Meng's name, one of the first times political name-calling was publicly condemned. "Very many people have criticized Wang Meng for having 'petty bourgeois' feelings. This is indeed blind labeling without any reason." They concluded with the plea, "Let us liquidate the subconsciousness of vulgar sociology from the minds of our writers, critics, editors, and readers." [68]

Wang Meng was the ostensible target, but behind the scenes Ch'in Ch'ao-yang was under severe pressure to renounce the ideas expressed in "Realism — The Broad Road" and to influence the young writers around him to accept the party's interpretation of literature. An indication of the pressures upon him and the self-hate they engendered can be seen in a letter he had sent to Liu Pin-yen in the later part of March 1957. He stated, "Since I wrote to you last December, I've been in the midst of a storm . . . I hate myself because I am not very wise nor very brave and am without strength . . . I am ashamed that I haven't had the power to change my environment." [69]

Apparently, in an effort to demonstrate his orthodoxy and save himself, Ch'in wrote an article in March 1957, "On 'Write the

Truth,' " in which he renounced the views he had expressed just six months earlier. He now rejected his own ideas on realism and upheld socialist realism. In contrast to his recent statements, he sharply criticized those writers, especially the younger ones, who treated the phrase "Write the Truth" to mean that they should express their own views. Though this was the way he had interpreted this slogan previously, he now insisted that it meant that one should write the truth as the party sees it. No longer does he tell young authors to write of love, of personal affairs, and of family life. Now he declared that "The emotions of real love should be expressed, but if they are separated from the important aspects of life and from the ideas of the times what significance would they have?" [70] Finally, Ch'in begged his readers not to forget the lessons of the Hu Feng campaign, lessons that only six months earlier he had belittled. "We must increasingly study and reform ourselves and remember party principles in literature." [71] At the same time that he renounced his own ideas on realism, he also condemned Wang Meng's story, the work he had encouraged. In the March issue of *Hsüeh-hsi*, he attacked Wang Meng for lacking ideological consciousness and for inadequate depiction of the positive characters in party organs.

After these articles of self-criticism appeared, Ch'in tried to justify his actions to his younger disciples. Another letter to Liu Pin-yen revealed that his public words had been a result of fear rather than any genuine ideological change. "After the Wang Meng affair developed, I felt the greatest and most troublesome intimidation, not so much from literary and art circles, but from the newspaper world, including *Chung-kuo ch'ing-nien pao* and *JMJP*." [72] Ch'in's last minute effort to abide by the will of the party and confess his "errors" had not saved him. Wang Meng was sent to the countryside to reform himself by contact with the masses. Gradually, the public attack shifted more and more to Ch'in. Though Ch'in's suggestions to Wang Meng had been mainly stylistic, the mistakes found in "The Young Newcomer in the Organization Department" were now attributed to Ch'in's revisions. By spring of 1957, Ch'in was being eased out of his position as editor of *Jen-min wen-hsüeh*.

As a result of these attacks against nonconforming writers, the literary cadres once again began to emphasize the need for ideological unity. Several literary journals began to express dissatisfaction with the exchange of diverse viewpoints. Of the discussion forums, an article in *Jen-min wen-hsüeh* observed that sometimes they "may have some positive results, but often there are not any results, just confusion." [73] The article pointed to the plethora of literary journals that had arisen spontaneously in the cities and universities as a reflection of this confusion. To counter what was considered ideological chaos, the phrase "poisonous weeds and flowers" was brought forth as the party's euphemism for incorrect and correct ideas. "What we need is the kind of attitude that supports the fragrant flowers in their struggle against the poisonous weeds and makes the poisonous weeds fertilizers of the fragrant flowers." [74] Consequently, the purpose of debate was increasingly defined as a way to achieve a unified view. While this goal had been somewhat ambiguous in 1956, it now became clearly the prime reason for discussion in the literary field. As stated by *Wen-i pao*, "The Hundred Flowers movement has aroused debate. This is necessary for literary creativity because only by going through this kind of debate can we gradually achieve unanimity of consciousness." [75]

Mao Tun, always atune to shifts in the party line, already in March of 1957 labeled those writers who were unwilling to work towards unanimity of beliefs rightists. In *JMJP*, he declared that "In the course of combating doctrinairism, rightist ideas have emerged." [76] He defined these "rightist ideas" as resistance to Marxist-Leninist study and emphasis on the special characteristics of literature and art. He charged that these concepts weakened party leadership and the ideological character of literature. Though he criticized Ch'en Ch'i-t'ung's article for its oversimplifications and for its intolerance of differing views, he applauded it for its zeal in defending the party line and fighting against "petty bourgeois" ideas. In conclusion, he stressed the need for writers to undergo ideological remolding and restated the absolutist alternatives open to Chinese intellectuals: "If they do not have a Marxist-Leninist outlook, then a nonproletarian outlook will guide them." [77]

The sudden letdown in the party's first genuine effort at relaxation apparently deflated the hopes of many intellectuals. This was particularly true in the literary realm, which Huang Ch'iu-yün described at this time as overhung with a "frightening atmosphere." [78] Once again, the writers were noticeably quiet.

Second Phase of the Hundred Flower Movement, April–June 1957

Party Policy

Then, just as suddenly as it had halted, the Hundred Flowers movement resumed with renewed vigor. The reasons for the regeneration of this policy are still not fully clear. There are indications that there may have been some form of intraparty struggle as seen in the sudden suspension of this policy earlier. However, one can only surmise from the facts that are available. On February 27, 1957, Mao Tsetung gave his famous speech "On Correcting Contradictions Among the People." He presented the theory that nonantagonistic contradictions can exist in Communist society and must be resolved by persuasion rather than force. This speech appears to have been, in part, a response to the critics of the Hundred Flowers policy and, in part, an effort to reassure the intellectuals.

Evidently, the increasing silence of the intellectuals in the beginning of 1957 and the continuing economic dislocations were some of the reasons behind Mao's efforts. He sought anew to mollify the dissatisfaction of the intellectuals in order to gain their cooperation. An equally significant factor was the impact of the Hungarian uprising on the Chinese intellectuals. In his speech of February 27, Mao frankly admitted that the "Events of Hungary caused some intellectuals to lose balance a bit." [79] The first reports on the uprising in Poland and Hungary had been treated favorably in the party press. The *New York Times* reported that there was widespread sympathy for the Hungarian rebels among informed Chinese circles.[80] *KMJP*, when later describing the reaction of the intellectuals to the Hungarian and Polish uprisings, admitted that the intellectuals were "ready to repudiate all their earlier confessions and admissions in political and ideological matters." [81] It also acknowledged that these events caused antagonisms between the intellectuals and the party officials.

The response of the intellectuals to these events, plus the disillusionment that had set in after the denunciation of Stalin and the interruption of the Hundred Flowers movement, apparently led Mao to advocate the further relaxation of party controls rather than the reimposition of stricter ones, as Ch'en Ch'i-t'ung and the group he represented were suggesting. Mao had attributed the Hungarian uprising to the cadres' isolation from the masses and to their over-bearing attitude toward the intellectuals. He believed that unless the mounting pressures of repressed discontent were released, a Hungarian-like crisis might occur in China. He stated that "If we persist in using methods of terror to solve internal antagonisms, it may lead to the transformation of these antagonisms into antagonisms of a nation-enemy type, as happened in Hungary." [82] Whereas the Hungarian uprising led Khruschev to halt the trend toward liberalization in the Soviet Union, it induced Mao to push it further in Communist China.

In this speech on contradictions, Mao also accepted the thesis for which Wang Shih-wei had been so brutally criticized in 1942, that the cohesiveness of society could be maintained more effectively by acknowledging that conflicts existed instead of covering them up. He stated that in China in 1956 "A small number of work-ers and students in certain places went on strike . . . The im-mediate cause was the failure to satisfy certain demands for material benefit. But a more important cause was the bureaucratism on the part of those in leadership positions." [83] By blaming the contradic-tions in society on the party cadres, Mao sought to channel popular discontent toward the bureaucracy rather than toward the system itself.

Though rectification of party cadres had been going on since mid-1956, Mao now served notice that it would be carried on in a much more systematic and thorough fashion. An intensified instead of desultory effort to rectify the cadres who had been unresponsive and often antagonistic toward the Hundred Flowers movement became a major difference between the first phase in 1956 and the second phase in the spring of 1957. Moreover, Mao now urged the intellec-tuals to criticize officials and show them how they had misused their power. As we have seen, Mao had been concerned about the shortcomings in the cadres before. As early as 1942, he feared that the cadres would become perfunctory in their duties in the manner of the old-style bureaucrats. From that time on, there had been periodic campaigns as seen in 1953 and the first half of 1954 to rejuvenate the cadres with the former spirit that once brought them close to the people. Also, Mao, like the Soviet leaders, apparently believed that opposition to bureaucratic practices would enhance his authority among the intellectuals. He even went further than the Soviet leaders at this time in encouraging direct criticism and inviting discussion of political issues. Nevertheless, Mao still remained suspicious of the intellectuals. They were still to be remolded, though this time by indirect methods. Their erroneous ideas were to be brought into the open by discussion, criticism, and reasoning, rather than by coercion.

Mao's speech seems to have had a delayed reaction. Though it was given in February, the echoes of opposition continued, though in muted tones, into April. Statements in official party organs contradicted Mao's words. Several editorials in *JMJP* imposed specific conditions and limitations on debate. Journals still focused on the cadres' criticism of the intellectuals, not the reverse. The April issue of *Hsüeh-hsi* said of the intellectuals, "We should look on them as old teachers, have them express their viewpoints, and afterwards help them analyse their mistakes . . . We should look on the struggle against erroneous thinking as opportunities for perfecting Marxism-Leninism." [84] Under these circumstances it is not surprising that intellectuals were slow to respond to Mao's call. Several expressed suspicion. Chang Po-chün, head of the CDL, said, "Many scientists say . . . some leaders pay lip service to the slogan [of a Hundred Flowers] without taking action. Precisely because of this, intellectuals are still groping for their way and speculate whether the policy is sincere or a gesture, whether it is an end or a means." [85]

Apparently, in response to this hesitation, Mao followed up his invitation to the intellectuals to air their grievances with concrete measures. In April, it was announced that a nationwide campaign to rectify party members from the municipal level to the top levels of government was to be launched immediately. Intellectuals no longer had to restrict themselves to the lower and middle levels, but were encouraged to criticize the leadership itself. Nonetheless, the directive cautioned that all levels of cadres could not be exposed to the same kind of denunciation that had been used against the intellectuals. "The campaign . . . should be carried out as gently as a breeze or as mild as rain . . . Large meetings of criticism and struggle should not be held." [86] In the belief that the ideological remolding drives had been effective, Mao expected that the criticisms of the leadership would be kept within bounds.

With Mao's full weight behind it, an organized drive was launched at the end of April to enlighten the cadres on the importance of the relaxation of control. An editorial in *JMJP*, on May 19, 1957, said of the cadres that "On hearing all kinds of opinions freely expressed and some views directed against them, they feel uneasy and panic-stricken, afraid this will force the leadership into a passive position . . . Many nonparty elements do not dare criticize leading person-nel for fear of reprisal; these anxieties must be removed." [87] This time, instead of the party leadership collaborating with the cadres to regulate the intellectuals, it collaborated with the intellectuals to control the bureaucratism among the cadres. The voices against liberalization and rightist thinking which had become louder in the beginning of 1957 were now directed primarily to the events in Eastern Europe. Within China itself, they died down to nothing more than a murmur in May of 1957.

Implementation of These Policies in the Literary Field

In contrast to his hesitation in the first phase of the Hundred Flowers movement, Chou Yang this time put Mao's ideas into effect, even before the launching of the rectification drive at the end of April. Consequently, the leadership in the literary realm was one of the first and one of the most active in the reinvigoration of the Hundred Flowers policy. Apparently, the Hungarian uprising, particularly the role of the Petofi Club in Hungary, had had a profound impact on China's writers. The Petofi Club was composed of old and young poets, playwrights, and novelists, who through their positions on newspapers and journals were able to publish direct criticism of the government. Its members had had a leading role in the rebellion and were responsible for fomenting student unrest. They also had had contacts with the working class. Fearing similar actions from China's writers, the leadership in the literary realm worked ener-getically to forestall any such eruption. Furthermore, since writers more than other intellectuals, had been victimized during the in-terregnum at the beginning of 1957, greater efforts had to be ex-pended to allay their fears and to encourage them to contend.

Though Chou Yang and his associates were the epitome of the organization men, they became the most outspoken critics of the bureaucracy. But their attacks were primarily on the middle and lower levels of the bureaucracy. As they stood aloof to rectify the mistakes of their underlings, they simultaneously elevated their own prestige. As early as April 9, 1957, Chou Yang condemned all the things for which he, himself, was most guilty. "Things disadvantageous to the development of literature, art, and science . . . include doctrinairism, sectarianism, and bureaucratic treatment of these fields with administrative orders." [88] Ch'en Ch'i-t'ung and his associates were being denounced everywhere. Their sharpest critics were among the literary leadership. Concomitantly, the cases of Wang Meng and Ch'in Chao-yang were temporarily shelved. Chou Yang's close associate, Lin Mo-han, vice-minister of culture, presented the definitive word on "The Young Newcomer in the Organization Department." Though he claimed the story had some faults, he commended it as a whole. Since the CC was no longer beyond criticism, he insisted that Wang Meng should not be attacked for his criticism of defects in a party office. He called those who denounced the story dogmatists and opponents of the Hundred Flowers movement.

Response of the Writers to the Reinvigoration of the Hundred Flowers Movement

Unlike the 1940's and the first half of the 1950's when left-wing writers had stepped forth as the chief critics of the regime, in the second phase of the Hundred Flowers Movement, it was the non-Communist intellectuals, particularly the leaders of the CDL, who led the attack on the party. Beguiled by the party leaders' criticism of the cadres and by their encouragement to speak out, these intellectuals gave vent to all the bitterness they had stored up for the last six years. Contention quickly spread from academic matters to state policy. Their anger could not be confined to the cadres and specific party officials. Inevitably, it led to denunciation of the party itself. The leaders of the CDL, Chang Po-chün, who was also Minister of Communications, and Lo Lung-chi, also Minister of the Timber Industry, held that it was not merely the bureaucratic methods of the cadres, but the privileged position of the party that was at the root of the contradictions between the leaders and the led. Whereas the principal criticism of the party hitherto had been on ideological and philosophical grounds, these "democratic" leaders for the first time attacked on political grounds. Though the implication of their words had the same effect, even the writers in 1956 had not hit directly at the political system itself.

One of the most incisive attacks on the party in the spring of 1957 came from the editor of *KMJP*, Ch'u An-p'ing. In April 1957 the leaders of the CDL attempted to run their organ, *KMJP*, independently and to abolish the party committee on the paper. Ch'u An-p'ing sent correspondents to the large cities to organize forums where nonparty members could express their criticisms. Full coverage was given to these forums. Suddenly, *KMJP* emerged as a powerful weapon of opposition. Along with the statements of other "democratic" leaders, Ch'u's speeches became the battle cry of the students and the intellectuals. In addition to condemning the incompetence and arrogance of party members, they attacked the party's monolithic structure, the identification of party and state, and the sham coalition government. Ch'u declared that the party sought "to bring about the monolithic structure of a one-family empire." [89] To counteract these phenomena, the "democratic" leaders demanded institutional changes in the governmental structure. Chang Po-chün asked that decisions be reached by legally-established institutions in which other parties had a voice.

Leaders of the CDL also reiterated several of the points that the revolutionary writers had made in the past. Principally, the plea that intellectuals be treated with respect and understanding. At a forum of intellectuals at Peking University on May 7, 1957, the chemist Fu Ying declared that "When an intellectual's knowledge is neglected, he then becomes passive . . . We only want schools to refrain from treating us like outsiders. When the Party treats us like outsiders, we cannot give all our strength." [90] Most intellectuals asked merely to be allowed to run their own affairs. At forum after forum, they demanded that the faculties and administrations of the universities be freed from party direction. The party should be in charge of political affairs, but academic pursuits should be left to the professors. There were others such as Lo Lung-chi who went further to add that scholars be given a role in government as they had in old China. He maintained that "During several thousand years of China's history, scholars have had some knowledge of the art of leadership." [91]

There was also a move afoot in the social sciences and in the arts in particular to lessen the dominance of party ideology. Several intellectuals questioned the need for any Marxist-Leninist doctrine in scholarship. This was particularly true among the historians who, even more than the writers, were restricted to fitting their material into an exact ideological mold. Professor Lei Hai-tsung, head of the history department at Nankai University, declared that "Marx and Engels constantly revised their own theories, but their successors thought they had solved all problems and that the social sciences could develop no further." [92] Another historian, Yang Hsiang-k'uei, went still further. He not only questioned whether Marxism-Leninism had relevance to academic issues, he also asked whether Mao did either. "Perhaps Mao does not have time to decide these problems for us . . . Academic problems should be solved by the scholastic world . . . The natural sciences are like this, the social sciences also should be like this." [93] Intellectuals in all disciplines challenged the party's qualifications to lead their fields.

While a large number of non-Communist intellectuals and members of the CDL were demanding radical political and cultural reforms, many of the writers still held back. If a leading literary official, like Ch'in Chao-yang, could not contend with impunity, then who could? Despite the assurances from Mao and Chou Yang and the boldness of some of their fellow intellectuals, a heavy atmosphere continued to pervade literary circles. A veteran writer, Yao Hsüeh-yin, asked why it was that during the Hundred Flowers movement "everyone expressed opinions in science, theater, or film, but in the areas of creative writing, there is silence? In private, many literary friends will grumble and discuss quite a few things which have aroused their resentment; but in public, it is as if everything were fine . . . There is a public literary world and a private one." [94] Yao pointed out that this divergence between what they thought and what they said was due to the fact that writers had been so persecuted in the past for offering criticism.

Even the literary bureaucrats themselves conceded that fear had inhibited writers from expressing their own true thoughts. Shao Ch'üan-lin, in attempting to explain their silence, said, "It is not that people do not understand the policy of the party, but that they fear that after they have bloomed and contended, they will be rectified." [95] Apparently, some writers were asking for much more than merely the party's promises of good faith before they ventured forth again. An article in *Wen-i pao* disclosed that "There were people who demanded that the leadership provide guarantees and make certain there are no repercussions; otherwise they will not contend." [96]

The silence of the revolutionary writers, who had been so bold in the past, was particularly conspicuous. At the climax of the Hundred Flowers movement there was hardly a public word uttered by the group of writers around Ting Ling. An article in *Hsin kuan-cha* (New observer) asked why was it that "In the commemoration of the Fifteenth Anniversary of Mao's Yenan 'Talks,' party members who are authors and who had participated in the original forum were asked to write, but many would not." [97]

The most outspoken writers in the second phase of the Hundred Flowers movement came from the generation trained by the party. The major spokesman of this group was again Liu Shao-t'ang, the young writer who had defended Wang Meng just a few months earlier. He was thirteen at the time of the party takeover. While in high school, he became a member of the Communist Youth League. Most of his knowledge of Western literature came from his study of Russian writers. From 1951 to 1954, his short stories closely followed the pattern laid out by the party's literary officials. His works were filled with idealized peasant heroes. He was singled out as one of Communist China's most promising writers. Then in 1955, his stories began to change. They became less concerned with large-scale political events and more concerned with individuals, family relationships, and love affairs. Though there was some criticism of his works at the time, he was praised once again at the outset of the Hundred Flowers movement because his writing coincided with the party's more relaxed line. In the first phase of the Hundred Flowers movement, he had written some stories indirectly critical of the party's programs. In one of them, "Clouds at Sundown in the Fields," he described a village going through the first great push in collectivization of China's agriculture in the latter part of 1955. Instead of showing the farmers overflowing with enthusiasm, as party propaganda portrayed them, he painted them as dejected, somber, and at times utterly without hope. Another story, "The Grass of Hsi yüan," was about students in a university. Here also he did not show the youth bubbling with joy and devoted to the party, but instead revealed them as resentful of the organized life that had been imposed upon them.[98]

In the spring of 1957, he was more daring. He directly attacked Mao's literary dicta in a bold essay, "The Development of Realism in a Socialist Period." As seen from the title, Liu was influenced by Ch'in Ch'ao-yang's "Realism — The Broad Road." He also claimed to have been affected by the intellectual stirrings in the Soviet Union and Eastern Europe. He, like Ch'in, attacked the stultifying effect which dogmatic formulas had in the development of China's cultural life. But he went further than Ch'in and explicitly mentioned the arbitrary application of Mao's "Talks on Art and Literature" as a direct cause of stagnation. He characterized Mao's literary doctrine as "emphasizing only the political nature of literature, not its artistic quality." He acknowledged that at one time it was necessary to give prominence to specific political questions in literature. "In the life and death struggle against feudalism and reactionary rule, the revolution demanded that literature be the quickest, most direct propaganda weapon. There was no time to spend long hours on a work to create beautiful images." But, in China of the 1950's, these "Talks" were not only inappropriate to literature, but even more important, he regarded them as inappropriate to the present ideological demands. He declared that "The theory [Mao's 'Talks'] . . . has now become conservative. It is far behind the situation now developing." [99]

In addition to criticizing Mao's "Talks" for not developing with changing conditions, he also attacked them for directing writers toward future ideals instead of present realities. In another article written a month later, he asserted that "To carry on the tradition of realism, we must be truly faithful to the realities of life . . . We should not in the name of 'realistic development of the revolution' whitewash life and alter the true face of life. The realities of life must have the characteristics of the age and the mark of the times; we cannot equate the realities of 1957 with those of 1967." [100]

Liu's criticism of Mao's "Talks," therefore, was not so much concerned with artistic values as with social and ideological issues. Like Huang Ch'iu-yün and Hu Feng, he denounced the party's literary theories because they directed writers and subsequently the reading

public away from the real problems before them. Liu demanded, in
the manner of Wang Shih-wei, that writers reveal the sufferings and
injustices around them so that they could be rectified. In his earlier
article, he declared that writers had a different function from other
intellectuals. "In the analysis and study of political and economic
systems of society, the social sciences prove the excellence of socialism, . . . but literature and art must be based on the living truths
of the present. Consequently, they must not only reflect the good
things in life, but also reflect the backward things in life truthfully
and strikingly." [101] Several in the literary world echoed Liu's rejection of Mao's "Talks" as the doctrine for literature.[102]

Another radical measure to be suggested during the Hundred
Flowers movement was the establishment of independent publishing
houses and journals. Though these demands were not so dramatic as
the pleas of the "democratic" leaders for a coalition government,
in effect they would have had the same impact. Once independent
organs of expression were established, they could bring pressure and
the weight of public opinion to bear on the government. The plea
for independent publications was actually a reiteration of Hu Feng's
proposal that journals compete freely with one another. Shu Wu,
Hu Feng's former colleague, now suggested that these journals also
become small publishing houses. Finally, writers demanded that
they receive salaries and working conditions comparable to those of
the scientists. While the salaries of scientists went up, writers' fees
and royalties were reduced by as much as one-half to two-thirds.[103]

Along with these demands, a ground swell developed to reopen
the cases of all those writers who had been made scapegoats of the
party's cheng feng campaigns. This movement, which crested at the
end of May 1957, captured the imagination of the youth, particularly those in the creative arts. Some pointed to Wang Shih-wei's
essay, "The Wild Lily," as a *tsa wen* to be imitated. Many began
to question the so-called ascetic life Mao supposedly led in Yenan.[104]
Li Hsi-fan's and Lan Ling's attack on Yü P'ing-po's study of *Hung
lou meng* was cited as an example of the dogmatism prevalent in
the literary world. *JMJP* published articles by intellectuals denouncing the crudity of their interpretation of *Hung lou meng*. A typical
criticism was that of Shu Wu: "Some students of *Hung lou meng*

have become intoxicated with extracts and comparisons of socio-logical, economic, historic, and political matters. They use these as substitutes for a profound study of the real material of a literary work." [105] Several writers complained that the one-sided praise of new writers, intensified by Li Hsi-fan and Lan Ling's attack on Yü P'ing-po, had led to disrespect for the older writers. Also, many spoke out in defense of Wang Meng's and Liu Pin-yen's attack on the bureaucratism in the party.

The loudest clamor of all went up in defense of Hu Feng. Now that Hu Feng's opinions, which the party had pronounced as heresy just a year earlier, were being debated and his terms such as "vulgar sociology" and "mechanized literature" were being mouthed by Communist leaders, there was a movement, especially among the youth, to re-examine the charges against him. The trial of Hu Feng in open court became a cause célèbre for the more independent young intellectuals. They compared the Hu Feng case to the Dreyfus affair. Like Dreyfus, they charged that Hu Feng had been falsely accused. Several students insisted that there was no proof that Hu's literary faction was counterrevolutionary. A wall newspaper at Tsing-hua University called on students to fight for justice for Hu Feng the way French liberals had fought for Dreyfus. It stated, "We do not want French capitalism, but the French spirit of seeking the truth and fighting for justice regardless of sacrifice is right indeed." [106] The most vocal member of this student movement was twenty-one-year-old party member Lin Hsi-ling, a student at People's University. She pointed out that the party's current Hundred Flowers policy actually was the implementation of Hu Feng's demands. Not only did she and her followers seek to vindicate Hu Feng's ideas, they also tried to redeem Hu Feng himself. His example had apparently inspired many youth in this period. At student gatherings, Lin was reported to have declared that history would judge Hu Feng to be one of the heroes of the age.

Concomitant with these protests against the activities of the party literary officials, went a barrage of criticism against the officials them-selves. It was in this aspect, more than in the sphere of ideas, that this second phase of the Hundred Flowers movement differed from the first. In 1956, there had been attacks on the injustices of the bureaucracy in general and on the underlings who carried out the orders in particular. Now the onus shifted and was placed directly at the very top of the bureaucracy.

Several "democratic" leaders had condemned the highest levels of political leadership. They interpreted Mao's statement in his speech of February 27, that "In some cases the responsibility for bureaucratic mistakes should be placed on high authority and those at lower levels should not be made to bear all the blame," [107] as a sanction for them to attack. Ch'u An-p'ing was reported to have even challenged Mao himself. "People lately have made suggestions to junior monks, but nothing to the senior monks, Mao and Chou [En-lai]." [108] Ch'u An-p'ing's challenge to the pinnacle of power most likely stimulated others to follow suit in their own organizations and disciplines.

One of the writers joining the attack on the top-level bureaucrats was Hsü Mou-yung, Lu Hsün's one-time colleague who in the mid-1930's had joined with Chou Yang against his old master. In the 1940's, he had worked with the Red Army in the North. When the party took over the mainland, he became chancellor of Wuhan University and at the end of 1955 was transferred to the Philosophy Institute of the Academy of Sciences. At various times during this period he was under surveillance by the party for supposedly "independent" activities. He had written virtually nothing for twenty years until the spring of 1957 when he suddenly issued a barrage of *tsa wen* on several subjects. Some stressed the universality of human emotions, others emphasized the need for friendly relationships among comrades reminiscent of Hsiao Chün, and a few described the constant state of anxiety under which intellectuals lived. One of his sharpest, "Random Notes from the Abode of a Noisy Cicada" was directed against the party's organization men, the group to which he once belonged. "I have seen some who do not read, but direct others to read and are good at criticizing the arguments derived from books by those who read and make conclusions." [109] In a devastating description of the opportunism of the party organization man, he wrote, "One year he was an advocate of the theory of no conflict. A year later, the Soviet Union began to oppose the theory of no conflict, so he, too, began to argue against it with all pomposity . . . Though the arguments of this kind of

Marxist leader undergo repeated changes, he never admits he is wrong. Every 180 degree turn of his is right. This man's thinking is characterized by following, he never thinks." [110]

There was no question by 1957 that Chou Yang was the chief organization man in the literary realm. He had demolished his competitors for power, Hu Feng and Feng Hsüeh-feng. There was evidence that he had had Ting Ling put under surveillance. Outside of Mao Tse-tung, Chou Yang was quoted most frequently as the final arbiter on all cultural matters. Such famous writers as Lao She, Mao Tun, and Pa Chin referred to Chou as the authority for their remarks. In September of 1956, Chou had been named alternate member of the CC. His official position had finally begun to coincide a little more closely with his actual power.

Hence, when members of the Writers' Union became more daring in May of 1957, Chou Yang was the natural target for their attacks. Their offensive began slowly at first and in a roundabout fashion. As the volleys against Mao's "Talks" and the party's interpretation of realism grew louder and echoed further, they converged increasingly on those officials in charge of implementing them. Huang Ch'iu-yün explained that sectarianism was more intense in literature than in other fields because "The damage done by sectarianism has deep historical roots in our literary world. It not only hinders the union of the party and nonparty writers, it also harms the union of party writers with one another." [111] Hence, whereas in other fields of intellectual endeavor, the complaint about the bureaucracy was mainly about the gap between the leaders and the led, in literature the complaints were also about the divisions within the leadership itself. Another division was between writers who came from Yenan and those who came from the KMT areas. The poet Tsang K'e-chia complained about literary officials who insisted that only those from Yenan were revolutionary, whereas the ones from the KMT areas were not to be trusted.[112]

As the writers' verbal slashes came closer to their targets, they revealed that the grumbling against Chou Yang was not merely because he was in a position of leadership. More significant was the disclosure that he had personally aroused a feeling of disgust among those whom he led. This dislike for Chou Yang had been publicly expressed by some of the revolutionary writers in the 1930's, particularly by Lu Hsün and Feng Hsüeh-feng, but these had been the individual views of writers who were in competition with Chou for power. Now, however, this animosity toward Chou was expressed from all sides and from people who had no personal contact with him. Actually, as far back as 1956, some writers had begun to complain about the ignorance of the literary bureaucrats, the chief allegation Feng Hsüeh-feng had leveled against Chou Yang in the past. An article in *Wen-i pao* on September 15, 1956, lamented the anti-intellectual approach of the literary bureaucrats, though no names were mentioned. "To be a leader of literature and art, one should understand the characteristics of literature and art. If he does not understand, then he should study them . . . How can one lead a factory or hospital without expending great effort in studying its special characteristics?" [113] Such efforts were even more necessary, this article claimed, for literature. However, "The person chosen for leadership is in the habit of establishing authoritarian views with a bamboo whip. He does not respect other people and their work and, therefore, cannot gain the respect of others." [114] The literary critic Huang Yao-mien charged that the officials of the Writers' Union were repugnant to others because of their officiousness, which he defined as "too much talk, too little thought." [115]

At first, several of Chou Yang's close associates were singled out as guilty of these faults, such as Ho Ch'i-fang and vice-minister of culture Liu Chih-ming, the one who had led the attack on Hsiao Chün. Gradually, the accusations finally shifted directly to Chou. The major charge against him, as the chief representative of the literary leadership, was that he only pretended to uphold the line of the Hundred Flowers movement, but, in reality, he treated this policy as detrimental to his own position. Huang Ch'iu-yün was one of the first to criticize Chou openly. He showed that instead of supporting the Hundred Flowers movement as Chou ostensibly claimed, he had actually tried to smother it. Huang asserted that "The fact that the rectification in literature and art could not develop satisfactorily and that the lower-level cadres had worries and little courage was due to the judgment of their superiors." [116] He presented the example of Chou Yang's treatment of Liu Shao-t'ang as evidence. "Not long ago, Chou Yang accused Liu Shao-t'ang as being a man who did not know how high the sky or how thick the earth . . . This can hurt one's positive nature." [117] In addition, Huang implied that Chou's rejection and then his subsequent approval of Wang Meng's novel were due to his opportunist attitude of moving along with each twist of the party line rather than to any real change of mind as to its value.

Two members of the editorial staff of *Chung-kuo ch'ing-nien*, one of them Liu Pin-yen, pointed to Chou Yang as a prime example of a doctrinaire with great power and influence. They explained that Chou achieved his unchallengeable position because of the party system. "The reason why there can be no person today like Lu Hsün, who twenty years ago dared to contend against Chou Yang, is because of the different position of a writer in relation to the Propaganda Department of the CC." [118] Lin Hsi-ling openly proclaimed that Hu Feng was attacked because he had offended Chou Yang and his associates.

The movement against Chou culminated with an article by T'ang Chih (T'ang Ta-ch'eng), an assistant editor of *Wen-i pao*. In castigating Chou, he also summed up the arguments against socialist realism. He charged Chou with evaluating literature purely in terms of its propaganda value. He asserted that Chou's insistence on the depiction of "correct" characters, meant that "a work no matter how lacking in characterization and in the real spirit of life, need only have new heroes to be praised." [119] In the words of Hu Feng, T'ang declared that Chou's formula led writers away from life's realities and rendered them incapable of absorbing its complexities. This approach, T'ang predicted, will lead to the writer's self-destruction, because the truthfulness of his literary images have been destroyed. When editorials in *JMJP* in the second week of June ended the Hundred Flowers movement, T'ang's article which appeared on June 9 was the last public criticism of Chou Yang at this time.

The blooming in literature in the first and second phases of the Hundred Flowers movement proved that despite years of indoctrination, for some dating back to the early 1940's, a large number of writers and intellectuals had essentially not abandoned their own views and literary concepts. What was even more significant was that fundamental criticism of the party came not only from the older party and nonparty intellectuals, but from young students who had been counted among the regime's most ardent supporters. Members of the younger generation who had been educated by the party were capable of producing their own heterodoxies. The Hundred Flowers movement showed that China's traditional humanitarian values, together with the spirit of revolutionary idealism and an appreciation for some Western intellectual and literary currents, had not necessarily been spent nor had their continuity been interrupted.

chapter nine

THE ANTIRIGHTIST DRIVE
AGAINST THE WRITERS,
1957–1958

Suddenly in June, the party turned from tolerance and relaxation to persecution and intransigence. There were many reasons for this sharp turn. The Hundred Flowers movement had developed a momentum of its own. In attempting to enlarge the role of the intellectuals, the party had opened the way for demands that constituted a challenge to its own competence. Having overestimated the effectiveness of its former indoctrination movements, the party's relative liberalization had released more pent-up dissatisfaction and bitterness than it had anticipated, especially from the youth and students. The recognition of differences of opinion had not enhanced the unity of the country as Mao Tse-tung had hoped; it did just the reverse. Since free discussion and criticism could not be confined, the flood of criticism spread well beyond the permitted limits. Although most intellectuals were only asking for a greater degree of freedom to pursue their own interests, the acceptance of their demands would have shaken the foundation of the regime.

The abrupt reversal in policy was also due to China's continuing economic difficulties. Cuts in capital construction and the expansion of the free market which had accompanied the relaxation in the intellectual sphere had not brought the improvements in the economy that the party had expected. Instead of seeking an explanation for their difficulties in their own economic policies, party leaders blamed the contending of the intellectuals. The country's economic disorders were attributed largely to the harmful effect of criticism, which weakened the single-minded zeal required for economic construction. In this way, the party hoped to channel discontent away from criticism of the regime. Furthermore, in the wake of repercussions from the uprisings in Hungary and Poland, China appeared anxious to minimize its ideological differences with the rest of the Communist bloc. At this time, China, no less than the Soviet Union, seemed concerned with maintaining solidarity. Both countries now stressed that revisionism was more of a danger than dogmatism. In the summer of 1957, relations between China and the Soviet Union were less strained than after Khruschev's de-Stalinization speech and than they were to be six months hence. It has also been suggested that Mao agreed to end the Hundred Flowers movement at this juncture in return for Soviet aid on nuclear weapons.[1]

Party leaders in all Communist countries endeavored in 1957 to tighten their control, but the swing of the pendulum in China was sharper than elsewhere, an indication of the seriousness with which the leadership regarded opposition within the country. Moreover, the reaction may have been greater because Mao had confidently lifted the lid, only to find disaffection hitherto kept underground. Although the Hundred Flowers movement was still heralded, its meaning was redefined. Chou Yang declared, "The slogan of a hundred flowers bloom, a hundred schools contend, is not a slogan of liberalization as certain bourgeois writers and newspaper reporters imagine, but a militant slogan for the development of socialist culture." [2]

First Phase of the Antirightist Drive

In June 1957, the rectification of the party turned into the rectification of the critics of the party. An editorial in *JMJP* on June 9, 1957, announced the reversal: "There must be active countercriticism as well as criticism." Party officials could now answer their critics. The editorial criticized those who "term all Marxist theories dogmas and denounce all socialist organs as bureaucracy." [3] A later editorial of *JMJP* on July 12, 1957, remarked that the party purposely let "evil spirits and demons" contend freely for a period without striking back. The purpose was to let the poisonous weeds gain a luxuriant growth so that people would be startled into taking action. Apparently, the people had not pulled out these weeds with the vigor the party had expected. Consequently, with the appearance of these *JMJP* editorials in the second week of June, a campaign against leading intellectuals was set in motion with an unexpected speed and intensity, suggesting that the party's response had been well planned. The intellectuals who had criticized were labeled rightists and the drive was called the antirightist campaign. It served the dual purpose of damaging the prestige of the intellectuals and providing a mechanism for the reaffirmation of the party's position. As the movement progressed, the emphasis shifted from the first to the second purpose.

On June 19, 1957, Mao's speech of the preceding February 27 on contradictions among the people was published. It was an amended text that contained six criteria for correct criticism, defining the limits to which criticism could go. The most important criteria were support for party leadership and maintenance of socialism. As in the cheng feng movements of 1942 and the early 1950's, the correct formula for discussion was now consolidation, criticism, and again consolidation. Even Chou En-lai, one of the chief architects of the previous liberalization policy, though repeating his warnings to Communist cadres against too much interference, now insisted on firm party control in all areas. The party explained that the discontent expressed during the Hundred Flowers movement was the voice of a small clique of unreformed intellectuals who were intent on undermining the socialist system. As in the campaign against Hu Feng, their criticisms were interpreted as political subversion. The June 24 editorial of *JMJP*, entitled "Unusual Spring," stated this very clearly in its charge that the intellectuals had "organized their own campaign to undermine socialism under the cloak of giving the party aid." [4]

The antirightist campaign followed the pattern of earlier thought reform drives. Sweeping attacks were directed against those who had been outspokenly critical and had not wholeheartedly accepted party leadership. A few important targets, representative of certain groups, were singled out as instigators and they and their followers were subjected to accusations until they at last confessed. Among the first to be selected for attack were the non-Communist leaders of the CDL, Chang Po-chün, Lo Lung-chi, and the editor of their newspaper *KMJP*, Ch'u An-p'ing. During the first month the full weight of the attack fell on the older leaders of the non-Communist intellectuals. Initially, charges were made by colleagues within the accused's own institution or political group. In the fear of being labeled anti-socialist and anti-Communist, members of "democratic" and professional organizations hastened to disassociate themselves from leading rightists and sought to advance their personal interests by attacking them.

The climax of this aspect of the campaign was reached at the meetings of the NPC on July 12, 1957, when Lu Ting-i summed up the charges against the "democratic" leaders and the non-Communist intellectuals. "These elements disseminated antisocialist views, attempted to seize leadership among the educated, journalists, and scientists, and sought to provoke student disturbances." [5] He also accused them of wanting to do away with the leadership of the proletariat and of seeking to sow discord between the Soviet Union and China. One of the most serious charges made against them was their desire to eliminate party leadership from the academic realm. As in the past, all their mistakes were traced back to the fact that they had not thoroughly reformed. "They have passed the tests of the three-anti movement and ideological remolding, but they are not basically changed." [6]

At the July 13 and 15 sessions of the NPC, Chang Po-chün and Lo Lung-chi finally made abject, sweeping confessions in which they admitted the mistakes with which the party had charged them and promised to reform. Ch'u An-p'ing had already criticized himself at the end of June. The leaders of the "democratic" parties not only renounced their own criticisms of the party, but all the "evils" the party was intent on eradicating. Chang confessed that he had been infected by the Soviet Twentieth Party Congress, the Polish and Hungarian uprisings, and Chinese traditions. Though no substantial evidence was brought forth of plotting against the regime, Lo confessed that he and Chang in contact with other intellectuals had formed antiparty committees in the schools and universities. Once again, the "democratic" parties reverted to their passive, unquestioning role under the party.

Considering the sharpness of their attack on the party and the charges against them, the leaders of the non-Communist intellectuals received relatively light treatment. They were subjected to criticism at various meetings, but these criticisms never reached the kind of unrelenting "public" denunciations that were Hu Feng's fate. Outside of being dismissed from their posts, few punitive measures were taken against them. Their confessions were eventually accepted as signs of repentance. Most likely, the party's forgiving attitude toward the leaders of the "democratic" parties was related to the pressing need for the full participation of the intellectuals, particularly the scientists, in China's modernization.

The Attack on Ting Ling and Her Colleagues

Ting Ling

Perhaps an even more pertinent reason for the relative mildness of the attack on the non-Communist intellectuals was that they were not to be the main focus of the antirightist movement. The chief scapegoats were to be the old revolutionary writers, Ting Ling and her colleagues Feng Hsüeh-feng, Ai Ch'ing, Hsiao Chün and Ch'en Ch'i-hsia. Ironically, outside of Ai Ch'ing and a few words from Feng Hsüeh-feng against unquestioning acceptance of Soviet culture, none of them had published any attacks on the party during the Hundred Flowers movement. In fact, since 1953 little had been heard from Ting Ling. Others in the literary realm, including some who had been far more outspoken in their public attacks on party ideology and leadership than Ting Ling and Feng Hsüeh-feng, suffered less cruel treatment.

Ting Ling was chosen for this role primarily because of her rivalry with Chou Yang and his group for power in cultural circles. There is evidence that in the final days of the Hundred Flowers movement, Ting Ling and her associates were engaged in a power struggle to wrest the cultural leadership from Chou and his followers. Up until the end of 1952, she and Chou competed on equal terms, but in 1953 Chou began to get the upper hand. His group sought to lessen Ting Ling's influence in the Central Literary Institute. Though Ting Ling had already started to withdraw from administrative duties to devote herself more to creative writing, she still spent considerable time at the Institute, guiding young writers in their literary work. Many young writers came to consider her their mentor and adviser. An indication of the esteem in which she was held can be seen in the reports that her picture was hung up in the classroom alongside that of Tolstoy.[7] Consequently, the Institute had become another important center from which she could influence literary circles. Apparently in an effort to undermine her position, the party committee of the Writers' Union and the Propaganda Bureau proposed in 1953 that the Institute give more emphasis to ideological remolding and political studies than to creative writing. The name of the Institute was changed to the Literary Study Institute of the Writers' Union and T'ien Chien, one of Chou Yang's cohorts, became the new head. Though Ting Ling resisted these changes, they were eventually implemented. Also, by the second half of 1953 Ting Ling's job as editor of *Jen-min wen-hsüeh* was taken over by Chou Yang's close associate, Shao Ch'üan-lin.

Another effort of Chou Yang's to undermine Ting Ling's power can be seen in an attack by some of his colleagues on her close friend Ch'en Ch'i-hsia, the assistant editor of *Wen-i pao*. It began early in 1954, before they had turned to Feng Hsüeh-feng. They charged Ch'en with crudely criticizing a young writer in *Wen-i pao*, thereby making it impossible for him to sell his works. Ting Ling immediately rushed to her friend's defense. She complained that he had been treated unfairly. Apparently, Ch'en refused to admit his "error" and published a letter in the Internal Correspondence of *Wen-i pao* supporting his position. Then in late 1954, when Chou Yang attacked Feng Hsüeh-feng and *Wen-i pao*, Ting Ling was also criticized because of her connections with *Wen-i pao* and its editors.

Initially, she was reluctant to confess to the party's accusations. Her first self-criticism was not accepted because she refused to acknowledge that the mistakes in *Wen-i pao* were the fault of herself or of her associates. Instead, she insisted that they were the result of factional conflict. She maintained that the party's investigations and not her colleagues' actions were to blame for the suppression of free discussion in *Wen-i pao*. Both she and Ch'en vigorously resisted the party's efforts to shift the blame onto them. Subsequently, party leaders managed to "help" her see the truth so that the final self-criticism they evoked from her at the close of the meetings on *Wen-i pao* was agreeable to the party.

Nevertheless, her confession and even the fact that she was connected with the case were not mentioned in the press at this time. Presumably, the party still hoped to gain her support for their own purposes, or perhaps Chou Yang may have been too unsure of himself and of the impact an attack on Ting Ling would have on the reading public. Whatever the reasons, Ting Ling, as in 1942, was shielded from public reprimand and from the verbal blows that were hurled at her friends. Moreover, these attacks did not prevent her election in 1954 as a representative from Shangtung to the NPC. She also remained a member of the presidium of the ACFLAC and vice-chairman of the Writers' Union. Ch'en, too, stayed on the editorial committee of *Wen-i pao*. Still, their replacement as editors of *Wen-i pao* and *Jen-min wen-hsüeh* by Chou Yang's adherents had removed them from the very center of power in the cultural realm and placed their antagonists in control.

Then, in January 1955 the Writers' Union, under the supervision of Chou Yang's group, convened an enlarged meeting specifically to condemn Ting Ling and Ch'en through an official resolution. At first, Ting Ling and Ch'en appeared to accept the resolution against them meekly. However, in April 1955 three anonymous letters, which Ch'en later confessed he wrote,[8] were sent to a "comrade at the center." The comrade was not mentioned by name, but was most likely a member of the Politburo. These letters supposedly denounced the Propaganda Department and the party committee of the Writers' Union for their actions against *Wen-i pao* and its editors. They alleged that the disciplinary measures were a result of personal animosities. Charging that such actions "destroy democracy," [9] Ch'en asked that the case against *Wen-i pao* be re-examined. Like Hu Feng, Ch'en apparently hoped to gain the support of some of the top leaders in his battle with Chou Yang's group.

As a result of these letters and of the Hu Feng campaign then underway, a series of sixteen enlarged meetings were held against Ch'en and Ting Ling from August to September 1955. At these meetings they were charged with many of the "crimes" they were to be accused of later: refusal to accept party leadership and supervision; expansion of the influence of their small group; encouragement of the cult of personality. Under such duress, both writers again confessed and promised to reform.

About six months later, at the third enlarged meeting of the Writers' Union in February–March 1956, Ting Ling was attacked once more. These were the same meetings at which Ai Ch'ing, Ch'en, and Feng Hsüeh-feng had been publicly attacked by Chou Yang and his colleagues, but again, not a word was said about Ting Ling in the press. Nevertheless, there was criticism of the idea of "one-bookism," a way of thinking later to be attributed to Ting Ling. The literary bureaucrats used this term to signify concern with artistic quality rather than with the propaganda value of a writer's work. In his speech at this meeting, Mao Tun had declared that "An evil, bourgeois concept has spread among the students, . . . "one bookism," it encourages the young writer to set as his goal the attainment of individual fame and status and personal 'immortality.' " [10] Though Ting Ling in the private debates supposedly insisted at first that she had not said anything about "one-bookism," she again, after some coercion, admitted her "mistakes." Apparently, at these meetings Ting Ling and Ch'en were for the first time described as leading an antiparty group. A subsequent report of the Writers' Union to the CC depicted Ting Ling as being against the party all her life.

During this whole period of investigation, Ting Ling wrote little that appeared in print. There was one speech of hers to a film study meeting, which, though it had gone through the hands of the censors, still spoke, albeit indirectly, against the party's insistence that everyone write in the literary form of socialist realism. Actually, her words expressed the same ideas articulated later by Lu Ting-i in his reinterpretation of socialist realism during the Hundred Flowers movement. She stated, "We advocate the creative method of socialist realism, but still each of us has his own creative road and uses a different method of expression. Although our stands are the same, each one has his own style and character and his own way of life." [11] While these views were to be acceptable a year later, they were not sanctioned during the strict orthodoxy of the campaign against Hu Feng. Surprisingly, however, they were printed at this time. Another section of Ting Ling's speech, however, was not. She had once again reiterated her old theme that one must live a long time in an area to know it, but she also added that one need not always live in the village. This phrase was cut out because, most likely, it was too close to Hu Feng's belief that the material for literature could be found everywhere, not merely among the workers and peasants. The only manifestation of any public criticism of Ting Ling at this time, as a matter of fact, was a cartoon in *Wen-i pao* obviously related to this incident. She was shown with a certificate giving her permission to move from one place to another. Presumably, this was a means of informing her that she herself should dwell in a village for a long time.[12]

In her speech before the film study group, she had admitted that although there were characters and material in her mind, she had not written anything recently. However, the September 1956 issue of *Jen-min wen-hsüeh*, at the time Ch'in Ch'ao-yang was editor, published a chapter from a new novel she was writing. This chapter described a village along the Sangkan River, the scene of her last novel, during the clash between the KMT and the Red Army in the later part of the 1940's. That was the extent of the writings after 1954 from one of China's hitherto most prolific writers.

During the Hundred Flowers movement, she gave an interview that was published in *Wen-i pao* in May 1957. In contrast to other statements being made by writers and intellectuals at this time, her words were innocuous. She stated that she had been living in a small village and had been ill. Probably, she had been sent there after her condemnation in 1956. In this interview, she urged writers to go to the countryside "to see the real beauty of the lives of the masses and the development of new types, of unselfish labor, and of pure, deep sentiments." [13] But this time, she was able to add because of the party's shift to the Hundred Flowers movement that there are many ways a writer can immerse himself in the lives of the masses. It was not necessary to go to a village or factory to do so. A writer should work with the material with which he is most familiar. She also observed that there were some writers who saw conflicts in society but were afraid to discuss them. Her remarks fully conformed to the current party line. In fact, similar ideas were articulated much more forcefully at this time even by Chou Yang and his followers. Obviously, Ting Ling herself was afraid to express her own conflicts and may have considered the party's plea for criticism as a trap to catch her and her friends.

Nevertheless, toward the end of May, carried along by the feeling of euphoria and optimism that prevailed in intellectual circles, Ting Ling's doubts appear to have been somewhat allayed. She had been at the meeting where Mao Tun, indirectly, and Huang Ch'iu-yün, directly, had attacked Chou Yang and his associates. Many of the forums had revealed a deep feeling of animosity toward Chou Yang by a large number of creative writers. Criticism and demands from the intellectuals had swelled to such a pitch that many truly expected the party would yield at this point to popular pressure and modify its absolute power and that of Chou Yang's. Consequently, Ting Ling began to speak out at small gatherings, where she described herself as oppressed by the party committee of the Writers' Union. She insisted that the leadership of literature be guided not by bureaucrats, but by writers themselves. However, she did not appear on any large platform. She and the older writers apparently still hesitated to uphold their views before a wide audience.

Rather, it was the younger writers who had been close to her when she was editor of *Wen-i pao* and director of the Central Literary Institute who were most active in criticizing the party's policies, particularly its treatment of Ting Ling. By the end of May, many voices demanded an airing of Ting Ling's and Ch'en Ch'i-hsia's case. Several editorial writers and reporters on the Shanghai *Wen-hui pao* and *Wen-i pao* spoke out in support of Ting Ling. Pu Hsi-hsiu, a reporter from *Wen-hui pao*, asked Shao Ch'üan-lin to publish the details of the case in the press. Shao refused.

Two editorial writers of *Wen-i pao*, T'ang Yin and T'ang Chih (T'ang Ta-ch'eng), who had openly criticized Chou Yang, led the counterattack on the party committee of the Writers' Union in late May. Both men were party members, but had been close to Ch'en when he was the editor of *Wen-i pao*. Although they had been criticized along with Ch'en in 1954 and were forced to write self-criticisms, the party had been lenient with them at that time. They were needed to fill important positions on the reorganized editorial board of *Wen-i pao*. Despite the party's conciliatory attitude toward them, these two writers remained loyal to Ting Ling and Ch'en. They looked upon the relaxation of the Hundred Flowers movement as an opportunity to redress the grievances of their mentors.

Hence, at the main rectification meeting of the editorial board of *Wen-i pao*, they demanded the withdrawal of the 1955 resolution against Ting Ling and Ch'en, criticized the party's handling of the affair, and asked that the record of the investigation be made public. Following their mentor's line, they declared that the mistakes in this case had not been made by the party itself, but by the leadership of the Propaganda Bureau and the Writers' Union, in other words, Chou Yang and his group. Supposedly, T'ang Yin was reported to have described the Writers' Union as "the police station of the Propaganda Department and *Wen-i pao* as the 'notice board' of the police station." [14] He insisted that injustices had occurred because leading comrades of the Propaganda Bureau, of the party committee of the Writers' Union, and of *Wen-i pao*'s editorial board had resisted the policy of the CC. Like Hu Feng with his report to the CC and Ch'en with his letters to a high official, these young editors attempted to draw the top leadership to their side and away from Chou Yang's group. They declared that the CC had received a distorted account of what happened on *Wen-i pao* because it had learned about it from Chou Yang's ally Lin Mo-han, head of the literary section of the Propaganda Bureau. They implied that the party committee's case against Ting Ling was based on trumped-up evidence. Therefore, they asked for a chance to present their side of the picture.

Several others echoed the arguments of these two editorial writers. *Wen-i pao* claimed that the impact of T'ang Yin's remarks, "sparked a big fire that spread into a holocaust against the party." [15] Probably, this was an exaggeration to show that the party had been victimized by powerful forces. Nevertheless, there is no doubt that T'ang Yin's attack on Chou Yang's group stirred up literary circles and paved the way for further blows at Chou Yang himself. As more and more criticisms were leveled at Chou Yang's literary theories and at the Propaganda Bureau, no voice was raised in rebuttal. Word spread that Chou Yang had been compelled to apologize openly to Ting Ling and her group and that the case against Ting Ling and Ch'en was about to be reviewed. It appeared at the end of May that Chou Yang had for the first time been forced to retreat.

Then suddenly on June 6 the party committee of the Writers' Union convened a series of meetings. They were convened a few days before the *JMJP* editorials abruptly marked the end of the Hundred Flowers movement. These meetings were called to denounce Ting Ling. Although they were presided over by Chou Yang's associates, Shao Ch'üan-lin, Lin Mo-han, Liu Pai-yü, and Ho Ch'i-fang, apparently Ting Ling, cheered on by a rush of popular enthusiasm to her side, displayed vigorous defiance from the very start of the sessions. Her speeches and those of her friends were never published, but their words and actions at these meetings can be pieced together from the accusations subsequently made against them. In the first three sessions, Ting Ling spoke out in her own behalf. She attacked the investigations made by the Propaganda Bureau and the Writers' Union in 1954 and demanded that the discussion of her case be reopened. As in the past, she did not criticize the party itself, but only the party members in charge of literature. She complained that "Chou Yang has ruled the literary world for twenty years," [16] and asserted that he had instigated the investigation of *Wen-i pao* for his own factional purposes. [17]

Apparently, the third speech she had made at these meetings was very emotional. She was reported to have denounced the antiparty charges against her by tearfully exclaiming that her disagreements with party officials were expressed through the legal means of writing and speaking, not through the illegal means of secret activity. [18] Her tactics reveal that she still suffered from the illusion that had led to her downfall in 1942 — that it was possible for dissident views to be expressed in a party-run society. Nevertheless, she apparently had been so forceful and so articulate in the public presentation of her own case that for a short time she was able to swing many of the participants in these meetings, supposedly Chou Yang's loyal supporters, to her side. This had been her intention all along. She had hoped to influence public opinion in the expectation that it could exert some pressure on the party's top leaders. Supposedly, at the earlier meeting in 1956 when she was first labeled an antiparty element, quite a few comrades had supported her. When they had been asked by the Writers' Union to write essays to be used in discussions against her, several had defended rather than attacked her. In an atmosphere still lingering with the spirit of the Hundred Flowers movement, it is most likely that Ting Ling expected an even more sympathetic response this time.

Another part of Ting Ling's planned counterattack on the party leaders in the Writers' Union was for her and Ch'en to withdraw publicly from the Writers' Union at the Third National Congress of Writers and Artists to be held in the fall of 1957. Since she considered herself the leader of a large public following, she anticipated that others would follow suit and thereby undermine the position of Chou Yang's group. All of these actions and plans of Ting Ling were, of course, motivated by her antipathy to Chou Yang and her desire to regain power. Still, as can be seen from her past writings, she also expected to reduce party controls over cultural circles and creative work. Ting Ling's methods indicate that even after many years of experience to the contrary, she still believed that public opinion and the views of the majority could influence the decisions of the party.

However, before Ting Ling's counterattack could be mobilized, Chou Yang with his full force behind him took the offensive at the fourth meeting on July 25. From then on, the atmosphere changed completely. Meetings against Ting Ling and Ch'en took place almost every day. By the end of July, the number of people attending each session expanded to over two hundred people and included members of the Propaganda Bureau, the Writers' Union, and the Ministry of Culture. This intensification, while due in part to Chou Yang's own desire to hit back at his enemies, was also encouraged by the party itself. At this time, Communist China was acting in closer concert with her East European brethren. In the summer of 1957 there was an acceleration in the campaign to discipline writers in most Communist countries. Khrushchev led the way by attacking nonconforming Soviet writers, particularly Ilya Ehrenburg.

Along with the stepping up of the meetings of the Writers' Union, the party for the first time publicized the news of Ting Ling's crimes. They were given wide coverage throughout China in the press and on the radio. Under this constant pressure, her colleague, Ch'en Ch'i-hsia, finally surrendered unconditionally on August 3. He confessed to all the crimes that the party claimed he had committed. He also accused Ting Ling of attempting to seize the leadership of literary circles and handed over his correspondence with Ting Ling and other members of his group to the party. As opposed to their earlier handling of the Hu Feng correspondence, party leaders did not publish these letters. Perhaps, they feared the publication of Ting Ling's letters would backfire, as had been the case with Hu Feng's letters in the Hundred Flowers movement, or maybe they feared that her letters might only enhance her popularity with the public. Nevertheless, they used quotes out of context as material against her.

While Ch'en had given in completely to the party's demands, the party was unable to force an acceptable confession from Ting Ling. Party leaders called her self-criticisms ambiguous, evasive, and dwelling on trivia. Probably, they would have been unacceptable no matter how abject they may have been, since at this point the party intended to use her as a prime example in its antirightist campaign. A still more significant reason was that despite the meekness of her colleagues and the penalties of resistance, Ting Ling refused to admit to the "crimes" the party charged against her, especially to the crime of being antiparty. She adamantly maintained that she had been a correct party member and had served her party well, which in her terms may have been true. She further insisted that she had opposed certain individuals, not the party, and that her relationship with Ch'en had been ideological, not conspiratorial. Throughout, she refused to hand over her correspondence as Ch'en had done. Her husband, Ch'en Ming, a party member, also refused to confess and continued to defend her. Lao She's speech at these meetings described the nature of Ting Ling's defiance. Addressing himself to her, he declared, "You always look down on us, so do you today. Your superiority complex has led you to make a demonstration to us when you are explaining your crimes, to show us how meticulous you are and how well you can write." [19]

After speeches by Communist China's principal writers and party officials and after twenty-five meetings over a period of three and a half months, the sessions finally concluded on September 16 and 17. There were 1,350 people at the last meeting to hear the concluding speeches by Lu Ting-i and Chou Yang. They included officials of the branches of the Writers' Union from all over the country and leaders of the Propaganda Departments in the provinces. The Third National Congress of Writers and Artists was postponed. Though this would have been an appropriate forum to attack Ting Ling, the party, perhaps, feared her supporters would use it to defend her.

Feng Hsüeh-feng

When Ch'en had confessed on August 3, he revealed that Feng Hsüeh-feng had been connected with Ting Ling in her "antiparty" plans. Apparently, party leaders wanted to include Feng in their campaign against Ting Ling. By the end of August, Feng had taken the place of Ch'en as Ting Ling's chief assistant in subversive activities.

Like Ting Ling, Feng had spoken out only occasionally since the investigation of *Wen-i pao*. After losing his editorship of the journal, he was made the director of the People's Literature Publishing House, but he was only a figurehead. The deputy director, Wang Jen-shu, whose pen name was Pa Jen, was actually in charge.[20] Feng seldom attended to even the routine duties. During the Hu Feng campaign, he had been ordered to write an essay against Hu. Presumably, he was under considerable pressure, since a denunciation of Hu Feng from a former colleague would have great propaganda value. He collected the material and wrote several drafts, but had difficulty writing an acceptable essay. Finally, one of his efforts appeared in *JMJP* on May 27, 1955. He condemned Hu as ordered, but his confession carried the implication that Hu's actions were not subversive. He wrote Hu "showed individuality, but throughout I thought he was following us politically, I did not think he was against the people." [21]

Unlike his friends Ting Ling and Ch'en, Feng after 1954 was still asked to speak at official meetings. At the start of the Hundred Flowers movement, he was invited to talk before a gathering of the editorial boards of the literary magazines. Though his speech was not published, some idea of its contents can be seen in excerpts that were reprinted later as evidence against him. Actually, his remarks appear to be no more inflammatory than the statements of other writers at this time. Like Huang Ch'iu-yün, Feng insisted that "Literary works should praise our socialistic construction and encourage people to progress, but we still cannot say that our people are not without hardship. The problem is how to understand this distress." [22] At another point, he declared that "If we are satisfied with the present, it is difficult to imagine why." [23] Feng continued to believe that literature should help solve some of China's current difficulties, but he complained that it was unable to do so in present-day China. "In history, great writers have pushed reality forward, but we have done away with the spirit of critical realism." [24] He blamed this on the fact that "The leadership superficially and crudely understands creative principles," [25] and that the writers do not dare write about the problems they see.[26] Not only Communist China, but also Soviet literature, Feng believed, suffered from the same malady. In Feng's view, the basic problem of Soviet literature was dogmatism, which he interpreted as separation from the basic concerns of mankind. By contrast, he believed that nine-teenth-century "Russian literature had a great humanistic spirit. Soviet literature should have more of this spirit." [27]

In addition, Feng was also concerned with literature as an art form. "Political standards are first. This is an unalterable principle, but literary works should also be artistic; if they are not, then they do not exist as literature." [28] Except for his blast at Soviet litera-ture, Feng's words echoed along the same wave length as Huang Ch'iu-yün's and Ch'in Ch'ao-yang's. Yet, whereas their utterances were to reach a crescendo at the height of the Hundred Flowers movement, these were the few public statements Feng made through-out this period. Moreover, his words had nowhere near the power of the direct denunciations that young men like Liu Shao-t'ang leveled against Mao's "Talks on Art and Literature."

Though not enjoying the wide audience and popularity of Ting Ling, he was still highly regarded in intellectual and literary circles. During the Hundred Flowers movement, several articles appeared that defended him against the abuses heaped upon him during the investigation of *Wen-i pao*. One of these was published in the same issue of *Jen-min wen-hsüeh* as Ch'in Ch'ao-yang's "Realism — The Broad Road." [29] Its author, Wu Ying, in giving examples of actions contrary to the spirit of the Hundred Flowers movement, cited a criticism that Li Hsi-fan, the initiator of the attack on Yü P'ing-po, had written of Feng's essay, "On the Tradition of Ah Q." He ad-vised Li to treat Feng as one who had been reformed and to give him the respect that was due him. Ch'en Yung, who had spoken out for artistic standards, also complained that Feng had been treated unfairly and called the method of handling the *Wen-i pao* case sectarian. Outside of these few statements undertaken in his behalf, Feng made little effort to defend himself publicly. In an interview with a reporter, he declared there should be more genuine scholars who spend several years in solid reading.[30] Apparently, this was the way Feng spent most of his time in the two years after his denunciation.

However, during the second phase of the Hundred Flowers movement in May 1957, Feng appears to have suddenly come alive. He was buoyed by the spirit of the times. Like his friend Ting Ling, he thought that some real reforms might occur. Probably because of his past experience, he too did not publicize his views, but worked behind the scenes. His major activity was the planning of an independent journal called *T'ung-jen k'an-wu* (Colleagues magazine), to be established in collaboration with Ch'en Yung, who, as we have shown, was very outspoken during this period, and with T'ang Yin and T'ang Chih (T'ang Ta-ch'eng), the two *Wen-i pao* editors who had sought to reopen Ting Ling's case. The journal was intended to present literary viewpoints different from those advocated by the party, but was still to be based on Marxist ideals. Its very name implied that it was for those primarily interested in literature, which by definition eliminated Chou Yang and the party leadership. The fact that he and some of his colleagues planned to set up a journal independent of party organs was not unusual in this period. Disaffected students and intellectuals organized a wide variety of independent journals in several large cities. Yet, these efforts received only minor attention in the antirightist campaign, whereas Feng's was made the prime target. The reasons apparently were the same as in Ting Ling's case and in the previous attacks on Feng, his reputation, his long-time conflict with Chou Yang and his group, and his challenge to their leadership.

In June, when the party committee of the Writer's Union, of which Feng was a member, began meetings on Ting Ling and Ch'en, Feng did not attend, most likely, because of loyalty to his old friends. As the campaign reached a climax and hit at Feng in the beginning of August, he immediately presented a preliminary self-examination in which he confessed to individualism and opposition to Mao's literary thoughts. However, like Ting Ling, his self-criticism was found unacceptable. There is some indication that Feng was more defiant this time under pressure than he had been in the past. He was quoted by Yüan Shui-p'o as having said at one of the meetings that "I did not know that to be anti-Chou Yang was to be anti-party." [31] Officials at the meetings were reported to have been greatly dissatisfied with his attitude and his evasion of the main issues.[32] Even into September, Feng only confessed that he opposed the party's policies in the cultural sphere. He still refused to acknowledge any connection with antiparty groups. By the end of these meetings, he was deposed as deputy to the NPC from Chekiang.

Other Colleagues

Concomitant with the sessions against Ting Ling and Feng, all those associated with Ting Ling in the Wang Shih-wei case in 1942 — Ai Ch'ing, Hsiao Chün, Lo Feng, and his wife Pai Lang — were subjected to renewed attacks. With the exception of Ai Ch'ing, they, like Ting Ling and Feng, had hardly written anything during the Hundred Flowers movement. Their chief crime was their dissension in the 1940's, not their activities in 1956 and 1957. Even the charges brought against Ai Ch'ing were not so much for his biting allegories made during the Hundred Flowers campaign as for his past friendship with Ting Ling and Feng.

Apparently, at the time that Ting Ling and Ch'en had been denounced in 1955, Ai Ch'ing, bitter over the treatment of his friends, spread the word among various artistic groups that the blows against Ting Ling and Ch'en were the result of "sectarianism." [33] He was especially friendly with Wu Tsu-kuang, the playwright, and with Chiang Fu, the artist who was assistant director of the Central Institute of Fine Arts. Because both of these men were outspoken during the Hundred Flowers movement, they too were charged with being allied with the Ting Ling-Ch'en conspiracy. During May 1957, Ai Ch'ing was also reported to have urged reporters on *Wenhui pao* to demand a re-examination of the Ting Ling case.[34] For these and other unrelated reasons, such as promiscuity and irresponsibility, Ai Ch'ing was forced to prepare a self-criticism in the middle of August. Like Feng, his first attempt was totally unsatisfactory. He too disclaimed any political intent and insisted he was merely acting against the factional squabbles in cultural circles. Moreover, he defended his friends, especially Wu Tsu-kuang, against charges of conspiracy. By September, however, Ai Ch'ing's self-criticisms conformed to the party's line.

Another participant in the Wang Shih-wei case attacked at this time was Hsiao Chün. The choice of Hsiao as a target for censure blatantly revealed the flimsiness of the party's charges of conspiracy and the fact that the attacks were used as a screen behind which Chou Yang and his associates could do away with their old enemies.

As mentioned previously, Hsiao had been sentenced to hard labor in a Manchurian mine for his insubordination during the rectification campaign of 1948. After two or three years he was released, at which time he went to live in Peking. Finally, in October 1954 he emerged from his long obscurity with a new edition of *Village in August*, revised in conformity with the criticisms of it in 1948. The following month a new novel of his was published, *Mines in May*, written under party guidance. It was presented as proof of Hsiao's complete ideological reform. *Mines in May* described the support of the miners for the liberation army in 1949 and extolled the party's stereotype of the model worker. Hsiao's broad humanitarian outlook had been eclipsed by a narrow, class-conscious view of reality.[35]

At first, Hsiao's novel received no hostile criticism and was found ideologically correct. However, in the wake of the Hu Feng campaign, when all "suspicious" people were assailed, the novel and Hsiao himself came under sudden attack. In December 1955, two unknown writers criticized the novel in *Wen-i pao*. Actually, their arguments sounded similar to Liu Chih-ming's earlier condemnation of *Village in August*, though *Mines in May* was very different in spirit. Hsiao, once again, was criticized because he described heroic feats carried out spontaneously by individual heroes instead of by the party organization and because he showed a nonparty hero, not the party cadres, as responsible for the increased production in the mines. Ironically, the party charged that he had painted his model worker too glowingly so that he emerged as a hero above the masses. Applying the criticism used against all people accused of thinking like Hu Feng, Hsiao's critics charged that he "shows that the working class does not need leadership, political consciousness, nor technical abilities, it only needs a strong subjective spirit." Without adding the usual "unless he reforms," they concluded that "We must punish this kind of writer." [36]

This attack was followed by others. Paradoxically, one of them came from the Shanghai writer Wang Jo-wang, who subsequently coined a famous statement used repeatedly by critics of the party during the Hundred Flowers movement: "A wall exists between the party and the masses, created not by stone and cement, but by ideas." [37] Now, however, he himself helped to create that "wall." Though Wang insisted in his article on Hsiao that "literature should reveal . . . the mistakes of our bureaucracy," [38] he criticized Hsiao for doing exactly this. He condemned Hsiao for showing party cadres who stifled the production enthusiasm of the workers and called it slander to describe some party leaders as "those who eat and do no work." [39] With the beginning of the Hundred Flowers movement, criticism of Hsiao's novel diminished.

Hsiao had said little during the Hundred Flowers period and appears to have had virtually no contact with Ting Ling and her associates after he was released from the mines. Yet, with the onset of the campaign against Ting Ling and Ch'en, his fate became inseparable from that of his former Yenan friends. Again, criticisms of his novels began to appear. This time they were described as "filled with wild, individualistic, anarchistic ideas." [40] Similarly, the case against his journal, *Wen-hua pao*, was reopened and some of its articles were reprinted so that they could be criticized. Once more, several meetings were convened against him "to dig out the roots of the poison that had not been completely removed." [41]

Another writer whom the party connected with Ting Ling and Feng Hsüeh-feng was Ch'en Yung. Although he had been in Yenan when Ting Ling and Wang Shih-wei had criticized the party in 1942, he had been only a boy in his late teens at that time. He had not taken an active role for or against their position. However, because of his supposed association with Feng in the intended publication of the "Colleagues Magazine," and because he had accepted some of Feng's interpretations of Lu Hsün, he was called Feng's protégé. It was especially to his views on Lu Hsün that the party directed most of its attention. Denunciations of Ch'en, as of Feng, were part of the party's effort to reinterpret Lu Hsün in line with its ideological outlook. Ch'en was attacked because he had shown Lu Hsün to be disinterested in the class struggle. Other writers were accused of putting Lu Hsün on a higher level than Mao.[42] The party attempted at this time to topple Lu Hsün from his pre-eminent position in intellectual circles. Obviously, it considered Lu Hsün's legacy a threat to its leadership.

Like Feng, Ch'en did not surrender at the initial meetings held to criticize him. From the party's account, he appears to have renewed his attack on the party's control of creative work. He acknowledged that the leadership was protective of its writers, but he claimed that this approach was not suitable to the needs of literature. He begged that writers be allowed to regulate themselves in their own endeavors.

By the conclusion of these struggle meetings, all the revolutionary writers had made some sort of public confession. Yet, of all of them, only Ch'en Ch'i-hsia's was found acceptable. The rest were found wanting. They were charged with having "avoided the serious for the trivial." [43] What this meant was that they had admitted to opposing party leadership in the cultural realm, but insisted it was for personal rather than for ideological reasons as the party maintained. Ting Ling apparently held out more obdurately than the rest. As late as October 6, an article in *Wen-i pao* implored her, "acknowledge your mistakes truthfully and hand yourself over to the organization; otherwise it means you wish to alienate yourself from the people and willingly bury yourself." [44] While the others were temporarily removed from their official posts and positions on editorial boards, and sent away to reform through work in the villages and factories, she was expelled from the party, the vice-chairmanship of the Writers' Union, the presidium of the ACFLAC, and the NPC. Her works, along with Ai Ch'ing's were prohibited in the schools and universities. She was deprived of her rights as a writer and a citizen and subjected to two years of labor reform at a desolate spot on the northern fringe of Manchuria. Most likely, because of her long fight with those in charge of the ideological remolding movements and because of her continuing refusal to submit to their demands, she, of all the leading writers, received the harshest treatment.

The Nationwide Campaign Against the Revolutionary Writers

In the fall of 1957, the party leadership launched a campaign to inform all intellectuals and all students of the "crimes" that this small group of writers supposedly carried out against the state. By charging them with these "crimes," many of which they had not committed, Chou Yang and his associates planned to do away with a group of disruptive rivals. Even more important, the leadership sought to re-establish the party's total control over the intellectuals which had been disrupted during the Hundred Flowers movement. So, once again, the party indoctrinated the public by systematically refuting the ideas of these revolutionary writers.

Ideological Charges

The main charge against this group was directed at its independent way of thinking and acting, an attitude that appeared among all segments of the intellectuals during the Hundred Flowers movement. Party leaders labeled as revisionism all the views which denied that literature and scholarship obey party leadership. Their prime example of revisionism was Ting Ling. She was described as outwardly following Marxism-Leninism, but actually retaining the "bourgeois" concept that culture need not serve political goals and that art and politics were distinct. What seems to have alarmed these leaders most was the subtle idea held by these writers, particularly by Ting Ling, that the writer is a special sort of person, engaged in a highly individual craft and sometimes possessing individual genius. This view carried implications similar to Pasternak's which had so disturbed the Soviet authorities — namely, that the writer has the right to stand outside events and judge them nonpolitically. The party charged that "Although they are party members, they believe that they cannot be controlled or investigated and that the party's organizational rules are inappropriate to them." [45] Actually, this ideological charge had validity. These writers were willing to follow party rules only to the point where they did not interfere with the development of their talents. They continued to regard themselves as special people who need not conform to the demands of the organization. Even after fifteen years of having been shown the contrary, they continued to believe that they could remain party members and still write as they pleased.

Another major argument against them was the one made against Hu Feng, their disregard of ideology. Their passive resistance to ideological remolding and their insistence that great works could be written by writers without knowledge of Marxism-Leninism were strongly attacked. An editorial in the literary journal, *Wen-i yüeh-pao* maintained that "They put the writers' study of Marxism-Leninism in an unimportant position and mistakenly claim that the writer in the process of writing and studying foreign literature can grasp a correct world view." [46] Ting Ling's works which previously had been praised were now condemned because they lacked an ideological basis. T'ien Chien declared that *Sun Over the Sangkan River* "cannot be considered a great book among our present-day literary works." [47] The explanation as to why this novel hitherto had been universally acclaimed was that the editorial boards of the literary journals had been controlled by Feng Hsüeh-feng. Therefore, dissenting views could not be published. Now that Feng had been exposed, party officials asserted that the "correct" interpretation could be presented. Consequently, Ting Ling's novel was criticized because although it depicted land reform, it did not describe "the past hatred of the peasants for the landlords, nor did it create models of new peasants and party leaders in the struggle for land reform." Furthermore, she pictured the peasants as "backward and vacillating." [48] As with Hsiao Chün's *Village in August*, evaluation of Ting Ling's novel depended on the party's view of the author's politics.

Ting Ling and her associates were also accused of following Hu Feng's precept to "write the truth" instead of portraying the class struggle. It was in this aspect of the campaign that Feng Hsüeh-feng was most severely denounced. A renewed effort was made to condemn the ideas associated with Hu Feng, which had excited so many intellectuals during the Hundred Flowers movement. By showing that Hu Feng's and Feng Hsüeh-feng's beliefs were the same, party leaders rebuked Hu Feng by attacking Feng Hsüeh-feng. In the 1954 campaign against Feng, there had been no mention of the similarities and connections between him and Hu Feng. Now, in addition to showing ideological affinities, several officials asserted that Feng and Hu Feng had worked together to disrupt the League of Left-wing Writers in the 1930's and caused dissension between the party and Lu Hsün.

Expectedly, Chou Yang was conspicuous in listing the various ways in which Feng and Hu Feng were alike. "Feng Hsüeh-feng opposes the Marxist world view for creative work, . . . advocates the subjective fighting spirit, disrespects national tradition and national form, and calls writers who seek to popularize and use national forms 'Party merchants'!" [49] Along with the two other major critics of Hu Feng, Lin Mo-han and Ho Ch'i-fang, Chou Yang again presented the very same arguments against Feng that had been used two years earlier against Hu Feng. To a lesser degree, Ai Ch'ing was also likened to Hu Feng. He, too, was accused of fostering the same subjective, spontaneous spirit.

Of the similarities between Hu Feng and Feng Hsüeh-feng the one that disturbed the authorities the most was that these two writers wished to dispense with Marxist-Leninist theories when creating art. One of Feng's letters on this subject, which was handed over to the party, was quoted as evidence against Feng. Sarcastically, Feng wrote, "It appears there was no truth before Marx, only total darkness. When a person isn't a Marxist he cannot achieve truth. I often heard people say that the reason Lu Hsün had defects in his earlier period was because he wasn't a Marxist. This is very funny. How can it be . . . that as soon as one learns Marxism, everything is correct? Don't Marxists commit mistakes? The criterion for correctness should not be whether one is a Marxist, but whether what he says is appropriate to science. So long as one's thought reflects objective reality, it is appropriate to science, it is truth. The greatness of Lu Hsün was that, even when he was not a Marxist, his ideas already reflected the objective reality of the Chinese revolution and were appropriate to science." [50] Actually, when the party accused Feng of believing that the creative writer could express more truth than a Marxist, its criticism had an element of truth.

The fact that a number of youth had turned against the party during the Hundred Flowers movement was blamed on the ideological influence of Ting Ling and her group. Though one of the most outspoken, Liu Shao-t'ang, had not studied with Ting Ling, nevertheless the attention given to her relationship with young writers indicates the deep impact she had on them. As the party was concerned that older writers had substituted Lu Hsün for Mao, it was similarly concerned that the younger generation had substituted the leadership of Ting Ling's group for the party's. Shao Ch'üan-lin declared, "Influenced by Ting Ling and her kind, a number of youth have taken the wrong path. They have refused party leadership and supervision and have opposed the power of the party group." [51] As a famous writer and an old party member, Ting Ling, the party complained, had attracted many youth to her side. "She seems to have cast a spell on a number of young people . . . and has duped them into believing in her with respect and affection." [52]

Her influence supposedly had induced many young writers to spend their time writing books rather than participating in political activities. Repeatedly, the refrain was heard, "Many young people want to write just one book, like *Sun Over the Sangkan River*." [53] To counter this approach, the party stressed that "Our line, as opposed to hers, is first to encourage infinite loyalty to the party and then seek innovations, creativity, and . . . attainment of professional knowledge and techniques." [54] Furthermore, literary officials incessantly warned the youth, as did K'ang Cho, that "those so-called architects of the souls of mankind, with Ting Ling as their leader, are merely a bunch of soul-corroding masters." [55]

Political Charges

At the time the party was conducting its meetings against Ting Ling, it was also carrying out an internal cheng feng movement against liberal and individualistic tendencies within the party. Consequently, Ting Ling not only became an example of a rightist intellectual, she also became the symbol of a rightist party member. In fact, this latter aspect of the campaign against Ting Ling was even more important than the former. A *JMJP* editorial of September 11, 1957, stated that "The writers inside the party do more harm than those outside. The easiest way to attack a fortress is to attack from within." [56] In the party's view, "The longer the rightists have had membership in the party, the higher the positions they hold, the greater their threat to the party." [57] Ting Ling's ideas had such a large market place, the party believed, because she could "use the authority of the party to delude the people." [58] Most likely, this explains why the party treated her and her colleagues more severely and went after them more zealously than the nonparty and younger intellectuals, who had actually presented the party with more radical demands.

As with Hu Feng, the activities of Ting Ling and her group in the literary realm were interpreted as political activities subversive to the regime. Ting Ling's wide personal influence among people in the creative arts was shown by the party to be politically disruptive. "She ignored organizational lines and rallied supporters around her, formed her private clique and created the impression that she was the literary czar." [59] The party admitted that her group was small, but claimed that because of its pivotal position in the area of communications, it could take over the leadership of the ideological front. It further contended that Ting Ling and Feng were plotting against the regime in alliance with the Chang Po-chün and Lo Lung-chi group of non-Communist intellectuals. This contention was based on the unsubstantial evidence that several reporters from the non-Communist newspaper *Wen-hui pao* had had some contacts with Ting Ling and her friends. Actually, there appears to have been little direct connection between these two groups.

Another way in which the party tried to prove the conspiratorial nature of Ting Ling's group was to point out its similarity to the Petofi Club, which had helped to initiate the revolt in Hungary. As Mao Tse-tung had stated in his speech of February 27, 1957, the Hungarian incident had unnerved many Chinese intellectuals. Through attacking Ting Ling and her associates, the party sought to condemn further the happenings in Hungary. Various statements were quoted out of context as proof of Feng Hsüeh-feng's sympathy for the Hungarian rebels. After the denunciation of Stalin and the end of the Hungarian uprising, Feng Hsüeh-feng was reported to have said that "Mankind has no hope" and that "The flood will break the dikes." [60] In addition, the party insisted that Ting Ling and other rightists had been profoundly influenced by Howard Fast's withdrawal from the Communist party after the suppression of the Hungarian rebellion and sought to do likewise. However, even if Ting Ling and Feng had been impressed by the events in Hungary and Fast's actions, the party did not present any concrete evidence that they had attempted to recreate a Hungarian-like incident in China or follow Fast's example.

Besides all these charges, Ting Ling's past activities which hitherto had gone unnoticed were now called traitorous. She was accused of betraying the party when under arrest in 1933. Feng was charged with collaborating with Hu Feng in his antiparty activities in the 1950's. Again, there was little evidence. In the 1950's, there had been hardly any communication between Hu Feng and Feng Hsüeh-feng or Ting Ling.

Therefore, while it was true, as the party claimed, that Ting Ling and her associates were guilty of independent thoughts, it did not follow that such thoughts had led them to antiparty activity. Likewise, while it was true that Ting Ling sought to undermine the leadership of the Writers' Union and even the Propaganda Bureau, this did not mean she sought to overthrow the political leadership. The major "crime" of Ting Ling and her associates was that they were a closely-knit group of friends who had been in personal conflict with Chou Yang and his supporters for many years and that they advocated a viewpoint that refused to conform to the party's. Their loyal following among a small but influential group of writers and intellectuals was another aspect of their "crime." The fact that their influence did not derive from the party and that they were an alternative focus of leadership particularly disturbed the party. Though, as we have shown, Ting Ling did not engage in any treasonable acts, still her efforts to dislodge the leadership in the cultural sphere loyal to the party and replace it by a group less willing to carry out the party's dictates would ultimately have undermined the party leadership.

Results of the Attack on Ting Ling and Her Associates

As in the Hu Feng case, it appears that the party had some difficulty foisting their picture of Ting Ling and her group as counterrevolutionary onto the intellectual community, especially the youth. Because of the wide appeal that Ting Ling's works had among the reading public and because the party's previous accusations against Hu Feng had been openly denounced as false, the party apparently encountered even firmer resistance to its efforts to imprint its extreme image of Ting Ling. Many frankly admitted that when they first read of the revelations about Ting Ling and her friends, they did not believe them. They asked, "How could such famous, respected artists do such things?" [61]

While the meetings against Ting Ling and her friends were in progress, party leaders such as Shao Ch'üan-lin frequently complained that "The struggle against the rightists in the literary and art circles is not developing sufficiently." [62] In fact, Hsiao Yeh-mu, now a redeemed rightist, claimed it had hardly developed at all. While expressing satisfaction that nonliterary circles were obeying party orders, he chastised his fellow writers for not following their example. He complained that "The antirightist struggle has already been carried on for over a month, but the literary and art world is still silent." [63] The party was especially irritated with those people who insisted, as did Ting Ling herself, that her conflict with party leaders was personal and did not have any subversive intent. Even on the last days of the meetings, when most of Ting Ling's group had presented some form of self-criticism, Kuo Mo-jo still found it necessary to exhort the participants: "We must understand that the counterattack against rightists should not have the slightest degree of sentimentalism." [64] At the same time a *JMJP* editorial of September 11, 1957, complained that many party members were reluctant to classify people as rightists and were particularly sympathetic with the veteran party members who were called rightists. After the meetings ended, this feeling of disbelief among the intellectuals and, even more significant, among party members, evidently continued.

Finally, in the beginning of 1958, the party made new moves in its effort to convince the literate public of the guilt of the revolutionary writers. The *tsa wen* that these writers had published in Yenan during the first cheng feng movement along with Mao's "Talks" were reprinted in the major literary and cultural journals. They were accompanied by voluminous pages of interpretation written by the literary bureaucrats. The whole issue of the February 1958 *Wen-i pao* was devoted to these essays. Some of the comments on Ting Ling's essay "Thoughts on March 8" in *Peiching wen-i* (Peking literature) were typical. The author claimed that Ting Ling's advice to women to use their own brains and stand by their own principles showed that "The rightist doctrine of 'independent thought' and 'daring to buck the tide' . . . originated with . . . Ting Ling sixteen years ago." [65] The publication of these articles was followed by the convening of forums in large cities to study and criticize them. At these sessions, comrades who had participated in the 1942 Yenan literary forum once more refuted the arguments of the revolutionary writers.

The primary purpose was to re-educate the youth who had never read these essays and still had a sentimental attachment to Ting Ling and her associates. Several of the confessions that filled the journals and newspapers at this time revealed the reluctance of the youth to accept the image of Ting Ling created by the party. A young writer wrote, "Previously, I worshipped Ting Ling and Ai Ch'ing as idols and considered them China's first-rate writers and poets of international fame. I regarded them as my mentors and example." When they were criticized, he wondered how "these old party members and party writers could be this way. I still sympathized with them and believed the charges against them were excessive." He also admitted that he had reread the stories of Ting Ling that had been criticized, but "I could not clearly see their poisonous points and in some areas, I thought she had written correctly." Finally, he added that only after having read the commentaries on the essays written in Yenan did he suddenly realize that "Although these people merely used their pens, they are far more insidious and frightening than enemies with guns." [66] By the conclusion of these forums on Ting Ling and her colleagues, reference to those who refused to call them rightists and antiparty elements had virtually disappeared from the press.

The Campaign Against Other Dissident Writers

The young writers who had bloomed so blatantly during the Hundred Flowers movement were treated less harshly than their quieter, senior brethren. Several sessions were also held against them in the summer of 1957, but the focus at first was on Ting Ling and her associates rather than on them. Moreover, they were found to be ideologically mistaken, but were not directly charged with counterrevolutionary activities. Lu Ting-i, in his concluding speech against Ting Ling on September 17, presaged the offensive against these younger writers when he stated, "In this struggle we can see that new intellectuals with bourgeois ideology may be produced even in a socialist society." [67]

From this group, Liu Shao-t'ang became the prime example of rightist thinking among the younger generation. He was used as a symbol in the re-education of younger writers in the same manner that Ting Ling and Feng Hsüeh-feng had been used to reeducate party members, writers, and intellectuals in general. Why he, of all the younger critical writers, should have been chosen is primarily a matter of speculation. Unlike the older generation, he had no record of conflict with the followers of Chou Yang. However, from the evidence the party presented, it seems that he, like the revolutionary writers, had captured the imagination of the youth. Of the younger writers, his works had been the most direct in its criticism. Spontaneous literary groups and semiautonomous literary magazines that arose used his article "Development of Realism in a Socialist Period" as its ideological base. Moreover, Liu put up a greater resistance than the other younger writers to presenting a "proper" self-criticism. His confession of August 3 was, in fact, another condemnation of the party's policies, rather than a surrender to them. Supposedly, he wrote that "If the author is a peasant or worker in origin or has a higher political cultivation, he will be spotted and loved immediately by the leadership; he will be introduced in many newspapers and journals and will make his name quickly." But, he declared, the way to produce better literature and art "is much more tortuous." [68]

Consequently, as soon as the meetings against Ting Ling and Feng had ended, the party, through the sponsorship of the Propaganda Department of the Communist Youth League, the young writers' committee of the Writers' Union and *Chung-kuo ch'ing-nien*, convened a series of discussions specifically on Liu in the beginning of October 1957. The discussions lasted for several days and were attended by more than a thousand youth. Among the speakers were the party's leading literary bureaucrats. Particularly vocal was Li Hsi-fan. Since his denunciation of Yü P'ing-po, he had assumed Chou Yang's role as the upholder of the party line among the younger generation. He is an example of how active participation in cheng feng movements was a path to upward mobility in the party.

The question was continually asked, why was it that during the Hundred Flowers movement youth brought up completely under the Communist system should become rightists? Throughout the fall of 1957, the party sought to provide the answers to this question in order that other youths could learn from them. In trying to supply the "correct" answers, party officials traced Liu's development into a rightist writer and inadvertently revealed some of the actual reasons a student such as he, educated entirely by the party, had come to question some of its principles. Liu's development showed increasing preoccupation with his own profession, that is with writing, and with Soviet and foreign culture.

As noted earlier, when Liu first began to write, his subject matter had been the good, hardworking peasant in the village, in line with the party's concept of socialist realism. The epilogue to his first book of stories, written at the age of eighteen, was filled with enthusiasm for the party. He wrote, "I hope these stories will reflect the happy life and lovable people of our Motherland. The Party has educated me . . . and opened my eyes to see the essence of things and an even more beautiful and better future. I am a young man directly nourished by the party and if I have any small achievement, they are all due to the efforts of the party." [69]

His next collection of short stories revealed that writing itself was becoming more and more important to him. He remarked, "I am now writing and will never stop." [70] The epilogue to a collection written around 1955 showed that his interest in writing was overshadowing his concern with party demands. "With the addition of years and of experience, I have gradually become dissatisfied with my own work and feel that the most fatal weakness of my writing is its deficiency in depicting reality . . . At present, I am thinking deeply about creative work; I wish to search for something and chase after something, but I still have not found my way. Nevertheless, I want to make demands of myself: I will reflect life more truthfully and my style will have more native [local] color." [71] In his letters to his publishers, Liu revealed more of his inner thinking. In one written in May 1957, at the height of the Hundred Flowers movement, Liu explained his "search" more specifically. "With a concern for artistic skill, I will study several classics. If I still have the strength I also hope to write essays on my research and study, but the object of all this is not to write essays, but to open up new horizons." [72]

Apparently, Liu was also influenced by the debates on literature going on in the Soviet Union. Some of the questions that were troubling Soviet and East European writers also disturbed him. The party acknowledged that the unorthodox views of writers and critics in the rest of the Communist world "had considerable support among writers, though Liu was the only one to write them down." [73] In fact, some of his remarks on Soviet literature sounded like an echo of the protests being made by the younger writers in Moscow. Like them, he too rejected the Stalinist interpretation of socialist realism and demanded the depiction of the truth. In his "The Development of Realism in the Socialist Period," he wrote that "The Soviet experience showed that when Stalin did not make mistakes and when subjective dogmatism did not have sway over creative writing, great literature was produced, such as Sholokhov's *Quiet Flows the Don* and *Virgin Soil* . . . But afterwards, when only the reflection of the excellence of socialism and service to abstract political propaganda were permitted, writers were not loyal to life and did not look truthfully at the internal conflicts of the people. The result was that literary works began to decorate life. The later twenty years [of Soviet literature] could not compare with the former." [74] For the same reasons, Liu believed works produced in China before 1942 were far better than those produced after.

Other outside influences also affected him. On October 25, 1956, at the time he began to formulate the ideas expressed in "The Development of Realism in the Socialist Period," he wrote to his publisher, "In the last year, I have felt the influence of Indian, Italian and French stories and films. They have opened my eyes to an artistic world and have aroused in me the desire to search for the truth of life, its romantic flavor and its infinite beauty." [75] Instead of being concerned about acquiring the "correct" ideology, Liu was preoccupied in the mid-1950's with reading more literature and developing literary techniques.

He was particularly interested in describing his life in the village from a different perspective than he had done in the early 1950's. In another letter to his publishers in May 1957 he wrote, "I wish to write of my home and of my landlord relatives . . . Perhaps I can develop new horizons for myself." [76] He wanted to describe more personal, individual events. The writer he sought to emulate was the Russian novelist Sholokhov, whose works were not restricted by socialist realist content and style. Liu admired Sholokhov's characters because they were living people concerned with moral problems and exhibiting cruelty as well as nobility in their daily lives. Sholokhov's depiction of Gregor, a Cossack landowner, as the hero of *Quiet Flows the Don* made an especially deep impression on him. Liu wrote of him, "Is Gregor a positive or negative person? It is said he represents the individual tragedy of a small, peasant landowner. Then why is it that he stands in people's eyes as a noble, brave rebel? Why is it that people do not hate him, but sympathize with him?" [77] Since the party at this juncture wanted to cooperate with the Soviet Union, it blamed the changes in Liu's thinking on bourgeois international thought. It did not yet refer directly to the influence of Soviet revisionism. However, it is likely that the beginning of the party's concern with the disruptive influence of Soviet culture on Chinese youth must have dated from its experience with students like Liu.

The party insisted that, as with the revolutionary writers, the acclaim of others was another reason for Liu's increasing estrangement from the party and the people. It declared that "After he wrote works which were well received, he gradually became conceited, refused the party's advice and ideological reform, and hated to study Marxism-Leninism." [78] In 1954 he was in the Chinese literature department at Peking University, but he left before the first year was up because, the party claimed, he believed that the political classes and organized life in the university were hindering his creative work. The party had then asked him to return to his village, but instead, it complained, he preferred "the slothful life of the city." [79] He was accused of bohemianism, extravagance, and licentiousness. These kinds of denunciations sounded like the ones concurrently leveled against the poet Yevtushenko by the Soviet bureaucrats. When in 1955 Liu did go to the countryside for a short time, the party declared that he went only to escape party supervision. The village party unit invited him to meetings, but he made excuses not to attend. Worst of all, the party declared, he failed to make contact with peasants and stayed in his own room all day. Using its standard ideological explanation, the party pointed to Liu's landlord background as also responsible for his nonconformity. As with all the rightists, another reason was said to be the influence of Hu Feng. The party could not prove any connection, however, between him and Hu Feng.

Finally, as with Ting Ling and her group, what appears to have most disturbed the party was that Liu had diverted the students' loyalty from the party to himself. Gathering followers around him, he had challenged the party-organized groups. The party accused him of forming a small clique of young writers which he called the Peking School. Supposedly, this school had also planned, like Feng Hsüeh-feng's group, to establish its own journal. The party complained that Liu wielded so much power because of his following that the editorial boards of journals and publishing houses were uncritical of his manuscripts and the organizations to which he belonged did not discipline him.

The man who appears to have had a greater impact on Liu than any of the older revolutionary writers was Ch'in Ch'ao-yang. Yet, for some reason, Ch'in received less attention. Perhaps this may have been because Ch'in had been accused so harshly during the suspension of the Hundred Flowers movement from January to March 1957. Though he was not denounced now as loudly as Liu, he was nevertheless criticized. Like Liu, Ch'in's opposition to some of the party policies was attributed to the fact that he had not been thoroughly reformed. Apparently, Ch'in had been disciplined even before 1957. Once during the land reform of 1947, he was punished because he had not carried out the tasks assigned to him by the party. At another time, because of a story he had written, "Reform," he had been sent to the countryside where he then wrote short vignettes of peasant life and was pardoned. Nevertheless, the party admitted that despite its efforts to "educate" him, his writings in 1956 proved that they had had no effect.

The main criticism of Ch'in, however, was not so much against what he wrote as against his policies as an editor. Though the meetings against him began in November 1957, after those against Liu Shao-t'ang, actually, it was not until 1958 that a large number of articles appeared against him. There may have been a delay so that the criticism of him would coincide more closely with the intensified drive to reform the editorial boards of the journals and newspapers launched at the end of 1957 and beginning of 1958. One of the party's first moves in its drive to re-establish tight control over its journals was to reduce the number. Another was to demonstrate that Ch'in was the kind of editor the party intended to eliminate. Though *Jen-min wen-hsüeh* was an organ of the Writers' Union and of the party, the party complained that Ch'in had resisted any party supervision. When the party had asked him to employ a larger number of writers from the peasants and workers, Ch'in had objected for fear that the standards of the journal would be lowered. The party charged that Ch'in preferred "bourgeois" writers who exposed the gloomy side of life and exaggerated the shortcomings of the regime. The party particularly held Ch'in to blame for encouraging and publishing Liu Pin-yen's "Our Paper's Inside News." The story was condemned for spreading the "bourgeois" concept of newspaper work.

As more meetings were convened in January 1958 against Ch'in, he presented a self-criticism. Still, he, like the others, did not accept the charges against him without some resistance. When he had been criticized earlier during the Hundred Flowers movement, he had written letters of protest to the literary bureaucrats. In one to Shao Ch'üan-lin of May 31, 1957, he had accused the party bureaucrats once more of dogmatism, sectarianism, and subjectivism. At the meetings in 1958 Ch'in asserted that he had published controversial articles and stories in order to stimulate discussions as the party had directed during the Hundred Flowers movement. Therefore, he insisted, he had not diverged from the party and Marxism-Leninism. Apparently, his disciple Liu Pin-yen put up even stiffer resistance. In an essay, "Coolness," which had been suppressed, Liu Pin-yen had accused the leaders in cultural circles of a lack of human feeling and compared them to " 'chameleons' who in spring allowed the youth to oppose the bureaucracy and then in autumn called them antibureaucratic." [80]

A final series of meetings were held against Ch'in and his disciple, Liu Pin-yen in July 1958. The one against Ch'in was called by the Writers' Union and was attended by over a hundred writers, reporters, and editors in Peking. Among the speakers were Lin Mo-han, Liu Pai-yü, and Chang Kuang-nien, now the editor of *Wen-i pao*. Shao Ch'üan-lin, who by the end of the 1950's appears to have become second in command to Chou Yang, gave the final summary. Simultaneously, meetings were convened by *Chung-kuo ch'ing-nien* to criticize Liu Pin-yen's literary works, his reporting, and his relations with Lin Hsi-ling, the defender of Hu Feng. These meetings probably brought the final, correct confessions from these two writers because little was heard of them after this.

One of the charges against Ch'in had been that in editing Huang Ch'iu-yün's article, "We Must Not Shut Our Eyes Before the Hardships of the People," he had changed the content. With this shift in responsibility, Huang fared much better than his associates. As opposed to them, he was still addressed as "comrade." Perhaps one of the reasons the party had diverted some of the blame away from Huang was because he had come forth with an acceptable self-criticism at the very beginning of the antirightist movement without resorting as had his colleagues to various kinds of resistance. His confession, published in September 1957, denied that writers should expose and criticize the hidden evils in society, the point he had made most convincingly in his article. He ascribed his mistaken views to the fact that as the translator of Romain Rolland, he had come to look at people and situations the way Rolland did, from a humanist standpoint and from the viewpoint of critical realism rather than in terms of class and the class struggle. What was especially interesting in his self-criticism was that he, like Liu Shao-t'ang, admitted that his study of Sholokhov's works had led him away from the party's literary line. Sholokhov's sympathetic treatment of Gregor, Huang confessed, had "confused me and caused me to have a dualistic view of life." [81] As early as 1958, there appears to have been a concerted effort by the party to diminish the influence of Sholokhov's writings. Huang also acknowledged that his defense of certain rightists had been wrong. It will be remembered that he had vigorously defended Liu Shao-t'ang when he had first been attacked. After another self-criticism in November 1957, there was only incidental criticism of him at meetings and in the press.

Second Phase of the Antirightist Drive

By late 1957, the cycle in the literary field had come around full turn to the strict rigidity of 1955. Once again, the party attempted to reindoctrinate writers with the party line on literature similar to the one imposed during the Hu Feng campaign. Party leaders sought to reaffirm all the aspects of the party's literary policies which had been denounced during the Hundred Flowers movement. Hence, once more, stress was put on party leadership of culture, the political and class nature of literature, the party interpretation of socialist realism, the necessity of popularization, and the importance of Mao's Yenan "Talks." Again, politics and art were pronounced inseparable and talent was given no objective value in itself. Shao Ch'üan-lin in his concluding speech against Ting Ling had informed the writers that they are "party members first, not writers first." [82] Instead of the party's withdrawing from the literary realm as the writers had asked, it now planned to increase its authority still further.

As usual, Chou Yang made the final summary of the arguments against the rightist writers, called "The Great Debate on the Literary Front." In essence, this work was a condensation of the speeches and articles against Ting Ling, Feng Hsüeh-feng, and the younger writers. It was published in *Wen-i pao* on March 11, 1958, and, soon after, in all the major journals. Party officials described it as "The first assessment of the historical struggle between the Marxist line and the bourgeois line in the proletarian literary movement of the last thirty years." [83] In response to the criticisms of Mao's "Talks" during the Hundred Flowers movement, this work was an attempt to update Mao's doctrine. Actually, Chou's literary theorizing added little to Mao's, except that the examples he presented to prove Mao's points were of more recent vintage. Although it was implicit in Mao's "Talks" that every writer should ultimately follow the party line, because his "Talks" were written in the period of the United Front, Mao found it expedient then to declare that every writer cannot be expected to have a similar stand. Chou Yang, writing in the period when the party had complete control, now demanded that all intellectuals have only a working-class stand.

"The Great Debate on the Literary Front" served a purpose similar to Mao's "Talks" in Yenan in 1942. After it was published, writers, artists, journalists, and all those involved in related intellectual endeavors gathered in study groups to discuss and write essays. This work of Chou Yang's, along with the usual cheng feng documents and the material on Hu Feng, were used as a basis for the criticism and self-criticism sessions. The party's crusade was carried out even more zealously than in the Hu Feng campaign. It was not just against a small group of dissident writers, but against critics in nearly all party organs and in all sections of the land.

In another important way, the antirightist campaign went beyond the scope of the Hu Feng drive. As the weight of the movement shifted from its negative to positive purpose, it elevated to a greater degree than in the previous remolding movements the importance of the culture of the masses and of the collective. Correspondingly the campaign belittled the work and the prestige of the intellectual and of the individual. Again, Ting Ling and her associates became the party's take-off point for this facet of the campaign. Referring to this group, Lu Ting-i asserted that it may be possible to foster intellectuals from the middle class, "but among bourgeois intellectuals, there is a group which is very difficult to reform. Some even unto death are not willing to reform . . . Some have joined the party, but even though they have gone through Communist education for a long time, they cannot reform themselves." [84] Hence, as opposed to earlier claims, the party now declared that not all the bourgeoisie can be transformed into the proletariat and that some intellectuals would remain irredeemably bourgeois.

Of all the segments of the population, the intellectuals were now regarded as the most untrustworthy. As stated in *KMJP*, "During the Hundred Flowers movement there were more rightists among the intellectuals than among the private businessmen; they were more violent and could argue more plausibly." [85] Among the intellectuals, of course, the most suspect were the writers. Lu Ting-i, in that same concluding speech against Ting Ling, maintained that "The occupation of a writer is honorable, but dangerous, because the mode of labor of a writer is that of a handicraft man, which tends to encourage individuality and liberalism." Furthermore, Lu continued, "A writer has many chances of winning fame and fame leads easily to arrogance and self-importance." [86] The remedies the party prescribed for the writer to rid himself of his suspicious nature, of course, would also rid him of his artistic nature.

As before, ideological remolding and political indoctrination sessions were carried out in the major cities and universities, but at the end of 1957 and in 1958, the main method of reform was through learning from the workers and peasants. Though the intellectuals had undergone continuous ideological reform for many years, the party claimed that their thinking was still "incorrect." Consequently, it insisted that they engage in the work of the common laborer. The study of Marxism-Leninism was now regarded as merely pretentious, when not accompanied by work in the countryside or factory. Chou Yang declared that "The main task now is in mixing the writers with the worker and peasant masses." [87] Writers were sent to the lowest echelons of the party in the countryside and factories. The Writers' Union adopted as its central task the dispatching of writers to do physical labor. Writing was to be put aside as writers went out to work for long periods, some for as long as from one to three years.

Along with the movement to the factories and villages, writers' fees were reduced still further. Their fees were considered to be too high in relation to the wages of workers and cadres. Therefore, the party sought to lessen this inequality. Publishers in Peking and Shanghai were reported to have reduced royalties by 50 per cent.[88] The party concluded that these measures would help transform writers into intellectuals of the working class. The aim apparently was to reduce everyone to a common denominator so that they would be easier to control. As Chou Yang stated, "Our ultimate goal . . . is to obliterate the boundary between mental labor and physical labor so that every one has culture and at the same time is a physical as well as mental laborer." [89]

With writers away undergoing labor reform and unable to carry out their official duties, party cadres took over their positions. The party transferred numbers of party members from high-level party and government organs to cultural and educational enterprises. *Wen-i pao* removed Ch'en Yung, Ai Ch'ing, Huang Yao-mien, and the well-known writer Hsiao Ch'ien, another critic of the regime, from the editorial board. Even *JMJP* was reorganized. This major shake-up in the party's cultural endeavors put the party cadres more firmly in control of the literary realm than ever before. Similar shake-ups occurred in other intellectual fields — in the social sciences and to a lesser degree in the natural sciences. In direct opposition to the pleas of the intellectuals during the Hundred Flowers movement, the party implemented the policy articulated by Kuo Mo-jo that "cultural work must be led by amateurs who have mastered Marxism-Leninism." [90]

Party leaders frankly admitted that the party cadres did not even have the modicum of knowledge necessary for their jobs. "To be leaders of professional people, the best thing is to have a high political level and fair academic level. But because of historical conditions, we have insufficient cadres who possess these two levels." [91] However, they optimistically believed that "Since they have the scientific basis of Marxism-Leninsm, . . . if they study diligently, they can learn." [92] The fact that under such circumstances, little or no writing would be produced, did not seem to disturb them. Chou Yang asserted that it was all right if writers did not write for a while as long as they absorbed material for creative work from the masses.[93] The antirightist movement widened the gap still further between the party and the intellectuals. Having once had their hopes aroused and then drastically shattered, the disillusionment of the intellectuals undoubtedly was more acute than ever before.

chapter ten

THE GREAT LEAP FORWARD
AND HO CH'I-FANG

The dispatch of intellectuals to factories and villages was not only to remold them through manual labor, but also to prepare the way for a new campaign to bring culture to the masses. This campaign was to accompany the party's mammoth production drive called the Great Leap Forward. The party's plan of ordered economic progress yielded in 1958 to a program envisaging rapid advances in industry and agriculture and the introduction of communes. In contrast to the Hundred Flowers movement, emphasis was on political reliability rather than professional skill. A new slogan was advanced which called on people in all walks of life — scientists, university professors, and professional people in particular — to become "Red and expert."

To a greater extent than ever before, the initiative and intelligence of the masses was accepted as articles of faith. Intelligence was now defined as political consciousness and was no longer considered the monopoly of a few. Peasants just emerging from illiteracy were praised as scientists, philosophers, and poets, and were held capable of almost any achievement. The party claimed that the peasants and workers were capable of great achievements because they approached all questions as proletarians. By contrast, the intellectuals were bound to fail because they were imbued with middle-class concepts of individualism, liberalism, and anarchism. As *KMJP* explained, the party wanted "to eliminate the concept of private ownership of knowledge" [1] and place knowledge in the hands of the collective mass.

The effect of this line was to make scholarship purely functional. All subjects were taught with production needs in mind. Academic study was coordinated with industrial practices. The importance of science and engineering grew still more, while the significance of the social sciences and humanities diminished further. Everything pertaining to schools, students, and teachers had to be produced in great quantities as fast as possible. As a result, academic standards were lowered. The five-year course in math, a basic subject for technical progress, was reduced to four years, and the study of scientific theory was slighted in order to concentrate on mastering technical skills. Even highly-specialized scientists and technicians were told to learn from the achievements of the ordinary peasant and worker. *Hung ch'i* (Red flag) which replaced *Hsüeh-hsi* as the party's main theoretical journal, directed these experts "to mingle with the masses and learn from them." [2]

The Great Leap Forward in Literature

A similar pattern was followed in harnessing literature to the GLF. Like others, writers were given plans to be fulfilled on schedule. There was no time to create slowly. One of China's most prolific writers, Pa Chin, who had produced little since the party's accession to power, pledged himself to write one long novel, three medium-length novels, and several translations in the course of a year. The Writers Union announced that in the year of the GLF it expected China's professional writers to produce thirty-eight full-length novels and seven hundred stories, plays, and poems. [3] All of them were to be easy to understand and were to reflect the kind of people and institutions the party sought to encourage. As enunciated by Chou Yang, "Writers have an obligation to provide timely reflections in all literary forms of the new heroes and new things." [4]

A development in the literary realm that occurred in other fields to a lesser extent was the projected increase not only in the number of works produced, but also in the number of participants. This was to be accomplished by incorporating thousands of loyal amateurs into the Writers Union. The distinction between professional writers and amateurs was obscured. Consequently, the number of "writers" jumped from 889 in 1957 to over 200,000 in 1958. [5] A nationwide drive of literary creation was launched. Meetings for amateur writers were held all over the country to encourage them in their endeavor. At one held May 28, 1958, these amateurs were informed that "The working class could be masters not only of politics and economics, but also . . . of literature and art." [6] At another meeting they were told that though they may have little education, they have an aptitude for writing. An editorial of *Jen-min wen-hsüeh* declared that "The time when literature and art were the possession of a minority is gone forever. It is time for the majority of workers to possess and to enjoy art." [7]

To these uneducated workers and peasants, the party proposed that they mass produce songs and poems in the old traditional styles. In line with the commune society it was building, the party advocated anonymous group creativity rather than individual literary achievement. What this meant in practice was that large meetings were convened throughout the land at which cadres suggested themes and ideas of poems to the assembled groups. The cadres would then write down the lines as the masses spoke them.[8] The party's intention was to manipulate the folk mentality and convert independent feelings into a collectivized consciousness. Hence, the party sought not only to control the physical activities, but also the mental processes of hundreds of thousands of people. Furthermore, by use of poetic and rhetorical verbiage, it sought to stimulate mass enthusiasm for an economic advance that was to be more rapid than at any time in its history. Finally, through the collective outpouring of feelings in mass poetry sessions, the emotional and physical strain of the GLF could be relieved. This purpose was explicitly stated by Shao Ch'üan-lin at a meeting of amateur poets: "For intellectuals, poetry writing is a tiring task, but your singing of songs is an act which relieves you of your exertions and increases your vigor." [9]

Poetry-writing by peasants had been used earlier as an effective means of organization, indoctrination, and mobilization of the masses, but never on such an intensive and widespread scale as in 1958. This movement reached unprecedented proportions. The mass production of spontaneous verse was stimulated by poetry contests held throughout the country. These poems and songs were broadcast over loudspeakers and pasted on walls. Shao Ch'üan-lin reported that in a village near Sian, there were plaques of homemade poems on the doors of all the houses. The creation of "millions of poems" was reported from working units in the same manner as production figures. The cultural official of Szechuan announced that his province had four million amateur writers who produced 78,450,000 literary works, most of them folk poems. Of these, 37,000 were considered worthy of publication.[10] Several literary journals competed in space devoted to workers' writings. *Jen-min wen-hsüeh*, China's foremost literary journal, gave itself over completely to publication of the songs of the workers and peasants. The ACFLAC made its central task the collecting, editing, and publicizing of folk literature. The major literary event of the year was the compilation of the best of these poems in the *Songs of the Red Flag*, edited by Chou Yang and Kuo Mo-jo. A representative example was one by an old worker:

> I am just sixty, but I can still work
> And I find it as easy as when I was young
> It's not that I am boasting of my strength
> But here in my heart I have Mao Tse-tung.[11]

As might be expected, Chou Yang had a leading role in the mass poetry movement. It exemplified his antiprofessional attitude. He published an article on the subject, "New Folk Songs Blaze a New Road in Poetry," in the first issue of *Hung ch'i*. This essay provided the theoretical framework for the movement and presented a supposedly new literary theory: "Literature should be the union of revolutionary realism with revolutionary romanticism." [12] Kuo Mo-jo was also active in promoting this new theory. Since his founding of the Creation Society, Kuo had embraced romanticism. He must have regarded the party's advocacy of romanticism as a personal triumph.

Though this theory was introduced as an original concept, in reality it was a restatement of the original Soviet concept of socialist realism. In fact, as early as 1934, Zhdanov had advocated revolutionary romanticism. He defined it as the projection of characters and events as they will exist in the ideal state of communism. By the late 1950's, however, Soviet writers had corrupted the original meaning of socialist realism. Their emphasis was more on the realism than on the socialism. Consequently, the party now attempted to reinvigorate the concept with its original meaning and at the same time disassociate it from its Soviet corruption by presenting it under a different name.

The introduction of the new formula was also a manifestation of Communist China's worsening relations with the Soviet Union and its inward withdrawal. The return to Soviet direction after the end of the Hundred Flowers movement in mid-1957 ended in 1958 with the launching of the GLF and the establishment of the communes. As with the communes, the party offered its new formula to demonstrate the superiority of the Chinese approach over the Russian. Kuo Mo-jo asserted that "the combination of revolutionary realism and revolutionary romanticism . . . is more perfect than socialist realism." [13] Chou Yang attributed this concept to Mao not only to enhance Mao's godlike image, but also to give it a uniquely Chinese origin. Incidentally, he also showed that he had finally reached the stage where he could speak directly for Mao instead of acting merely as his interpreter. The introduction of the theory of revolutionary realism and revolutionary romanticism was another effort to update Mao's "Talks" and answer the challenge to socialist realism presented during the Hundred Flowers movement. In 1942, Mao had proposed a similar combination of the real with the ideal, but had spoken of these ingredients in somewhat equal proportions. Now, the stress was on the ideal almost to the exclusion of the real. Chou contended that literature was not supposed to present a complete, true picture of reality. Instead of dealing with suffering and despair, literary works were to arouse enthusiasm and passion for the revolution. They were to capture in ordinary life the mystical élan of the future. In the party's view, the people's poems were best suited for this purpose.

Armed with this supposedly new dictum, party cadres encouraged the production of do-it-yourself poetry. As the amateur writers increasingly served the needs of the regime, the importance of the trained writer diminished more and more. The central figure in literature was no longer the writer who had mastered Communist ideology; it was now the worker-writer. Chou Yang had declared in a speech on August 29, 1958, that in the new epoch of the GLF, "the experience of the old writers can give us little help . . . Poems written by the masses are better than those written by the poets." [14] In fact, not only did the party's literary leaders consider the people's poems better, they considered them the main basis for Chinese poetry. The layman's quantitative output was exalted at the expense of the professional's qualitative product.

Ho Ch'i-fang after 1942

The writers in the Communist literary world who in the past had dared to express their concern about the lowering of artistic and professional standards were not heard from during the GLF. Most of them had been deported to work projects. At first there was virtually no resistance to the party's effort to depreciate the professional writer. Then, suddenly, in the middle of 1958, the last of the revolutionary writers from Yenan and the one who had most vociferously and loyally carried out the party's line since the 1942 cheng feng movement, Ho Ch'i-fang, stepped forth to protest the eclipse of literary standards. His protest was the counterpart in the cultural sphere to the economists' opposition to the party's extravagant production targets in the economic and scientific sphere.

For over fifteen years, Ho had been a trusted henchman of Chou Yang, a spokesman for the party's line in culture, and an active leader in its organizational work. How then can this sudden change be explained? A look at Ho's work after 1942 provides some answers. His writings, more than those of any of his former friends in Yenan, express the conflicting beliefs held by an individual who seeks to follow every twist and turn of party policy but still retains some appreciation for the inherent values of art. An example of his twisting can be seen in his interpretation of *Hung lou meng*. In 1951, his interpretation was close to that of Yü P'ing-po's. He wrote, "*Hung lou meng* . . . reveals the author's sincere nostalgia for some of the life of the feudal class." [15] But in 1954, in line with the party's efforts to reinterpret *Hung lou meng*, Ho, in direct opposition to his earlier comments, described *Hung lou meng* as a work that fought against the decadence and bankruptcy of feudal society. Also as we have seen, Ho was a prime mover in the periodic remolding campaigns against his fellow intellectuals and was one of the harshest critics of Hu Feng and Feng Hsüeh-feng. Yet, on several literary questions his views coincided with theirs. His fervent espousal of the party line and relentless attacks on these writers contrasted sharply with his unceasing concern with artistic values.

There was a hard core in Ho's thinking which appears not to have changed. This was his concern with poetry as a craft that must be consistently practiced and perfected. Unlike some of his associates in charge of the cheng feng movements, Ho, before he came under party rule, had been a prolific writer and had experimented with poetic forms. Most of his time after 1942 was spent in writing tracts to publicize the party's principles and in organizing cheng feng movements. Yet, his continued interest in poetic values was revealed in several ways. Perhaps the most personal was his distress over no longer being able to write poetry. In *On Realism*, a collection of essays written in the mid-1940's against Hu Feng's followers and Feng Hsüeh-feng, Ho asked himself why he had not written any poetry for so many years. He admitted in one of his essays that "After the Yenan meetings on art and literature, I was one of those who lagged behind in creativity." He explained that Mao's "Talks" had shown him that he did not have the right kind of material for creative writing. Obliged to write of the "heroes" of the period, he confessed that he could not because "I really knew too little about the workers, peasants, and soldiers, and their struggles." [16]

Having gone through repeated and supposedly successful thought reform, Ho, by the 1950's, could no longer blame his lack of creativity on his inability to abide by Mao's doctrine. Now, his justification most frequently was the pressure of organizational and party work. Consequently, in another collection of essays published in 1952 entitled *Hsi-yüan chi* (Hsi-yüan collection) he once again expressed despair at his inability to write poetry, but this time blamed the considerable time spent in party activities and constant exposition of the party line. In his introduction, dated January 19, 1952, he explained that he had presented the party literary line in *On Realism* in the expectation that "After I had published my views in this way, . . . I could devote my leisure time to creative work. But events ran counter to my wishes. For the past two or three years, I am still writing essentially the same kind of discussion of art." [17]

At this point, Ho was not only disturbed by his inability to write poetry, he was even dissatisfied with these essays. He complained that they lacked individual viewpoint and were not derived from his own inspiration. He wrote, "In my view, a person who genuinely devotes himself to theoretical criticism, should, like the creative writer who writes poetry, novels, and plays, write with a feeling of joy; but my essays do not have any independent creative views and, moreover, are not essays of beauty." This latter point concerned him particularly. Distressed by the lack of time to perfect his craft, he stated, "When I write, I only extend my efforts to speak comparatively clearly and correctly; consequently, in most of my essays, after I have finished writing I lose interest in them . . . Furthermore, many of them were written in haste; the time for fermentation and enrichment was insufficient." In conclusion, he expressed the same yearnings to write creatively as expressed in Ting Ling's essays in the early 1950's. "I wish to stop publishing discussions temporarily and arrange my time to do a bit of creative work . . . Now I have much hope to write some works which have fervent feelings and ideas and which I can offer to the readers without shame." [18]

Yet, as the first half of the 1950's went by, Ho was still turning out literary discussions prescribed by the party. In a long essay written in 1953, "On Writing and Reading Poetry," and in another collection published in 1956 under the same title as the essay, he was still lamenting the fact that his official duties had led him further and further away from creativity. He wrote in the essay, "Sometimes from observations of life and from newspapers, I grasp some feelings and wish to express them in poetry. But I am so busy that I do not have time to let them ferment and cannot elevate and enrich them. I cannot even take up a pen to write down these feelings." [19] In the collection, he added another misgiving, that he did not even have time to give proper attention to the reading of literature.

Ho also was sensitive to the fact that he was directing others in a craft which he himself was not practicing. This was in contrast to some of his colleagues. Chou Yang and Shao Ch'üan-lin, who had never been poets nor serious students of poetry, had no qualms about giving advice in this area. But Ho rhetorically asked, "What can a person who is unable to study deeply and to create contribute to students who write poetry?" [20] In Ho's view, those who direct literature should write it. To those writers, including himself, who gave forth with authoritative literary theories and criticisms, he advised, "They still should use their creative works to prove their theories and use their literary works as a form of criticism of the works with which they disagree." [21] His concept of leadership in the cultural realm opposed the party's practice of putting organization men in charge of academic and creative endeavors.

There was only one area in which Ho blamed the defects in literature directly on party policies rather than on the pressures of party work. This was in the party's effort to impose political demands on the techniques of writing poetry. As a poet, Ho was disturbed by the party's insistence that all poets must write in styles familiar to the ordinary peasants. After Ho participated in the cheng feng movement of 1942, he had intellectually accepted the party's dictum that poetry should be written in national forms, but he himself seemed unable to express himself in these forms. In October 1944 he wrote, "Europeanized poetic forms will not be accepted by the broad reader, but I still cannot find another substitute for them." [22]

The party authorities sought to help him in his dilemma. It suggested that he write specifically in the traditional meter of the old folk song, 5 or 7 characters to each line. The party was to prescribe this form as the main pattern for poetry during the GLF. This meter gave poetry a definite regularity, especially in tone pattern, in the number of syllables per line, and in the rhyme scheme. Through the use of this meter, which the masses readily enjoyed, the party believed it would have a powerful instrument of propaganda at its command that would have a deeper impact on the masses than its own wordy directives. In looking back over his efforts to write with 5/7 characters to each line, Ho observed, "I experimented with it, but when I wrote, I felt unnatural . . . Of course, I was dissatisfied." [23]

From this time on, Ho carried on his own individual campaign against forcing writers to use the 5/7 character line. His reasons for rejecting this style, at first sight, seem to have been merely technical. He believed that this meter, which was based on the old classical language, was unsuitable to the construction of China's modern language. The 5/7 character line, Ho declared, "was established essentially on the foundation of the literary language which took one character as a unit; the basis of our present-day language of poetry takes the oral language of 2 characters or more as a unit." [24]

However, Ho opposed the 5/7 syllable line not just because the spoken language had to be twisted and turned to conform to its structure. Even more significant, he opposed it because he believed that "to reflect the rich, new social life and complicated struggle of the masses, the 5/7 character line is inappropriate." [25] In Ho's view, a new way of life requires new forms, new language, and new syntax. Moreover, whereas in the old language, an idea could be expressed by using only 7 characters, in the modern language of 2 characters to a word, it was impossible to set forth a thought with just two or three words in a line. Such a technique limited poetry to jingly, slogan-like verses rather than to the reflection of the complicated, modern life. In effect, therefore, Ho's opposition to the party's stress on the 5/7 character line was because it changed poetry from an art form into an instrument of propaganda.

He also protested against the imposition of a specific meter on poets, because he feared that one national form would stunt the development of individual talent. Paradoxically, Ho's ideas on poetic style resembled those of the very victims against whom he helped to organize campaigns, another illustration of the contradictory nature of his thinking. At the same time that Ho was worrying about the dilution of poetry, Feng Hsüeh-feng expressed similar sentiments using virtually the same words. Feng wrote, "We . . . should not revive the old Chinese poetry of 5 and 7 characters to a line. Only on the basis of the living, rich language of the Chinese people do we have the possibility of establishing new poetic rules." [26]

After 1942, Ho often talked disparagingly of some of the poetry of the May Fourth movement. Following the party line, he claimed that it reflected the ideas and feelings of middle-class intellectuals. Nevertheless, he never condemned the May Fourth tradition outright as many of the party's literary officials did and, in fact, defended the modernization of Chinese literature. He declared that "Some people only respect the tradition of old poetry and forget that new poetry since the May Fourth movement also has a tradition of its own." [27] In his view, poetry should not be written just so it could be appreciated by the masses. "Actually, present-day China has different reading masses, different writers, and different traditions; the forms of the new poetry cannot be very quickly merged into one." [28] Concomitantly, he questioned why literature should be brought down to the level of the masses and suggested instead that the effort be made to lift their cultural standard. He asserted that "The cultural level of the masses can be gradually elevated; we cannot say that they cannot accept new poetic forms." [29]

In urging writers to use various styles, he refrained from favoring any one kind "because down to the present, I cannot through my own work prove whether my views are correct or not." [30] He suggested that the choice should come naturally from the individual author himself. He only requested that they experiment with new techniques: "A genuine artist should be very self-conscious, absorb the rich material of all kinds of literary inheritance, and yet break down the limitation of this literary inheritance." [31] He, like Feng Hsüeh-feng, looked to the great poets as examples to be followed. Although the 5/7 character line was predominant in the T'ang period, he declared that "the greatest poets of the T'ang, Li Po and Tu Fu, often broke through the constrictions of the 5/7 line poems." [32] To create new poetic forms, he urged Chinese poets not only to look toward their own cultural inheritance for inspiration, but to the poetic forms of other countries. He urged them to study foreign languages so they could learn from the literature of other cultures. He particularly urged them to study the poetry of the Soviet poet, Mayakovsky. In Ho's view, a poet "should have knowledge of all kinds of literature and all forms of poetry." [33] This demand was certainly at variance with the orthodox approach of the literary officials, which was to shun any experimentation or innovation, not only because it would not appeal to the masses, but because it would be disruptive to the party's control.

Though Ho advocated experimentation in technique, he did not talk of innovation in subject matter. It could be argued that experimentation in form inevitably leads to changes in subject matter, but Ho never conceded this point. On the contrary, he loudly asserted that the content of poetry should only express the party line: "I still uphold my opinion . . . that the forms of literature can be many, but the content and object can only be one; that is, the material of literature can be taken only from the [lives of the] people." [34]

Related to Ho's resistance to the limitations of the 5/7 character line was his desire to see Communist China produce a brilliant period of poetry. This was also the desire of his former colleagues Hu Feng and Ting Ling. But, whereas they attributed the sterility of Communist China's literature to the restrictions of ideology, he blamed it on lack of concern for literary techniques. He did not take the next logical step — that disregard for artistic values might stem from the imposition of a political ideology. Nevertheless, he did stress that while "A high degree of ideology is very important in writing poetry . . . it is not, however, equal to the preparation and conditions involved in writing poetry. There still must be artistic and poetic nourishment." [35]

"The preparation and conditions" that Ho referred to were years of study of the literature of all ages and all nations and diligent, consistent work. He pointed to Pushkin's revision of a poem ten times and Tolstoy's six years on *War and Peace* as examples of the kind of work he meant. Ho, like Ai Ch'ing and Feng Hsüeh-feng, wanted recognition of the fact that poetry was not a little ditty that a miner might compose while he was digging for coal or a farmer might rhyme while out in the field. In his view, "writing poetry is a special kind of work and is an unusually delicate, painstaking activity. Without definite preparation and attention what is produced is not appropriate to the rules of poetry and cannot strictly be called poetry at all." [36]

Consequently, he was concerned with the quality of literature as opposed to the quantity, another emphasis that differed from that of his fellow bureaucrats. Right after the establishment of the regime, he criticized the shoddy work that was being published by some of China's writers. He quoted the remarks made by Yü P'ing-po after the May Fourth movement because he believed them appropriate in 1950: "We cannot recklessly send poetry to newspapers for publication. I feel that restricting the number of poems can protect the 'name' of *pai-hua* poetry." [37] So, too, Ho was anxious to protect the name of poetry. "The positive method is certainly to write better poetry, but if we actually cannot write good poetry, this negative method can be adopted." [38] Perhaps this was one of the reasons he himself remained silent. He wrote, "Because I am so serious about poetry, I do not wish to corrupt its name." [39]

His stress on quality was related to his concept of poetry. Of all the artistic forms, Ho believed that poetry was most concerned with feeling. He wrote in 1953, "The novel and the play express the writer's ideas and emotions indirectly through characters; this is not like poetry, which usually expresses emotion directly." [40] Yet, he was strongly against the methods later used in the GLF of having people merely pour out their feelings onto paper. In his view, these emotions must be controlled by clear-cut rules relating to meter, rhythm, stanza, and metaphor. Moreover, poetry must have "beauty, richness of images, discipline of language, harmony and proper tone." [41] Unless poets developed these skills, in Ho's view, their writings could not be considered poetry.

To learn these poetic techniques required time, education, and culture, qualities the ordinary working man did not have. He was not against workers becoming poets, but was against their becoming poets while remaining workers. The implication of his view, though he never expressed it explicitly, was that poetry could only be the preserve of the professional writer. He beckoned all writers, himself included, "to elevate our general literature and poetic cultivation and accumulate writing experience. There are no short cuts, only to read much and to write much." [42] How Ho and his fellow writers who were constantly engaged in thought remolding drives and organizational work were to carry on these scholarly activities that Ho demanded was a question he never attempted to resolve.

He published new poetry only once during the whole period in which he acted as a spokesman for the party. This occasion was the publication of three poems in *Jen-min wen-hsüeh* in October 1954. These poems had been written during the brief respite of 1953 and early 1954. They appeared as an effort to exemplify the high standards he had set for poetry and did not conform in any way to the party's ideological strictures he was imposing on other writers. Just before Ho had written these poems, he stated that he had finally discovered the poetic style he had been searching for since he had rejected the form of free verse in 1942. He wrote, "Only in the last year or so have I had fairly definite ideas [on poetic form]; because of this, I wish very much to write poetry again according to these ideas." [43]

The longest of these poems, "Reply," is impressive even by Western standards. The rhythms in this poem are carefully measured and the language is melodious. Yet, Ho goes beyond just presenting a well-constructed, smoothly-phrased poem. Though it speaks of "My great fatherland, the great era of Mao Tse-tung," [44] it is almost devoid of ideological content; instead, it is a highly personal work, filled with the suffering of an intellectual who was no longer able to work at his craft. It connotes somewhat the same melancholy suggested in his "How Many Times I Have Left My Everyday Life" published just before the promulgation of Mao's "Talks." "Reply" is an ambiguous poem which can be variously interpreted. Perhaps this was Ho's intention.

The title, "Reply," supposedly signifies that this is Ho's response to the party officials, who since 1942 had persistently asked why he had stopped writing. His first stanzas are especially ambiguous:

> A strange wind blows from somewhere
> And makes the canvas of my ship tremble incessantly.
> My heart is thumping now
> It feels sweet but also a little bit afraid.
>
> Please blow a little softer and allow me to
>   sail bravely
> In my own river with your help.
> Do not blow so violently that my mast will
>   break
> And that I will lose my direction in the
>   waves.

What is the "strange wind"? Could it be the imposition of a political doctrine on his poetry, enforced "so violently" that he had lost his capacity to express himself?

The next stanza begins with two more rather mysterious lines:

> Here is one single word which is burning
>   like fire,
> But I let it become silent on my lips.

From the next two lines, it would appear that his burning word had been silenced by the restrictions of dogma:

> Here is a feeling as deep as the ocean
> But it is so narrow-minded and so fault-
>   finding.

Though in his forties, Ho, several phrases later, reflects the depression of old age and the coming of death, certainly not acceptable themes for Chinese Communist poetry. He expresses the dissatisfaction of a man who sees himself growing older without having created anything he himself considers worthwhile.

> The days have fallen beside me
> As numerous as leaves.
> But why are the fruits that I have given
> > birth to so few.
> Could it be that I am a barren tree?

After acknowledging the sterility of his own creativity, he laments the lack of vitality in present-day Chinese literature, particularly its inability to produce any great works of art. He is able to reflect the cultural stagnation with merely a few sharp images:

> How many heroes we have blooming like flowers
> > in the spring,
> We ought to compose immortal poems to praise
> > them.
> To have their names pass down for thousands
> > and thousands of years.
> Yet our songs today are so feeble and lost.
> Where can we find the minstrel of the ancient
> > ballads?
> The voice of her singing when she finishes
> Still lingered continuously for days along the
> > rafters.

The next few stanzas talk of his love of the countryside:

> I love the small villages hidden in the woods
> And the sound of the turning of the wheels, of a
> > small cart during the harvest season,
> And the low humming of the bellows in the peasant
> > home.

He also describes his love for the large expanse and variety of his nation:

> How broad is the span of my fatherland.
> When it is snowing in Peking, the ragflower
> > is blooming in Canton.
> I wish to walk all over the nation,
> Not caring which piece of land my head
> > will use as a pillow.

He then returns to the party's constant question: Why, if he has such feelings, does he not express them in verse?

> Then why are you so silent?
> Don't you think that for the sake of our young
> Republic,
> You should soar and sing like a bird
> Until you have sung out completely the blood in
> your breast?

When Ho answers this time, he no longer pleads the incapacities of old age or overwork, but instead uses metaphors that can lead to contradictory interpretations. They reveal a sense of frustration and distress at being unable to do either what he himself wants to do or what the party expects of him:

> My wings are so heavy,
> As if mud and dirt or some kind of grief have
> Loaded me down so I can only walk on the earth.
> But I also want to exert my best efforts to
> fly up to the sky.

What is this "mud and dirt"? Is it the weight of his "bourgeois" values that have rendered him unable to rise up to the party demands, or is it the suppression of his own individual feelings that has made it impossible for him to practice his craft and reach for excellence? It could be both, but in the earlier stanzas Ho implies that the "mud and dirt" were thrown on him by the party rather than by himself.

Such a poem, even by one of the party's most devoted and trusted representatives, could not go unnoticed. Hence, at the height of the Hu Feng campaign in which Ho himself took such an active part, he was criticized in the major literary journals. The editors of *Wen-i pao* and *Jen-min wen-hsüeh* claimed that they had received a great many criticisms of "Reply." Two of them were published in *Jen-min wen-hsüeh*. One was by Sheng Ch'üan-sheng, a high school teacher, and another by Yeh Kao, an educational worker. The attention given to the laymen's opinion was obviously to underline the party's antiprofessional, ideological view of literature. Both articles grudgingly admired Ho's poetic style, particularly his care with the construction of the verses and with the smoothness of his rhythm. However, as Sheng Ch'üan-sheng wrote, "Because the feelings of the poem are unhealthy, are inconsistent with the beauty of our age, and are obscure and hard to understand, all the structural beauty and rhythmic beauty are of secondary importance." [45]

This was the main line of criticism. The unhealthy feelings he referred to, of course, were the sense of sadness, depression, and personal dissatisfaction pervading the poem. Yeh Kao stated the party's view of such feelings. "The reader expected the poet to sing as a bird; however, he did just the opposite." [46] Ho's critics asked how he could talk of old age, death, and grief in the midst of China's dynamic socialist revolution? They asserted the party's belief that such emotions were inappropriate to progress and, therefore, should not be mentioned. Ho's use of the words "feeble" and "lost," they claimed, did not apply to Chinese Communist culture, but to Ho himself. They even chastised him for his phrase "lying down on a pillow" as a sign that he lacked "a passion to fight" [47] and was filled with self-pity

The party was not only upset with Ho's expression of feelings which it wanted to eliminate or at least ignore, it was also disturbed by his nostalgia for his old life in the village. Sheng Ch'üan-sheng declared, "Carts and bellows are still used, but they are backward labor tools." [48] In Communist China, there could be no glorification of outmoded ways of life nor idle dreaming on the beauties of nature. Ho should sing of "the roaring of motors, not the low humming of bellows." [49] Hence, he was criticized as he had criticized his former colleagues, for reflecting one's own feelings rather than the party's.

The sharpest point of the whole attack against Ho, however, was directed at the obscurity and ambiguity of his images. The vagueness and subtlety of Ho's verse did not serve the party's propaganda purposes and, in fact, ran counter to them. Most annoying was his unwillingness to define the meaning of the "strange wind" and the "mud and dirt." Such images, the party charged, led readers to interpretations that directed them away from the party instead of toward it.

Some of Ho's poems written before 1942 were also attacked at this time. Yet, despite these criticisms, Ho appears to have suffered

little diminution in rank or influence. Though nonconformity was
one of the major targets in the campaign against Hu Feng, undoubtedly Ho's leadership role in this campaign immunized him from
such an attack. In fact, in the following period of relaxation in the
Hundred Flowers movement, there were essays that countered
what they termed the "crudity" and "insensitivity" of the blows
directed against Ho's "Reply." One writer, Ch'ing I, in *Jen-min
wen-hsüeh* in November 1956, though conceding that the poem was
filled with obscure symbols and was difficult to understand, accused
Ho's critics of a stereotyped view of poetry. He advised them to
evaluate "Reply" in its own terms. Since it was essentially a lyrical
poem, Ch'ing I felt that it should be viewed as an expression of
the writer's internal feelings and not be judged by the standards
of socialist realism. To portray these innermost feelings, it was
necessary to use imaginative, albeit obscure, language. Ch'ing I declared, "It is regrettable that this kind of lyrical poetry is rejected." [50]

Yet, while some writers defended Ho during the Hundred
Flowers movement, there were many others who attacked him for
exemplifying the very traits he was particularly sensitive about.
They charged him with discussing topics on which he had only
superficial understanding, doing slipshod research, and showing a
lack of concern for artistic values. Here was an example of Ho's
contradictory position exposing him to attacks from both sides.
Many of those who criticized the party's policy in literature at
this time first attacked Ho before moving on to Chou Yang. Evidently, they used Ho as a test case to see how far they could go in
their denunciations.

Several scholars attacked Ho for his supposedly authoritative
interpretations of China's classical literature. In 1949, Ho had been
made vice-director of the Literary Research Institute of Peking
University and eventually became the director. Consequently, he
had the official voice in this area. A scholar of ancient literature
complained in *Hsüeh-hsi* that essays by specialists on the classics were
rejected by leading journals, but that Ho, who dealt primarily in
modern and Western literature, was praised everywhere as having
written the definitive work on the subject.[51] At one of the various
forums convened during the Hundred Flowers period, it was

pointed out that "For many years, Ho Ch'i-fang has not done any research himself. Everyone would write several essays and then he would summarize their points." [52] Apparently, there was some factional bickering involved in these criticisms. The literary historian Wang Yao declared at this same forum that members of the literary faculty of Peking University were made to feel that Ho Ch'i-fang's Literary Research Institute was "Marxist," while they in the university were "bourgeois." [53]

Hence, criticism converged on Ho from all sides, first because he was too concerned with artistic values and then because he was not. Yet, Ho was able to hold onto his powerful position in the party's hierarchy and remain among Chou Yang's chief lieutenants. Even his poem "Reply," which certainly went further than any of Ting Ling's public utterances in criticizing the regime and depicted, more vividly than Hu Feng's report to the CC, the despair of the intellectual, did not prevent him from becoming the editor of a new literary magazine, *Wen-hsüeh p'ing-lun* (Literary criticism). The journal appeared in the second half of 1958 and was to rank with *Wen-i pao* and *Jen-min wen-hsüeh* as one of the most influential cultural journals in Communist China.

Ho Ch'i-fang's Attack on the GLF in Poetry

Perhaps it was his ability to maintain his high place in the hierarchy, despite noncomformity on certain artistic matters and attacks on him from all sides, that led Ho to object strongly when the party introduced its policy of a GLF in poetry. As we have seen, Ho had obliquely been attacking the party's program to dilute poetry as an art form since 1942. Yet, it was not till 1958 that his approach and the party's met head on. Before 1958, the production of people's poems had been only one strain in the party's cultural policy, but with the launching of the GLF, it became the main focus for Communist China's cultural development. It was inevitable that Ho's consistent opposition would become more vigorous when the party attempted to make poetry the domain of the nonprofessionals and to decree that people's poetry become the mainstream of Chinese literature. Also, in light of

Ho's expressed discomfort at speaking out on subjects with which he was not well acquainted, it is likely that the criticism of him during the Hundred Flowers movement for this very failing hit a sensitive nerve. Subsequently, he spoke less and less on topics outside his major interest and devoted himself more and more to questions of poetry. Moreover, now he was in control of a powerful journal, *Wen-hsüeh p'ing-lun*, which he could use specifically as a vehicle for his own ideas.

His first comments on the wave of people's poems which poured forth in 1958 were printed in an article entitled "On a Hundred Flowers Bloom in New Poetry." [54] It was written in answer to an attack made upon him in *Jen-min wen-hsüeh* in May 1958 by the poet and critic Kung Mu,[55] who accused Ho of opposing the new popular ballads. Compared with his earlier comments on this aspect of the party's literary policy, his reply was low-keyed and expressed only partial opposition. He avoided discussing the content of the people's poems and merely criticized the meter of 5/7 characters to a line. Again, he repeated his old argument that this form had limitations in expressing the complexities of present-day life. His reply had been written to defend himself, not to attack the party's program for poetry.

Yet, as soon as these words were published, a large-scale, star-studded offensive was launched against him for his comments on poetic meter. Ho was later to write, "I simply could not have imagined that this small essay would have aroused such a storm." [56] As this offensive developed, it emerged as an effort to "educate" the people, particularly the intellectuals, to an appreciation of the "value" of the people's poems. *Wen-i pao* acknowledged that disrespect for literature of the people was widespread, especially in the literary world and among students. Through an attack on Ho's high standards, the party could enhance the literary efforts of the masses.

There were other campaigns going on in the literary realm at the same time. Among those under attack in 1958 was the literary historian Wang Yao, for having written favorably about such writers as Feng Hsüeh-feng, Hu Feng, and Ting Ling before the party had attacked them. Since even Mao Tse-tung had praised Ting Ling highly before the antirightist campaign, this was merely a trumped-up charge. Pa Chin was also criticized, his "mistake" being sympathy for Howard Fast when he was supposed to be denouncing him. Others found wanting in ideological correctness were the literary historian Li Ho-lin, the literary critic Pa Jen, and the *tsa wen* writer of the Hundred Flowers movement Hsü Mou-yung. They were called revisionists because they had advocated that literature depict the similarities among people instead of the differences.

These campaigns ran their course without encountering any outright resistance. All of these writers confessed to the "crimes" of which they were accused. By contrast, the campaign against Ho's views turned into a fiery debate. Ho did not publicly confess. Even more important, he rebuffed the charges made against him. Why Ho was able to attack one of the party's major programs without being silenced is not totally clear. It could be that his close relationship with Chou Yang for so many years shielded him from reprisal. But there were others close to Chou who were felled for less heterodoxy.[57] Perhaps the main reason was the party's own policy at the end of 1958 and the beginning of 1959. As the GLF began to fail, the party was forced to modify some of its policies, particularly the development of communes. Because of its indecision over its policies, there was a brief respite.

The party reduced its extreme emphasis on the innate knowledge and ability of the working man and increased its reliance on the services of the intellectuals and professionals. Although the party still insisted that the intellectuals learn from the masses, it now also maintained that the experts too had talents to contribute to China's development. Furthermore, Chou En-lai, in April 1959, issued a call for another period of contending and blooming in culture and science. Articles appeared once again attacking the dogmatic thinking of the cadres. They accused the cadres of being unwilling to listen to criticism, to read books, and to acknowledge differing views. In a gesture aimed at appeasing the intellectuals, several groups of rightists were released. Economists were allowed to criticize the economic irrationality of the GLF and the communes.

Within this less repressive atmosphere, Ho, with *Wen-hsüeh p'ing-lun* at his command, was able to fight back. Though the party's policy relaxed enough to allow Ho to express his divergent views, it did not relax to the point where it had forsaken its emphasis on the people's poetry. Other poetic forms were permitted, but this kind of poetry remained the focus of the party's literary policy. Lined up against Ho were virtually all of Communist China's literary officials and most of its famous poets, Kuo Mu-jo, T'ien Chien, and Tsang K'e-chia. Paradoxically, Chou Yang remained relatively quiet in the debate with Ho. Though he regarded the people's poetry as the realization of his literary ideas and was obviously opposed to Ho's position, he did not engage in the same kind of personal invective as some of his lieutenants. In addition to attacks by the major literary journals, *Wen-i pao, Jen-min wen-hsüeh*, and *Shih k'an* (Poetry), Ho was also criticized by the official organs of the CC, *JMJP*, and *Hung ch'i*. Ostensibly, the party denounced Ho for his opposition to the 5/7 meter, but behind its denunciation was another effort to demolish further the professional and artistic standards that still were important to China's writers and intellectuals. Essentially, then, this debate was a return to the basic question of the conflict between artistic and political values.

The attitude of the officials in their attacks on Ho was blatantly anti-intellectual and antiforeign. Shao Ch'üan-lin insisted that "folk poems express the ideas and emotions of the working classes more fully than the poetry of the intellectuals . . . To ignore this and only wrangle over the problem of 5 or 7 words is bookish." [58] Ho's critics ridiculed him for being scholarly and pedantic. In line with the tendency of the Chinese Communists to turn inward during the GLF, Shao Ch'üan-lin also asserted that the denial of the value of the 5/7 character line was equivalent to "Europeanizing" Chinese culture. Actually, Ho had asked poets to study the literary techniques and poetry styles used by writers in other countries. But, outside of this one area, he said little about learning from the West. The party's tactic was to isolate Ho and his views from the rest of the population. Worker-poets and intellectuals at large-scale meetings and in the literary journals, acting as "representatives" of the masses, joined in the denunciations of Ho.

Ho was accused of virtually the same gamut of charges as he delivered against his own victims. He was denounced for subjectivism, individualism, resistance to ideological remolding, disapproval of the proletarianization of poets, lack of class analysis, exclusivism, ivory towerism, nihilism, an aristocratic attitude, overemphasis on artistic technique, and, finally, wearing the mantle of Hu Feng and Feng Hsüeh-feng in his effort to negate folk literature. Apparently, Ho had even been charged with opposing Mao's poetic efforts, because at one point he felt called upon to declare, "To say the structure of old poetry limits ideas is not meant to injure the classical poetry of Mao." [59] Nevertheless, the party's censure did not go so far as to label him antiparty or a counterrevolutionary.

Literary officials were put somewhat on the defensive by Ho's assertion that Chinese culture, particularly its poetry, could not develop within the limitations of folk poetry. Therefore, in the process of condemning Ho, they attempted to show that, on the contrary, Chinese culture would progress much faster. As in other fields, party officials tried to blend the methods of the professional with those of the peasants and workers. This was one of their techniques for eliminating the distinction between the intellectuals and the masses. The editor of *Shih k'an*, the poet Tsang K'e-chia, described how this approach would work. "On the one hand, specialized, intellectual poets will gradually assimilate new things from the people's poems and gradually reform their own poetic spirit; on the other, the creativity of the working people daily progresses. I feel that in the future these two will combine and will be able to produce a national form enjoyed by the whole nation." [60]

Ho's response was angry and incisive. Judging from his actions in the past, it is most likely that if the party had struck at him on any issue other than the artistic standards of poetry, he would have readily spouted the party's line. Apparently, however, though Ho had surrendered every other part of his thinking to the party, poetic values continued to hold deep meaning for him. He was unwilling to abandon or even modify them no matter how they conflicted with his other expressed views. He used his journal, *Wen-hsüeh p'ing-lun* to win public support for his side. He had very little help in his endeavor. The only well-known writer to support him openly was an old friend of his from the 1930's, Pien Chih-lin, who had been profoundly influenced by Western literary techniques.[61] The other famous name to oppose the people's poetry was the aesthetician Chu Kuang-ch'ien. However, his help was of dubious value because of his well-known indifference to Marxist literary theory.

Ho's counterattack was waged on two fronts; one was against the party's current stress on the people's poetry and the other against the kind of attack that had been leveled against him for his differing opinions. He expressed forthright disapproval of every aspect of the mass production of poetry. His sharpest jab was directed at the party's basic assumption that the worth of a literary work be measured by the degree to which the masses appreciate it. Using the example of Lu Hsün, he claimed that "At present, the working people still have difficulty enjoying Lu Hsün's work, but regardless of this we cannot lower our estimate of his writings." He therefore concluded that "In evaluating literature and art, in addition to consideration of mass acceptance, there are scientific [artistic] standards. We should combine these two together." [62] Hence, Ho for the first time expressed himself ideologically in opposition to one of Mao's fundamental tenets. Instead of acknowledging the precedence of political standards over artistic ones, he now asserted that they had more or less equal importance.

Disregarding the party's injunction that poetry be a vehicle for propaganda and control, Ho told poets that "the important thing is to write better poetry." [63] In fact, he now seemed unconcerned with poetry as anything other than an end in itself. His chief interest was to make poetry express the spirit of the times and to enhance its tone, beauty, and rhythm. The people's poems, he firmly believed, could not do this. He was dismayed by the mass creativity sessions. Citing Lenin's statement that of all production, literature was the most unsuited for standardization, he warned that the production of communal folk poetry would drown the effort of individual genius before it even appeared on the surface.

He again replied, as he had done in the early 1950's to those who alleged that foreign poetry and the new poetry after the May Fourth movement had a negative effect on Chinese culture. Just because techniques are absorbed from abroad, he asserted, does not necessarily mean that a work loses the spirit of its nation. Again using Lu Hsün, he pointed out that "Lu Hsün's short stories assimilated quite a few elements from abroad and were very different from our own classical stories, but they still had heavy national characterics." [64]

He spent the major part of his rebuttal, however, debunking the party's contention that new poetry, with certain rules on meter, rhythm, tone, and rhyme, could eventually evolve from the mass creativity movement. He claimed that from his observations, "To write in accordance with the already established forms of folk songs and classical poetry, not elevating them, not changing them — this cannot be said to be development." [65] It was impossible, he insisted, to bring new forms out of what he considered to be stagnant, out-of-date literary styles. Citing the poetry of his literary-bureaucrat associates, specifically Yüan Shui-p'o and T'ien Chien, the latter one of his severest critics, Ho demonstrated that their attempt to mix together the forms of the people's poems with the new styles introduced after the May Fourth movement had produced discordant sounds. In his view, the poet may receive inspiration from the people's poems, but "All great poets do not mechanically imitate the songs of the people. They elevate and develop them in content and form and have their own creativeness." [66]

Actually, Ho's objection to this fusion was similar to the protests of intellectuals in other fields. He, like the scientists and the economists, wanted a division between the professional and the amateur so that standards would not be lowered and abilities wasted. Peasants and workers could write folk songs, but professional poets should be allowed to write more accomplished works with more varied meters, richer language, and more sophisticated imagery. He called for an enactment of the Hundred Flowers in poetry in the true sense of the slogan. The people's poems should exist only as one branch among many different poetic forms, rather than as the mainstream of China's poetic development. He declared, "We must open a new era of poetic spirit. This is not merely to have clear-sounding slogans, but to have great works which can be achieved only through an abundance of creativity." [67] As Ho saw it, the problem was not to evolve poetry from the people's songs, but to establish new poetic forms outside of them. He only asked that the poetry of professional poets be accepted along with the people's poems as part of Chinese culture. With obvious emotion, he said of these two kinds of poetry, "Even if they are different in spirit and in form, cannot both kinds exist at the same time? Why must we struggle so that one dies and the other lives?" [68] Actually, Ho was echoing the demands of the writers during the Hundred

Flowers movement and seconding Hu Feng's criteria for judging the value of a work of art. He asserted, "The form of poetry I advocate and the form of the people's poems can . . . compete with each other . . . Let us see which better expresses our present-day life." [69]

Ho struck out with equal force on the other front of his counter-attack. His blows at the literary bureaucracy likewise carried some of the critical spirit of the Hundred Flowers movement. He charged that his critics were not just considering the issues in the debate, but were attacking him as an individual. He asserted that "If a person's nervous system is somewhat weakened, he could become muddled or confused by this kind of criticism. According to 'the logic' of these writers, I dare to say that in any literature, . . . they can find defects and implicate their writers in all kinds of crimes . . . How can a person defend himself against this?" [70] Thus, he found himself a victim of the very same name-calling and character assassination he had perpetrated on others, particularly on Hu Feng. But whereas his victims had no way to fight back, he was able to use his journal to reveal what he termed the "deceit" of his opponents and to return their blows. Apparently, there was a factional squabble between him and the editor of *Wen-i pao*, Chang Kuang-nien, that had exacerbated the whole debate and may have given rise to the personal invective used by both sides. The reasons behind this conflict are not wholly apparent. Nonetheless, the fact that it existed is evident. It could be that both their journals competed for leadership of cultural circles. When Ho talked of the perfidy of his opponents, he most often referred to Chang Kuang-nien as his harshest critic, although other ·literary officials were equally loud in their denunciations.

Ho expressed shock and indignation at being ridiculed and rejected for merely advocating stricter poetic form. After many years of engaging in these kinds of tactics himself, he now asked why it was done. One of the reasons he gave was similar to Ting Ling's and Hu Feng's explanation, simply that in the Communist regime particular people are assigned to make scapegoats of others. Then he made perhaps the most piercing blow of his whole offensive, which in effect was also an attack on himself. He condemned the practice by which officials attacked the views and works of others without having studied or worked in the subject themselves. From his own experience of being criticized by uninformed critics, he was now appalled by this practice among others. He wrote, "A person who writes an article criticizing another and who does not look at the other person's original manuscript — this is absurd." [71] He maintained that those who shouted the loudest about how the people's poems did not limit creativity "have not gone through the difficult task of writing poetry." [72] He objected to the fact that certain officials were concerned only with making a name for themselves rather than with seriously studying the matters under their jurisdiction. "There are some people who only show interest in arguing or quarreling. Genuine, worthwhile discussions of concrete problems seldom occur." [73] Hence, he suggested that his critics had no right to attack his views on poetry, since their arguments could not compare to his own considered judgments. He asserted that "My study of poetic forms has gone through a long period of searching and thinking; my views can be criticized, but before doing so, my critics must also do some research and study themselves." [74]

Not only did he call for a more scholarly approach from those in charge of intellectual and creative work, he also demanded more tolerance of diverse viewpoints. Here again, his recent experience at the hands of his colleagues led him to condemn the very practices he himself had indulged in for many years. "Now that I have suggested the possibility of establishing another form of poetry in addition to the people's poems, it has been made to appear that I am committing a mistake in principle. Everybody has risen up to attack me." [75] Because of this treatment, Ho once more asked for the resurrection of the Hundred Flowers movement. However, he kept his demand specifically within the context of poetry. "To claim that one's idea is the only right one and not allow other people to have different attitudes in their research — this is not beneficial to the development of poetry." [76]

As soon as Ho stated his position in the first two numbers of *Wen-hsüeh p'ing-lun* in 1959, Li Hsi-fan, who personified the very kind of critic Ho had condemned, replied. His response demonstrated that Ho's critics were, as he claimed, becoming more concerned with denouncing him than discussing the issues. Even Li's title signifies this, "We Should Have A Correct Attitude in the

Treatment of Criticism." Li turned Ho's arguments back onto Ho. Instead of others failing to carry out the spirit of the Hundred Flowers movement, Li insisted that it was Ho himself who was guilty. Magnanimously, Li admitted that some of those who had attacked Ho had added and cut things out of Ho's statements "according to their own ideas and distorted the original meaning." [77] He asserted that Ho certainly had the right to counter the attack of his critics, but his mistake was that "When he rejected other people's criticism, he did not adopt a comradely attitude in discussing problems, but assumed a sneering, satiric, and disdainful attitude." [78] Unwillingness to accept denunciations with an air of repentance was also one of the complaints that had been made against the rightist writers. Li charged that Ho "not only adopted an individualistic attitude in the treatment of criticism, he even led debates on questions of principle into a mire of unprincipled, personal squabbles." [79] Expressing concern that the youth would be corrupted by his example, Li pontificated that "Ho, this famous critic and Marxist, who has been engaged in literary criticism for so many years, by adopting this kind of an attitude . . . could promote a bad spirit and mislead youth in their treatment of criticism." [80]

Toward the middle of 1959, there was another switch in party policy. Because of further deterioration of Sino-Soviet relations and the need to combat revisionist thinking, there was a return to the downgrading of intellectual endeavor, though to a lesser degree than in the earlier period. Still, many of the ingredients were at hand for the launching of one of the party's periodic thought reform drives. Some of the writers who were criticized for revisionist thought in 1958, particularly Hsü Mou-yung and Pa Jen, were attacked more intensively. On the whole, however, the party appeared reluctant to press the attack on the critics of the GLF into a full-scale drive. It needed their help more than ever in order to straighten out the dislocations created by the GLF. Hence, though the economic critics of the GLF were criticized and some lost their positions, no organized campaign was carried out against them in the later half of 1959.

Even more restraint was shown toward Ho. On April 12 and 14, 1959, an editorial meeting of his journal *Wen-hsüeh p'ing-lun* was convened to discuss orders sent down by Chou Yang. At this meeting, Shao Ch'üan-lin announced that Chou Yang and the top leadership had decreed a division of labor between Communist China's main cultural organs. *Wen-hsüeh p'ing-lun* was ordered to restrict itself to research, while *Wen-i pao* was directed to provide the leadership of the current literary movement. In effect, Ho and his journal were relegated to a subordinate position beneath their rivals Chang Kuang-nien and *Wen-i pao*. This appears to have been one of the party's methods for reprimanding Ho. However, despite this action and sporadic criticism in *Wen-i pao*, Ho seems to have returned to the fold as one of the party's trusted literary officials. In 1960, he was reappointed to his position on the secretariat of the Writers' Union along with some of his chief accusers, Chang Kuang-nien and Tsang K'e-chia. Furthermore, he once again became active in party organizations and in ideological rectification. He was named chairman of the Thirtieth Anniversary celebration of the League of Left-wing Writers, which was made another occasion to condemn Hu Feng and Feng Hsüeh-feng. Nevertheless, the problems that Ho had raised had not been resolved. Thus, as in previous years, though he vigorously implemented the party policies toward the intellectuals, his support of artistic criteria for poetry remained consistent.

Hence, the one member from the group of revolutionary writers in Yenan who had been able to move the highest and stay the longest in the party's ruling circles eventually suffered similar though less lethal blows. His experience shows that despite abandoning his friends after 1942, he had not completely abandoned his old patterns of thinking. He had kept inviolate a small segment of his thinking, his concern for artistic standards. Like his former friends, he had not entirely lost the spirit of intellectual defiance.

chapter eleven

THE SIGNIFICANCE OF
LITERARY DISSENT

The lives of the revolutionary writers in Communist China have more importance than their literary works. Despite the party's determination to eliminate them as a distinct group and to incorporate all intellectuals into the state bureaucracy, they were an amorphous, yet independent, island in the vast sea of the bureaucracy. Like the Russian intelligentsia whom they so admired, this handful of writers held true to the values they imbibed at an early stage. At times, they compromised and even betrayed their former friends. Yet, essentially, they remained alienated intellectuals who found themselves as alienated from the institutions and values of the new society they helped to establish as from the old ones they helped to destroy.

Their humanistic aspirations had not been weakened under Communist rule. A common theme that ran through their diverse criticisms was a concern with individual rights in the face of an increasingly monolithic society. True, their criticisms were inextricably connected with the desire to break down the authority of their old literary foes. Yet they were also motivated by a sincere belief in some degree of freedom and independence as prerequisites not only for creative and intellectual activity, but for life itself. They were appalled by the party's attempt to control human feelings and individual thought. Their criticism of the indifference, arbitrariness, and ignorance of the literary bureaucracy was an indictment of the party's entire bureaucratic system.

Their denunciations of Chou Yang and his group brought to light the existence of a power structure headed by men who abused the system instead of serving it. Speaking in a vein similar to that of Djilas in *The New Class,* they complained that their Communist ideal of a democratic, equalitarian society had not been realized. Instead, a new class of rulers had emerged with its own vested interests and prerogatives. They described its new leadership as an isolated elite, as much in conflict with those whom they led as the old rulers had been. Even more significant, some of them implied that this was not merely an isolated phenomenon nor a survival from the old society, but was due to the operation of the party itself. They suggested that the party's mechanisms of control in the literary realm permitted and even encouraged the advancement and leadership of mediocre, opportunistic bureaucrats at the expense of more skilled, better-trained intellectuals. They inferred that this tension between professional and party men and its accompanying factional warfare characterized all facets of life in Communist China.

They resisted the encompassing power of the party apparatus by demanding the separation of artistic and intellectual activity from party control. In contrast to their previous efforts to subordinate everything to a world view with a simple, all-embracing principle, these writers sought in the 1940's and 1950's to cut off some of the areas under party jurisdiction into semiautonomous units. Beginning with Wang Shih-wei's "Statesmen and Artists" through to Ho Ch'i-fang's protest against people's poetry, the revolutionary writers in various periods and in differing contexts suggested that art become an independent area of human inquiry with its own discipline, subject matter, and intrinsic purposes. They argued that it should be a realm where the writer is free to experiment and express an individual view of human experience. Moreover, it should be at least one sphere where criticism might be expressed, even if subtly. Their pleas that the party relax the tight controls over literature, lessen the exclusive rule of socialist realism, allow Western cultural influences, and modify its thought reform program were attempts in this direction. The desire to detach themselves from politics did not mean a withdrawal from the political struggle, but was, in fact, the assertion of a political stand. It sought to delineate the limits of the party's authority.

Their unceasing assaults on the formidable Chinese Communist monolith were not so futile as they might appear. It is true that the match between the party bureaucrats, represented by Chou Yang, and the revolutionary writers, represented by Ting Ling and Hu Feng, was unequal. We have seen that the struggle between these two groups for power and for the support of the top leadership was definitely weighted on the side of the more orthodox literary bureaucrats. The latter had become deeply entrenched in the party structure. Nevertheless, the revolutionary writers did not have to surrender unconditionally. The party leadership was aware of the danger of producing an atmosphere which stifled the initiative and creativity of the intellectuals. In certain periods, the party permitted and, during the Hundred Flowers movement, even encouraged chastisement of the bureaucracy. Then, the leadership used the intellectuals to help relax the grip of the routinized bureaucrats and, even more important, shake them out of their indifference and self-importance. As we have seen, this led to a pattern of oscillation, particularly in the 1950's, between pressure and relaxation. The drive against scholars in the early 1950's yielded to a slight respite in 1953 and the first half of 1954. This was followed by the severe repression of the Hu Feng campaign. In turn, this was succeeded by the liberalization of the Hundred Flowers movement, counteracted by the antirightist campaign, followed by a brief rest in 1959 and the early 1960's.

It was when the party allowed criticism of the bureaucracy and encouraged intellectual ferment that the revolutionary writers took the opportunity to speak out on questions that were important to them. Unlike similar intervals in the Soviet Union, these periods of relative relaxation were too short to make the writing of comparatively long, complex works possible. Still, in speeches, essays, and sometimes short stories, these writers presented publicly what they had thought secretly or spoken only to trusted friends. Moreover, in these intervals they answered the accusations made against them in previous campaigns. They brought the sharp conflicts going on behind the scenes out into the open and sought support for their cause by pleading their cases before a wider audience. Once they had been given a platform, several refused to be pushed off even when aware of the consequences. As writers, they could not help but express themselves. As Hsü Mou-yung explained his own actions in his "Random Notes from the Abode of a Noisy Cicada," "The cicada has shrieked too long. I had better stop, but still I want to chirp some more." [1]

Furthermore, though the literary bureaucrats used the cheng feng movements as a cover for eliminating their personal enemies, the revolutionary writers, with the exception of Wang Shih-wei and Hu Feng, inevitably returned to the literary scene and spoke out again during periods of relaxation. Even Ting Ling recovered in the early 1960's from her personal disgrace and was accepted back into literary circles. The ideological remolding campaigns do not appear to have been successful in changing the psychological and mental attitudes of these writers. Instead of inspiring them with faith in party doctrine, they filled them, as revealed in the correspondence between Hu Feng and his followers, with a sense of loneliness, depression, fear, and suspicion. This had the effect of curbing them temporarily, but their resistance broke out again once the pressure was eased. The revolutionary writers, for the most part, lived underground existences, but intermittently had the chance to flare out into the open.

Thus, the party's policy toward the intellectuals has had within it elements that make it impossible to check altogether the underlying forces which contribute to the emergence of heresy. This policy highlights the dilemma in which the party finds itself: How to promote and utilize intellectual ferment without producing criticism that could endanger its whole system of controls, and how to develop the talents of the intellectuals without producing a professional elite committed to its own standards.

Perhaps even more important than the party's contradictory policies in explaining the continuing role of the revolutionary writers has been the party's inability to incorporate the intellectual community effectively into its regime. Even the scientists and engineers, whose talents have been crucial to the modernization of China and who, therefore, have been treated more favorably than other intellectuals, similarly suffered from the harassment of the ideological remolding drives, the loss of intellectual freedom, and particularly the management of their fields of work by untutored cadres. Hence, they, along with other intellectuals, have had a bond with the revolutionary writers and have identified in part with their alienation.

The revolutionary writers were unable to solve the problems that disturbed China's intellectuals, but they were at least able to articulate them. Through their works and acts, they expressed for the intellectuals and probably for the more thoughtful part of the reading public their own repressed hopes and feelings, a dedication to truthfulness and sincerity, and the right to think and create freely. They reflected the feelings of the individual confronted with an oppressive bureaucracy. That these writers had a profound influence on the educated community and spoke for a much larger group than their own is demonstrated by the recurring campaigns against them, ever widening in scope and increasing in intensity.

What was the impact of this small number of writers on the regime itself? Their disaffection did not mean they were an organized political opposition; that would have required leadership capable of providing an alternative ideology and able to organize mass support, both of which were impossible in Communist China. In fact, they were not even united among themselves. The circle around Hu Feng, the Ting Ling–Feng Hsüeh-feng faction, the younger followers of Liu Shao-t'ang, and the writers guided by Ch'in Ch'ao-yang were diverse groups which had little contact with one another. They also did not present any program of their own. They were unable to find a formula to reconcile the humanistic values they found in Marxism with the restrictive organizational apparatus inherent in the party. Moreover, their moral exhortations and reforming zeal did not inspire any institutional changes within the party. Nevertheless, their *tsa wen*, allegories, poems, stories, and editorial activities corroded the ideological orthodoxy of the party, exposed the habitual slogans, and fostered dissatisfaction with party practices. They unmasked the differences between party propaganda on the one hand and the reality of life and art on the other. The integrity of their vision exposed the party's betrayal of truth, stimulated questioning, and helped to keep the spirit of inquiry alive.

Though they were unable to change or even reform the system directly, their survival as a critical minority eventually contributed to the downfall of their opponents, the literary bureaucrats. Some mention should be made of the fate that befell Chou Yang and his followers during the Cultural Revolution, though this event is outside the time span of this book. These powerful officials who, as we have seen, had ruthlessly purged the ranks of China's most creative writers for more than thirty years became the public target of the Cultural Revolution in the summer of 1966.[2] The attack on Chou may have been caused in part by his maneuvering in the power structure, but, perhaps more important, it was a reflection of the fact that dissident intellectuals continued to exist in Communist China.[3] Chou became the scapegoat for the party's inability to produce obedient intellectuals. Obviously unable to blame the regime or himself, Mao lashed out at Chou, the very one most conspicuous in implementing his policies toward the higher intellectuals.

However, the attack on Chou did not mean that the regime had placed the leadership of the literary realm into the hands of those who opposed Chou and his group. There was no attempt to rehabilitate the writers purged by him. In fact, in the summer of 1966, there were renewed attacks on Hu Feng, Feng Hsüeh-feng, and Ting Ling. Moreover, the regime made no effort to revive literary criteria or divorce literature from propaganda. Quite the contrary, after years of bitter conflict with the writers, it apparently concluded that not only writers, but literature itself was subversive. The chief obstacle to the control of literature was that literary creativity in itself was a highly individual skill. Pre-revolutionary literature and Western literature were proscribed in the summer of 1966. This was even true of *Hung lou meng* and the literary theories of the nineteenth-century Russian literary critics Chernyshevski and Belinsky whose work formed the basis for socialistic realism. As long as novels like *Hung lou meng* and Russian works were available, the reader could learn of humanitarian aspirations and critical standards by which to judge society as well as literature. Party reinterpretations did little to lessen their ideological or emotional effect.

The party, in seeking to produce literature devoid of this background, could not trust even such a devoted servant as Chou Yang to take the lead. Despite his purge of nonconforming writers and unorthodox ideas, he himself had studied these works and even translated Chernyshevski and Tolstoy. Furthermore, though Chou and his associates were first and foremost organization men, they had participated in the cosmopolitan, relatively free cultural life of Shanghai of the 1930's. Hence as urban, pseudo-intellectuals, they presumably had been tainted by bourgeois and revisionist ideas. A literary tradition that includes the great writers of nineteenth-century Russia and even Soviet literature of the 1950's is subversive to a cultural revolution trying to eliminate Western culture and trying to replace individual writers with amateur writing collectives under the direction of party cadres.

Still, if the events traced here are any guide to the future, this swing toward doctrinaire excess should be followed by a move toward relative relaxation. Granted that those who have assumed the leadership of the literary realm may know less about literature than Chou and his associates, it does not mean the end of literary dissent in China. The party's undulating policy makes it impossible to eliminate diversity and criticism. More important, the story of the revolutionary writers has shown that the party's imposition of totalitarian rule has not resulted in the destruction of the alienated intellectual in Communist China. Moreover, the death or disposal of these old revolutionary writers does not mean an end to their tradition. The Hundred Flowers period revealed that the burden of the struggle which they carried for so many years was taken on by a rising generation of authors who appeared willing and even eager to accept their legacy. Despite the Cultural Revolution, it is likely that their struggle will persist. One day it may be shown that China's writers, under overwhelming pressures, kept alive a sense of freedom and an appreciation for human and artistic values. In the West, where writers have been free to say what they please, composing a poem or writing a literary criticism is not a rebellious act, but in Communist China it can be an act of courage and fortitude.

NOTES, BIBLIOGRAPHY,
GLOSSARY AND INDEX

ABBREVIATIONS IN NOTES

CB	*Current Background*
CFJP	*Chieh-fang jih-pao*
ECMM	*Extracts From China Mainland Magazines*
JMJP	*Jen-min jih-pao*
KMJP	*Kuang-ming jih-pao*
LWHC	*Hu Feng wen-i ssu-hsiang p'i-p'an lun-wen hui-ch'i*
NCNA	New China News Agency
SCMP	*Survey of the China Mainland Press*
TKTL	*Chung-kuo hsien-tai wen-hsüeh shih ts'an-k'ao tzu-liao*

NOTES

Chapter 1: The Conflict Between the Party and Revolutionary Writers

1. Hu Feng, *Tsai hun-luan li-mien* (In confusion; Shanghai, 1946), p. 21.

2. Ho Tan-jen (Feng Hsüeh-feng), "Kuan-yü 'Ti-san-chung wen-hsüeh' ti ch'ing-hsiang yü li-lun" (Concerning the tendencies and theories of "The Third Kind of Literature"), in *TKTL*, I, 492.

3. Hu Feng, *Mi-yün ch'i feng-hsi hsiao-chi* (Studies in a cloudy period; Hankow, 1938). This book contains both Hu Feng's and Chou Yang's articles on this subject.

4. *Lu Hsün ch'üan-chi* (Complete works of Lu Hsün; Peking, 1958), VI, 437–438.

5. Ting Ling and Ai Ch'ing were imprisoned by the KMT at this time so did not participate in the controversy.

6. Lu Hsün, "Lun hsien-tsai wo-men ti wen-hsüeh yün-tung" (On our present literary movement), in *TKTL*, I, 545–547. This is Lu Hsün's open letter to Hsü Mou-yung. Part of this letter is translated in C. T. Hsia's *A History of Modern Chinese Fiction 1917–1957* (New Haven, 1961), pp. 297–299.

7. Lü K'e-yü (Feng Hsüeh-feng) "Tui-yü wen-hsüeh yün-tung chi-ke wen-t'i ti i-chien" (Opinions on several problems in the literary movement), in *TKTL*, I, 569. Printed originally in *Tso-chia* (The writer), September 1936.

8. *TKTL*, I, 575.

9. *Ibid.*, p. 573.

10. *Ibid.*, p. 574.

11. Shao Ch'üan-lin, "The Struggle Between Two Trends in Literature," *Chinese Literature*, No. 1:139 (1958).

12. The group of writers around Hu Feng came to be known as the Ch'i-yüeh (July) poetry group. Among them were the poets Li Yüan and Lu Li. This group and its journal were regarded by literary critics to have promoted the development of modern poetry in China.

13. Feng Hsüeh-feng, *Kuo-lai ti shih-tai* (Time past; Shanghai), p. 100.

14. Feng Hsüeh-feng, *Hsiang-feng yü shih-feng* (Spirit of country and city; Shanghai, 1948), p. 76. Both this book and the one above are compilations of Feng's essays written in the 1930's and early 1940's.

15. Hu Feng, *Hu Feng wen-chi* (Hu Feng's collected essays; Shanghai, 1947), p. 114.

16. *Ibid.*, p. 140.

Chapter 2: Literary Opposition During the Yenan Period

1. There were previous campaigns against intellectuals. For example, there was one in the late 1920's against the followers of Ch'en Tu-hsiu and another in the late 1930's against the followers of Wang Ming. But these were drives

against the individual followers of an opposing faction, they were not directed against intellectuals as a group.

2. Robert Lifton, *Thought Reform and the Psychology of Totalism* (New York, 1960). This book describes the psychological techniques used by the party to remold the intellectuals.

3. For a description of these various stages, see *CFJP* (Apr. 3, 1942), p. 2; (Apr. 22, 1942), p. 3; (Apr. 24, 1942), p. 1; (May 13, 1942), p. 1. See also Boyd Compton, *Party Reform Documents 1942–1944* (Seattle, 1952), p. xxxv.

4. Among the prescribed readings were Mao Tse-tung's "Correcting Unorthodox Tendencies in Learning, The Party, and Literature and Art," and "Opposing Party Formalism." Also Liu Shao-ch'i's "On the Training of a Communist Party Member" and "On the Intra-Party Struggle."

5. News release, *CFJP* (Apr. 8, 1942), p. 2.

6. *Ibid.* (Apr. 3, 1942), p. 2.

7. Conrad Brandt, Benjamin Schwartz and John K. Fairbank, *A Documentary History of Chinese Communism* (Cambridge, Mass., 1952), p. 338.

8. *Ibid.*, p. 360.

9. News release, *CFJP* (Feb. 10, 1942), p. 4.

10. Wang Shih-wei, "Yeh pai-ho-hua" (The wild lily), *CFJP* (Mar. 13, 1942), p. 4. This article is written in two parts. The second part appeared March 23, 1942. The author, Wang Shih-wei, expressed the hope that the party would listen to dissident views. Similar hopes were voiced by others.

11. Nym Wales, *My Yenan Notebooks* (printed for private distribution, 1961), p. 156.

12. Another one of her stories, "When I was in Hsia Village," was also attacked at these meetings. This story written in 1940 is discussed by T. A. Hsia in "Twenty Years after the Yenan Forum" in *The China Quarterly*, No. 13:241–242 (January–March 1963).

13. Ting Ling, "San-pa-chieh yu kan" (Thoughts on March 8), *CFJP* (Mar. 9, 1942), p. 4.

14. *Ibid.*

15. T. A. Hsia, "Twenty Years after the Yenan Forum," p. 242.

16. Lo Feng, "Hai-shih tsa-wen ti shih-tai" (Still a period of *tsa wen*), *CFJP* (Mar. 12, 1942), p. 4.

17. *Ibid.*

18. *Ibid.*

19. Wang Shih-wei, "Yeh pai-ho-hua," *CFJP* (Mar. 13, 1942), p. 4.

20. *Ibid.* (Mar. 23, 1942), p. 4.

21. *Ibid.*

22. *Ibid.* (Mar. 13, 1942), p. 4.

23. *Ibid.*

24. *Ibid.* (Mar. 23, 1942), p. 4.

25. *CFJP* (May 26, 1942), p. 4.

26. "Statesmen and Artists" was originally published in *Ku yü* (Grain rains), but copies of *Ku yü* are not available. Nevertheless, lengthy excerpts were reprinted in *CFJP*. Several excerpts were in Chin Ts'an-jan, "Tu Shih-wei t'ung-chih ti 'Cheng-chih-chia, i-shu-chia' hou" (After reading Comrade Shih-wei's "Statesmen and Artists"), *CFJP* (May 26, 1942), p. 4.

27. *Ibid.*

28. *Ibid.*

29. *Ibid.*

30. Hsiao Chün, "Lun chung-shen ta-shih" (On marriage), *CFJP* (Mar. 25, 1942), p. 4.

31. Hsiao Chün, "Lun t'ung-chih chih ai yü nai" (On love and patience among comrades), *CFJP* (Apr. 8, 1942), p. 4.

32. *Ibid.*

33. *Ibid.*

34. *Ibid.*

35. Ai Ch'ing, "Liao-chieh tso-chia, tsun-chung tso-chia" (Understand and respect writers), *CFJP* (Mar. 11, 1942), p. 4.

36. *Ibid.*

37. *Ibid.*

38. Ho Ch'i-fang, "Tuo-shao-tz'u a wo li-k'ai le wo jih-ch'ang ti sheng-huo" (How many times I have left my everyday life), *CFJP* (Apr. 3, 1942), p. 4.

39. Ho Ch'i-fang, "Yung Mao Tse-tung ti wen-i li-lun lai kai-chin wo-men ti kung-tso" (Improve our work with Mao Tse-tung's literary theory), *Wen-i pao*, No. 1:5 (1952). This article describes the public support given to the revolutionary writers in Yenan in 1942.

40. Wen Chi-tse, "Tou-cheng jih-chi" (Diary of struggle), *CFJP* (June 28, 1942), p. 4.

41. *CFJP* (May 4, 1942), p. 4.

42. *Ibid.*

43. Mao Tse-tung, *On Art and Literature* (Peking, 1960), p. 83.

44. *Ibid.*, p. 104.

45. *Ibid.*, p. 111.

46. *Ibid.*, p. 112.

47. *Ibid.*, p. 113.

48. Wang Yao, *Chung-kuo hsin wen-hsüeh shih-kao* (Draft history of China's new literature; Shanghai, 1954), II, 427.

49. Ch'en Po-ta, "Kuan-yü Wang Shih-wei" (Concerning Wang Shih-wei), *CFJP* (June 15, 1942), p. 4.

50. *Ibid.*

51. A diary was kept of these meetings and was published in *CFJP* (June 28, 1942), p. 4, and (June 29, 1942), p. 4. It was by Wen Chi-tse, called "Tou-cheng jih-chi" (Diary of struggle).

52. Wen Chi-tse, in *CFJP* (June 29, 1942), p. 4.

53. Speech by Fan Wen-lan at discussion meeting of Institute, in *CFJP* (June 29, 1942), p. 4.

54. Since the views of the party critics overlap, their arguments will be discussed as a whole. Among these critics were the historian Fan Wen-lan whose views were published in *CFJP* (June 9, 1942), p. 4, and (June 29, 1942), p. 4; the ideologist Ch'en Po-ta, *CFJP* (June 9, 1942), p. 4, and (June 15, 1942); the writer Chou Wen, *CFJP* (June 16, 1942), p. 4; the literary bureaucrat Chou Yang, *CFJP* (July 28, 1942), p. 4.

55. Lo Man, "Lun Chung-yang yen-chiu yüan ti ssu-hsiang lun-chan" (On the ideological polemic in the Central Research Institute), *CFJP* (June 28, 1942), p. 4.

56. Speech by Fan Wen-lan, in *CFJP* (June 29, 1942), p. 4.

57. Liao Ying, "Jen tsai chien-k'u chung sheng-chang" (Men grow out of adversity), *CFJP* (June 10, 1942), p. 4.

58. Ting Ling, "Wen-i chieh tui Wang Shih-wei ying-yu ti t'ai-tu chi fan-hsing" (The attitude and self-introspection that the literary circles should take toward Wang Shih-wei), *CFJP* (June 16, 1942), p. 4.

59. *Ibid.*

60. Gunther Stein, *The Challenge of Red China* (New York, 1945), pp. 256–257.

61. *Ibid.*

62. Ai Ch'ing, "Wo tui-yü mu-ch'ien wen-i shang chi-ko wen-t'i ti i-chien" (My opinion about some of the problems in current literature and art), *CFJP* (May 15, 1942), p. 4.

63. *Ibid.*

64. *Ibid.*

65. Ai Ch'ing, "Hsien-shih pu jung-hsü wai-ch'ü" (Reality doesn't allow distortion), *CFJP* (June 24, 1942), p. 4.

66. Robert Payne, *Journey to Red China* (London, 1947), p. 155.

67. Ho Ch'i-fang, "Yung Mao Tse-tung ti wen-i li-lun lai kai-chin wo-men ti kung-tso," p. 5.

68. Hsiao Chün, "Tui-yü tang-ch'ien wen-i chu wen-t'i ti wo-chien" (My views about the problems in the present art and literature), *CFJP* (May 14, 1942), p. 4.

69. *Ibid.*

70. *Ibid.*

71. Hsiao Chün, "Wen-t'an shang ti 'Pu-erh-pa' ching-shen" (The "Bulba" spirit in literary and art circles), *CFJP* (June 13, 1942), p. 4.

72. Chou Yang, *Piao-hsien hsin ti ch'ün-chung ti shih-tai* (To express the new age of the masses; Peking, 1948), p. 1. In this book, Chou discusses in detail his views on a national literary style for modern Chinese literature.

73. Wales, p. 51.

74. Chou Yang, *Piao-hsien hsin ti ch'ün-chung ti shih-tai*, p. 91.

75. *Ibid.*, p. 32.

76. *Ibid.*, p. 49.

77. *Ibid.*, p. 53.

Chapter 3: Conflicts Between Left-Wing Writers in the KMT Area and the CCP

1. Hu Feng, "Chih-shen tsai wei min-chu ti tou-cheng li-mien" (Placing oneself in the democratic struggle), *Hsi wang* (Hope), 1.1:4 (January 1945).

2. Victor Erlich, "Social and Aesthetic Criteria in Soviet Russian Criticism," in E. S. Simmons, ed., *Continuity and Change in Russian and Soviet Thought* (Cambridge, 1955), p. 412.

3. Feng Hsüeh-feng, *Kuo-lai ti shih-tai*, p. 73.

4. Feng Hsüeh-feng, *Lun min-chu ke-ming ti wen-i yün-tung* (On the literary movement of the democratic revolution; Shanghai, 1949), p. 49.

5. Hu Feng, *Chien wen-i jen-min* (Sword, literature and people; Shanghai, 1950), p. 33.

6. *Wen-hsüeh p'ing-lun* (Literary criticism), No. 1:48 (1959).

7. Hu Feng, *Wei-le ming-t'ien* (For tomorrow; Shanghai, 1950), p. 349.

8. *Hsin-hua jih-pao* (New China news; Apr. 10, 1943), p. 4.

9. *Ibid.* (Feb. 6, 1943), p. 4.

10. "Kuan-yü Hu Feng fan tang chi-t'uan ti i-hsieh ts'ai-liao" (Some materials concerning the Hu Feng antiparty clique), *Wen-i pao* (Literary gazette), Nos. 9 and 10:33 (1955). This letter is dated Oct. 26, 1943. Letters between Hu Feng and his followers, dating from the early 1940's down to 1955, were confiscated from them and reprinted in *Wen-i pao* when they were attacked in 1955.

11. *Ibid.* This letter is dated Jan. 4, 1944.

12. Lu Hsün wrote a letter to Hu Feng on Sept. 12, 1935, in which he said, "I have the feeling that I am tied down by iron chains with a foreman standing behind me, lashing me all the time. No matter how hard I have worked the whipping would continue." Compilation of letters of Lu Hsün, *Lu Hsün ch'üan-chi*, II, 947–948, tr. Yang I-fan in *The Case of Hu Feng* (Hong Kong, 1956), p. 29.

13. "Kuan-yü Hu Feng fan tang chi-t'uan ti i-hsieh ts'ai-liao," p. 31. This letter is dated May 25, 1944.

14. *Hu Feng wen-chi*, p. 139.

15. "Kuan-yü Hu Feng fan tang chi-t'uan ti i-hsieh ts'ai-liao," p. 33. This letter is dated May 27, 1944.

16. *Ibid.* This letter is dated Nov. 1, 1944.

17. Hu Feng, "Chih-shen tsai wei min-chu ti tou-cheng li-mien," p. 3.

18. Shu Wu, "Lun chu-kuan" (On subjectivism), *Hsi wang*, 1.1:84 (January 1945).

19. *Ibid.*, pp. 76–77.

20. *Ibid.*, p. 79.

21. *Ibid.*, p. 80.

22. *Ibid.*, p. 81.

23. *Ibid.*, p. 83.

24. "Kuan-yü Hu Feng fan tang chi-t'uan ti i-hsieh ts'ai-liao," p. 32. This letter is dated Jan. 18, 1945.

25. *Ibid.* This letter is dated Jan. 24, 1945.

26. *Ibid.* This letter is dated Jan. 24, 1945.

27. *Ibid.*, p. 31. This letter is dated April 13, 1945.

28. *Ibid.*, p. 32. This letter is dated July 29, 1945.

29. *Ibid.*, p. 29. This letter is dated Nov. 17, 1945.

30. Ho Ch'i-fang, "Hsien-shih chu-i ti lu hai shih fan hsien-shih chu-i ti lu?" (The road of realism or the road of antirealism), in *LWHC*, II, 90.

31. Joseph Schyns, *1500 Modern Chinese Novels and Plays* (Peking, 1948), pp. 33–34.

32. Feng Hsüeh-feng, *K'ua ti jih-tzu* (Days of transition; Shanghai, 1946), p. 105.

33. Feng Hsüeh-feng, *Hsiang-feng yü shih-feng*, p. 146.

34. Feng Hsüeh-feng, *Lun min-chu ke-ming ti wen-i yün-tung*, p. 57.

35. *Ibid.*, p. 61.

36. *Ibid.*, p. 83.

37. *Ibid.*, p. 86.

38. *Ibid.*, p. 91.

39. Wang Yao, II, 248.

40. Hua Shih (Feng Hsüeh-feng), "T'i-wai ti hua" (Irrelevant words), in *TKTL*, II, 428–429.

41. Ho Ch'i-fang, "Tui Hu Feng chi-t'uan ti fang-tung wen-i szu-hsiang ti tou-cheng" (The struggle against the reactionary literary ideas of the Hu Feng

clique), in *TKTL*, II, 348–361. Reprinted from *Hsin-hua jih-pao* (Feb. 9, 1946), literary supplement.

42. "Kuan-yü Hu Feng fan ke-ming chi-t'uan ti ti-san p'i ts'ai-liao" (The third collection of materials concerning the Hu Feng antirevolutionary clique), *Wen-i pao*, No. 11:15 (1955).

Chapter 4: Resumption of Thought Reform Drives in 1948

1. A drive was carried out in the Soviet Union at this time by the literary czar, Andrei Zhdanov, against nonconformist writers whose cases were used to whip up the flagging spirits of the nation and consolidate the dominance of the Soviet Communist party.

2. Articles from *Ta-chung wen-i ts'ung-k'an* (Digest of mass literature), were collected into a book entitled *Ta-chung wen-i ts'ung-k'an p'i-p'ing lun-wen ch'üan-chi* (Collected criticisms from popular literature; Hong Kong).

3. Shao Ch'üan-lin (Ch'üan-lin), "Lun chu-kuan wen-t'i" (On the problem of subjectivism), in *TKTL*, II, 378.

4. Lin Mo-han (Mo-han), "Ko-hsing chieh-fang yü chi-t'i chu-i" (The liberation of individuality and collectivism), in *TKTL*, II, 407.

5. Hu Ch'iao-mu (Ch'iao-mu), "Wen-i ch'uang-tso yu chu-kuan" (Literary creation and subjectivism), in *TKTL*, II, 402.

6. "Kuan-yü Hu Feng fan tang chi-t'uan ti i-hsieh ts'ai-liao," p. 30. This letter is dated Oct. 26, 1948.

7. *Ibid.*, p. 31. This letter is dated Oct. 26, 1948.

8. *Ta-chung wen-i ts'ung-k'an p'i-p'ing lun-wen ch'üan-chi*, p. 76. Also in Wang Yao, II, 250.

9. Hsiao Chün, "Cheng chiao fan-t'an" (Talk on government and education), in *TKTL*, II, 266. A reprint of Hsiao Chün's article. Since copies of *Wen-hua pao* are not available, it is necessary to quote from reprints or excerpts.

10. Hsaio is quoted in Liu Chih-ming, *Hsiao Chün p'i-p'an* (Criticism of Hsiao Chün; Hong Kong, 1949), p. 42.

11. Hsiao Chün, "Ta-yung-che ti ching-shen" (The spirit of the great brave man), *Wen-ts'ui* (Articles digest), 1.1:19 (Oct. 9, 1945).

12. *Ibid.*

13. Quoted in Chang Ju-hsin, "P'ing Hsiao Chün ti she-hui kuan yü jen-hsing lun" (On Hsiao Chün's outlook toward society and his theory of human nature), *Ch'ün-chung* (The masses), 3.21:18 (May 19, 1949).

14. From the third chapter of *Village in August*, reprinted in *Living China*, ed. Edgar Snow (New York, 1936), pp. 212–213.

15. These sentiments were expressed by prisoners of war from Manchuria during the Korean War. Allen Whiting, "The New Chinese Communists," *World Politics*, 7.4:601–603 (July 1955).

16. Quoted in Huang Mo, "I-yeh tou-cheng li-shih" (An historical page of struggle), *Wen-i pao*, No. 17:16 (1955).

17. Liu Chih-ming, *Hsiao Chün p'i-p'an*, p. 39.

18. *Ibid.*, p. 40.

19. Quoted in Chang Ju-hsin, "P'ing Hsiao Chün ti she-hui kuan yü jen-hsing lun," p. 20.

20. Hsiao Chün, "Hsia-yeh ch'ao chih san" (Notes on summer nights, No. 3), *TKTL*, II, 266.

21. Wang Yao, II, 244.

22. Liu Chih-ming, *Hsiao Chün p'i-p'an*, p. 48.

23. Quoted in Yen Wen-ching and Kung Mo, "Hsiao Chün ssu-hsiang tsai p'i-p'an" (Recriticism of Hsiao Chün's thought), *Wen-i pao*, No. 7:38 (1958).

24. Hsiao Chün, "Ch'ou-chiao tsa-t'an" (Talk on clowns), in *TKTL*, II, 268.

25. Whiting, p. 600.

26. Quoted in Yang Yen-nan, *Chung-kung tui Hu Feng ti tou-cheng* (The struggle against Hu Feng by the Chinese Communists; Hong Kong, 1956), p. 179.

27. Liu Chih-ming, *Hsiao Chün p'i-p'an*, p. 46.

28. Hsiao Chün, "Cheng chiao fan-t'an," *TKTL*, II, 266.

29. Hsiao Chün, "Hsia-yeh ch'ao chih san," *TKTL*, II, 265.

30. Liu Chih-ming, "Tung-pei san-nien lai wen-i kung-tso ch'u-pu tsung-chieh" (A preliminary summation of the literary work in the Northeast for the past three years), in *TKTL*, II, 166.

31. *Hsiao Chün ssu-hsiang p'i-p'an* (Criticism of Hsiao Chün's ideas; Peking, 1949), p. 250. This book contains the criticisms made against Hsiao Chün during the 1948 campaign.

32. Liu Chih-ming, *Hsiao Chün p'i-p'an*, p. 48.

33. *Ibid.*, and "Hsiao Chün ssu-hsiang tsai p'i-p'an," p. 41.

34. Liu Chih-ming, *Ch'ing-suan Hsiao Chün ti fan-tung ssu-hsiang* (Liquidate Hsiao Chün's reactionary ideas; Hong Kong, 1949), p. 225.

35. *Wen-hua pao*, No. 60.

36. Liu Chih-ming, *Hsiao Chün p'i-p'an*, pp. 4–9.

37. *Ibid.*, p. 9.

38. Chang Ju-hsin, "P'ing Hsiao Chün ti she-hui kuan yü jen-hsing lun," p. 22.

39. *Ibid.*

40. *Hsiao Chün ssu-hsiang p'i-p'an*, p. 178. Since copies of *Sheng-huo pao* are not available, it is necessary to quote from reprints and excerpts.

41. *Ibid.*, p. 139.

42. *Ibid.*, p. 138.

43. Liu Chih-ming, *Hsiao Chün p'i-p'an*, p. 37.

44. *Ibid.*, p. 40.

45. Chang Ju-hsin, "P'ing Hsiao Chün ti she-hui kuan yü jen-hsing lun," p. 18.

46. *Ibid.*

47. *Hsiao Chün ssu-hsiang p'i-p'an*, p. 132.

48. Ting Ling, *K'ua-tao hsin-ti shih-tai lai* (Leap into the new period; Peking, 1951), p. 87. This book is a collection of Ting Ling's essays written in the 1940's.

49. *Ibid.*, p. 83.

50. *Ibid.*, p. 88.

51. Liu Chih-ming, *Ch'ing-suan Hsiao Chün ti fan-tung ssu-hsiang*, p. 65.

52. *Ibid.*

Chapter 5: Re-emergence of Literary Factions, 1949–1952

1. "Intellectuals and People of All Circles Should Persistently Reform Their Ideology" (*KMJP* editorial, July 1, 1952); in *CB*, No. 200:32.

2. "Six Thousand College Teachers in Peking and Tientsin Conduct Study Campaign," NCNA (Nov. 12, 1951); in *SCMP*, No. 214:26.

3. "Teachers of Physics Department of Tsinghua Understand More about the Soviet Union," NCNA (Jan. 22, 1952); in *SCMP*, No. 261:6.

4. Shen Yin-mo, "This Man Hu Shih," *Ta-Kung pao* (Shanghai, Dec. 16, 1951); in *CB*, No. 167:4.

5. Chou Yang, *Chien-chüeh kuan-ch'e Mao Tse-tung wen-i lu-hsien* (Steadfastly carry out Mao Tse-tung's line in literature and art; Peking, 1952), p. 94.

6. *Ibid.*, p. 102.

7. Chou Wen, "Kuan-yü Wu Hsün ti 'k'u-hsing' ho 'hsing-hsüeh' " (About Wu Hsün's "ascetic behavior" and "establishment of schools"), *Hsüeh-hsi* (Study), 4.5:22 (1951).

8. Kuo Mo-jo, "Self-Examination in Connection with the Criticism of Wu Hsün," *JMJP* (June 7, 1951); in *CB*, No. 113:15.

9. *Wo ti ssu-hsiang shih tsen-yang chuan-pien kuo-lai ti* (How my ideas have changed; Peking, 1952), p. 178.

10. *Wen-i pao*, 5.4:18 (Dec. 10, 1951).

11. T. A. Hsia, "Twenty Years After the Yenan Forum," *The China Quarterly*, No. 13:246 (January–March 1963).

12. Ting Ling, *K'ua-tao hsin-ti shih-tai lai*, p. 256.

13. Examples: *SCMP*, No. 342:4; *SCMP*, No. 657:17; *SCMP*, No. 663:15.

14. Ting Ling, *Tao ch'ün-chung chung ch'ü lo-hu* (Go into the dwellings of the masses; Peking, 1954), p. 87.

15. Yang Erh, "Shih-t'an T'ao Hsing-chih hsien-sheng piao-yang 'Wu Hsün ching-shen' yu wu chi-chi tso-yung" (On whether there is anything positive in T'ao Hsing-chih's praise of "The Spirit of Wu Hsün"), *Wen-i pao*, 4.2:26–27 (May 10, 1951) and Chia Chi, "Pu-tsu wei-hsün ti Wu Hsün" (Wu Hsün is hardly to be emulated), *Wen-i pao*, 4.1:7–11 (Apr. 25, 1951).

16. Chou Yang, *Chien-chüeh kuan ch'e Mao Tse-tung wen-i lu-hsien*, p. 91.

17. Yü Tzu, "Ou-yang Shan teng jen ti li-tzu cheng-ming liao shen-mo?" (What does the example of Ou-yang Shan and others prove?), *Wen-i pao*, No. 4:11 (1952). Ou-yang Shan was also one of the writers criticized at this time.

18. This story is discussed by C. T. Hsia, pp. 474–475.

19. Ting Ling, *Tao ch'ün-chung chung ch'ü lo-hu*, p. 18.

20. *Ibid.*

21. Ting Ling, "Tso-wei i-chung ch'ing-hsiang lai-k'an" (To view it as a tendency), *Wen-i pao*, 4.8:9 (Aug. 10, 1951).

22. Ting Ling, "Wei t'i-kao wo-men k'an-wu ti ssu-hsiang-hsing, chan-tou-hsing erh tou-cheng" (Struggle for the elevation of consciousness and fighting spirit of our journals), *Wen-i pao*, 5.4:16 (Dec. 10, 1951).

23. *Ibid.*

24. Wang Shu-ming, "Ts'ung *Wen-hsüeh p'ing-lun* pien-chi kung-tso chung chien-t'ao wo ti wen-i p'i-p'ing ssu-hsiang" (An examination of my ideas of literary criticism from the editorial work in *Literary Criticism*), *Wen-i pao*, No. 1:17 (1952).

25. Ting Ling, "*Shan-pei feng-kuang* chiao-hou chi shuo kan" (Thoughts after proofreading *Sketches of Northern Shensi*), *Jen-min wen-hsüeh* (People's literature), 2.2:33 (1950).

26. Ting Ling, *Sun Over the Sangkan River*, in *Chinese Literature*, No. 1:42 (1953).

27. *Ibid.*

28. Ting Ling, *K'ua-tao hsin-ti shih-tai lai*, pp. 265–266.

29. Ting Ling, *Tao ch'ün-chung chung ch'ü lo-hu*, p. 84.

30. *Ibid.*, p. 103.

31. *Ibid.*, p. 101.

32. Ting Ling, *K'ua-tao hsin-ti shih-tai lai*, p. 212.

33. *Ibid.*, p. 210.

34. Ting Ling, *Tao ch'ün-chung chung ch'ü lo-hu*, p. 29.

35. *Ibid.*, p. 30.

36. *Ibid.*, p. 31.

37. *Ibid.*, p. 34.

38. *Ibid.*, p. 26.

39. *Ibid.*, p. 102.

40. *Ibid.*

41. *Chinese Literature*, No. 1:26 (1953).

Chapter 6: The Relaxation of 1953 and the Campaign Against Feng Hsüeh-feng in 1954

1. "Teachers of Institutions of Higher Education in Peking Carry Out Study of *On Practice* and *On Contradiction*," *JMJP* (Sept. 23, 1953); in *SCMP*, No. 664:34.

2. *SCMP*, No. 602:7.

3. "All-China Federation of Literary and Arts Circles Holds Reporting Forum," NCNA (Peking, Nov. 24, 1953); in *SCMP*, No. 696:26.

4. Chou Yang, "Literary Work in Past Four Years," speech at Second All-China Conference of Writers and Artists, NCNA (Sept. 24, 1953); in *SCMP*, No. 658:14.

5. "Strive to Develop Literary and Art Creation," *JMJP* editorial (Oct. 8, 1953); in *SCMP*, No. 668:16.

6. "Measured Advance in the Promotion of Pedagogical Reform in Higher Engineering Schools," *JMJP* editorial (Aug. 16, 1953); in *SCMP*, No. 648:21.

7. "The Whole Teaching Emulation Campaign Should be Stopped," *Jen-min Chiao-Yu* (People's education; August 1953); in *SCMP*, No. 653:18.

8. "Strengthen the Ideological Leadership Over Teachers of Institutions of Higher Education," *JMJP* editorial (Dec. 22, 1953); in *SCMP*, No. 720:24.

9. *Ibid.*, p. 25.

10. "Higher Education Must Follow General Line of the State," *KMJP* (Nov. 8, 1953); in *SCMP*, No. 741:28.

11. "Struggle for the Victorious Fulfillment of this Year's Plan for Cultural and Educational Enterprise," *JMJP* editorial (Mar. 25, 1954); in *SCMP*, No. 777:20.

12. Yen Feng, "T'i-ch'ang ta-tan yen-chiu wen-t'i ti ching-shen" (Advocate the spirit of studying problems boldly), *Hsüeh-hsi*, No. 5:42 (1954).

13. "Struggle for the Victorious Fulfillment of this Year's Plan for Cultural and Educational Enterprise," p. 20.

14. Yen Feng, p. 42.

15. "Strive to Develop Literary and Art Creation," p. 16.

16. *Ibid.*, p. 17.

17. Mao Tun, "New Realities, and New Tasks," speech delivered at Second All-China Conference of Writers, NCNA (Sept. 26, 1953); in *SCMP*, No. 658:18.

18. Mao Tun, "New Realities and New Tasks," *JMJP* (Oct. 10, 1953); in *CB*, No. 282:4.

19. Chou Yang, "Wei ch'uang-tsao keng-to ti yu-hsiu ti wen-hsüeh i-shu tso-p'in erh fen-tou" (To struggle for the creation of more outstanding works of art and literature), *Wen-i pao*, No. 19:10 (1953).

20. *Ibid.*, p. 11.

21. *Ibid.*, p. 16.

22. Chou Yang, "Literary Work in Past Four Years," p. 13.

23. Kuo Mo-jo, "Report Concerning the Basic Conditions of the Chinese Academy of Sciences," *JMJP* (Mar. 26, 1954); in *CB*, No. 359:22.

24. "Liang Shu-ming Makes Self-Review at CPPCC National Committee," NCNA (Feb. 4, 1956); in *SCMP*, No. 1235:48. There is a discussion of his case in Theodore H. E. Chen, *Thought Reform of the Chinese Intellectuals* (Hong Kong, 1960), pp. 46–49; pp. 91–92.

25. For a discussion of their cases, see Theodore H. E. Chen, p. 49.

26. Jerome Grieder analyzes the party's interpretation of *Hung lou meng* in "The Communist Critique of *Hung lou meng*," *Papers on China*, 10:142–169 (Harvard University, East Asian Research Center, 1956).

27. Kuo Mo-jo, "Cultural and Academic Circles Should Launch Struggle Against Bourgeois Thought," *KMJP* (Nov. 8, 1954); in *SCMP*, No. 935:35.

28. "Record of Forum Held for the Study of *The Dream of the Red Chamber*," *KMJP, Literary Heritage Supplement* (Nov. 14, 1954); in *CB*, No. 315:61.

29. Chou Yang, "Wo-men pi-hsü chan-tou" (We must fight), *Wen-i pao*, Nos. 23 and 24:14 (1954).

30. "Record of Forum Held for the Study of *The Dream of the Red Chamber*," p. 39.

31. Lu K'an-ju, "Hu Shih fan-tang ssu-hsiang kei-yü ku-tien wen-hsüeh yen-chiu ti tu-hai" (The poison rendered the study of classical literature by the reactionary thought of Hu Shih), *Wen-i pao*, No. 21:4 (1954).

32. "Record of Forum Held for the Study of *The Dream of the Red Chamber*," p. 62.

33. *Ibid.*, p. 59.

34. *Ibid.*, p. 63.

35. "Criticism of the Writer Feng Hsüeh-feng," NCNA (Aug. 27, 1957); in *SCMP*, No. 1607:9.

36. Feng Hsüeh-feng, *Lun min-chu ke-ming ti wen-i yün-tung*, pp. 133–135.

37. "All-China Association of Literary Workers Reorganized," NCNA (Mar. 29, 1953); in *SCMP*, No. 541:21.

38. Pa Jen (Wang Jen-shu), "Tu 'Ch'u Hsüeh' " (Reading "First Snow"), *Wen-i pao*, No. 2:19–20 (1954). Pa Jen was labeled a rightist in the late 1950's.

39. Feng Hsüeh-feng, *Lun wen-chi* (Collection of essays; Peking, 1952), I, 239.

40. Feng Hsüeh-feng, *Lun 'Pao-wei Yenan'* (On Defend Yenan; Shanghai, 1956), p. 29.

41. Quoted in "P'i-p'an Feng Hsüeh-feng fan Ma-k'e-ssu-chu-i ti wen-i ssu-hsiang" (Criticism of the Anti-Marxist literary ideas of Feng Hsüeh-feng), *Jen-min wen-hsüeh*, No. 12:98 (1957).

42. Quoted in Pa Jen, "Shih hsien-shih chu-i hai-shih fan hsien-shih chu-i" (Is this realism or antirealism?), *Wen-hsüeh p'ing-lun*, No. 1:54 (1959).

43. Ching Tzu, review of 'Hung lou meng' yen-chiu (A study of The Dream of the Red Chamber) by Yü P'ing po; in Wen-i pao, No. 9:39 (1953).

44. Editorial note to Li Hsi-fan and Lan Ling, "Kuan-yü 'Hung lou meng chien-lun' chi ch'i-t'a" (Concerning "A Short Study of The Dream of the Red Chamber" and other views), Wen-i pao, No. 18:31 (1954).

45. "Preserve the Noble Qualities of Communist Party Members, Oppose the Base Individualism of the Bourgeois Class," JMJP editorial (Apr. 13, 1954); in SCMP, No. 793:16.

46. "Record of Forum Held for the Study of The Dream of the Red Chamber," p. 63.

47. Yüan Shui-p'o, "Chih wen 'Wen-i pao' pien-che" (An inquiry of the editors of Wen-i pao), Wen-i pao, No. 20:4 (1954).

48. Decision of joint meeting of presidiums of All-China Federation of Literary and Art Circles and Union of Chinese Writers concerning "Literary Gazette," NCNA (Dec. 8, 1954); in SCMP, No. 960:28.

49. Ibid., p. 27.

50. "Tui 'Wen-i pao' ti p'i-p'ing" (Criticisms of Wen-i pao), Wen-i pao, No. 22:3 (1954).

51. Chou Yang, "Wo-men pi-hsü chan-tou," p. 16.

52. News release, Wen-i pao, No. 22:46 (1954).

53. Kuo Mo-jo, "San-tien chien-i" (Three suggestions), Wen-i pao, Nos. 23 and 24:8 (1954).

54. Ibid., p. 9.

55. Feng Hsüeh-feng, "Chien t'ao wo-tsai 'Wen-i pao' so-fan ti ts'o-wu" (Criticism of my errors committed on Wen-i pao), Wen-i pao, No. 20:5 (1954).

56. News release, Wen-i pao, No. 22:46 (1954).

Chapter 7: The Hu Feng Campaign of 1955

1. Hu Feng, Ts'ung yüan-t'ou tao hung-liu (From the source to the flood; Shanghai, 1952), p. 64.

2. Ibid., p. 106.

3. Ibid., p. 108.

4. "Kuan-yü Hu Feng fan ke-ming chi-t'uan ti ti-erh-p'i ts'ai-liao" (The second collection of materials concerning the Hu Feng antirevolutionary clique), Wen-i pao, No. 11:19 (1955). This letter is dated Aug. 26, [195?].

5. Ibid.

6. Ibid., p. 12. This letter is dated Aug. 22, 1951.

7. Ibid.

8. Ibid., p. 17. This letter is dated Feb. 18, 1951.

9. Ibid. This letter is dated Apr. 16, 1950.

10. Ibid., p. 25. This letter is dated Aug. 29, 1950.

11. Ibid., p. 14. This letter is dated Nov. 15, 1950.

12. Ibid., p. 19. This letter is dated Jan. 16, 1951.

13. Ibid., p. 21. This letter is dated Feb. 26, [195?].

14. Ibid., p. 24. This letter is dated Aug. 24, 1950.

15. Ibid., p. 25. This letter is dated Aug. 29, 1950.

16. Ibid. This letter is dated Feb. 16, [195?].

17. "Kuan-yü Hu Feng fan tang chi-t'uan ti i-hsieh ts'ai-liao," p. 30. This letter is dated Mar. 29, 1950.

18. "Kuan-yü Hu Feng fan ke-ming chi-t'uan ti ti-erh-p'i ts'ai-liao," p. 19.

19. This is reprinted in Yüan Shui-p'o, "Ts'ung Hu Feng ti ch'uang-tso k'an t'a-ti li-lun ti p'o-ch'an" (The bankruptcy of Hu Feng's theories as seen in his writings), in *LWHC*, III, 108.

20. "Kuan-yü Hu Feng fan-ke-ming chi-t'uan ti ti-erh-p'i ts'ai-liao," p. 19. This letter is dated Jan. 18, 1950.

21. In the 1930's, A Lung had written under the pen name Shou Mei and S. M.

22. "Kuan-yü Hu Feng fan-ke-ming chi-t'uan ti ti-erh-p'i ts'ai-liao, p. 19.

23. Li Hsi-fan, "Tui-yü wo-hsiao wen-i chiao-hsüeh wen-t'i ti chi-tien i-chien" (Some suggestions concerning the instruction of aesthetics at our school), *Wen-i pao* No. 2:30 (1952).

24. Lu Hsi-chih, "Wai-ch'ü hsien-shih ti 'hsien-shih chu-i' " (The "realism" that distorts reality), *Wen-i pao*, No. 9:25–26 (1952).

25. *Ibid.*, p. 26.

26. *Ibid.*, p. 28.

27. "Kuan-yü Hu Feng fan-ke-ming chi-t'uan ti ti-erh-p'i ts'ai-liao," p. 23. This letter is dated May 29, 1952.

28. *Ibid.*

29. *Ibid.*, p. 25.

30. *Ibid.*, p. 23. This letter is dated Apr. 16, 1952.

31. "Kuan-yü Hu Feng fan-ke-ming chi-t'uan ti ti-san p'i ts'ai liao," p. 8. This letter is dated May 7, 1952.

32. *Ibid.*, p. 22. This letter is dated May 9, 1952.

33. Note to Shu Wu's, "Ts'ung-t'ou hsüeh-hsi 'tsai Yenan wen-i tso-t'an hui-shang' ti chiang-hua" (Thoroughly study "Talks at the Yenan Forum on Art and Literature"), in *LWHC*, II, 109.

34. "Kuan-yü Hu Feng fan-ke-ming chi-t'uan ti ti-erh-p'i ts'ai-liao," p. 25.

35. Shu Wu, "Chih Lu Ling ti kung-k'ai hsin" (Open letter to Lu Ling), in *LWHC*, II, 138.

36. Ho Ch'i-fang, "Hsien-shih chu-i ti lu hai-shih fan hsien-shih chu-i ti lu?" p. 69.

37. *Ibid.*, p. 70.

38. Lin Mo-han, "Hu Feng ti fan Ma-k'e-ssu chu-i ti wen-i ssu-hsiang" (The anti-Marxist literary ideas of Hu Feng), in *LWHC*, II, 59.

39. Ho Ch'i-fang, "Hsien-shih chu-i ti lu hai shih fan hsien-shih chu-i ti lu?", p. 76.

40. Lin Mo-han, "Hu Feng ti fan Ma-k'e-ssu chu-i ti wen-i ssu-hsiang," p. 63.

41. Ho Ch'i-fang, "Hsien-shih chu-i ti lu hai shih fan hsien-shih chu-i ti lu?", p. 87.

42. *Ibid.*, p. 69.

43. "Kuan-yü Hu Feng fan ke-ming chi-t'uan ti ti-erh-p'i ts'ai-liao," p. 20.

44. "Kuan-yü Hu Feng fan ke-ming chi-t'uan ti ti-san p'i ts'ai-liao," p. 9. There are conflicting reports as to whether Hu was ever a member of the CCP. To apply for membership in the party may refer to admission or reinstatement.

45. "Kuan-yü Hu Feng fan ke-ming chi-t'uan ti ti-erh-p'i ts'ai-liao," p. 20.

46. "Hu Feng tui wen-i wen-t'i ti i-chien" (Hu Feng's literary opinions), supplement to *Wen-i pao* (January 1955).

47. *Ibid.*, p. 34.

48. *Ibid.*, p. 9.

49. *Ibid.*, p. 14.

50. *Ibid.*, p. 8.

51. *Ibid.*, p. 19.

52. *Ibid.*

53. *Ibid.*, p. 20.

54. *Ibid.*, p. 21.

55. *Ibid.*, p. 111.

56. *Ibid.*, p. 24.

57. *Ibid.*, p. 80.

58. *Ibid.*, p. 51.

59. Speech by Lu Ting-i, to the National People's Congress *JMJP* (July 27, 1955); in *CB*, No. 350:14.

60. "Kuan-yü Hu Feng fan ke-ming chi-t'uan ti ti-erh-p'i ts'ai-liao," p. 26. This letter is dated Oct. 27, 1954.

61. *Ibid.*

62. "Tui *Wen-i pao* ti p'i-p'ing," p. 9.

63. *Ibid.*, p. 13.

64. *Ibid.*, p. 11.

65. *Ibid.*, p. 12.

66. *Ibid.*, p. 14.

67. "Kuan-yü Hu Feng fan ke-ming chi-t'uan ti ti-erh-p'i ts'ai-liao," p. 27. This letter is dated Dec. 13, 1954.

68. *Ibid.*

69. *Ibid.* This letter is dated Jan. 20, 1955.

70. Chow Ching-wen, *Ten Years of Storm* (New York, 1960), p. 150. Also, this was the belief of intellectuals who escaped to Hong Kong.

71. Hu Feng's self-criticism, *Wen-i pao*, Nos. 9 and 10:21-26 (1955).

72. *JMJP* (Apr. 1, 1955).

73. *SCMP*, No. 1090:45; NCNA (Peking, July 16, 1955).

74. BBC, World News Broadcasts, No. 473:11.

75. There have been conflicting accounts of what happened to Hu Feng. *Time* on June 24, 1957, reported that he had been released from prison in June 1957 as a symbol of the party's relaxation during the Hundred Flowers movement. A *New York Times* release on June 11, 1957, gave similar information. However, a later report in the *New York Times* on July 19, 1957, stated that Hu was still in prison. Chow Ching-wen in *Ten Years of Storm* wrote, "According to reliable sources, Hu Feng became mentally deranged while in prison," p. 153.

76. Kuo Mo-jo, Report to Inaugural Meeting of Departments of Chinese Academy of Sciences, *JMJP* (June 12, 1955); in *CB*, No. 359:13.

77. BBC, World News Broadcasts, No. 472:13.

78. "Raise Vigilance, Eliminate All Hidden Counterrevolutionaries Within the Ranks of Scientific Circles," editorial in *K'o-hsüeh T'ung-pao* (Journal of science), No. 9 (September 1955); in *ECMM*, No. 18:48 (1955).

79. "Hu Feng's 'On Human Nature' Just a Lie" *Chung-kuo Ch'ing-nien* (China youth), No. 18 (1955); in *ECMM*, No. 15:7.

80. "Kuan-yü Hu Feng fan ke-ming chi-t'uan ti ti-erh-p'i ts'ai-liao," p. 18.

81. "Kuan-yü Hu Feng fan tang chi-t'uan ti i-hsieh ts'ai-liao," p. 32.

82. BBC, World News Broadcasts, No. 471:29.

83. *Ibid.*, No. 469:29.

84. Lu K'uei-jan, *Hu Feng shih-chien ti ch'ien-yin hou-kuo* (The cause and effect of the Hu Feng case; Hong Kong, 1956), pp. 8–9.

85. *Union Research Service* (Hong Kong), 10.1:5.

86. *Ibid.*

87. "Kuan-yü Hu Feng fan ke-ming chi-t'uan ti ti-erh-p'i ts'ai-liao," p. 28.

88. *Ibid.*

89. "Kuan-yü Hu Feng fan ke-ming chi-t'uan ti ti-san p'i ts'ai-liao," p. 9.

90. "Kuan-yü Hu Feng fan ke-ming chi-t'uan ti ti-erh-p'i ts'ai-liao," p. 28.

91. *Ibid.*, p. 27.

92. *SCMP*, No. 1068:19; NCNA (June 10, 1955).

93. Speech by Lu Ting-i to the National People's Congress, *JMJP* (July 27, 1955); in *CB*, No. 350:12.

94. Wang Tzu-yeh, "Are There Any Merits on the Part of Double-Crossers?" *Chung-kuo Ch'ing-nien*, No. 14 (July 16, 1955); in *ECMM*, No. 4:4 (1955).

95. Robert Guillain, *Six Hundred Million Chinese* (New York, 1957), p. 176.

96. *Ibid.*

Chapter 8: Writers Bloom in the Hundred Flowers Movement

1. "Symposium at Headquarters of CDL on the Problem of Uniting and Transforming Intellectuals," *KMJP* (Dec. 3, 1955); in *SCMP*, No. 1190; 5.

2. Cheng Chu-chang, "Lun Chung-kung t'ung-chih ts'e-lüeh ti chuan-pien" (On the change of the leadership policy of the Chinese Communists), *Min-chu p'ing-lun* (Democratic review), 7.16:15 (1956).

3. An Chao-tsun, "Make Better Use of Technical Persons," *JMJP* (Jan. 12, 1956); in *CB*, No. 379:1.

4. Shih P'ing, "Tang ti ling-tao tui tzu-jan k'o-hsüeh ti i-i" (The significance of party leadership to the natural sciences), *Hsüeh-hsi* No. 1:22 (1956).

5. *Union Research Service*, II, 154.

6. "Promote Independent Thinking and Free Discussion Among Cadres in Their Theoretical Study," *Hsüeh-hsi* No. 10 (Oct. 2, 1956); in *ECMM*, No. 65:30.

7. Lin K'o, "Yeh-shih tso-chia-men ti tse-jen" (It is also the responsibility of the writers), *Wen-i pao*, No. 1:36 (1956).

8. Chou Yang, "Building a Socialist Literature," *Chinese Literature*, No. 4:216 (1956).

9. *Ibid.*

10. Chou Yang, "Building a Socialist Literature," excerpts, *JMJP* (Mar. 25, 1956); in *CB*, No. 385:11.

11. *Ibid.*, p. 17.

12. "Pien-che ti hua" (Words from the editor), *Wen-i pao*, No. 9:21 (1956).

13. Wang Yü, "I-shu hsing-hsiang ti ko-hsing-hua" (The individualization of artistic images), *Wen-i pao*, No. 10:28 (1956).

14. Shen Yen-ping (Mao Tun), "Wen-hsüeh i-shu kung-tso chung ti kuan-chien-hsing wen-t'i (The key problems in art and literature), *Wen-i pao*, No. 12:3 (1956).

15. "Chung-kuo tso-chia hsieh-hui yen-chiu chih-hsing 'pai-hua ch'i-fang, pai-chia cheng-ming' ti fang-chen" (The Chinese Writers' Union is studying the

implementation of the principles of the "Hundred Flowers, Hundred Schools"), *Wen-i pao*, No. 14:20 (1956).

16. Shen Yen-ping (Mao Tun), "Wen-hsüeh i-shu kung-tse chung ti kuan-chien-hsing wen-t'i," p. 3.

17. "Chung-kuo tso-chia hsieh-hui yen-chiu chih-hsing 'pai-hua ch'i-fang, pai-chia cheng-ming' ti fang-chen," p. 21.

18. "This is No Small Clique," *Chung-kuo Ch'ing-nien pao* (China youth newspaper; July 17, 1956); in *SCMP*, No. 1343:2.

19. Chou Yang, "The Important Role of Art and Literature in the Building of Socialism," *Chinese Literature*, No. 1:184 (1957).

20. "Measures Adopted to Ensure Intellectuals of Time for Their Specialized Activity," *KMJP* (Nov. 22, 1956); in *SCMP*, No. 1434:11.

21. Lu Ting-i, "Speech in Commemoration of the Twentieth Anniversary of Death of Lu Hsün," NCNA (Oct. 19, 1956); in *SCMP*, No. 1404:16.

22. Chou Yang, "The Important Role of Art and Literature in the Building of Socialism," p. 187.

23. For a discussion of the impact of Soviet literary happenings on Communist Chinese literary circles in this period, see D. W. Fokkema, *Literary Doctrine in China and The Soviet Influence 1956–1960* (The Hague, 1965).

24. Ch'iu-yün (Huang Ch'iu-yün), "Pu-yao tsai jen-min ti chi-k'u mien-ch'ien pi-shang yen-ching" (We must not close our eyes to the hardships of the people), *Jen-min wen-hsüeh*, No. 9:58 (1956).

25. *Ibid.*

26. *Ibid.*

27. *Ibid.*

28. *Ibid.*

29. *Ibid.*, p. 59.

30. Ch'in Ch'ao-yang, *Village Vignettes* (Peking: Foreign Language Press, 1955).

31. Chou Yang, "Building a Socialist Literature," p. 218.

32. *Ibid.*, p. 211.

33. Ho Chih (Ch'in Ch'ao-yang), "Hsien-shih chu-i — kuang-k'uo ti tao-lu" (Realism — the broad road), *Jen-min wen-hsüeh*, No. 9:2 (1956).

34. *Ibid.*, p. 4.

35. *Ibid.*, p. 3.

36. *Ibid.*, p. 8.

37. *Ibid.*, p. 9.

38. *Ibid.*, p. 8.

39. *Ibid.*, p. 13.

40. *The Selected Works of Lu Hsün* (Peking: Foreign Language Press, 1956), III, 22.

41. Ch'en Yung, "Kuan-yü wen-hsüeh i-shu t'e-cheng ti i-hsieh wen-t'i" (Some problems concerning the characteristics of art and literature), *Wen-i pao*, No. 9:33 (1956).

42. *Ibid.*, p. 37.

43. Ch'en Yung's report, in *Ch'üan-kuo ch'ing-nien wen-hsüeh ch'uang-tso che hui-i pao-kao fa-yen chi* (A collection of reports of the meetings of China's young creative writers; Peking, 1956), p. 62.

44. Ch'en Yung, "Wei wen-hsüeh i-shu ti hsien-shih chu-i erh tou-cheng ti

Lu Hsün" (Lu Hsün struggles for literary and artistic realism), *Jen-min wen-hsüeh*, No. 10:12 (1956).

45. Ch'en Yung's report, p. 64.

46. Hsiao Yeh-mu, " 'Pai-hua ch'i-fang, pai-chia cheng-ming' yu kan" (Thoughts on "The Hundred Flowers, Hundred Schools"), *Jen-min wen-hsüeh*, No. 7:58–59 (1956).

47. Chu Kuang-ch'ien, "Ts'ung chieh-shen ti ching-yen t'an pai-chia cheng-ming" (On the "Hundred Flowers" from personal experience), *Wen-i pao*, No. 1:10 (1957).

48. Ai Ch'ing, "T'an-t'an hsieh shih" (Talk about writing poetry), in *Tso-chia t'an ch'uang-tso*, p. 113.

49. Ai Ch'ing's speech, in *Chung-kuo tso-chia hsieh-hui ti-erh tz'u li-shih-hui hui-i k'uo-ta pao-kao fa-yen chi* (A collection of speeches of the second meeting of the Chinese Writers' Union; Peking, 1956), p. 338.

50. "Fei-t'eng ti sheng-huo ho shih" (Seething life and poetry), *Wen-i pao*, No. 3:26 (1956). Discussions of poets in the Chinese Writers' Union.

51. Ai Ch'ing, "Huang niao" (The yellow bird), reprinted in *Tang t'ien-hsia yü tang kuo-chia* (Party world and party state), ed. I Ch'ung-kuang (Hong Kong, 1958), II, 161.

52. Ai Ch'ing, "Yang-hua jen ti meng" (The dream of the gardener), *Wen-i yüeh-pao* (Literary and art monthly; Shanghai), No. 2:22 (1957).

53. Ho Chih (Ch'in Ch'ao-yang), "Lun 'Chien-jui' chih feng" (On the spirit of "Sharpness"), *Wen-i hsüeh-hsi* (Literary study), No. 8:3 (1956).

54. Ho Chih (Ch'in Ch'ao-yang), "Lun 'Ch'üeh-shao shih-chien' " (On "The Lack of Time"), *Jen-min wen-hsüeh*, No. 6:1–2 (1956).

55. Ho Yu-hua (Ch'in Ch'ao-yang), "Ch'en mo" (Silence), *Jen-min wen-hsüeh*, No. 1:26–27 (1957).

56. Liu Pin-yen, "Pen-pao nei-pu hsiao-hsi" (Our paper's inside news), *Jen-min Wen-hsüeh*, No. 6:6–21 (1956).

57. Quoted by Chang Kuang-nien in *Wen-i pien-lun chi* (Literary debates; Peking, 1958), p. 143.

58. Discussed by R. David Arkush in "One of the Hundred Flowers: Wang Meng's 'Young Newcomer,' " *Papers on China*, 18:155–186 (Harvard University, East Asian Research Center, 1964). Also in Fokkema, pp. 99–103.

59. "Don't Be Afraid of Opposing Views," *JMJP* editorial (Oct. 9, 1956); in *SCMP*, No. 1397:5.

60. "Positively Better the Working and Living Condiitons for Teachers in Institutions of Higher Education," *KMJP* editorial (April 17, 1956); in *SCMP*, No. 1279:3–4.

61. Ch'en Ch'i-t'ung, Ch'en Ya-ting, Ma Han-ping, Lu Le, "Some of Our Views on Current Literary and Art Work," *JMJP* (Jan. 7, 1957); in *SCMP*, No. 1507:18–19.

62. "Ministry of Education Issues Notification of Strengthening of Ideological and Political Indoctrination in Middle Schools" *Chiao Shih pao* (Teachers' news; Jan. 22, 1957); in *SCMP*, No. 1480:5.

63. "Kuan-yü 'Tsu-chih pu hsin-lai ti ch'ing-nien jen' ti t'ao-lun" (Discussion of "A Young Newcomer in the Organization Department"), *Wen-i hsüeh-hsi*, No. 2:11 (1957).

64. *Hsüeh-hsi*, No. 6:23 (1957).

65. Huang Ch'iu-yün, "Tz'u tsai na-li?" (Where is the thorn?), *Wen-i hsüeh-hsi*, No. 6:8 (1957).

66. Liu Shao-t'ang and Ts'ung Wei-hsi, "Hsieh chen-shih — she-hui chu-i hsien-shih chu-i ti sheng-ming he-hsin" (Write the truth — the living core of Socialist realism), *Wen-i hsüeh-hsi*, No. 1:17 (1957).

67. *Ibid.*, p. 18.

68. *Ibid.*

69. Quoted in Chang Kuang-nien, p. 144.

70. Ho Chih (Ch'in Ch'ao-yang), "Kuan-yü 'hsieh chen-shih' " (On "Write the Truth"), *Jen-min wen-hsüeh*, No. 3:3 (1957).

71. *Ibid.*

72. Quoted in Chang Kuang-nien, p. 148.

73. Chien Yü, " 'Hsien chuang' ou-kan erh-tse" (Two impromptu pieces on the "status quo"), *Jen-min wen-hsüeh*, No. 3:57 (1957).

74. Li Chien-feng, "Hsiang-hua ho tu-ts'ao" (Fragrant flowers and poisonous weeds) in *Jen-min wen-hsüeh*, No. 3:59 (1957).

75. "Cheng-ch'ü she-hui chu-i wen-hsüeh i-shu ti kao-tu fan-jung" (Strive for the flourishing of Socialist literature and art), *Wen-i pao* editorial, No. 1:2 (1957).

76. Mao Tun, "Carry Out the Line of Letting All Flowers Bloom Together, Oppose Doctrinairism and the Rightist Ideas of the Petty Bourgeoisie," *JMJP* (Mar. 18, 1957); in *SCMP*, No. 1507:13.

77. *Ibid.*

78. Huang Ch'iu-yün, "Tz'u tsai na-li?", p. 8.

79. Mao Tse-tung, "On the Correct Handling of Contradictions Among the People," NCNA (June 18, 1957); in Roderick MacFarquhar, *The Hundred Flowers* (London, 1960), p. 267.

80. *New York Times* (Feb. 24, 1957), p. 20.

81. "Should Bourgeois Intellectuals Not be Included in Ranks of Exploiting Classes?" *KMJP* (July 25, 1958); in *SCMP*, No. 1838:6.

82. Mao Tse-tung, "On the Correct Handling of Contradictions Among the People," p. 270.

83. *Ibid.*, p. 276.

84. Han Yü-chung, "T'an-t'an hsüeh-hsi Ma-k'e-ssu-lieh-ning chu-i ching-tien chu-tso ho tu-li ssu-k'ao" (On the Marxist-Leninist texts and independent thinking), *Hsüeh-hsi*, No. 8:11 (1957).

85. "Many Scientists Think that Line of Letting All Flowers Bloom Should be Further Implemented," NCNA (Peking, Apr. 21, 1957); in *SCMP*, No. 1529:12.

86. "Party Directive on Rectification Campaign," NCNA (Apr. 30, 1957); in *SCMP*, No. 1523:41.

87. "Continue to Contend, Aid the Rectification Campaign," *JMJP* editorial (May 19, 1957); in *SCMP*, No. 1537:3.

88. "Chou Yang Answers Questions on Literary and Art Work," *Wen-hui pao* (Shanghai, Apr. 9, 1957); in *CB*, No. 452:29.

89. "Refutation of the Preposterous Idea of 'Party Empire,' " *Hsin Chien-sheh* (New construction), No. 1 (January 1958); in *ECMM*, No. 123:3.

90. "Peking University Holds Forum to Discuss Contradictions Within the Ranks of the People," NCNA (May 7, 1957); in *SCMP*, No. 1545:5.

91. Lo Lung-chi, "Band the Non-Party Intellectuals Closer With the Party," *JMJP* (Mar. 23, 1957); in *CB*, No. 444:21.

92. "Tientsin Professors' Views on Contention of Diverse Schools of Thought," NCNA (Apr. 22, 1957); in *SCMP*, No. 1529:20.

93. "Kao-chi chih-shih fen-tzu tso-t'an Ma-Lieh chu-i li-lun hsüeh-hsi" (High-level intellectuals discuss the study of Marxist-Leninist theory), *Hsüeh-hsi*, No. 11:6 (1957).

94. Yao Hsüeh-yin, "Ta-k'ai ch'uang-hu shuo liang-hua" (Open the window and tell the truth), *Wen-i pao*, No. 7:10 (1957).

95. Shao Ch'üan-lin is quoted in an account of a meeting of editors by Huang Mo, "Pien-chi kung-tso i-ting yao shih-ho tang-ch'ien hsin hsing-shih" (Editorial work must suit the current new situations), *Wen-i pao*, No. 4:2 (1957).

96. Cheng Nung, "Yeh t'an 'pai-hua ch'i-fang, pai-chia cheng-ming'" (Also on the "Hundred Flowers, Hundred Schools"), *Wen-i pao*, No. 8:3 (1957).

97. "When the Buds Blossom," *Hsin kuan-cha* (New observer), No. 10 (May 16, 1957); in *ECMM*, No. 97:7.

98. Fokkema, p. 178. Mr. Fokkema discusses the criticism of these stories.

99. Liu Shao-t'ang, "Hsien-shih chu-i tsai she-hui chu-i shih-tai ti fa-chan" (The development of realism in a period of socialism), *Pei-ching wen-i* (Peking literature), No. 4:9, 11 (1957).

100. MacFarquhar, p. 180.

101. Liu Shao-t'ang, "Hsien-shih chu-i tsai she-hui chu-i shih-tai ti fa-chan," p. 9.

102. Among them were Yao Hsüeh-yin and the playwright Wu Tsu-kuang who claimed that such writers as Li Po and Tolstoy did not need doctrine or leadership to produce great works.

103. *Communist China 1949–1959* (Hong Kong, 1961), p. 166.

104. Dennis Doolin, *Communist China, The Politics of Student Opposition* (Stanford, 1964), p. 63.

105. Speech of Shu Wu, *Chung-kuo tso-chia hsieh-hui ti-erh tz'u li-shih-hui hui-i k'uo-ta pao-kao fa-yen chi*, p. 316.

106. Doolin, p. 55.

107. Mao Tse-tung, "On the Correct Handling of Contradictions Among the People," p. 276.

108. Quoted in Cheng Hsüeh-chia, *The So-Called Enlightened Despotism* (Taiwan, 1957), p. 39.

109. Hsü Mou-yung, "Ch'an-tsao chü man-pi (Random notes from the abode of a noisy cicada), *Jen-min wen-hsüeh*, No. 7:155 (1957).

110. *Ibid.*

111. Huang Ch'iu-yün, "Tz'u tsai na-li?", p. 8.

112. Tsang K'e-chia, "Ko-jen ti kan-shou" (My individual impressions), *Wen-i pao*, No. 8:3 (1957).

113. I Sung, "Pu-hao ling-tao" (Leadership is not easy), *Wen-i pao*, No. 17:3 (1956).

114. *Ibid.*, p. 4.

115. "Chinese Writers' Union Forum on Rectification," NCNA (May 22, 1957); in *SCMP*, No. 1556:12.

116. *Communist China 1957* (Hong Kong, 1958), p. 143.

117. *Ibid.*

118. "*Chung-kuo ch'ing-nien pao* Editorial Department Examines Itself," NCNA (July 10, 1957); in *SCMP*, No. 1576:24.

119. T'ang Chih, "Fan-suo kung-shih k'o-i chih-tao ch'uang-tso na?" (Can elaborate formulas lead creative writing?), *Wen-i pao*, No. 10:2 (1957).

Chapter 9: The Antirightist Drive Against the Writers, 1957–1958

1. *New York Times* (Sept. 2, 1963). The article was written by Harry Schwartz.

2. Chou Yang, "Speech at Meeting of Writers and Artists to Celebrate the Fortieth Anniversary of the October Revolution," *JMJP* (Nov. 9, 1957); in *SCMP*, No. 1664:5.

3. "There Must Be Active Criticism as well as Correct Counter-Criticism," *JMJP* editorial (June 9, 1957); in *SCMP*, No. 1553:4.

4. *New York Times* (June 24, 1957), p. 7.

5. *New York Times* (July 12, 1957), p. 4.

6. "Which Should Come First — 'Becoming Red' or 'Becoming an Expert'?", *Chung-kuo ch'ing-nien*, No. 23 (Dec. 1, 1957); in *ECMM*, No. 121:10.

7. Sun Hsiao-p'ing, "Ting Ling kuan-hsin kuo ch'ing-nien tso-che ma?" (Has Ting Ling ever been concerned about young writers?), *Meng-ya* (Sprouts), No. 20:6 (1957).

8. "The Writers' Association Combats Ting Ling's and Ch'en Ch'i-hsia's Anti-Party Activities," NCNA (Aug. 6, 1957); in *SCMP*, No. 1590:31.

9. *Ibid.*, p. 30.

10. Mao Tun, "P'ei-yang hsin-sheng li-liang, k'uo-ta wen-hsüeh tui-wu" (Cultivate new strength, broaden the ranks of literature), in *Chung-kuo tso-chia hsieh-hui ti-erh tz'u li-shih hui hui-i k'uo-ta pao-kao fa-yen chi*, p. 45.

11. Ting Ling, "Sheng-huo, ssu-hsiang yü jen-wu" (Life, thought and characters), *Jen-min wen-hsüeh*, No. 3:120 (1955).

12. *Wen-i pao*, No. 1:266 (1956).

13. *Wen-i pao*, No. 7:3 (1957).

14. "Turn Around the Bourgeois Tendency of *Wen-i pao*," NCNA (July 12, 1957); in *SCMP*, No. 1580:9.

15. Ho Chin-ching, "1954 nien chien-ch'a *Wen-i pao* ti chieh-lun pu-neng t'ui-fan" (The conclusion reached after the investigation of *Wen-i pao* in 1954 cannot be overthrown), *Wen-i pao*, No. 22:6 (1957).

16. "Wen-i chieh cheng-tsai chin-hsing i-ch'ang ta pien-lun" (A great debate is going on in art and literary circles), *Wen-i pao*, No. 20:2 (1957).

17. Ho Ch'i-fang, "Pao-wei tang ti yüan-tse, pao-wei she-hui chu-i ti wen-i shih-yeh" (Defend the party's principles, defend the Socialist literary undertaking), *Wen-i pao*, No. 20:7 (1957).

18. *Ibid.*, p. 6.

19. Lao She, "Shu-li hsin feng-ch'i" (Establish a new trend), *Wen-i pao*, No. 25:9 (1957).

20. He was an old literary theorist from the 1930's in Shanghai, who was later to be accused of revisionist thinking.

21. Feng Hsüeh-feng's self-criticism in "Kuan-yü Hu Feng fan ke-ming huo-tung ti i-hsieh shih-shih" (Some facts concerning Hu Feng's antirevolutionary activity), *Wen-i pao*, No. 12:20 (1955).

22. Feng Hsüeh-feng is quoted in "Wen-hsüeh shang ti hsiu-cheng chu-i ssu-

ch'ao ho ch'uang-tso ch'ing-hsiang" (The revisionist stream of thought and tendency of writing in literature), *Jen-min wen-hsüeh*, No. 11:110 (1957).

23. Feng Hsüeh-feng is quoted in "P'i-p'an Feng Hsüeh-feng fan Ma-k'e-ssu chu-i ti wen-i ssu-hsiang" (Criticism of Feng Hsüeh-feng's anti-Marxist literary thought), *Jen-min wen-hsüeh*, No. 12:94 (1957).

24. Feng Hsüeh-feng is quoted in "Feng Hsüeh-feng tsai san-ko wen-t'i shang ti hsiu-cheng chu-i kuan-tien" (The revisionist views of Feng Hsüeh-feng on three problems), *Jen-min wen-hsüeh*, No. 12:114 (1957).

25. *Ibid.*

26. "P'i-p'an Feng Hsüeh-feng fan Ma-k'e-ssu chu-i ti wen-i ssu-hsiang," p. 94.

27. "Feng Hsüeh-feng tsai san-ko wen-t'i shang ti hsiu-cheng chu-i kuan-tien," p. 113.

28. "P'i-p'an Feng Hsüeh-feng fan Ma-k'e-ssu chu-i ti wen-i ssu-hsiang," p. 100.

29. Wu Ying, "Pai-chia cheng-ming'i-wai chung-chung" (In spite of the "Hundred Schools Contend"), *Jen-min wen-hsüeh*, No. 9:54-57 (1956).

30. Yang Chih-i, "T'a-men che-yang tsai 'kuan-hsin' ch'ing-nien jen" (They are so "concerned" about young men), *Wen-i pao*, No. 23:5 (1957).

31. Yüan Shui-p'o, "Fan-tu Feng Hsüeh-feng ti wen-i lu-hsien" (Against Feng Hsüeh-feng's line of literature and art), *Wen-i yüeh-pao*, No. 10:10 (1957).

32. "Criticism of the Writer Feng Hsüeh-feng," NCNA (Aug. 27, 1957); in *SCMP*, No. 1607:6.

33. News item, *Wen-i pao*, No. 22:2 (1957).

34. *Ibid.*, p. 3.

35. Leo Ou-fan Lee discusses this novel in "Hsiao Chün, The Man and His Works," Seminar paper (Harvard University, 1964).

36. "Hsiao Chün ti *Wu-yüeh ti k'uang-shan* wei-shen-mo shih yu-tu ti?" (Why is Hsiao Chün's *Coal Mines in May* poisonous?), *Wen-i pao*, No. 24:44, 47 (1955).

37. *Tang-t'ien hsia yü tang kuo-chia*, I, 102.

38. Wang Jo-wang, "I-pu wu-mieh tang, wu-mieh kung-jen chieh-chi ti fan-tung hsiao-shuo" (A reactionary novel which slanders the party and the working class), *Wen-i hsüeh-hsi*, No. 1:17 (1956).

39. *Ibid.*

40. "Hsiao Chün ssu-hsiang tsai p'i-p'an," p. 41.

41. *Ibid.*

42. Wang Ming t'ang, "Hsü Chung-yü ti 'Lu Hsün yen-chiu'" (Hsü Chung-yü's "A Study of Lu Hsün"), *Wen-i yüeh-pao*, No. 9:16 (1957).

43. News item, *Wen-i pao*, No. 22:2 (1957).

44. "Ting Ling ni chiao-au hsieh shen-mo?" (Ting Ling, What are you proud of?), *Wen-i pao*, No. 26:7 (1957).

45. Huai Hai, "'Tso-i' ch'eng-wei 'yu-i'" ("Left-wing" into "right-wing"), *Jen-min wen-hsüeh*, No. 10:13 (1957).

46. "Chien-ch'ih she-hui chu-i ti wen-i lu-hsien" (Insist on the Socialist literary line), *Wen-i yüeh-pao*, No. 10:3 (1957).

47. Tien Chien, "Chieh-ch'uan Ting Ling ti wei-chuang" (Take off Ting Ling's camouflage), *Wen-i pao*, No. 21:6 (1957).

48. Chu K'o-yu, "Lun *T'ai-yang chao-tsai sang-kan-ho shang*" (On the Sun Over the Sangkan River), *Jen-min wen-hsüeh*, No. 10:126 (1957).

49. Chou Yang, "Wen-i chan-hsien shang ti i-ch'ang ta pien-lun" (A great debate on the literary front), *Wen-i pao*, No. 5:7 (1958).

50. Feng Hsüeh-feng is quoted in Pa Jen, "Shih hsien-shih chu-i hai-shih fan hsien-shih chu-i," p. 43.

51. Shao Ch'üan-lin, "The Struggle Between Two Trends in Literature, p. 138.

52. K'ang Cho, "Liquidate the Evil Influence of 'Soul-corroding Master' Ting Ling," *Chung-kuo ch'ing-nien*, No. 17 (Sept. 1, 1957); in *ECMM*, No. 114:21. K'ang Cho was an associate of Chou Yang.

53. Ha Hua, "Fan-tang fen-tzu Ting Ling ti ch'ou-o ling-hun" (The ugly soul of the antiparty Ting Ling), *Meng ya*, No. 17:3 (1957).

54. K'ang Cho, p. 21.

55. *Ibid.*, p. 16.

56. *Union Research Service*, VIII, 425.

57. "Handle Inner-Party Rightists Sternly," *JMJP* editorial (Sept. 11, 1957); in *SCMP*, No. 1616:3.

58. Chu Ching-hua and Pao Ming-lu, "Shen k'e ti i-k'e" (A profound lesson), *Wen-i pao*, No. 27:2 (1957).

59. K'ang Cho, p. 18.

60. "Ting Ch'en fan-tang chi-t'uan t'ou shih" (Looking through the antiparty clique of Ting Ch'en), *Wen-i pao*, No. 24:5 (1957).

61. Letter to the editor, entitled "'Tsai p'i-p'an' pang-chu wo t'i-kao le jen-shih" ("Recriticism" has helped elevate my consciousness), *Wen-i pao*, No. 6:31 (1958).

62. Ch'üan-lin (Shao Ch'üan-lin), "Tou-cheng feng-mang chih-hsiang yu p'ai" (The sword of struggle is pointed toward the rightists), *Wen-i pao*, No. 14:2 (1957).

63. Hsiao Yeh-mu, "Pu yau tsai ch'en-mo le!" (Don't be silent any more!), *Wen-i pao*, No. 15:8 (1957).

64. Kuo Mo-jo, "Strive to Remold Ourselves into Cultural Workers for the Proletariat," *JMJP* (Sept. 23, 1957); in *SCMP*, No. 1629:10.

65. "Ting Ling chieh-ch'i ti i-mien fan-tang hei-ch'i" (An antiparty black flag that Ting Ling has hoisted), *Pei-ching wen-i*, No. 2:8 (1958).

66. Li Yün, "Yu shou-tao i-tz'u chiao-yü" (I got another education), *Wen-i pao*, No. 6:32 (1958).

67. Lu Ting-i, Kuo Mo-jo, et al., "Great Victory Won in Struggle by Literary and Art Circles Against Ting Ch'en Antiparty Group," *JMJP* (Sept. 27, 1957); in *SCMP*, No. 1629:15.

68. Liu Shao-t'ang is quoted in Kuo Hsiao-ch'uan, "Ch'en-chung ti chiao-hsün" (A heavy lesson), *Wen-i pao*, No. 28:8 (1957).

69. Liu Shao-t'ang is quoted in Hsiao Li, "Tang-hsing, sheng-huo ho chen-shih" (Party spirit, life and reality), *Wen-i yüeh-pao*, No. 1:83–84 (1958).

70. *Ibid.*, p. 84.

71. *Ibid.*

72. "Liu Shao-t'ang tsai 't'an-so' shen-mo?" (What is Liu Shao-t'ang "searching for"?), *Wen-i yüeh-pao*, No. 1:86 (1958).

73. Mao Tun, "Distinguish Between the Right and Wrong Among Great Issues," *Wen-i pao*, No. 25 (Sept. 29, 1957); in *ECMM*, No. 111:7.

74. Liu Shao-t'ang, "Hsien-shih chu-i tsai she-hui chu-i shih-tai ti fa-chan," p. 10.

75. "Liu Shao-t'ang tsai 't'an-so' shen-mo?", p. 85.

76. *Ibid.*, pp. 85–86.

77. Liu Shao-t'ang is quoted in Ha Hua, "Yu-p'ai fen-tzu Liu Shao-t'ang tui Su-lien wen-hsüeh ti fei-pang" (Rightist Liu Shao-t'ang's slander of Soviet literature), *Meng ya*, No. 19:3 (1957).

78. "Yao tso wu-ch'an chieh-chi ti hsin-sheng li-liang!" (We want to be the newborn force of the proletariat), *Meng ya*, No. 18:3 (1957).

79. Kung Mu, "To-lo ti chiao-yin, ch'en-t'ung ti chiao-hsün" (A decadent footprint, a painful lesson), *Wen-i hsüeh-hsi*, No. 11:23 (1957).

80. "*Chung-kuo ch'ing-nien pao* Writer Liu Pin-yen Exposed as Mouthpiece in the Party for Bourgeois Rightists," *JMJP* (July 20, 1957); in *SCMP*, No. 1583: 16.

81. Huang Ch'iu-yün, "P'i-p'an wo tzu-chi" (Criticizing myself), *Wen-i hsüeh-hsi*, No. 9:28 (1957).

82. Shao Ch'üan-lin, "Tou-cheng pi-hsü keng shen-ju" (The struggle must penetrate more deeply), *Wen-i pao*, No. 25:5 (1957).

83. "Peking Writers and Artists Discuss Chou Yang's Report," *Chinese Literature*, No. 5:139 (1958).

84. "Lu Ting-i, Chou Yang tsai tso-hsieh tang-tsu k'uo-ta hui-i shang tso chung-yao chiang-hu" (Lu Ting-i and Chou Yang made important speeches to enlarged sessions of the party branch of the Writers' Union), *Wen-i pao*, No. 25:1 (1957).

85. "Should Bourgeois Intellectuals Not Be Included in Ranks of Exploiting Classes?", p. 10.

86. Lu Ting-i, Kuo Mo-jo, et al., "Great Victory Won in Struggle by Literary and Art Circles Against Ting Ch'en Antiparty Group," p. 18.

87. *Ibid.*, p. 21.

88. *New York Times* (Nov. 29, 1958), p. 16.

89. Chou Yang, "Build China's Own Marxist Literary Theory and Criticism," *KMJP* (Aug. 29, 1958); in *SCMP*, No. 1861:16.

90. Kuo Mo-jo, "Hit Back with a Vengeance at the Rightist!" NCNA (July 15, 1957); in *SCMP*, No. 1580:16.

91. Chiang I-wei, "Chi-shu yü cheng-chih" (Skill and politics), *Hsüeh-hsi*, No. 16:13 (1957).

92. Mao I-sheng, "Tang shih wan-ch'üan neng-kou ling-tao k'o-hsüeh shih-yeh ti" (The Party is totally capable of leadership of scientific work), *Hsüeh-hsi*, No. 20:9 (1957).

93. *Union Research Service*, 11.14:181.

Chapter 10: The Great Leap Forward and Ho Ch'i-fang

1. *Union Research Service*, 17.17:109.

2. "The Road of Development of Our Country's Scientific and Technical Work," *Hung-ch'i* (The red flag), No. 9 (Oct. 1, 1958); in *ECMM*, No. 154:12.

3. "Famous Writers Plans for This Year," NCNA (Mar. 8, 1958); in *SCMP*, No. 1731:23.

4. "Chou Yang on Leap Forward Literature," NCNA (Mar. 30, 1958); in *SCMP*, No. 1749:7.

5. S. H. Chen, "Poetry and The Great Leap Forward," *The China Quarterly*, No. 3:4 (1960).

6. "Amateur Worker-Writers Meet in Tientsin," NCNA (May 28, 1958); in *SCMP*, No. 1785:40.

7. "*People's Literature* Devoted to Writings by Workers, Peasants, and Soldiers," NCNA (Aug. 4, 1958); in *SCMP*, No. 1835:35.

8. S. H. Chen, p. 5. Mr. Chen describes this process.

9. "Vice Chairman of Writers' Union Participates in Peasants' Poetry Contest in Village Near Sian," NCNA (July 30, 1958); in *SCMP*, No. 1826:9.

10. *New York Times* (Dec. 1, 1958), p. 13.

11. *Songs of The Red Flag*, comp. by Chou Yang and Kuo Mo-jo (Peking, 1961), p. 10.

12. This article was incorporated into Chou Yang's *A Great Debate on the Literary Front* (Peking, 1958), p. 30.

13. Kuo Mo-jo, "Chiu mu-ch'ien ch'uang-tso chung ti chi-ke wen-t'i ta *Jen-min wen-hsüeh* pien-che wen" (Answer to questions by editors of *People's Literature* on some problems in current creative writing), *Jen-min wen-hsüeh*, No. 1:4 (1959).

14. Chou Yang, "Build China's Own Marxist Literary Theory and Criticism," p. 20.

15. Ho Ch'i-fang, *Hsi-yüan chi* (Hsi-yüan collection; Peking, 1952), p. 158.

16. Ho Ch'i-fang, *Kuan-yü hsien-shih chu-i* (On realism; Shanghai, 1950), p. 33.

17. Ho Ch'i-fang, *Hsi-yüan chi*, p. 1.

18. *Ibid.*, pp. 1-2.

19. Ho Ch'i-fang, "Kuan-yü hsieh-shih ho tu-shih" (On writing and reading poetry), *Tso-chia t'an ch'uang-tso*, p. 112.

20. Ho Ch'i-fang, *Kuan-yü hsieh-shih ho tu-shih* (On writing and reading poetry; Peking, 1956), p. 2.

21. Ho Ch'i-fang, *Hsi-yüan chi*, p. 74.

22. Ho Ch'i-fang, "Kuan-yü shih-ko hsing-shih wen-t'i ti cheng-lun" (Controversy concerning the problem of poetic forms), *Wen-hsüeh p'ing-lun*, No. 1:17 (1959).

23. *Ibid.*

24. Ho Ch'i-fang, *Hsi-yüan chi*, p. 87.

25. *Ibid.*, pp. 88-89.

26. Feng Hsüeh-feng, *Lun-wen chi*, p. 239.

27. Ho Ch'i-fang, *Hsi-yüan chi*, p. 90.

28. *Ibid.*, p. 93.

29. Ho Ch'i-fang, *Kuan-yü hsieh-shih ho tu-shih*, p. 64.

30. *Ibid.*, p. 73.

31. Ho Ch'i-fang, *Hsi-yüan chi*, p. 148.

32. *Ibid.*, p. 87.

33. Ho Ch'i-fang, *Kuan-yü hsieh-shih ho tu-shih*, p. 69.

34. Ho Ch'i-fang, *Hsi-yüan chi*, p. 92.

35. Ho Ch'i-fang, "Kuan-yü hsieh-shih ho tu-shih," *Tso-chia t'an ch'uang-tso*, p. 101.

36. *Ibid.*, p. 99.

37. Ho Ch'i-fang, *Hsi-yüan chi*, p. 95.

38. *Ibid.*

39. Ho Ch'i-fang, *Kuan-yü hsieh-shih ho tu-shih*, p. 105.

40. Ho Ch'i-fang, "Kuan-yü hsieh-shih ho tu-shih," *Tso-chia t'an ch'uang-tso*, p. 97.

41. Ho Ch'i-fang, *Kuan-yü hsieh-shih ho tu-shih*, p. 99.

42. Ho Ch'i-fang, "Kuan-yü hsieh-shih ho tu-shih," *Tso-chia t'an ch'uang-tso*, p. 101.

43. *Ibid.*, p. 111.

44. Ho Ch'i-fang, "Hui-ta" (Reply), *Jen-min wen-hsüeh*, No. 10:46 (1954).

45. Sheng Ch'üan-sheng, "Yao-i pu-hsiu ti shih-p'ien lai ou-ko wo-men ti shih-tai" (To eulogize our era with immortal poems), *Jen-min wen-hsüeh*, No. 4:137 (1955).

46. Yeh Kao, "Che pu-shih wo-men ch'i-tai ti hui-ta" (This is not the reply we expected), *Jen-min wen-hsüeh*, No. 4:138 (1955).

47. Sheng Ch'üan-sheng, p. 137.

48. *Ibid.*

49. *Ibid.*

50. Ch'ing I, "Wei 'Hui-ta' pien-hu" (A defense for "Reply"), *Jen-min wen-hsüeh*, No. 11:47 (1956).

51. "Kao-chi chih-shih fen-tzu tso-t'an Ma-Lieh chu-i li-lun hsüeh-hsi, p. 4.

52. "Chiao-t'iao chu-i ho tsung-p'ai chu-i tsu-ai che wen-hsüeh yen-chiu kung-tso ti k'ai-chan" (Dogmatism and factionalism block the way to the development of literary research work), *Wen-i pao*, No. 9:13 (1957).

53. *Ibid.*

54. This article was published in *Ch'u-nü ti* (Virgin land), No. 7 (1958).

55. Kung Mu was to be accused of being a rightist.

56. Ho Ch'i-fang is quoted in Li Hsi-fan, "Tui-tai p'i-p'ing ying-tang yu cheng ch'üeh ti t'ai-tu" (A correct attitude should be taken toward criticism), *Shih-k'an* (Poetry), No. 4:91 (1959).

57. The best example is Shao Ch'üan-lin who at the end of the 1950's appeared second to Chou Yang in the literary hierarchy. Yet, in the socialist education campaign of the mid-1960's, he became one of the chief targets for attack.

58. Shao Ch'üan-lin, "Min-ko, lang-man chu-i, kung-ch'an chu-i feng-ko" (Folk song, romanticism, Communist style), *Shih-k'an*, No. 10:60 (1958).

59. Ho Ch'i-fang, "Kuan-yü shih-ko hsing-shih wen-t'i ti cheng-lun," p. 19.

60. "Kuan-yü hsin-shih fa-chan wen-t'i ti lun-cheng" (Polemics concerning the development of new poetry), *Shih-k'an*, No. 2:99 (1959).

61. C. T. Hsia describes his poetry in *A History of Modern Chinese Fiction 1917–1957*, p. 137.

62. Ho Ch'i-fang, "Tsai-t'an shih-ko hsing-shih wen-t'i" (Again on the problem of poetic forms), *Wen-hsüeh p'ing-lun*, No. 2:63 (1959).

63. *Ibid.*, p. 68.

64. *Ibid.*, p. 73.

65. Ho Ch'i-fang, "Kuan-yü shih-ko hsing-shih wen-t'i ti cheng-lun," p. 12.

66. Ho Ch'i-fang, "Tsai-t'an shih-ko hsing-shih wen-t'i," p. 67.

67. Ho Ch'i-fang, "Kuan-yü shih-ko hsing-shih wen-t'i ti cheng-lun," p. 3.

68. *Ibid.*, p. 20.

69. *Ibid.*, p. 18.

70. *Ibid.*, pp. 2–3.

71. Ho Ch'i-fang, "Tsai-t'an shih-ko hsing-shih wen-t'i," p. 56.

72. *Ibid.*, p. 58.

73. *Ibid.*, p. 71.

74. Ho Ch'i-fang, "Kuan-yü shih-ko hsing-shih wen-t'i ti cheng-lun," p. 18.

75. Ho Ch'i-fang, "Tsai-t'an shih-ko hsing-shih wen-t'i," p. 70.

76. *Ibid.*, p. 71.
77. Li Hsi-fan, "Tui-tai p'i-p'ing ying-tang yu cheng-ch'üeh ti t'ai-tu," p. 90.
78. *Ibid.*, p. 92.
79. *Ibid.*, p. 91.
80. *Ibid.*, p. 93.

Chapter 11: The Significance of Literary Dissent

1. Hsü Mou-yung, p. 157.
2. Among Chou Yang's associates who were attacked in the mid-1960's were Shao Ch'üan-lin, Lin Mo-han, Yuan Shui-p'o, K'ang Cho, T'ien Han, and Hsia Yen.
3. For further discussion of the purge of Chou Yang and his group see Merle Goldman, "The Fall of Chou Yang," *The China Quarterly* (July–September 1966).

BIBLIOGRAPHY

The Chinese characters in the Bibliography are written in
both regular and abbreviated style. Names of persons
and journals which appear in the original source in both
forms are written here in the regular form. Characters
printed only in the abbreviated form in the original are
written here in the abbreviated form.

Unsigned translated articles receive full citation in the
Notes but are not included in the Bibliography.

Ai Ch'ing 艾青. "Liao-chieh tso-chia, tsun-chung tso-chia" 瞭解
作家,尊重作家 (Understand and respect writers); Chieh-fang
jih-pao (Mar. 11, 1942), p. 4.

------"Wo tui-yü mu-ch'ien wen-i shang chi-ko wen-t'i ti i-chien"
我對於目前文藝上幾個問題的意見 (My opinion
about some of the problems in current literature and art); Chieh-
fang jih-pao (May 15, 1942), p. 4.

------"Hsien-shih pu jung-hsü wai-ch'ü" 現實不容許歪曲
(Reality doesn't allow distortion); Chieh-fang jih-pao (June 24,
1942), p. 4.

------"T'an-t'an hsieh shih" 談談寫詩 (Talk about writing poetry),
in Tso-chia t'an ch'uang-tso, pp. 113-126.

------"Yang-hua jen ti meng" 養花人的夢 (The dream of a gardener);
Wen-i yüeh-pao, No. 2 (1957).

------"Huang-niao" 黄鳥 (The yellow bird); reprinted in Tang t'ien-hsia
yü tang kuo-chia. Hong Kong, 1958.

An Chao-tsun. "Make Better Use of Technical Persons," Jen-min
jih-pao (Jan. 12, 1956); in Current Background, No. 379:1.

Arkush, R. David. "One of the Hundred Flowers: Wang Meng's
'Young Newcomer,'" Papers on China, 18:155-186. Harvard
University, East Asian Research Center, 1964.

British Broadcasting Corporation. World News Broadcasts.

Brandt, Conrad, Benjamin Schwartz and John K. Fairbank. A
Documentary History of Chinese Communism. Cambridge,
Mass., 1952.

CB: Current Background (Hong Kong: United States Consulate-General).

CFJP: Chieh-fang jih-pao 解放日報 (Liberation daily). Official newspaper of the Chinese Communist Party in Yenan.

Chang Ju-hsin 張如心. "P'ing Hsiao Chün ti she-hui kuan yü jen-hsing lun" 評蕭軍的社會觀與人性論 (On Hsiao Chün's outlook toward society and his theory of human nature); Ch'ün-chung, 3.21:18-22 (May 19, 1949).

Chang Kuang-nien 張光年. Wen-i pien-lun chi 文艺辯論集 (Literary debates). Peking, 1958.

Chen, S. H. "Poetry and The Great Leap Forward," The China Quarterly, No. 3:1-15 (1960).

Chen, Theodore H. E. Thought Reform of the Chinese Intellectuals. Hong Kong, 1960.

Ch'en Ch'i-t'ung, Ch'en Ya-ting, Ma Han-ping and Lu Le. "Some of Our Views on Current Literary and Art Work," Jen-min jih-pao (Jan. 7, 1957); in SCMP, No. 1507:17-19.

Ch'en Po-ta 陳伯達 (Po-chao 佰剑), "Chi 'Tu Yeh pao-ho-hua yu kan' chih-hou" 繼'讀野百合花有感'之後 (Additional thoughts on "After Reading The Wild Lily"); Chieh-fang jih-pao (June 9, 1942), p. 4.

------"Kuan-yü Wang Shih-wei" 關於王實味 (Concerning Wang Shih-wei); Chieh-fang jih-pao (June 15, 1942), p. 4.

Ch'en Yung 陈涌. "Kuan-yü wen-hsüeh i-shu t'e-cheng ti i-hsieh wen-t'i" 关于文学藝術特征的一些問題 (Some problems concerning the characteristics of art and literature); Wen-i pao, No. 9:33-37 (1956).

------"Wei wen-hsüeh i-shu ti hsien-shih chu-i erh tou-cheng ti Lu Hsün" 为文学艺术的現实主义而斗争的鲁迅 (Lu Hsün struggles for literary and artistic realism); Jen-min wen-hsüeh, No. 10:1-20 (1956).

Cheng Chu-chang 鄭竹章. "Lun Chung-kung t'ung-chih ts'e-lüeh ti chuan-pien" 論中共統治策略的轉變 (On the change of the leadership policy of the Chinese Communists); Min-chu p'ing-lun, 7.16:13-16 (1956).

"Cheng-ch'ü she-hui chu-i wen-hsüeh i-shu ti kao-tu fan-jung" 争取社会主义文学艺术的高度繁荣 (Strive for the flourishing of Socialist literature and art); Wen-i pao editorial, No. 1:1-3 (1957).

Cheng Hsüeh-chia. The So-Called Enlightened Despotism. Taiwan, 1957.

Cheng Nung 征農. "Yeh t'an 'Pai-hua ch'i-fang, pai-chia cheng-ming'" 也談'百花齊放,百家爭鳴' (Also on "The Hundred Flowers, Hundred Schools"); Wen-i pao, No. 8:13 (1957).

Chia Chi 賈霽. "Pu-tsu wei-hsün ti Wu Hsün" 不足為訓的武訓 (Wu Hsün is hardly to be emulated); Wen-i pao, 4.1:7-11 (Apr. 25, 1951).

Chiang I-wei 蔣一葦. "Chi-shu yü cheng-chih" 技術与政治 (Skill and politics); Hsüeh-hsi, No. 16:11-14 (1957).

"Chiao-t'iao chu-i ho tsung-p'ai chu-i tsu-ai che wen-hsüeh yen-chiu kung-tso ti k'ai-chan" 教条主义和宗派主义阻碍着文学研究工作的开展 (Dogmatism and factionalism block the way to the development of literary research work); Wen-i pao, No. 9:13 (1957).

Ch'iao-mu, see Hu Ch'iao-mu.

Chieh-fang jih-pao, see CFJP.

"Chien-ch'ih she-hui chu-i ti wen-i lu-hsien" 堅持社会主义的文艺路綫 (Insist on the Socialist literary line); Wen-i yüeh-pao, No. 10:1-3 (1957).

Chien Yü 鑒余. "'Hsien chuang' ou-kan erh-tse" '現狀'偶感二則 (Two impromptu pieces on the "status quo"); Jen-min wen-hsüeh, No. 3:57-58 (1957).

Chin Ts'an-jan 金燦然. "Tu Shih-wei t'ung-chih 'Cheng-chih-chia, i-shu-chia' hou" 讀實味同志'政治家藝術家'後 (After reading Comrade Shih-wei's "Statesmen and Artists"); Chieh-fang jih-pao (May 26, 1942), p. 4.

Ch'in Chao-yang 秦兆陽. Village Vignettes. Peking: Foreign Language Press, 1955. Translation.

------(Ho Chih 何直). "Lun 'Ch'üeh-shao shih-chien'" 論'缺少時間' (On "The Lack of Time"); Jen-min wen-hsüeh, No. 6:1-2 (1956).

------(Ho Chih). "Lun 'Chien-jui' chih feng" 論'尖銳'之風 (On the spirit of "Sharpness"); Wen-i hsüeh-hsi, No. 8:3 (1956).

------(Ho Chih). "Hsien-shih chu-i--kuang-k'uo ti tao-lu" 現实主义一广闊的道路 (Realism--The broad road); Jen-min wen-hsüeh, No. 9:1-13 (1956).

------(Ho Yu-hua 何又化). "Ch'en-mo" 沉默 (Silence); Jen-min wen-hsüeh, No. 1:26-27 (1957).

Chinese Literature, a monthly literary journal published in English by the Chinese Communist Party.

Chinese Writers' Union Forum on Rectification. New China News
  Agency (May 22, 1957); in SCMP, No. 1556:12-14.

Ching Tzu 靜之. Review of "Hung-lou meng yen-chiu" 紅樓夢研
  究 (A study of The Dream of the Red Chamber) by Yü P'ing-po
  俞平伯 ; in Wen-i pao, No. 9:39 (1953).

Ch'ing I 清一. "Wei 'Hui-ta' pien-hu" 为'回答'辯护 (A defense
  for "Reply"); Jen-min wen-hsüeh, No. 11:47-49 (1956).

Ch'iu-yün, see Huang Ch'iu-yün.

Chou Wen 周文. "Ts'ung Lu Hsün ti tsa wen t'an-tao Shih-wei"
  從魯迅的雜文談到實味(From Lu Hsün's tsa wen to
  Wang Shih-wei); in Chieh-fang jih-pao (June 16, 1942), p. 4.

------"Kuan-yü Wu Hsün ti 'k'u-hsing' ho 'hsing-hsüeh'" 關於武訓
  的'苦行'和'興學'(About Wu Hsün's "ascetic behavior" and
  "establishment of schools"); Hsüeh-hsi, 4.5:19-22 (1951).

Chou Yang 周揚. "Wang Shih-wei ti wen-i-kuan yü wo-men ti wen-i-
  kuan" 王實味的文藝觀與我們的文藝觀
  (Wang Shih-wei's literary views and our literary views); in
  Chieh-fang jih-pao (July 28, 1942), p. 4.

------Piao-hsien hsin ti ch'ün-chung ti shih-tai 表現新的羣眾的
  時代 (To express the new age of the masses). Peking, 1948.

------ Chien-chüeh kuan-ch'e Mao Tse-tung wen-i lu-hsien 堅決貫澈
  毛澤東文藝路線(Steadfastly carry out Mao Tse-tung's
  line in literature and art). Peking, 1952.

------"Wei ch'uang-tsao keng-to ti yu-hsiu ti wen-hsüeh i-shu tso-p'in
  erh fen-tou" 為創造更多的優秀的文學藝術作品而奮
  鬥 (To struggle for the creation of more outstanding works of
  art and literature); Wen-i pao, No. 19:7-16 (1953).

------"Literary Work in Past Four Years," speech at Second All-China
  Conference of Writers and Artists. New China News Agency (Sept.
  24, 1953); in SCMP, No. 658:13-15.

------"Wo-men pi-hsü chan-tou" 我們必須戰鬥(We must fight);
  Wen-i pao, Nos. 23 and 24:13-19 (1954).

------"The Task of Building Socialist Literature," Jen-min jih-pao
  (Mar. 25, 1956); in Current Background, No. 385:7-17. An
  excerpted version of "Building a Socialist Literature."

------"Building a Socialist Literature," Chinese Literature, No.
  4:198-222 (1956). Translation of a report to the Second Council
  Session of the Union of Chinese Writers on Feb. 27, 1956.

------"The Important Role of Art and Literature in the Building of
  Socialism," Chinese Literature, No. 1:179-188 (1957).

------"Answers Questions on Literary and Art Work, " Wen-hui pao (Shanghai, Apr. 9, 1957); in Current Background, No. 452:27-33.

------"Speech at Meeting of Writers and Artists to Celebrate the Fortieth Anniversary of the October Revolution, " Jen-min jih-pao (Nov. 9, 1957); in SCMP, No. 1664:5-9.

------"Build China's Own Marxist Literary Theory and Criticism, " Kuang-ming jih-pao (Aug. 29, 1958); in SCMP, No. 1861:13-23.

------"Wen-i chan-hsien shang ti i-ch'ang ta pien-lun" 文艺战线 上 的 一 場 大 辯論 (A great debate on the literary front); Wen-i pao, No. 5:2-14 (1958).

------A Great Debate on the Literary Front. Peking: Foreign Language Press, 1958. Translation of "Wen-i chan-hsien shang ti i-ch'ang ta pien-lun. "

Chow Ching-wen.   Ten Years of Storm.   New York, 1960.

Chu Ching-hua 朱靖华 and Pao Ming-lu 鮑明路. "Shen-k'e ti i-k'e, " 深 剜 的 一 課 (A profound lesson); Wen-i pao, No. 27:1-2 (1957).

Chu K'o-yü 竹可羽. "Lun T'ai-yang chao-tsai Shang-kan-ho shang" 論太陽照在桑乾河上 (On The Sun Over the Sangkan River); Jen-min wen-hsüeh, No. 10:113-126 (1957).

Chu Kuang-ch'ien 朱光潛. "Ts'ung chieh-shen ti ching-yen t'an 'pai-chia cheng-ming'" 從切身的經驗談百家爭鳴 (On the "Hundred Flowers" from personal experience); Wen-i pao, No. 1:10 (1957).

Ch'üan-kuo ch'ing-nien wen-hsüeh ch'uang-tso che hui-i pao-kao fa-yen chi 全國青年文学創作者會議報告.發言集 (A collection of reports of the meetings of China's young creative writers). Peking, 1956.

Ch'üan-lin, see Shao Ch'üan-lin.

Ch'ün-chung 群衆 (The masses). Hong Kong.

Chung-kuo hsien-tai wen-hsüeh shih ts'an-k'ao tzu-liao, see TKTL.

Chung-kuo tso-chia hsieh-hui ti-erh tz'u li-shih-hui hui-i k'uo-ta pao-kao fa-yen chi 中国作家协会第二次理事会会议(扩大)报告發言集(A collection of reports and speeches of the second meeting of the Board of Directors of the Chinese Writers' Union). Peking, 1956.

"Chung-kuo tso-chia hsieh-hui yen-chiu chih-hsing 'pai-hua ch'i-fang, pai-chia cheng-ming' ti fang-chen" 中国作家协会研究执行 ﹑百花齐放,百家争鳴的方針 (The Chinese Writers' Union is studying the implementation of the principles of the "Hundred Flowers, Hundred Schools"); Wen-i pao, No. 14:20-21 (1956).

Communist China, 1957. Hong Kong, 1958.

Communist China, 1949-1959. Hong Kong, 1961.

Compton, Boyd. Party Reform Documents, 1942-1944. Seattle, 1952.

Current Background, see CB.

Djilas, Milovan. The New Class. New York, 1957.

Doolin, Dennis. Communist China, The Politics of Student Opposition. Stanford, 1964.

Dorrill, William. "Study of the Cheng Feng Movement of the CCP." M.A. thesis; University of Virginia, 1954.

ECMM-Extracts from China Mainland Magazines. Hong Kong: United States Consulate-General.

Erlich, Victor. "Social and Aesthetic Criteria in Soviet Russian Criticism," in E.S. Simmons ed. Continuity and Change in Russian and Soviet Thought. Cambridge, Mass., 1955.

Extracts from China Mainland Magazines, see ECMM.

Fan Wen-lan 范文瀾 . "Lun Wang Shih-wei t'ung-chih ti ssu-hsiang i-shih" 論王實味同志的思想意識 (On the ideology of Comrade Wang Shih-wei); Chieh-fang jih-pao (June 9, 1942), p. 4.

------"Tsai Chung-yang yen-chiu yüan liu-yüeh shih-i-jih tso-t'an hui shang ti fa-yen" 在中央研究院六月十一日座談會上的發言 (Speech given at the discussion meeting of the Central Research Institute on June 11, 1942); Chieh-fang jih-pao (June 29, 1942), p. 4.

Feng Hsüeh-feng 馮雪峰 (Ho Tan-jen 何丹仁). "Kuan-yü 'Ti-san-chung wen-hsüeh' ti ch'ing-hsiang yü li-lun" 关于 '第三种文学' 的傾向与理論 (Concerning the tendencies and theories of "The Third Kind of Literature"); in TKTL, I, 486-495.

------(Lü K'e-yu 呂克玉). "Tui-yü wen-hsüeh yün-tung chi-ke wen-t'i ti i-chien," 对于文学运动几个問題的意見 (Opinions on several problems in the literary movement); in TKTL, I, 567-575.

------(Hua Shih 画室). "T'i-wai ti hua" 題外的話 (Irrelevant words); in TKTL, II, 428-430.

------K'ua ti jih-tzu 跨的日子 (Days of transition). Shanghai, 1946.

------Kuo-lai ti shih-tai 過來的時代 (Time past). Shanghai, 1948.

------Hsiang-feng yü shih-feng 鄉風與市風 (Spirit of country and city). Shanghai, 1948.

------Lun min-chu ke-ming ti wen-i yün-tung 論民主革命的文藝運動 (On the literary movement of the democratic revolution). Shanghai, 1949.

------Lun wen-chi 論文集 (Collection of essays). Peking, 1952.

------"Chien t'ao wo-tsai Wen-i pao so-fan ti ts'o-wu" 檢討我在‘文藝報’所犯的錯誤 (Criticism of my errors committed on Wen-i pao); Wen-i pao, No. 20:4-5 (1954).

------"Kuan-yü Hu Feng fan ke-ming huo-tung ti i-hsieh shih-shih" 關於胡風反革命活動的一些事實 (Some facts concerning Hu Feng's antirevolutionary activity); Wen-i pao, No. 12:19-20 (1955).

------Lun Pao-wei Yenan 論保衛延安 (On Defend Yenan). Shanghai, 1956.

"Feng Hsüeh-feng tsai san-ko wen-t'i shang ti hsiu-cheng chu-i kuan-tien" 馮雪峰在三个問題上的修正主義观点 (The revisionist views of Feng Hsüeh-feng on three problems); Jen-min wen-hsüeh, No. 12:109-114 (1957).

Fokkema, D.W. Literary Doctrine in China and The Soviet Influence, 1956-1960. The Hague, 1965.

Grieder, Jerome. "The Communist Critique of Hung lou meng, " Papers on China, 10:142-169. Harvard University, East Asian Research Center, 1956.

Guillain, Robert. Six Hundred Million Chinese. New York, 1957.

Ha Hua 哈华. "Fan-tang fen-tzu Ting Ling ti ch'ou-o ling-hun" 反党分子丁玲的丑恶灵魂(The ugly soul of the antiparty Ting Ling); Meng-ya, No. 17:2-3 (1957).

------"Yu-p'ai fen-tzu Liu Shao-t'ang tui Su-lien wen-hsüeh ti fei-pang" 右派分子刘紹棠对苏联文学的誹謗 (Rightist Liu Shao-t'ang's slander of Soviet literature); Meng-ya, No. 19:2-4 (1957).

Han Yü-chung 韓愚仲. "T'an-t'an hsüeh-hsi Ma-k'e-ssu lieh-ning chu-i ching-tien chu-tso ho tu-li ssu-k'ao" 談談学習馬克思列宁主义经典著作和独立思考 (On the Marxist-Leninist texts and independent thinking); Hsüeh-hsi, No. 8:11 (1957).

Ho Ch'i-fang 何其芳. "Tuo-shao-tz'u a wo li-k'ai le wo jih-ch'ang ti sheng-huo" 多少次啊我離開了我日常的生活(How

many times I have left my everyday life); Chieh-fang jih-pao
(Apr. 3, 1942), p. 4.

------Kuan-yü hsien-shih chu-i 關於現實主義 (On realism).
Shanghai, 1950:

------"Yung Mao Tse-tung ti wen-i li-lun lai kai-chin wo-men ti
kung-tso" 用毛澤東的文藝理論來改進我們的工作
(Improve our work with Mao Tse-tung's literary theory);
Wen-i pao, No. 1:5-9 (1952).

------Hsi-yüan chi 西苑集 (Hsi-yüan collection). Peking, 1952.

------"Hsien-shih chu-i ti lu hai shih fan hsien-shih chu-i ti lu?"
現實主義的路還是反現實主義的路
(The road of realism or the road of antirealism); in LWHC, II,
69-92.

------"Kuan-yü hsieh-shih ho tu-shih" 關於寫詩和讀詩
(On writing and reading poetry); in Tso-chia t'an ch'uang-tso,
pp. 91-112.

------"Hui-ta" 回答 (Reply); Jen-min wen-hsüeh, No. 10:45-47 (1954).

------"Tui Hu Feng chi-t'uan ti fan-tung wen-i ssu-hsiang ti tou-cheng"
对胡風集团的反动文艺思想的斗争 (The struggle
against the reactionary literary ideas of the Hu Feng clique); in
TKTL, II, 348-361.

------ Kuan-yü hsieh-shih ho tu-shih 关于写诗和读诗
(On writing and reading poetry). Peking, 1956.

------"Pao-wei tang ti yüan-tse, pao-wei she-hui chu-i ti wen-i shih-
yeh" 保衛党的原则,保衛社会主义的文艺事业
(Defend the party's principles, defend the socialist literary undertaking); Wen-i pao, No. 20:6-7 (1957).

------"Kuan-yü shih-ko hsing-shih wen-t'i ti cheng-lun" 关于诗歌
形式问题的争论 (Controversy concerning the problem of
poetic forms); Wen-hsüeh p'ing-lun, No. 1:1-22 (1959).

------"Tsai-t'an shih-ko hsing-shih wen-t'i" 再谈诗歌形式问题
(Again on the problem of poetic forms); Wen-hsüeh p'ing-lun,
No. 2:55-75 (1959).

------Wen-hsüeh i-shu ti ch'un-t'ien 文学艺术的春天 (Springtime
of literature and art). Peking, 1964.

Ho Chih, see Ch'in Chao-yang.

Ho Tan-jen, see Feng Hsüeh-feng.

Ho Yu-hua, see Ch'in Chao-yang.

Hou Chin-ching 侯金鏡. "1954 nien chien-ch'a Wen-i pao ti chieh-lun pu-neng t'ui-fan" 1954年檢查文艺报的結論不能推翻 (The conclusion reached after the investigation of Wen-i pao in 1954 cannot be overthrown); Wen-i pao, No. 22:6-7 (1957).

Hsi-wang 希望 (Hope).

Hsia, C.T. A History of Modern Chinese Fiction, 1917-1957. New Haven, 1961.

Hsia, T.A. "Lu Hsün and the Dissolution of the League of Leftist Writers." Monograph; University of Washington, 1958.

------"Twenty Years After the Yenan Forum," The China Quarterly, No. 13 (January-March 1963).

Hsiao Chün 蕭軍. "Lun chung-shen ta-shih" 論終身大事 (On marriage); Chieh-fang jih-pao (Mar. 25, 1942), p. 4.

------"Lun t'ung-chih chih ai yü nai" 論同志之'愛'與'耐' (On love and patience among comrades); Chieh-fang jih-pao (Apr. 8, 1942), p. 4.

------"Tui-yü tang-ch'ien wen-i chu wen-t'i ti wo-chien" 對於當前文藝諸問題的我見 (My views about the problems in the present art and literature); Chieh-fang jih-pao (May 14, 1942), p. 4.

------"Wen-t'an shang ti 'Pu-erh-pa' ching-shen" 文壇上的'布爾巴'精神 (The "Bulba" spirit in literary circles); Chieh-fang jih-pao (June 13, 1942), p. 4.

------Village in August, tr. Evan King with introduction by Edgar Snow. New York, 1942.

------"Ta-yung-che ti ching-shen" 大勇者的精神 (The spirit of the great brave man); Wen-ts'ui, 1.1:17-19 (Oct. 9, 1945).

------"Cheng chiao fan-t'an" 政教泛談 (Talk on government and education); in TKTL, II, 266.

------"Hsia-yeh ch'ao chih san" 夏夜抄之三 (Notes on summer nights, No. 3); in TKTL, II, 266.

------"Ch'ou-chiao tsa-t'an" 丑角杂談 (Talk on clowns); in TKTL, II, 267-268.

Hsiao Chün ssu-hsiang p'i-p'an 蕭軍思想批判 (Criticism of Hsiao Chün's ideas). Peking, 1949.

Hsiao Li 曉立. "Tang-hsing, sheng-huo ho chen-shih" 党性、生活和真实 (Party, life and reality); Wen-i yüeh-pao, No. 1:81-84 (1958).

Hsiao Yeh-mu 蕭也牧. "'Pai-hua ch'i-fang, pai-chia cheng-ming' yu kan" 百花齐放、百家争鳴'有感 (Thoughts on "The

Hundred Flowers, Hundred Schools"); Jen-min wen-hsüeh, No. 7:58 (1956).

------"Pu yau tsai ch'en-mo le!" 不要再沈默了 (Don't be silent any more!); Wen-i pao, No. 15:8 (1957).

Hsin-hua jih-pao 新華日報 (New China news). Communist newspaper in Chungking.

Hsü Mou-yung 徐懋庸. "Ch'an-tsao chü man-pi" 蟬蝶居漫笔 (Random notes from the abode of a noisy cicada); Jen-min wen-hsüeh, No. 7:154-157 (1957).

Hsüeh-hsi 學習 (Study).

Hu Ch'iao-mu (Ch'iao-mu) 胡喬木. "Wen-i ch'uang-tso yu chu-kuan" 文艺創作与主观 (Literary creation and subjectivism); in TKTL, II, 389-406.

Hu Feng 胡風. Mi-yün ch'i feng-hsi hsiao-chi 密雲期風習小記 (Studies in a cloudy period). Hankow, 1938.

------"Chih-shen tsai wei min-chu ti tou-cheng li-mien" 置身在為民主的鬥爭裏面 (Placing oneself in the democratic struggle); Hsi-wang, Vol. 1, No. 1 (January 1945).

------Tsai hun-luan li-mien 在混亂裏面 (In confusion). Shanghai, 1946.

------Hu Feng wen-chi 胡風文集 (Hu Feng's collected essays). Shanghai, 1947.

------Wei-le ming-t'ien 為了明天 (For tomorrow). Shanghai, 1950.

------Chien, wen-i, jen-min 劍, 文藝, 人民 (Sword, literature, and people). Shanghai, 1950.

------Ts'ung yüan-t'ou tao hung-liu 從源頭到洪流 (From the source to the flood). Shanghai, 1952.

------"Wo-ti tzu-wo p'i-p'an" 我的自我批判 (My self-criticism); Wen-i pao, Nos. 9 and 10:21-28 (1955).

"Hu Feng tui wen-i wen-ti ti i-chien" 胡風對文藝問題的意見 (Hu Feng's literary opinions); supplement to Wen-i pao (January 1955), pp. 1-165.

Hu Feng wen-i ssu-hsiang p'i-p'an lun-wen hui-chi, see LWHC.

Hua Shih, see Feng Hsüeh-feng.

Huai Hai 懷海. "'Tso-i' ch'eng-wei 'yu-i'" '左翼' 成為 '右翼' ("Left wing" into "right wing"); Jen-min wen-hsüeh, No. 10:12-13 (1957).

Huang Ch'iu-yün 黄秋耘. "Pu-yao tsai jen-min ti chi-k'u mien-
  ch'ien pi-shang yen-ching" 不要在人民的疾苦面前
  閉上眼睛 (We must not close our eyes to the hardships of the
  people); Jen-min wen-hsüeh, No. 9:58-59 (1956).

------"Tz'u tsai na-li?" 刺在哪里 (Where is the thorn?); Wen-i
  hsüeh-hsi, No. 6:8 (1957).

------"P'i-p'an wo tzu-chi" 批判我自己 (Criticizing myself);
  Wen-i hsüeh-hsi, No. 9:24-29 (1957).

Huang Mo 黄沫. "I-yeh tou-cheng li-shih" 一頁鬥爭歷史
  (An historical page of struggle); Wen-i pao, No. 17:15-18 (1955).

------"Pien-chi kung-tso i-ting yao shih-ho tang-ch'ien hsin hsing-shih
  編輯工作一定要適合当前新形势 (Editorial work
  must suit the current new situation); Wen-i pao, No. 4:2 (1957).

Huang Sung-k'ang. Lu Hsün and The New Culture Movement of Modern
  China. Amsterdam, 1957.

Hung Ch'i 紅旗 (The red flag).

I Sung 抱松. "Pu-hao ling-tao" 不好領导 (Leadership is not
  easy; Wen-i pao, No. 17:3-4 (1956).

Jen-min jih-pao, see JMJP.

Jen-min wen-hsüeh 人民文學 (People's literature).

JMJP: Jen min jih-pao 人民日報 (People's daily).

Johnson, Chalmers. Communist Policies Toward the Intellectual Class.
  Hong Kong, 1959.

K'ang Cho. "Liquidate the Evil Influence of The 'Soul-Corroding Master'
  Ting Ling, " Chung-kuo Ch'ing-nien, No. 17 (Sept. 1, 1957); in
  ECMM, No. 114:16-22.

"Kao-chi chih-shih fen-tzu tso-t'an Ma-Lieh chu-i li-lun hsüeh-hsi"
  高級知識分子座談馬列主义理論学習
  (High-level intellectuals discuss the study of Marxist-Leninist
  theory); Hsüeh-hsi, No. 11:2-11 (1957).

Klein, Donald. "Biographies of Chinese Communist Leaders."
  Tokyo, 1959; available at Harvard University, East Asian Research
  Center.

KMJP: Kuang-ming jih-pao 光明日報 (Kuangming daily).

"Kuan-yü hsin-shih fa-chan wen-t'i ti lun-cheng" 关于新詩发展
  問題的論爭 (Polemics concerning the development of

new poetry); Shih-k'an, No. 2:96-100 (1959).

"Kuan-yü Hu Feng fan tang chi-t'uan ti i-hsieh ts'ai-liao" 關於胡
風反黨集團的一些材料 (Some materials concerning
the Hu Feng antiparty clique); Wen-i pao, Nos. 9 and 10:28-33
(1955).

"Kuan-yü Hu Feng fan ke-ming chi-t'uan ti ti-erh-p'i ts'ai-liao"
關於胡風反革命集團的第二批材料
(The second collection of materials concerning the Hu Feng
antirevolutionary clique); Wen-i pao, No. 11:18-28 (1955).

"Kuan-yü Hu Feng fan ke-ming chi-t'uan ti ti-san p'i ts'ai-liao"
關於胡風反革命集團的第三批材料
(The third collection of materials concerning the Hu Feng antirevolutionary clique); Wen-i pao, No. 11:4-17 (1955).

"Kuan-yü 'Tsu-chih pu hsin-lai ti ch'ing-nien jen' ti t'ao-lun"
关于'組織部新來的青年人'的讨论
(Discussion of "A Young Newcomer in the Organization
Department"); Wen-i hsüeh-hsi, No. 2:9-19 (1957).

Kuang-ming jih-pao, see KMJP.

Kung Mu 公木. "To-lo ti chiao-yin, ch'en-t'ung ti chiao-hsün"
隨落的脚印, 沉痛的教訓 (A decadent footprint, a
painful lesson); Wen-i hsüeh-hsi, No. 11:2-25 (1957).

Kuo Hsiao-ch'uan 郭小川. "Ch'en-chung ti chiao-hsün" 沉重
的教訓 (A heavy lesson); Wen-i pao, No. 28:8-9 (1957).

Kuo Mo-jo 郭沫若. "Self-Examination in Connection With the
Criticism of Wu Hsün," Jen-min jih-pao (June 7, 1951); in
Current Background, No. 113:15-16.

------"Report Concerning the Basic Conditions of the Chinese Academy
of Sciences, " Jen-min jih-pao (Mar. 26, 1954); in Current
Background, No. 359:15-22.

------"Cultural and Academic Circles Should Launch Struggle Against
Bourgeois Thought, " Kuang-ming jih-pao (Nov. 8, 1954); in
SCMP, No. 935:33-35.

------San-tien chien-i 三點建議 (Three suggestions); Wen-i pao,
Nos. 23 and 24 (1954), pp. 6-10.

------"Report to Inaugural Meeting of Departments of Chinese Academy
of Science, " Jen-min jih-pao (June 12, 1955); in Current Background,
No. 359:3-13.

------"Hit Back with a Vengeance at the Rightists!" New China News
Agency (July 15, 1957); in SCMP, No. 1580:16.

------"Strive to Remold Ourselves into Cultural Workers for The Proletariat, " Jen-min jih-pao (Sept. 23, 1957); in SCMP, No. 1629:8-13.

------"Chiu mu-ch'ien ch'uang-tso chung ti chi-ke wen-t'i ta Jen-min wen-hsüeh pien-che wen" 就目前創作中的几个問題答 '人民文学' 編者問 (Answer to questions bv editors of People's Literature on some problems in current creative writing); Jen-min wen-hsüeh, No. 1:4-9 (1959).

Lao She 老舍. "Shu-li hsin feng-ch'i" 树立新風气 (Establish a new trend); Wen-i pao, No. 25:9 (1957).

Lee, Leo Ou-fan. "Hsiao Chün, The Man and His Works." Seminar paper; Harvard University, 1964.

Li Chien-feng 李健風. "Hsiang-hua ho tu-ts'ao" 香花和毒草 (Fragrant flowers and poisonous weeds); Jen-min wen-hsüeh, No. 3:59 (1957).

Li Hsi-fan 李希凡. "Tui-yü wo-hsiao wen-i chiao-hsüeh wen-t'i ti chi-tien i-chien" 對於我校文藝教學問題的幾點意見 (Some suggestions concerning the instruction of aesthetics at our school); Wen-i pao, No. 2:30-32 (1952).

------"Tui-tai p'i-p'ing ying-tang yu cheng-ch'üeh ti t'ai-tu" 对待批評应当有正确的态度 (A correct attitude should be taken toward criticism); Shih-k'an, No. 4:89-93 (1959).

Li Hsi-fan and Lan Ling 藍翎. "Kuan-yü 'Hung-lou meng chien-lun' chi ch'i-ta" 關於 '紅樓夢簡論' 及其他 (Concerning "A Short Study of The Dream of The Red Chamber, " and other views); Wen-i pao, No. 18:31-36 (1954).

Li Yün 李云. "Yu shou-tao i-tz'u chiao-yü" 又受到一次教育 (I got another education); Wen-i pao, No. 6:32-33 (1958).

Liao Ying 燎熒. "Jen tsai chien-k'u chung sheng-chang" 人在艱苦中生長 (Men grow out of adversity); Chieh-fang jih-pao (June 10, 1942), p. 4.

Lifton, Robert. Thought Reform and the Psychology of Totalism. New York, 1960.

Lin K'o 林可. "Yeh-shih tso-chia-men ti tse-jen" 也是作家們的責任 (It is also the responsibility of the writers); Wen-i pao, No. 1:35-36 (1956).

Lin Mo-han (Mo-han) 林默涵. "Ko-hsing chieh-fang yü chi-t'i chu-i" 个性解放与集体主义 (Individual liberation and collectivism); in TKTL, II, 406-411.

------"Hu Feng ti fan Ma-k'e-ssu chu-i ti wen-i ssu-hsiang" 胡風的
反馬克思主義的文藝思想 (The anti-Marxist literary
ideas of Hu Feng); in LWHC, II, 49-68.

Liu Chih-ming 劉芝明. Ch'ing-suan Hsiao Chün ti fan-tung ssu-
hsiang 清算蕭軍的反動思想 (Liquidate Hsiao Chün's
reactionary ideas). Hong Kong, 1949.

------Hsiao Chün p'i-p'an 蕭軍批判 (Criticism of Hsiao Chün).
Hong Kong, 1949.

------"Tung-pei san-nien lai wen-i kung-tso ch'u-pu tsung-chieh"
東北三年来文艺工作初步总結 (A preliminary
summation of the literary work in the northeast for the past
three years); in TKTL, II, 162-180.

Liu Pin-yen 刘宾雁. "Pen-pao nei-pu hsiao-hsi" 本报内部
消息 (Our paper's inside news); Jen-min wen-hsüeh, No. 6:6-21
(1956).

Liu Shao-t'ang 刘绍棠. "Hsien-shih chu-i tsai she-hui chu-i shih-tai
ti fa-chan"现实主义在社会主义时代的發展
(The development of realism in a period of socialism); Pei-ching
wen-i, No. 4:9-11 (1957).

Liu Shao-t'ang and Ts'ung Wei-hsi 从维熙. "'Hsieh chen-shih'--
she-hui chu-i hsien-shih chu-i ti sheng-ming he-hsin" 写真实—
社会主义现实主义的生命核心 ("Write the Truth"--
the living core of Socialist realism); Wen-i hsüeh-hsi, No.
1:17-18 (1957).

"Liu Shao-t'ang tsai 't'an-so' shen-mo?" 刘绍棠在'探索'什么?
(What is Liu Shao-t'ang "searching for?"); Wen-i yüeh-pao,
No. 1:85-86 (1958).

Lo Feng 羅烽. "Hai-shih tsa wen ti shih-tai" 還是雜文的時代
(Still a period of tsa wen); Chieh-fang jih-pao (Mar. 12, 1942), p. 4.

Lo Lung-chi 羅隆基. "Band the Non-Party Intellectuals Closer with
the Party," Jen-min jih-pao (Mar. 23, 1957); in Current Background,
No. 444:17-22.

Lo Man 羅邁. "Lun Chung-yang yen-chiu yüan ti ssu-hsiang lun-chan"
論中央研究院的思想論戰 (On the ideological polemic in
the Central Research Institute); Chieh-fang jih-pao (June 28, 1942),
p. 4.

Lu Hsi-chih 陸希治. "Wai-ch'ü hsien-shih ti 'hsien-shih chu-i'"
歪曲現實的'現實主義'(The "realism" that distorts reality);
Wen-i pao, No. 9:25-28 (1952).

Lu Hsün 魯迅. "Lun hsien-tsai wo-men ti wen-hsüeh yün-tung" 論現在我們的文學運動 (On our present literary movement); in TKTL, I, 545-547.

Lu Hsün ch'üan-chi 魯迅全集 (Complete works of Lu Hsün). New ed., 10 vols.; Peking, 1956.

Lu Hsün, Selected Works of. Peking: Foreign Language Press, 1956.

Lu K'an-ju 陸侃如. "Hu Shih fan-tang ssu-hsiang kei-yü ku-tien wen-hsüeh yen-chiu ti tu-hai" 胡適反黨思想給予古典文學研究的毒害 (The poison rendered the study of classical literature by the reactionary thought of Hu Shih); Wen-i pao, No. 21:4-5 (1954).

Lu K'uei-jan 魯喟然. Hu Feng shih-chien ti ch'ien-yin hou-kuo 胡風事件的前因後果 (The cause and effect of the Hu Feng case). Hong Kong, 1956.

Lu Ting-i. "Speech to the National People's Congress," Jen-min jih-pao (July 27, 1955); in Current Background, No. 350:8-14.

------"Speech in Commemoration of the Twentieth Anniversary of Death of Lu Hsün," New China News Agency (Oct. 19. 1956); in SCMP, No. 1404:14-16.

Lu Ting-i, Kuo Mo-jo, et al., "Great Victory Won in Struggle by Literary and Art Circles Against Ting Ch'en Antiparty Group," Jen-min jih-pao (Sept. 27, 1957); in SCMP, No. 1629:14-22.

"Lu Ting-i, Chou Yang tsai tso-hsieh tang-tsu k'uo-ta hui-i shang tso chung-yao chiang-hua" 陸定一.周揚在作協黨組扩大会議上作重要講話 (Lu Ting-i and Chou Yang made important speeches to enlarged sessions of the party branch of the Writers' Union); Wen-i pao, No. 25:1-3 (1957).

Lü K'e-yu, see Feng Hsüeh-feng.

LWHC: Hu Feng wen-i ssu-hsiang p'i-p'an lun-wen hui-chi 胡風文藝思想批判論文彙集 (Collection of criticisms of Hu Feng's literary ideas). 5 vols.; Peking, 1955.

MacFarquhar, Roderick. The Hundred Flowers. London, 1960.

Mao I-sheng 茅以升. "Tang shih wan-ch'üan neng-kou ling-tao k'o-hsüeh shih-yeh ti" 党是完全能够領导科学事業的 (The party is totally capable of leadership of scientific work); Hsüeh-hsi, No. 20:7-10 (1957).

Mao Tse-tung. On Art and Literature. Peking, 1960.

------"On the Correct Handling of Contradictions Among the People,"
New China News Agency (June 18, 1957); in Roderick MacFarquhar,
The Hundred Flowers.

Mao Tun 茅盾. "New Realities and New Tasks," speech delivered
at Second All-China Conference of Writers, Jen-min jih-pao
(Oct. 10, 1953); in Current Background, No. 282:1-19. Also
reported by NCNA (Sept. 26, 1953); in SCMP, No. 658:18.

------(Shen Yen-ping 沈雁冰) "Wen-hsüeh i-shu kung-tso chung
ti kuan-chien hsing wen-t'i" 文学艺术工作中的关键性
問題 (The key problems in art and literature); Wen-i pao,
No. 12:3-4 (1956).

------"Carry Out the Line of Letting All Flowers Bloom Together,
Oppose Doctrinairism and the Rightist Ideas of the Petty
Bourgeoisie," Jen-min jih-pao (Mar. 8, 1957); in SCMP,
No. 1507:13-16.

------"P'ei-yang hsin-sheng li-liang, k'uo-ta wen-hsüeh tui-wu"
培养新生力量，擴大文学隊伍 (Cultivate new
strength, broaden the ranks of literature); in Chung-kuo tso-chia
hsieh-hui ti-erh tz'u li-shih hui hui-i k'uo-ta pao-kao fa-yen chi,
pp. 39-52.

------"Distinguish Between the Right and Wrong Among Great Issues,"
Wen-i pao, No. 25 (Sept. 29, 1957); in ECMM, No. 111:5-9.

Meng-ya 萌芽 (Sprouts). Published by the Shanghai branch of the
Writers' Union.

Min-chu p'ing-lun 民主評論 (Democratic review), a Hong Kong
bimonthly.

Mo-han, see Lin Mo-han.

New York Times, The.

Pa Jen 巴人 (Wang Jen-shu 王任叔). "Tu 'Ch'u hsüeh'" 讀'初
雪' (Reading "First Snow"); Wen-i pao, No. 2:19-20 (1954).

------"Shih hsien-shih chu-i hai-shih fan hsien-shih chu-i" 是現
实主义还是反現实主义 (Is this realism or
antirealism?); Wen-hsüeh p'ing-lun, No. 1:39-62 (1959).

Payne, Robert. Journey to Red China. London, 1947.

Pei-ching wen-i 北京文藝 (Peking literature).

Po-chao, see Ch'en Po-ta.

"Record of Forum Held for the Study of The Dream of the Red Chamber,"
Kuang-ming jih-pao, Literary Heritage Supplement (Nov. 14,
1954); in Current Background, No. 315:39-63.

Schwartz, Benjamin. "The Intelligentsia in Communist China,"
Daedalus (Summer 1960), pp. 604-622.

Schyns, Joseph. 1500 Modern Chinese Novels and Plays. Peking,
1948.

SCMP: Survey of The China Mainland Press (Hong Kong: United States
Consulate-General).

Shao Ch'üan-lin (Ch'üan-lin) 邵荃麟. "Lun chu-kuan wen-t'i"
論主觀問題 (On the problem of subjectivism); in TKTL, II,
361-388.

------"Tou-cheng feng-mang chih-hsiang yu-p'ai" 斗争鋒芒指
向右派 (The sword of struggle is pointed toward the rightists);
Wen-i pao, No. 14:2 (1957).

------"Tou-cheng pi-hsü keng shen-ju" 斗争必須更深入 (The
struggle must penetrate more deeply); Wen-i pao, No. 25:4-6
(1957).

------"Min-ko, lang-man chu-i, kung-ch'an chu-i feng-ko" 民歌.
浪漫主义、共産主义风格 (Folk song, romanticism,
Communist style); Shih-k'an, No. 10:59-64 (1958).

Shen Yen-ping, see Mao Tun.

Shen Yin-mo, "This Man Hu Shih," Ta kung pao (Shanghai, Dec.
16, 1951); in Current Background, No. 167:3-5.

Sheng Ch'üan-sheng 盛荃生. "Yao-i pu-hsiu ti shih-p'ien lai
ou-ko wo-men ti shih-tai" 要以不朽的詩篇來謳歌
我們的時代 (To eulogize our era with immortal poems);
Jen-min wen-hsüeh, No. 4:136-137 (1955).

Shih-k'an 詩刊 (Poetry).

Shih P'ing 施平. "Tang ti ling-tao tui tzu-jan k'o-hsüeh ti i-i"
党的領導对自然科学的意义 (The significance
of party leadership to the natural sciences); Hsüeh-hsi,
No. 1:20-22 (1956).

Shu Wu 舒蕪. "Lun chu-kuan" 論主觀 (On subjectivism);
Hsi-wang, Vol. 1, No. 1 (January 1945).

------"Ts'ung-t'ou hsüeh-hsi 'Tsai Yenan wen-i tso-t'an hui-shang'
ti chiang-hua" 從頭學習在延安文藝座談會上的講話
(Thoroughly study "Talks at the Yenan Forum on Art and
Literature"); in LWHC, II, 108-114.

------ "Chih Lu Ling ti kung-k'ai hsin" 致路翎的公開信
(Open letter to Lu Ling); in LWHC, II, 115-139.

Snow, Edgar, ed. Living China. New York, 1936.

Songs of the Red Flag, comp. by Chou Yang and Kuo Mo-jo. Peking,
1961.

Stein, Günther. The Challenge of Red China. New York, 1945.

Sun Hsiao-p'ing 孫肖平. "Ting Ling kuan-hsin kuo ch'ing-nien
tso-che ma?" 丁玲关心过青年作者嗎?
(Has Ting Ling ever been concerned about young writers?);
Meng-ya, No. 20:6-7 (1957).

Survey of The China Mainland Press, see SCMP.

Ta-chung wen-i ts'ung-k'an p'i-p'ing lun-wen ch'üan-chi 大眾文藝
叢刊批評論文全集 (Collected criticisms from popular
literature). Hong Kong.

Tagore, Amitendramath. "Left-wing Literary Debates in Modern
China, 1918-1937." Ph.D. dissertation presented to Visva
Bharati, September 1962.

Tang t'ien-hsia yü tang kuo-chia 黨天下與黨國家 (Party
world and party state), ed. I Ch'ung-kuang 易重光. 2 vols.;
Hong Kong, 1958.

T'ang Chih 唐摯. "Fan-suo kung-shih k'o-i chih-tao ch'uang-tso
ma?" 煩瑣公式可以指导創作嗎?(Can elaborate
formulas lead creative writing?); Wen-i pao, No. 10:1-2 (1957).

Tien Chien 田間. "Chieh-ch'uan Ting Ling ti wei-chuang" 揭穿
丁玲的偽裝 (Take off Ting Ling's camouflage); Wen-i pao,
No. 21:6 (1957).

"Ting Ch'en fan-tang chi-t'uan t'ou-shih" 丁陳反党集团透視
(Looking through the antiparty clique of Ting Ch'en); Wen-i pao,
No. 24:5-6 (1957).

Ting Ling 丁玲. "San-pa-chieh yu kan" 三八節有感 (Thoughts
on March 8); Chieh-fang jih-pao (Mar. 9, 1942), p. 4.

------ "Wen-i chieh tui Wang Shih-wei ying-yu ti t'ai-tu chi fan-hsing"
文藝界對王實味應有的態度及反省 (The attitude
and self-introspection that the literary circles should take
toward Wang Shih-wei); Chieh-fang jih-pao (June 16, 1942), p. 4.

------ "Shan-pei feng-kuang chiao-hou chi sho-kan" '陝北風光'
校後記所感 (Thoughts after proofreading Sketches of
Northern Shensi); Jen-min wen-hsüeh, 2.2:33-34 (1950).

------"K'ua-tao hsin-ti shih-tai lai" 跨到新的時代來
    (Leap into the new period) . Peking, 1951.

------"Tso-wei i-chung ch'ing-hsiang lai-k'an" 作為一種傾向
    來看 (To view it as a tendency); Wen-i pao, 4.8:7-10
    (Aug. 10, 1951).

------"Wei t'i-kao wo-men k'an-wu ti ssu-hsiang-hsing, chan-tou-hsing
    erh tou-cheng" 為提高我們刊物的思想性、戰鬥性而
    鬥爭 (Struggle for the elevation of consciousness and fighting
    spirit of our journals); Wen-i pao, 5.4:14-17 (Dec. 10, 1951).

------Sun Over the Sangkan River, in Chinese Literature, No. 1:26-312
    (1953).

------Tao ch'ün-chung chung ch'ü lo-hu 到羣衆中去落戶
    (Go into the dwellings of the masses). Peking, 1954.

------"Sheng-huo, ssu-hsiang yü jen-wu" 生活.思想與人物
    (Life, thought and characters); Jen-min wen-hsüeh, No. 3:120-128
    (1955).

"Ting Ling chieh-ch'i ti i-mien fan-tang hei-ch'i" 丁玲揭起的
    一面反党黑旗 (An antiparty black flag that Ting Ling has
    hoisted); Pei-ching wen-i, No. 2:7-8 (1958).

"Ting Ling, ni chiao-au hsieh shen-mo?" 丁玲,你驕傲些什么？
    (Ting Ling, what are you proud of?); Wen-i pao, No. 26:6-7
    (1957).

"Ting Ling t'ung-chih t'an shen-ju sheng-huo" 丁玲同志談深入
    生活 (Comrade Ting Ling talks about living deeply); Wen-i pao,
    No. 7:3 (1957).

TKTL: Chung-kuo hsien-tai wen-hsüeh shih ts'an k'ao tzu-liao 中国
    現代文学史參考資料 (Research materials on the history
    of modern Chinese literature), ed. Peking Shih-fan ta-hsueh Chung-
    wen hsi hsien-tai wen-hsüeh chiao-hsüeh kai-ke hsiao-tsu 北京师
    范大学中文系現代文学教学改革小組
    (Committee on Revision of the Teaching of Modern Literature,
    Department of Chinese Literature, Peking Normal University).
    2 vols.; Peking, 1960.

Tsang K'e-chia 臧克家. "Ko-jen ti kan-shou" 个人的感受
    (My individual impressions); Wen-i pao, No. 8:2-3 (1957).

Tso-chia t'an ch'uang-tso 作家談創作 (Writers talk on creative
    writing). Peking, 1955.

"Tui Wen-i pao ti p'i-p'ing" 對文藝報的批評 (Criticisms of
    Wen-i pao); Wen-i pao, No. 22:3-22 (1954).

Wales, Nym. My Yenan Notebooks. Printed for private distribution, 1961.

Wang Jo-wang 王若望. "I-pu wu-mieh tang, wu-mieh kung-jen chieh-chi ti fan-tung hsiao-shuo" 一部污衊党．污衊工人階級的反動小說(A reactionary novel which slanders the party and the working class); Wen-i hsüeh-hsi, No. 1:17-20 (1956).

Wang Meng 王蒙. "Tsu-chih-pu hsin-lai-te ch'ing-nien-jen" 組織部新來的青年人 (The young newcomer in the organization department); Jen-min wen hsüeh, No. 9:29-43 (Sept. 8, 1956).

Wang Ming t'ang 王明堂. "Hsü Chung-yü ti 'Lu Hsün yen-chiu'" 徐中玉的·魯迅研究 (Hsü Chung-yü's "A Study of Lu Hsün"); Wen-i yüeh-pao, No. 9:16-18 (1957).

Wang Shih-wei 王實味. "Yeh pai-ho-hua" 野百合花 (The wild lily), 2 Pts.; Chieh-fang jih-pao (Mar. 13, 1942), p. 4; ibid. (Mar. 23, 1942), p. 4.

Wang Shu-ming 王淑明. "Ts'ung Wen-hsüeh p'ing-lun pien-chi kung-tso chung chien-t'ao wo ti wen-i p'i-p'ing ssu-hsiang" 從'文學評論'編輯工作中檢討我的文藝批判思想 (An examination of my ideas of literary criticism from the editorial work on Literary Criticism); Wen-i pao, No. 1:17-20 (1952).

Wang Tzu-yeh, "Are There Any Merits on the Part of Double-Crossers?" Chung-kuo Ch'ing-nien, No. 14 (July 16, 1955); in ECMM, No. 4:4-5 (1955).

Wang Yao 王瑤. Chung-kuo hsin wen-hsüeh shih-kao 中國新文學史稿 (Draft history of China's new literature). 2 vols.; Shanghai, 1954.

Wen Chi-tse 溫濟澤. "Tou-cheng jih-chi" 鬥爭日記 (Diary of struggle), 2 Pts.; Chieh-fang jih-pao (June 28, 1942), p. 4; ibid. (June 29, 1942), p. 4.

Wen-hsüeh p'ing-lun 文學評論 (Literary criticism).

"Wen-hsüeh shang ti hsiu-cheng chu-i ssu-ch'ao ho ch'uang-tso ch'ing-hsiang" 文學上的修正主義思潮和創作傾向 (The revisionist stream of thought and tendency of writing in literature); Jen-min wen-hsüeh, No. 11:109-126 (1957).

"Wen-i chieh cheng-tsai chin-hsing i-ch'ang ta pien-lun" 文艺界正在进行一場大辯論 (A great debate is going on in art and literary circles); Wen-i pao, No. 20:1-3 (1957).

Wen-i hsüeh-hsi 文藝學習 (Literary study). Literary journal of the Communist Youth League.

Wen-i pao 文藝報 (Literary gazette).

Wen-i yüeh-pao 文藝月報 (Literary monthly). Shanghai.

Wen-ts'ui 文萃 (Articles digest). Hong Kong.

Whiting, Allen. "The New Chinese Communists," World Politics, Vol. 7, No. 4 (July 1955).

Wo ti ssu-hsiang shih tsen-yang chuan-pien kuo-lai ti 我的思想是怎樣轉變過來的 (How my ideas have changed). Peking, 1952.

Wu Ying 伍郢. "'Pai-chia cheng-ming' i-wai chung-chung" 百家爭鳴'以外种种 (In spite of the "Hundred Schools Contend"); Jen-min wen-hsüeh, No. 9:54-57 (1956).

Yang Chih-i 楊志一, "T'a-men che-yang tsai 'kuan-hsin' ch'ing-nien jen" 他們这样在'关心'青年人 (They are so "concerned" about youth); Wen-i pao, No. 23:5 (1957).

Yang Erh 楊耳. "Shih-t'an T'ao Hsing-chih hsien-sheng piao-yang 'Wu Hsün ching-shen' yu wu chi-chi tso-yung" 試談陶行知先生表揚'武訓精神'有無積極作用 (On whether there is anything positive in T'ao Hsing-chih's praise of "The Spirit of Wu Hsün"); Wen-i pao, 4.2:26-27 (May 10, 1951).

Yang I-fan. The Case of Hu Feng. Hong Kong, 1956.

Yang Yen-nan 楊燕南. Chung-kung tui Hu Feng ti tou-cheng 中共對胡風的鬥爭 (The struggle against Hu Feng by the Chinese Communists). Hong Kong, 1956.

Yao Hsüeh-yin 姚雪垠. "Ta-k'ai ch'uang-hu shuo liang-hua" 打开窗户说亮话 (Open the window and tell the truth); Wen-i pao, No. 7:10-12 (1957).

"Yao tso wu-ch'an chieh-chi ti hsin-sheng li-liang!" 要做无产阶级的新生力量 (We want to be the newborn force of the proletariat!); Meng-ya, No. 18:2-3 (1957).

Yeh Kao 葉高. "Che pu-shih wo-men ch'i-tai ti hui-ta" 这不是我們期待的回答 (This is not the reply we expected); Jen-min wen-hsüeh, No. 4:138-139 (1955).

Yen Feng 嚴鋒. "T'i-ch'ang ta-tan yen-chiu wen-t'i ti ching-shen" 提倡大胆研究問題的精神 (Advocate the spirit of studying problems boldly); Hsueh-hsi, No. 5:42 (1954).

Yen Hsüeh 晏學 and Chou P'ei-t'ung 周培桐. "Hsiao Chün ti Wu-yüeh ti k'uang-shan wei-shen-mo shih yu-tu ti?" 蕭軍 的'五月的礦山'為什么是有毒的(Why is Hsiao Chün's Coal Mines in May poisonous?); Wen-i pao, No. 24:43-47 (1955).

Yen Wen-ching 严文井 and Kung Mu 公木. "Hsiao Chün ssu-hsiang tsai p'i-p'an" 蕭軍思想再批判 (Recriticism of Hsiao Chün's thought); Wen-i pao, No. 7:36-41 (1958).

Yü Tzu 于子. "Ou-yang Shan teng jen ti li-tzu cheng-ming liao shen-mo?" 歐陽山等人的例子証明了什麼? (What does the example of Ou-yang Shan and others prove?); Wen-i pao, No. 4:10-12 (1952).

Yüan Shui-p'o 袁水拍. "Chih-wen Wen-i pao pien-che" 質問 '文藝報'編者 (Query of the editor of Wen-i pao); Wen-i pao, No. 20:3-4 (1954).

------"Ts'ung Hu Feng ti ch'uang-tso k'an t'a-ti li-lun ti p'o-ch'an" 從胡風的創作看他的理論的破產 (The bankruptcy of Hu Feng's theories as seen in his writings); in LWHC, III, 100-122.

------"Fan-tui Feng Hsüeh-feng ti wen-i lu-hsien" 反对馮雪峰 的文艺路綫 (Against Feng Hsüeh-feng's line of literature and art); Wen-i yüeh-pao, No. 10:8-11 (1957).

"Yung-hu wen-i chieh cheng-feng hsüeh-hsi" 擁護文藝界整 風學習 (Uphold rectification and study in literary and art circles); Wen-i pao, 5.4:18 (Dec. 10, 1951).

GLOSSARY

A Lung 阿瓏
Ai Szu-ch'i 艾思奇

Chang Chung-hsiao 張中曉
Chang Po-chün 張伯鈞
Ch'en Ch'i-hsia 陳企霞
Ch'en Ch'i-t'ung 陳其通
Ch'en Ming 陳明
Ch'en Tu-hsiu 陳獨秀
cheng-feng 整風
Ch'i-tien 起點
Ch'i-yüeh 七月
Chiang Feng 江豐
Ch'u An-p'ing 儲安平
Chuang Yung 莊湧
Chung-kuo ch'ing-nien 中國青年
Chü-pen 劇本
Ch'ü Ch'iu-pai 瞿秋白

Fang Jan 方然

Hou Chin-ching 侯金鏡
Hsi-wang 希望
Hsia Yen 夏衍
Hsiao Ch'ien 蕭乾
Hsin chien-she 新建設
Hu Ch'iu-yüan 胡秋原
Hu Shih 胡適
Huang Yao-mien 黃藥眠

Huang Yuan 黃源
Hung lou meng 紅樓夢

Jen-min jih-pao 人民日報

K'ang Cho 康濯
K'o-hsüeh t'ung-pao 科學通報
Ku-yü 穀雨
Kuang-ming jih-pao 光明日報
kung-tso che 工作者

Lin Hsi-ling 林希翎
Liu Hsüeh-wei 劉雪葦
Liu Pai-yü 劉白羽
Lu Ling 路翎
Lu Tien 蘆甸
Lü Ying 呂熒

Ni-t'u she 泥土社

Pa Chin 巴金
pai-hua 白話
Pai Lang 白朗
Pei-ching jih-pao 北京日報
P'eng Po-shan 彭柏山
Pien Chih-lin 卞之琳

Sheng-huo pao 生活報
Su Wen 蘇汶
Sun Yü 孫瑜

329

Ta-chung wen-i 大衆文藝   Wang Jen-shu 王任叔 [Pa Jen 巴人]

Ta kung pao 大公報   Wang Jung 王戎

T'ang Yin 唐因   Wang Meng 王蒙

T'ien Chien 田間   Wen-hua pao 文化報

T'ien Han 田漢   Wen-hui pao 文匯報

tsa wen 雜文   Wen-i chen-ti 文藝陣地

T'sao Yü 曹禺   Wen-i tsung-k'an 文藝叢刊

tso-chia 作家   Wu Hsün 武訓

T'ung-jen k'an wu 同人刊物   Wu Tsu-kuang 吳祖光

INDEX

Academy of Sciences, xvii; Institute of Literary Research, 171; Philosophy Institute, 198

ACFLAC, *see* All-China Federation of Literary and Art Circles

Aesthetics, 172–173

Agriculture: collectivization, 113–114, 158–159; cooperatives, 144; and expansion of free market, 159; and Great Leap Forward, 243

Ai Ch'ing, xi, 2, 9, 14, 37, 102; and cheng feng movement of *1942*, 21, 29–30, 57; "Understand and Respect Writers," 29; rebuked by Mao, 35–36; and Wang Shih-wei, 39; and thought reform, 44–45; party posts, 94; and literary cheng feng (*1951–1952*), 99; and attack on Hu Feng (*1955*), 148, 174; Chou Yang's criticism of (*1956*), 162, 174, 209; during Hundred Flowers campaign, 166, 174–176; and poetic techniques, 174; opposition to bureaucratic control, 175; "The Yellow Bird," 175–176; "The Dream of a Gardener," 175, 176; and antirightist movement of *1957*, 207, 220, 226, *1958*, 241; self-criticism, 220

Ai Szu-ch'i, xiv, 33, 48, 54, 89; and censure of Wang Shih-wei, 38; and *Chieh-fang jih-pao*, 43; criticism of Wu Hsün, 92

All-China Federation of Literary and Art Circles (ACFLAC), xvii, 90; and Ting Ling, 94, 96, 209, 223; and re-education of writers, 96; and collective leadership of *Wen-i pao*, 127; and Hu Feng, 117, 149–150; during Great Leap Forward, 246

Allegory, 175–176, 220, 276

A Lung, 134, 135, 146, 171

Anti-Americanism, *see* "Resist America" campaign

Antirightist movement (*1957–1958*), 223–229, 231–238, 274; and Hundred Flowers campaign, 203–204; and non-Communist intellectuals, 205–207; scapegoats, 207, 220–223; power struggle, 207–209, 212–213, 219; Ting Ling's counterattack,

213–216; and Feng Hsüeh-feng, 216–220; ideological charges, 224–227; political charges, 227–229; results, 229–231, 242; and young writers, 231–238; second phase (*1958*), 238–242; scope of, 240

Association of Literary Workers, 90, 94–95; and Ting Ling's literary standards, 101; renamed Chinese Writers Union, 112; and Feng Hsüeh-feng, 120

Balzac, Honoré de, 6, 53, 141

Belinsky, Vissarion Grigorievich, 6, 277

Buddhism, 7, 73

Bureaucracy, 18, 56, 88, 272–274, 276; literary cadres of, 109–111, 276 (*see also* Chinese Communist party, cadres); opposition of writers to control of (*1956*), 165–180; response to Hundred Flowers campaign, 180–187; popular discontent with (*1957*), 188, 197–198; Mao's discontent with (*1957*), 188–189, 198; Chou Yang's criticism of, 190–191; Ho Ch'i-fang's attack on (*1959*), 268–271

Byron, George Gordon, xi

Capitalism, 129

CC, *see* Chinese Communist party, Central Committee

CCP, *see* Chinese Communist party

CDL, *see* Chinese Democratic League

Central Committee, CCP, *see* Chinese Communist party, Central Committee

Central Institute of Fine Arts, 220

Central Literary Institute, 94, 96, 207–208, 212; becomes Literary Study Institute of the Writers' Union, 208

Central Research Institute, 31, 32; and Wang Shih-wei, 37–38, 42

Chang Chung-hsiao, 131–133, 145, 153; criticism of Hu Feng, 155–156

Chang Ju-hsin, 80, 82, 83

Chang Kuang-nien, 237; and Ho Ch'i-fang, 268, 271

Chang Po-chün, 189; criticism of party

(1957), 191; in antirightist drive of *1957*, 205, 228; self-criticism, 206

Chekov, Anton, 6

Ch'en Ch'i-hsia, 21, 94, 105, 125; Chou Yang's criticism *(1956)*, 162; denunciation of *(1955)*, 207–209, 212–214; self-criticism, 209, 215–216, 223

Ch'en Ch'i-tung, 181–182, 186, 187; denunciation of *(1957)*, 191

Ch'en Ho-ch'in, 115

Ch'en Ming, 216

Ch'en Po-ta, xv, 48, 54, 89, 283n54; and Wang Shih-wei, 37–38; and ideological orthodoxy among intellectuals, 90

Ch'en Tu-hsiu, 38, 281n1

Ch'en Yung, 167, 219; and literary standards, 171–172; and debate on aesthetics, 172; defends Feng Hsüeh-feng, 218; and antirightist movement of *1957*, 222–223, *1958*, 241; public confession, 223

Cheng feng movements, 18–22, 31–32, 35, 80–81, 83, 86, 196, 205, 230, 232; Ting Ling's criticism, 22–24; and Lo Feng, 24–25; and Wang Shih-wei, 25–27, 32, 38; and Hsiao Chün, 27–29, 46; and Ai Ch'ing, 29–30; and Ho Ch'i-fang, 30–32, 251; party's response to opposition of, 32–36, 41, 274–275; and cultural reorientation, 49; in Chungking, 54–66; and ideological conformity, 56; *1948* drive, 67–86; and university professors, 88, 91; as training ground for post-takeover officials, 89; literary of *1951–1952*, 93–100, 108, 173; internal of *1957*, 227. *See also* Thought reform

Chernyshevski, Nikolai Gavrilovich, xv, 6, 49, 277

Chiang Fu, 220

Chiang Kai-shek, 40, 75, 82, 154

Chieh-fang jih-pao (Liberation daily), xiv, 21, 24, 29, 43, 93, 94; and opposition to cheng feng movement *(1942)*, 32; criticism of Wang Shih-wei, 38

Chin Ts'an-jan, 282n26

Ch'in Ch'ao-yang, 2, 127, 167, 191, 193, 276; and Chou Yang, 168–169; "Village Vignettes," 168; and socialist realism, 169, 170, 176–185, 218; and *Jen-min wen-hsüeh*, 169, 176, 179, 185, 211, 236–237; "Realism – The Broad Road," 169, 184, 195, 218; repudiation of Mao's principles on literature, 169–170, 171; as leader of "angry young men," 170, 236–238; opposition to bureaucratic controls *(1956)*, 176–177; "On the Spirit

of Sharpness," 177; "The Lack of Time," 177; "Silence," 177–178; and Liu Pin-yen, 178–179; criticized by party, *1956*, 181, 184, *1957*, 236; "On 'Write the Truth,'" 185; self-criticism, 185, 237; "Reform," 236

Ch'in Mu, 115

Ch'i tien (Starting point), 133

Ch'i-yüeh (July), 15, 48, 281n12

China University, Peking, xv

Chinese Communist party (CCP), xi, xiii, xv, 129; Party Training School, xiv, xv; Propaganda Department, xv, xvi, 31, 37, 90, 94, 116, 117, 150, 201, 209, 216; Central Committee, xv, 78, 80, 124, 140, 143–145, 147–148, 159, 163–164, 169, 199, 210, 213; Politburo, xv, 209; cadres, 2, 21, 109–111, 113, 120, 125, 135, 159–160, 166, 173, 180–187, 241–242, 245; and writers, 2–17, early *1950's*, 104–105, 116–118, *1956*, 161–165, *1957*, 224; and socialist realism, 8, 10, 34, 49, 113, 138, 141, 161, 163, 165–167, 173, 233, 238; and national forms, 15–17; during Sino-Japanese War, 18, response to writers in Yenan cheng feng, 32–36; policy toward literature and scholarship, 34–35, 39, 44, 46, 48–49, 56–57, 137, 143–144; power struggles within, 37, 187; educational policies, 50, 88–89, 91; and non-Communist intellectuals *(1948)*, 67–68; in rectification campaign of *1948*, 81, 85–86; take-over, 87; policy toward intellectuals, *1949–1952*, 87–89, *1953–1954*, 106–113, *1956*, 159–160, *1957–1958*, 238–239, *1959*, 263, 268, 270; "Common Program," 87; Committee of Cultural and Educational Affairs, 90, 94; Department of Economic Affairs, 107; displacement of older intellectuals, 118–119; Creative Work Committee, 120–121; internal policy *(1955)*, 144; and Hu Feng movement *(1955)*, 149, 151–154, 156–157; Eighth Congress *(1956)*, 164, 181; Hundred Flowers movement, 158–161, 184, 187–190, 204; and bloc solidarity, 204, 215, 235; and Ting Ling's "crimes," 215–216; and antirightist movement of *1957*, 224–226, 230, *1958*, 238–242; and Great Leap Forward, 243–244, 251, 263; dilemma in policy for intellectuals, 275; impact of writers on, 276–277

Chinese Democratic League (CDL), 107, 172, 189; in Hundred Flowers move-

ment (*1957*), 191, 193; in antirightist
drive of *1957*, 205
Chinese Literary Workers, 12
Chinese Literature (party's English-lan-
guage journal), 104
Chinese People's Political Consultative
Conference (CPPCC), xvii; National
Committee conferences, 88; and re-education of intellectuals, 89
Chinese People's Republic (CPR), 87, 171;
and USSR, 73, 246; Ministry of Culture,
90, 94, 215; economic development, 106,
113, 149, 158, 203; Five-Year Plans, 106,
108, 114, 144, 151; Ministry of Education, 182. *See also* Chinese Communist
party; Sino-Soviet relations
Chinese Writers' Resistance movement,
48
Chinese Writers Union, 112, 118, 123,
139, 241; and Feng Hsüeh-feng, 121;
and collective leadership of *Wen-i pao*,
127; and Hu Feng, 140, 147, 148, 149–
150, 156; and Hundred Flowers policy,
162, 164, 173; Secretariat, 162; and Ai
Ch'ing, 174; and Chou Yang, 199–200;
pressure on Central Literary Institute,
208; and Ting Ling, 209, 212–216, 219,
223, 229; young writers' committee, 232;
and denunciation of Ch'in Ch'ao-yang,
237; literary goals in Great Leap Forward, 244; incorporation of amateurs
into, 244–245; and Ho Ch'i-fang, 271
Ch'ing I, 260
Chou Ch'i-ying, *see* Chou Yang
Chou En-lai, 22, 29, 136, 205; and attack
on Hu Feng (*1955*), 148, 161; approach
to intellectuals, *1956*, 159, 161, 165, 180,
181, *1959*, 263
Chou Wen, 30, 92, 283n54
Chou Yang, xv–xvi, 5, 9, 10, 11, 30, 34, 51,
57, 59, 63, 105, 114, 129, 130, 220, 273,
283n54; *1935* debate with Hu Feng,
11–14; disbands League of Left-wing
Writers, 12; "Opinions on Several
Problems in the Literary Movement,"
13; and national forms, 15, 17, 49–50,
108; and Wang Shih-wei, 48–50; and
1948 rectification campaign, 68–69, 80,
82; and ideological orthodoxy, 89–93,
96, 98; and Ting Ling, 95, 99, 207, 214–
216, 229; quoted on impact of ideological remolding of, 96; and literary cheng
feng (*1951–1952*), 99, 134, 136; self-criticism, 99; and literary profession, 112–
113, 250; and Yü P'ing-po controversy,

116–119, 124–126; and Chinese Writers
Union, 121; and denunciation of Feng
Hsüeh-feng, 124–127, 208; attacks on Hu
Feng, *1952*, 137, 139, 143, *1955*, 147–148,
1956, 162; and thought reform campaign
of *1955*, 144, 145, 155; and Hundred
Flowers movement policy, 162, 164, 165,
166, 190, 193; and Ch'in Ch'ao-yang,
168–169; target of writers' attacks
(*1957*), 199–201, 212–213; redefinition of
Hundred Flowers slogan, 204; and *1957*
nationwide campaign against writers,
223, 225–226, 239, 241–242; "The
Great Debate on the Literary Front,"
239; and Great Leap Forward in
Literature, 244, 246; "New Folk Songs
Blaze a New Road in Poetry," 246; and
revolutionary romanticism, 247; and Ho
Ch'i-fang, 264; downfall in Cultural
Revolution of *1966*, 276–278
Chow Ching-wen, 293n75
Chuang Yung, 155
Chu Kuang-ch'ien, 172; opposition to
party control (*1956*), 173–174; opposition
to mass poetry in GLF, 265–266
Chu Teh, 44
Ch'u An-p'ing, 192, 198; in antirightist
drive of *1957*, 205; self-criticism, 206
Ch'ü Ch'iu-pai, 10, 11, 34, 49; and national
forms controversy, 15
Chü-pen (Theater book), 126
Chungking, 51; cheng feng movement in,
54, 66, 67, 89, 135
Chung-kuo ch'ing-nien (China youth), 156,
164, 178, 185, 201, 232; criticism of
Liu Pin-yen, 237
"Colleagues Magazine," *see* *T'ung-jen
k'an-wu*
Collectivization, *see* Agriculture; Land re-
form
Comintern, xii, 10, 15; and United Front,
12
Commerce, socialization of, 144
Communes, 243, 245, 247; and party
policy modification, 263. *See also* Great
Leap Forward
Communism, 41, 55, 59; intellectuals'
utopian view of, 3, 8; Hu Feng's view,
140–141, 142
Communist bloc, 204, 215, 235
Communist Youth League, xiii, 182, 194;
Propaganda Department, 232
Confucianism, 1, 114; and social criticism,
7
Counterrevolution, 150–151, 153–154, 156,

159; and Ting Ling, 227–229; and young writers, 231. *See also* Antirightist movement

CPPCC, *see* Chinese People's Political Consultative Conference

CPSU, *see* Soviet Union, Communist party of

Creation Society, xvi, 246

Creativity, 1–2, 274; and party solidarity, 20; Ai Ch'ing's view of, 30, 44; view of Chungking writers, 51–52; Feng Hsüeh-feng on, 53; Hsiao Chün on, 77; Ting Ling's view, 101, 103–104; and Hu Feng, 131–132, 138–139, 143–144, 155; and attack on socialist realism (*1956*), 170–171; of the masses during GLF, 245; Ho Ch'i-fang's view, 249–250, 256–257, 267

Criticism, intellectual, 2, 272, 273; literature as vehicle for, 8; and cheng feng of *1942*, 19–21, 24, 25, 27, 33; Mao on, 36; and rectification drive of *1948*, 69; and Hu Feng's thought reform, 137; during Hundred Flowers campaign, 166, 190–191, 203; Mao's correct criteria for, 205; Ho Ch'i-fang's view, 270. *See also* Self-criticism

Cultural Revolution (*1966*), xv, xvi; and fate of Chou Yang, 276–278

Dante, 121

Debate, 160–161, 164–165, 166, 186; on aesthetics, 172–173

"Defend Yenan," 121–122

Democracy, 26–27, 40, 272

Democratic centralism, 40

Democratic Revolution, 162

Dialectical materialism, xiv, 107

Djilas, Milovan: *The New Class*, 25, 272

Dogmatism, 20, 70, 204; "subjective," 56; of party leaders, 58, 166; Shu Wu on, 58–59; "mechanical," 59, 63; and Feng Hsüeh-feng, 63; and Hu Feng, 142–143, 145; and Hundred Flowers campaign, 182; in Soviet literature, 218

Dostoevsky, Fedor, 6

Dreyfus, Alfred, 197

Dudinstev, Vladimir: *Not by Bread Alone*, 183

East China Cultural Department, 139

Egalitarianism, 25–26, 40, 272

Ehrenburg, Ilya, 100, 215

Emotionalism, 151

Engels, Friedrich, 53, 193

Factionalism, 4, 9–17, 273

Fang Jan, 149

Fan Wen-lan, 38, 283n54; and denunciation of Wang Shih-wei, 42; criticism of Wu Hsün, 92

Fast, Howard, 228, 263

Feng Hsüeh-feng, xi, xiii, 2, 9–13, 21, 102, 114–115, 145, 156, 172, 174, 276; withdrawal from party pressure, *1936*, 14–15, *1940*, 17, *1954*, 127; and national forms controversy, 15–16, 37, 62; on internationalization of culture, 16, 62; and role of subjective spirit, 51–54, 63–64, 225; in Chungking, 55, 61, 65; and Ting Ling, 62, 94; *K'ua ti jih-tzu* (Days of transition), 62; *Hsiang-feng yü shih-feng* (Spirit of country and city), 62; "On the Literary Movement of the Democratic Revolution," 62–64; and role of intellectual, 62, 72; and Hu Feng, 63–64, 217; attacks Mao's literary policy, 64–65; "Irrelevant Words," 64–65; ambivalence in Hu Feng campaign (*1945*), 65; party criticism of, 65; and Yenan cheng feng, 66; and *1948* rectification drive, 68; and literary cheng feng of *1951*, 96; and *Wen-i pao*, 105, 119, 122–128, 169; "Reminiscences of Lu Hsün," 120; power in party hierarchy, 120–121, 225; concern with literary standards, 121–122, 125, 217–218; party denunciation of, 122–128, 225; basis of campaign against, 126–127, 129; and Chou Yang, 162, 200; and antirightist movement of *1957–1958*, 207, 209, 216–220, 225–226, 228; "On the Tradition of Ah Q," 218; on Hungarian uprising, 228; concern with poetry, 252–253; in Cultural Revolution of *1966*, 277

Five-anti movement, 89

Five-year Plans, 106, 108, 114; Lu Ting-i on, 144; and Hu Feng movement, 151. *See also* Chinese People's Republic, economic development

Flaubert, Gustave, xiii

Folk culture, *see* National forms

Formulism, 162

Freud, Sigmund, 6

Fu Ying, 192

Gide, André: *Return From the USSR*, 131

GLF, *see* Great Leap Forward

Goethe, Johann Wolfgang, xvi

Gogol, Nikolai: *Tarus Bulba*, 47
Gorki, Maxim, xiii, 6, 72, 77
Great Leap Forward, 243; proletarian emphasis of, 243–244; theoretical framework of, 246; and Ho Ch'i-fang, 248–261; and party's prescription for poetry, 251, 261; modification of party policy, 263–266; critics of, 266–270
Guillain, Robert: *Six Hundred Million Chinese*, 157

Harbin, 67, 71, 79, 80, 85, 89; White Russians in, 74. *See also* Manchuria
Heine, Heinrich, xvi
Heterodoxy, 20; in Chungking, 61; and *1948* rectification campaign, 68; and *1955* thought reform campaign, 144, 147, 149
Hitler, Adolf, 131
Ho Chih, *see* Ch'in Ch'ao-yang
Ho Ch'i-fang, xii, 2, 60, 65, 137–138, 140, 141, 200, 248–261; and criticism of Yenan cheng feng movement, 21, 30–32; "How Many Times I Have Left My Everyday Life," 31, 255; thought reform, 47–48, 249; and Yü Ping-po controversy, 119; and criticism of Hu Feng, 121; *On Realism*, 134, 249; and Hu Feng campaign (*1955*), 144, 145, 225, 248; and denunciation of Ting Ling, 213; protests GLF policy in literature, 248, 254, 261–271; view of creativity, 249–253; *Hsi-yüan chi* (Hsi-yüan collection), 249; "On Writing and Reading Poetry," 250; and literary techniques and standards, 253–255, 266–268, 271, 273; "Reply," 255–259, 260–261; criticism, 258–266; attack on literary bureaucracy, 268–271
Hong Kong, 65; *1948* rectification campaign in, 67, 79, 133
Ho Tan-jen, *see* Feng Hsüeh-feng
Hou Chin-ching, 127
Ho Yu-hua, *see* Ch'in Ch'ao-yang
Hsia, T. A., 282n12
Hsia, Yen, 305n2
Hsiao Ch'ien, 241
Hsiao Chün, xii–xiii, 2, 9, 12, 14, 37, 42, 58, 88, 95, 98, 104, 152, 153, 198; *Village in August*, xii, 71, 73–74, 81–82, 221, 225; in Yenan cheng feng movement (*1942*), 21, 27–29, 57; and Lo Feng, 24; and role of intellectual, 28–29, 72; "On Love and Patience Among Comrades," 28; and Mao's literary theories, 35, 36, 46;

resistance to party demands, 45, 73, 83; thought reform, 45–46, 76–77; "The 'Bulba' Spirit in Literary and Art Circles," 46–47; and *Ch'i-yüeh*, 48; and *1948* rectification campaign, 67, 70, 78, 221; and *Wen-hua pao*, 71, 222; "Talk on Government and Education," 71, 77; and nationalism, 72–74; criticism of CCP policy, 73–78, 79; "Different Shades of Imperialim," 74; urges conciliation with KMT, 75, 82; belief in multiparty system, 75; "Talk on Clowns," 76; criticism of land reform drive, 76–77; as scapegoat (*1948*), 80–86; and antirightist movement of *1957*, 207, 220–222; *Mines in May*, 221
Hsiao Yeh-mu, 97–98, 104; "Between Husband and Wife," 97; opposition to party control, 173; on antirightist drive of *1957*, 229–230
Hsieh Tao, 131
Hsin chien-shen (New construction), 116
Hsin-hua jih-pao (New China news), Chungking, 45, 54, 57; publishes Mao's "Talks," 56; attacks Hu's journal (*Hsi-wang*), 59–60; Feng Hsüeh-feng's attack on Mao's literary policy in, 64–65
Hsin kuan-cha (New observer), 194
Hsi wang (Hope), 56–57, 59, 62, 68, 132; Hu Feng's "Placing Oneself in the Democratic Struggle," 57–58; suppressed by party, 60; and *1948* rectification drive, 68
Hsü Mou-yung, 13, 80, 198–199; "Random Notes from the Abode of a Noisy Cicada," 198, 274; party criticism of, *1958*, 263, *1959*, 270
Hsüeh-hsi (Study), xv, 183, 185; criticism of Wu Hsün, 92; criticism of cadres, *1953*, 110, *1956*, 159–160; on independent thinking, 160–161; criticism of intellectuals (*1957*), 189; replaced by *Hung Ch'i*, 243; criticism of Ho Ch'i-fang, 260
Huang Ch'iu-yün, 167; "We Must Not Close Our Eyes to the Hardships Among the People," 167, 169, 238; criticism of socialist realism, 167–168, 195, 217–218; urges traditional realistic literature, 168; on stifling of Hundred Flowers spirit, 183, 186; on sectarianism in literature, 199; criticizes Chou Yang, 200–201, 211; and antirightist drive (*1957*), 238; self-criticism, 238
Huang Yao-mien, 172, 202, 241

Huang Yüan, 12

Hua Shih, *see* Feng Hsüeh-feng

Hu Ch'iao-mu, 60, 68, 89, 93; and ideological orthodoxy among intellectuals, 90; and *Hung lou meng* controversy, 116–117

Hu Ch'iu-yüan, 10–11

Hu Feng, xiii, 2, 9, 10, 13, 21, 48, 72, 102, 104, 114–115, 121, 160, 161, 167, 171–172, 184, 196, 209, 260, 268, 273, 275, 276, 293n75; *1935* debate with Chou Yang, 11–14; and Chinese Literary Workers, 12–13; withdrawal from factional squabbles, 15; and Ch'i-yueh, 15, 48; and national forms controversy, 15–17, 37; "Questions on National Forms," 16; and subjective spirit, 51–54, 57, 64, 130, 134, 138; on Lu Hsün, 53; in Chungking, 55, 65; and cheng feng movement, 55–56, 61, 66; and *Hsi wang*, 56–57, 59–60; "Placing Oneself in the Democratic Struggle," 57–58; on his own defiance, 60–61; denunciation of, 64, 65, 206; and *1948* rectification campaign, 67, 68–70, 78–79, 80, 83, 84, 86; describes coercion used against him, 70; resistance to party's literary dictates, 129–139, 195, 268; *Ts'ung yüan-t'ou tao hung-liu* (From the source to the flood), 129; and party's political line, 129–130, 151, 153, 154; "Time Begun" (poem), 133–134; critical report to Central Committee (*1954*), 140–144, 163–164, 169, 213; negation of party's literary concepts (*1954*), 141–144, 153; and campaign of *1955*, 144–157, 169, 185, 205, 210, 217, 221, 225, 274; attacks literary hierarchy, 145–147, 163; charged with counterrevolution, 153–154; results of campaign against, 155–157, 158, 164; attempts to redress excesses of campaign against (*1956*), 163–164; attempts to vindicate (*1957*), 197; and antirightist drive of *1957*, 225–226, 228, 235; in Cultural Revolution of *1966*, 277

Humanitarianism, 6–8, 73, 141–142, 166, 202, 277

Hundred Flowers campaign, 2, 110, 113, 158–202, 205, 232, 237, 239, 260; general party policy, 158–161, 184, 187–190, 274; policy toward writers, 161–165, 190–191, 238; response of writers, 165–180, 191–202, 224; reaction of bureaucracy, 180–187; and reversal of policy (*1957–1958*), 203–204; in poetry, 267–270

Hungary, 187–188, 190, 203, 206; Petofi Club, 190, 228

Hung Ch'i (Red flag), xv, 246; becomes party's main theoretical journal, 244; criticism of Ho Ch'i-fang, 264

Hung lou meng (Ts'ao Hsüeh-ch'in) (The dream of the red chamber), 101–102, 115–119, 122–123, 196–197; party's early interpretation of, 117; Ho Ch'i-fang's interpretation, 248; interpretation during Cultural Revolution of *1966*, 277. *See also* Yü P'ing-po

Hu Sheng, 88; criticism of Wu Hsün, 92

Hu Shih, 14, 16, 114, 145; party criticism of, 33; denunciation of (early *1950*'s), 88; and Yü P'ing-po, 115, 118, 128; party's view of (*1954*), 118–119; and Hu Feng movement, 148, 155

Idealism, 6–7, 41

Ideology, xiv, 3, 4, 25, 33; remolding campaigns, xvi, 35, 47, 87–89, 95, 96, 107, 108, 110, 113–115, 160, 206, 240, 269, 275 (*see also* Thought reform); and revolutionary writers, 2–9, 13, 29, 35; and *tsa wen* (essays), 21; and cheng feng movements, 33, 56; Trotsky's view, 40; and Lu Hsün, 53–54; and Hsiao Chün, 83; and party's "Common Program," 87; study movements (*1953*), 107; and reinterpretation of Chinese classics, 115; and Feng Hsüeh-feng, 123, 125; and Hu Feng, 129, 138, 146, 151–154; in Hundred Flowers movement, 160, 193; in *1957* antirightist drive, 224–227, 231

Imperialism, 74, 83, 121, 129

Individualism, 63, 81, 102, 264

Industrialization, 1, 106, 158; role of intellectuals in, 67, 88, 113–114. *See also* Chinese People's Republic, economic development

Industry: socialization of, 144; light, 159; and Great Leap Forward, 243

Intellectuals, 272; and ideological remolding campaigns, 1, 33–34, 49; and oscillation of party pressure, 1–2; relations with party, 3, 22, 39, 62, 157, 273, 275; effect of Russian intellectuals on, 6, 273; as social critics, 7; Wang Shih-wei's view, 27, 41; and Hsiao Chün, 28–29, 71–72; Feng Hsüeh-feng's view, 62; disillusionment with KMT (*1940*'s), 67; and *1948* rectification campaign, 78, 85–86; party policy for, *1949–1952*, 87–89,

1953-1954, 106–113; and Common Program, 87; enhancement of prestige (*1953*), 109; displacement of older, 118, 119; and *1955* thought reform campaign, 144, 148–149, 156; effect of Hu Feng campaign upon, 157, 158; and Hundred Flowers campaign, 160, 181, 187, 189; impact of Hungarian uprising on, 187; non-Communist in *1957* antirightist drive, 205–207, 228; effect of antirightist campaign on, 240 242, 243; party's attempt to appease (*1959*), 263; downgrading of (*1959*), 270

Jen-min jih-pao (JMJP) (People's daily), xv, 92, 96, 134, 185; on artists' lack of enthusiasm (*1953*), 108; on role of intellectual, 109, 189; criticism of cadres, *1953*, 111, *1956*, 159, 180, *1957*, 190; criticizes "independent kingdoms within party," 124; "Thoroughly Study 'Talks at the Yenan Forum on Art and Literature'" (Shu Wu), 136–137; criticism of Hu Feng (*1955*), 148–150, 156; criticizes intellectuals' interpretation of *Hung lou meng*, 196; heralds antirightist drive (*1957*), 204; criticizes intellectuals (*1957*), 204; criticizes "rightist" writers, 227, 230; reorganized (*1958*), 241; criticism of Ho Ch'i-fang, 264

Jen-min wen-hsüeh, 94–95, 97, 139, 236–237, 255; and Ting Ling, 99, 105, 126, 208–209, 211; and Hu Feng, 140, 148; and Ch'in Ch'ao-yang, 169, 176, 179, 185; and Ai Ch'ing, 174; on value of debate, 186; on writers in GLF, 245; and amateurs in GLF, 246; criticism of Ho Ch'i-fang, 258

JMJP, *see Jen-min jih-pao*

K'ang Cho, 127, 227, 305n2
Kao Kang, 124
Khrushchev, Nikita, 167, 204; and Hungarian uprising, 188; and nonconforming writers, 215
KMJP, *see* Kuang-ming jih-pao
KMT, *see* Kuomintang
K'o-hsüeh t'ung-pao (The journal of sciences), 151
Korean War, 87
Kuang-ming jih-pao, 91, 99–100, 205; on Soviet model for intellectuals, 107; on value of "old teachers," 110; criticism of *Hung lou meng*, 116, 124; on role of intellectual (*1955*), 158; criticism of

cadres (*1956*), 181; on impact of Hungarian and Polish uprisings, 187; denunciation of party (*1957*), 192; on rightist intellectuals (*1958*), 240; on Great Leap Forward, 243
K'un Lun (film studio), 91, 92
Kung Mu, 262
Kuo Mo-jo, xvi–xvii, 61, 65–66, 94, 145; in *1948* rectification campaign, 68; and ACFLAC, 90; and criticism of Wu Hsün, 92; and Yü P'ing-po controversy, 117, 126, 128; and attack on Hu Feng (*1955*), 148, 149, 151; in antirightist drive, *1957*, 230, *1958*, 241; and GLF in literature, 246, 264
Kuomintang, xii, xiii, xiv, xv, 67, 70, 75; and revolutionary writers, 2–3, 10; and Hu Feng, 11, 14; Sino-Japanese War, 18; and cheng feng movement (Yenan), 21, 24; satirized by left-wing writers, 55; disillusionment with (*1948*), 67; and nationalism, 80–81; defeated, 87; and three-anti movement, 89; and conter-revolutionary charge against Hu Feng, 153–154. *See also* Chungking
Ku yü (Grain rain), 29, 282n26

Land reform, 68, 87; in Manchuria, 76, 79; and *Sun Over the Sangkan River* (Ting Ling), 94, 100, 225
Lan Ling, 117, 118, 123–125, 196, 197
Lao She, 121, 199; and attack on Hu Feng (*1955*), 148; and attack on Ting Ling, 216
League of Left-wing Writers, 9–11, 225, *1960*, 271; disbanded, 12. *See also* Chou Yang
Lei Hai-tsung, 193
Lenin, Nikolai, 19; concept of party discipline, 20; view of poetry production, 266
Liang Sou-ming, 114–115
Liberalism, 20, 88
Li Ho-lin, 263
Li Hsi-fan, 117, 118, 122–125, 135, 196, 218; and Wang Meng controversy, 183, 197; and antirightist drive of *1957*, 232; "We Should Have A Correct Attitude in the Treatment of Criticism," 269–270
Lin Hsi-ling, 197, 201, 237
Lin Mo-han, xvi, 137–138, 140, 141, 225, 305n2; and *1948* rectification drive, 68; and *1955* thought reform drive, 144, 145; and Hundred Flowers movement, 191; and denunciation of Ting Ling,

213; denunciation of Ch'in Ch'ao-yang, 237

Li Po, 253

Literary Heritage (supplement of KMJP), 117

Literary Study Institute of the Writers Union, *see* Central Literary Institute

Literature, 162; as vehicle for criticism, 8; representative character controversy, 11–14; national forms controversy, 15; Western influence on Chinese, 40, 278; Mao's view of function of, 36, 39, 47; and role of subjective spirit, 51–54; Ting Ling's view, 103; paucity of output (*1956*), 161; and Great Leap Forward, 244–247; and cultural standards of masses, 252; in Cultural Revolution of *1966*, 277. *See also* Writers (left-wing)

"Literature for National Defense," 12; and Ting Ling, 48

Literature, Philosophy, and History (Shantung University journal), 117, 123

Liu Chih-ming, 80–82; 200; on Hsiao Chün, 83, 85, 86, 221

Liu Hsüeh-wei, 139

Liu Pai-yü, 30; and denunciation of Ting Ling, 213; and denunciation of Ch'in Ch'ao-yang, 237

Liu Pin-yen, 180, 184, 185, 197, 201; "Our Paper's Inside News," 178, 237; and Ch'in Ch'ao-yang, 237; "Coolness," 237; denunciation of, 237

Liu Shao-ch'i, 19, 124; "On the Training of a Communist Party Member," 20; "On the Intra-Party Struggle," 20

Liu Shao-t'ang, 2, 200–201, 226, 238, 276; and Wang Meng controversy, 183–184; and Hundred Flowers movement, 194; "Clouds at Sundown in the Fields," 194; "The Grass of Hsi yüan," 194–195; "The Development of Realism in a Socialist Period," 195, 232, 234; criticizes Mao's literary doctrine, 195–196, 218; in antirightist movement (*1957–1958*), 231–236; self-criticism, 232; literary standards, 233; literary influences on, 233–234; denunciation of, 235; influence on youth, 236

Li Yuan, 281n12

Lo Feng, 21, 24–25, 46; "Still a Period of *Tsa wen*," 24; and antirightist campaign of *1957*, 220

Lo Lung-chi, 191; in antirightist drive of *1957*, 205, 228; self-criticism, 206

Long March, xi, 14

Lu Hsün, xi, xvi, 48, 53, 55, 61, 64, 79, 80, 103, 155, 165, 175, 200, 226, 266; *Village in August* (with Hsiao Chün), xii, 71, 73–74; and factionalism, 9–14; death, 14; and Yenan writers, 21, 24, 25, 28, 51; party's analysis of writing of, 36, 49; as embodiment of revolutionary writer, 72, 102, 170–171, 222; and Feng Hsüeh-feng, 120–121; *Ah Q*, 142; and Ch'en Yung, 171, 222

Lu Hsün Academy of Art, 29, 30, 38, 48; Western influence at, 47; Chou Yang's reforms, 50

Lukacs, Georgy, 52

Lü K'e-yü, *see* Feng Hsüeh-feng

Lu Li, 281n12

Lu Ling, 55, 64, 65, 121; party criticism of, 61; and *1948* rectification drive, 68; and Hu Feng campaign, 133, 135–137, 139, 148; "The Children of a Rich Man," 171

Lunarcharsky, Anatoli Vasilievich, 51–52

Lu Tien, 136; and Tientsin Writers Union, 139

Lu Ting-i, 90, 144, 156; and Hundred Flowers campaign, 160, 162, 164, 165; 180; and antirightist drive of *1957–1958*, 206, 216, 231, 240; reinterpretation of socialist realism, 210

Lü Ying, 135, 156

Lü Yuan, 133

Manchuria, 70–71, 76, 82–83, 87; and Russian presence, 73–74; *1948* party program in, 78–86

Mao Tse-tung, xv, 19, 37, 69; "The Position of the Chinese Communist Party in the National War," 15–16; cultural policies, 17, 48–49, 56, 65; "Talks on Art and Literature," 21, 34–36, 37, 38, 44, 46, 49, 51, 56, 64, 72, 93, 102–103, 130–131, 169, 194, 230, 239; and Ting Ling, 22, 37, 93, 262; and policy for intellectuals (*1950's*), 88, 129–131, 138; on realism and ideology, 141; and attack on Hu Feng, 149; and Hundred Flowers campaign, 160, 162, 180, 193, 203; "On Correcting Contradictions Among the People," 187–189, 205; interpretation of Hungarian uprising, 187–188, 228; concern with cadres, 188–190; and revolutionary romanticism, 247; and Cultural Revolution (*1966*), 277

Mao Tun, xvi, xvii, 61, 66, 94, 102, 174,

199; in *1948* rectification campaign, 68; and Ministry of Culture, 90; and literary cheng feng of *1951–1952*, 99; on professional standards (*1953*), 111–112; and Chinese Writers Union, 121; and attack on Hu Feng, 148; attacks literary hierarchy (*1956*), 163, 211; and rightists, 186; on "one-bookism," 210

Marx, Karl, 6, 52, 53, 75, 139, 193; "scholasticization" of, 146

Marxism-Leninism, *see* Ideology

Materialism, 57, 63. *See also* Dialectical materialism

Maupassant, Guy de, xiii

Mayakovsky, Vladimir, xi, 253

May Fourth movement, 7, 15, 16, 152; and poetry, 252, 266

May 30th strike (*1925*), xiii

Nankai University, 193

National Congresses of Writers and Artists: September *1953*, 101, 107; and Mao Tun, 111–112; cancellation, fall *1957*, 214, 216

National forms, 15–17, 34, 95; and Feng Hsüeh-feng, 15–16, 37, 62, 225; and Ho Ch'i-fang, 30, 251, 265; and Wang Shih-wei, 37; and Chou Yang, 49–50, 108; and Hu Feng, 142; in poetry, 251–252, 265, 267–268

Nationalism, 72–73, 75, 80–81, 82; and Soviet scholarship, 88

National People's Congress (NPC), 140, 206; and Ting Ling, 209, 223; and Feng Hsüeh-feng, 220

New China News Agency, 150

New Democracy, 79–80, 174

New Literary and Art Publishing House, Shanghai, 139

New York Times, 187

Ni-t'u she (Earth society), 133

North China's Associated Universities, 90

Northern Expedition, xv

Northeast Propaganda Bureau, 78

NPC, *see* National People's Congress

Objectivism, 57, 63

Orthodoxy, 1–2, 13, 276

Pa Chin, 12, 121, 199; and Hu Feng, 148; during Great Leap Forward, 244, 263

Pai-hua style, 15, 254 *See also* National forms

Pai Lang, 220, 263

Pa Jen, *see* Wang Jen-shu

Pasternak, Boris, 224

Payne, Robert, 45

Peiching jih-pao (Peking news), 175

Peiching wen-i (Peking literature), 230

Peking School (writers' group), 236

Peking Study Committee on Literature and Art, 99

Peking University, xii, 114, 192, 235; Literary Research Institute, 260

P'eng Po-shan, 139

People's China, 116

People's Liberation Army, 181

"People's Literature of the National Revolutionary Struggle," 12

People's Literature Publishing House, 217

People's University, 118, 131, 174, 197

Petofii Club, Hungary, *see* Hungary

Pien Chih-lin, 265

Pilgrimage to the West, 132

Plekhanov, Georgi, 9

Poetry, 276; during GLF, 245–247, 251, 261–267; and Ho Ch'i-fang's concern for, 248–249, 251–261, 266, 269, 273

Poland, 187, 203, 206

Pragmatism, 58, 63, 102, 118, 148, 152

Propaganda, 22, 276; and Ai Ch'ing, 29; Bureau, 139, 208, 213, 214, 215, 229; and Hu Feng, 156; through poetic meter, 251, 266; in Cultural Revolution (*1966*), 277. *See also* Chinese Communist party, propaganda department

Pu Hsi-hsiu, 212

Pushkin, Aleksander, xi, 6, 254; *Eugene Onegin*, 142

Realism, Western, 6, 8, 42–43, 49; and national forms controversy, 15–16; and Hu Feng, 141; and Huang Ch'iu-yün, 168. *See also* Socialist realism

Rectification campaigns, 18, 32, 56; of *1948*, xiii, 67–86, 167, 221; and Hu Feng's group, 68–70; and Hsiao Chün, 77–78; of *1951–1952*, 96; and cadres, 110, 181, 188; of *1954*, 113–115; as source of hierarchical mobility, 118; in Hundred Flowers movement, 189–191; of party critics (*1957*), 204–207. *See also* Cheng feng movements

Red Army, 35, 71

"Resist America" campaign, 87, 121

Revisionism, 182, 204, 224, 270; Soviet, 235

Revolutionary realism, *see* Socialist realism

Rightists, 205–207, 270; Ting Ling as symbol of, 227–231; and Liu Shao-t'ang, 231–236. *See also* Antirightist movement

Rodin, François, 60

Rolland, Romain, 6, 72, 238; *Jean Christophe*, 167

Romanticism, revolutionary, 246–247

Scholars, university, 88, 91–92, 106, 108–109, 148–149, 274; relaxation in policy for (*1956–1957*), 159–160, 192–193

Scientists, 33, 118, 151, 158, 275; during Hundred Flowers movement, 165

Second World War, 74

Sectarianism, 153, 156, 199, 220

Self-criticism, 19–20, 32; Mao on, 36, 88; and Ting Ling, 43, 102, 208, 209, 210, 216; Ho Ch'i-fang's, 47–48; in Chungking, 54; and Hu Feng, 55, 139, 149; and Hsiao Chün, 77, 84–85; and post-takeover re-education policy, 88–89, 91; during literary cheng feng (*1951–1952*), 98–99; and Feng Hsüeh-feng, 127, 219; Shu wu's, 136; Ai Ch'ing's, 174–175, 220; Ch'in Ch'ao-yang's, 185; in *1957* antirightist drive, 206–207, 209, 220; and Liu Shao-t'ang, 232; Huang Ch'iu-yün, 238; and "The Great Debate on the Literary Front" (Chou Yang), 239

Shakespeare, William, 53

Shanghai, 65, 277; University, xiii; and *1948* rectification campaign, 67, 79; and followers of Hu Feng, 139–140; terror in following Hu Feng campaign (*1955*), 157

Shantung, 7; University, 117, 135, 156; *Literature, Philosophy, and History* (University journal), 117, 123

Shao Ch'üan-lin, xvi, 89, 120, 126, 237, 250, 271, 304n57, 305n2; and *1948* rectification drive, 68, 70, 83; on rational consciousness, 69; and Chinese Writers Union, 121, 162; and thought reform campaign of *1955*, 144; on fear during Hundred Flowers campaign, 193; during antirightist drive of *1957*, 208, 212, 229; and denunciation of Ting Ling, 213, 239; on Ting Ling's influence on youth, 226; and denunciation of Ch'in Ch'ao-yang, 237; on amateur poets in GLF, 245, 264

Shelley, Percy Bysshe, xvi

Sheng Ch'üan-sheng, 258–259

Sheng-huo pao (Life gazette), 80, 82–84

Shensi-Kansu-Ninghsia Border Region,

xvi; Government Assembly, 28, 29, 93; and Chou Yang, 49–50

Shih k'an (Poetry), 29, 264, 265

Sholokhov, Mikhail A., 238; *Quiet Flows the Don*, 234, 235; *Virgin Soil*, 234

Shu Wu, 55, 57, 70; "On Subjectivism," 58–59, 61, 69, 133, 145; criticism of leadership's dogmatism, 59; criticized by party, 61; and *1948* rectification drive, 68; and Hu Feng, 133; self-criticism (*1952*), 136–137; suggests independent publishing houses (*1957*), 196

Sino-Japanese War, xi, xii, 11, 14, 18, 71

Sino-Soviet relations, 246, 270; alliance, 73; and bloc solidarity, 204; and aid programs, 204. *See also* Chinese People's Republic; Soviet Union

Socialist realism, 201, 247, 273; party interpretation, 8, 10, 34, 233, 238–239; and Chou Yang, 49, 113; and Hu Feng, 138, 141; and Chou En-lai, 161; during Hundred Flowers period, 163, 165, 176; writers' criticism of (*1956–1957*), 166–167, 173; Soviet writers' criticism of, 166; Huang Ch'iu-yün's definition of, 167–168; and Ch'in Ch'ao-yang, 169, 170, 185; and Ting Ling, 210; Soviet view, 234, 246; and revolutionary romanticism, 246; in Cultural Revolution, 277

Socialist revolution, 162

Songs of the Red Flag (Chou Yang), 246

Soviet Union, 75, 129, 274; purges of *1930*'s, 38, 40; nonconforming intellectuals in, 49, 273; alliance with CCP, 73; and Manchuria, 73–74, 82–83; as model for post-takeover thought reform, 88–89, 95, 107; Communist party of, 89; as economic model, 108; post-Stalin relaxation, 108; literary criticism in, *1954*, 122, *1956*, 166, 169; Writers Association, 148; as literary model, 163, 166; Twentieth Party Congress, 167, 206; parallel to Hundred Flowers, 183; and Hungarian uprising, 188; concern with bloc solidarity (*1957*), 204; aid to China, 204; literary debates (*1957*), 233–234; relations with China (*1958*), 246

Stalin, Josef, 3, 4, 19, 38; purge of Trotskyites, 40; death, 108, 166; denunciation of by Khrushchev, 167, 187, 228

Stalin prize, xiv, 94

Stein, Gunther, 43

"Story of Wu Hsün" (film), 90–91

Subjectivism, 51–54, 57, 63–64, 102; as issue of *1948* rectification campaign, 69, 70, 83; and thought reform of Hu Feng, 130, 134, 138, 151; as issue in *1957* antirightist drive, 225–226; as issue in Ho Ch'i-fang campaign, 264

Sun Yat-sen, 75; "The People's Livelihood," 58

Sun Yat-sen University, xv

Sun Yü, 91, 92, 98

Su Wen, 10–11

Ta-chung wen-i (Mass literature), 30

Ta-chung wen-i ts'ung-k'an (Digest of mass literature), 68

Ta Hsia, Great China University, Shanghai, xv

Ta-kung pao, 91

T'ang Chih (T'ang Ta-ch'eng), 201, 212, 219

T'ang Yin, 212–213, 219

Tagore, Sir Rabindranath, xvi

Taiwan, 154

Taoism, 7, 73

Thought reform, 3–5, 17, 50, 273; resistance of writers to, 20; and Ting Ling, 43–44, 95, 103; Ai Ch'ing's, 44–45; and Hsiao Chün, 45–46, 76, 77; and Hu Feng, 53, 55, 56, 69–70, 129, 130, 142, 143, 153; and Feng Hsüeh-feng, 53, 70; in *1948* drive, 67, 69, 70–71; in Manchuria, 79; post-takeover policy for intellectuals, 88–89; of scholars, 88, 134; and Wu Hsün campaign, 90–93; of *1954*, 114, 117–118; of *1951*, 134; campaign of *1955*, 144–151; in Hundred Flowers campaign, 166. *See also* Cheng feng movements; Rectification campaigns

Three-anti movement, 89, 206

T'ien Chien, 208, 225; and GLF in poetry, 264, 267

T'ien Han, 126, 305n2

Tientsin Writers Union, 139

Ting Ling, xiii–xiv, 2, 9, 14, 37, 174, 180, 273, 275, 276; *Sun Over the Sangkan River*, xiv, 93–94, 100, 104, 225, 227; and Yenan cheng feng movement, 21–26, 30, 57; and Mao Tse-tung, 22, 37, 93, 262; "In the Hospital," 22–23, 42, 101, 178; "Thoughts on March 8," 23, 93, 230; on Lu Hsün, 24; and Hsiao Chün, 28, 45, 84–86; and Mao's cultural policy, 34; and Wang Shih-wei, 39, 102; and thought reform, 42–44; and Ch'i-

yüeh, 48; and Feng Hsüeh-feng, 62, 120; and *1951–1952* literary cheng feng movement, 93–100, 135; authority in party, 94, 121, 126, 207–208; criticism of Hsiao Yeh-mu, 97–98, 173; contradictory views, 100–105; *K'ua-tao hsin ti shih-tai lai* (Leap into the new period), 101; speech commemorating Tenth Anniversary of Mao's "Talks," 102–103; and artistic professionalism, 111–112, 121, 210–211, 224; in thought reform drive of *1955*, 148; during Hundred Flowers campaign, 194, 211, 226; denunciation of (*1955*), 207–216; and "one-bookism," 210, 227; defiance of denunciation of, 213–215, 223; ideological charges against, 224-225; influence on young writers, 226–227, 229–231; as symbol of "rightist" writer, 227–229, 240; results of *1957* campaign against, 229–231; in Cultural Revolution, 277

Tolstoy, Leo N., xiii, 6, 53, 141–142, 277; *Anna Karenina*, xv; *War and Peace*, 254

Trotsky, Leon, xiv, 35; and Wang Shih-wei, 38, 39; Western view of literature, 40

Tsang K'e-chia, 199, 271; and GLF in poetry, 264–265

Tsao Yü, 12

Ts'ao Hsüeh-ch'in, 116

Tsa wen (satirical essays), 21–24, 28, 33, 196, 198, 230, 276; publication stopped (*1942*), 31; Mao's interpretation, 120; during Hundred Flowers campaign, 166, 177

Tsing-hua University, 197

Ts'ung Wei-hsi: "Write the Truth — The Living Core of Socialist Realism," 184

Tu Fu, 253

T'ung-jen k'an-wu (Colleagues Magazine), 219, 222

Turgenev, Ivan Sergeevich, 6

Union of Chinese Writers, *see* Chinese Writers Union

United Association of Chinese Writers, 12. *See also* Chou Yang

United Front, xiv, 40, 48, 81; cultural policy of, 12, 239; and Wang Shih-wei, 38

United States, 154. *See also* "Resist America" campaign

Versailles, Treaty of, 7

Wang Jen-shu (Pa Jen), 217, 270
Wang Jo-wang, 221–222
Wang Jung, 155
Wang Meng, 191, 197, 201; "A Newcomer in the Organization Department," 179–180, 185; debate on work of, 182–183, 185; defended by young writers, 183; Ch'in Ch'ao-yang's criticism of, 185
Wang Ming, 281n1
Wang Pei-chang, 116
Wang Shih-wei, xiv, 2, 29, 54–55, 61, 66–67, 71, 79, 83, 98, 102, 104, 146, 153, 180, 187, 220, 275; criticism of Yenan cheng feng movement, 21, 25–27; "The Wild Lily," 25, 27, 58, 196, 282n10; on youth, 26, 29; "Artists and Statesmen," 26–27, 167, 273, 282n26; and role of intellectual, 27, 41; attacks leadership cadres, 32, 59, 100; rebuked by Mao's policy for arts, 34–36; public censure, 37–42; "On National Forms of Literature," 37; withdrawal from party, 38; effect of denunciation of, 42–48, 49, 50, 57
Wang Yao, 133, 261; party attack on (1958), 262
Wen-hsüeh p'ing-lun (Literary criticism), 261–263, 265, 269; "On a Hundred Flowers Bloom in New Poetry," 262; party restrictions on, 270–271
Wen-hua pao (Cultural news), 71, 73–76, 80, 222, 228; party reaction to anti-Soviet articles in, 74; discontinuance of party support, 84
Wen-hui pao, 91, 212
Wen-i chen-ti (The literary base), 23, 30; attack on Hsi wang (Hu Feng's journal), 59–60
Wen-i hsüeh-hsi (Literary study); and Wang Meng controversy, 182–183
Wen-i pao (Literary gazette), xii, 95, 96; criticism of Wu Hsün, 92–93, 221; and Ting Ling, 94, 96, 99, 105, 135, 210, 212; and criticism of Hsiao Yeh-mu, 97–98; and censure of Feng Hsüeh-feng, 120, 121, 123–128, 169; reorganization (1954), 127; and Hu Feng, 133, 134, 137, 147–148; and Lü Ying, 135–136; "Internal Correspondence," 136, 146, 208; on paucity of literary criticism (1956), 161; urges writers to freer expression, 163; and Ch'en Yung, 171;

and Huang Yao-mien, 172; on value of debate, 186; on silence of writers (1957), 194; criticism of literary bureaucrats, 200; and antiparty charges against Ting Ling (1955), 208–209, 212–213, 217; during antirightist drives, 1957, 230, 1958, 239, 241; criticism of Ho Ch'i-fang, 258, 264; role in GLF, 271
Wen-i yüeh-pao (Literary and art monthly), 176; on writers' disregard for ideology, 224–225
Whitman, Walt, xi, xvi
Women, 23–24, 28; and Ting Ling's thought reform, 43, 93
Women's National Salvation Association, 22
World War II, see Second World War
Writers (left-wing), 2–17, 272–278; as party scapegoats, 4; ideological conflict with party, 5–9, 224; concept of literature, 6; factional conflict with party, 9–17; and Yenan cheng feng movement, 21–22; and 1948 rectification drive, 67–86; post-takeover re-education, 87–89; and rectification of 1951–1952, 97; and literary standards, 111, 172–173, 224; and Hundred Flowers movement, 161–165; response to Hundred Flowers policy, 165–180, 190–202; impact of Hungarian uprising on, 190; nationwide campaign against (1957), 223–229; reduction of fees and royalties (1958), 241; nonprofessional, 245–246; as alienated intellectuals, 272–273; articulation of intellectuals' problems by, 275–276; impact on regime, 276–277
Writers Publishing House, 115
Writers Union, see Chinese Writers Union
Wuhan University, 198
Wu Hsün: campaign against, 91–93, 104, 108, 135; and Ting Ling, 96
Wu Tsu-hsiang, 123–124
Wu Tsu-kuang, 220, 298n102
Wu Ying, 218

Yang Hsiang-k'uei, 193
Yao Hsüeh-yin, 193, 298n102
Yeh Kao, 258, 259
Yenan, xi, xiii–xvi, 14, 40, 48; University of, xvi, 48; during Sino-Japanese War, 18; cheng feng movement of 1942, 21, 23–26, 30–31, 38, 189; and Ai Ch'ing's thought reform, 44–45

Yevtushenko, Yvigny, 183, 235

Youth, 26, 28, 31; impact of Wang Shih-wei upon, 41; and dislodging of older intellectuals, 118; criticism during Hundred Flowers movement, 201–202, 203, 226; and Ting Ling, 226–227, 229–231; and antirightist movement of *1957–1958*, 231–238; and Liu Shao-t'ang, 236; and Ho Ch'i-fang, 270

Yüan Shui-p'o, xvi, 121, 134, 136–137, 267, 305n2; "An Inquiry of the Editors of *Wen-i pao*," 125; and thought re-form of *1955*, 144, 145; attack on Hu Feng, 147–148; on being antiparty, 219

Yugoslav Communist party, 25

Yü P'ing-po, 114, 115, 122, 135, 145, 156, 175, 218, 254; and interpretation of *Hung lou meng*, 115–117, 122–126, 128, 183, 196–197, 248; party goals in criticism of, 117–118, 129

Zhdanov, Andrei, 34, 95, 286n1; and revolutionary romanticism, 246

Zola, Émile, 6, 61

Merle Goldman was educated at Sarah Lawrence College and Harvard University. She is a member of the Harvard East Asian Research Center and is an Instructor of Chinese History at Northeastern University.

Atheneum Paperbacks

THE WORLDS OF NATURE AND MAN

5   OF MEN AND MOUNTAINS *by William O. Douglas*
18 THE SUDDEN VIEW *by Sybille Bedford*
22 SPRING IN WASHINGTON *by Louis J. Halle*
33 LOST CITY OF THE INCAS *by Hiram Bingham*
45 THE SEA SHORE *by C. M. Yonge*
61 THE NEW YORK TIMES GUIDE TO DINING OUT IN NEW YORK
    edited by Craig Claiborne
81 THE NEW YORK TIMES GUIDE TO HOME FURNISHING *edited by*
    Barbara Plumb and Elizabeth Sverbeyeff
82 BIRDS AND MEN *by Robert H. Welker*
95 THE FIRMAMENT OF TIME *by Loren Eiseley*

LITERATURE AND THE ARTS

1   ROME AND A VILLA *by Eleanor Clark*
8   THE MUSICAL EXPERIENCE OF COMPOSER, PERFORMER, LISTENER
     by Roger Sessions
11   THE GRANDMOTHERS *by Glenway Wescott*
12   i: SIX NONLECTURES *by e. e. cummings*
14   THE PRESENCE OF GRACE *by J. F. Powers*
18   THE SUDDEN VIEW *by Sybille Bedford*
25   THE ROBBER BRIDEGROOM *by Eudora Welty*
29   CONTEXTS OF CRITICISM *by Harry Levin*
36   GEORGE BERNARD SHAW *by Hesketh Pearson*
37   THE TERRITORY AHEAD *by Wright Morris*
39   THE LETTERS OF VINCENT VAN GOGH *edited by Mark Roskill*
42   THE GREEN MARE *by Marcel Aymé*
50   AMERICAN ARCHITECTURE AND OTHER WRITINGS *by Montgomery*
     Schuyler, edited by William H. Jordy and Ralph Coe;
     abridged by William H. Jordy
66   SELECTED POEMS INCLUDING THE WOMAN AT THE WASHINGTON ZOO
     by Randall Jarrell
76   THE SINGER OF TALES *by Albert B. Lord*
96   CONRAD THE NOVELIST *by Albert J. Guerard*
99   MARK TWAIN *by Henry Nash Smith*
102 EMILY DICKINSON *by Thomas H. Johnson*
112 THE LIFE OF THE DRAMA *by Eric Bentley*
114 SELECTED MARK TWAIN-HOWELLS LETTERS *edited by Frederick*
     Anderson, William Gibson, and Henry Nash Smith
122 REPORTING THE NEWS *edited by Louis M. Lyons*
131 WHAT IS THEATRE? (*incorporating* THE DRAMATIC EVENT)
     by Eric Bentley
135 THE HERO OF THE WAVERLY NOVELS *by Alexander Welsh*
143 POETS OF REALITY *by J. Hillis Miller*
158 LANGUAGE AND SILENCE *by George Steiner*
159 THE IMMEDIATE EXPERIENCE *by Robert Warshow*
165 MOVIES: A PSYCHOLOGICAL STUDY *by Martha Wolfenstein and*
     Nathan Leites
168 LITERARY DISSENT IN COMMUNIST CHINA *by Merle Goldman*

Atheneum Paperbacks

HISTORY

3   SIX MEDIEVAL MEN AND WOMEN *by H. S. Bennett*

10   TRAVEL AND DISCOVERY IN THE RENAISSANCE *by Boies Penrose*

30   GHANA IN TRANSITION *by David E. Apter*

58   TROTSKY'S DIARY IN EXILE—1935 *translated by Elena Zarudnaya*

63   THE SINO-SOVIET CONFLICT 1956–1961 *by Donald S. Zagoria*

83   KARAMZIN'S MEMOIR ON ANCIENT AND MODERN RUSSIA
      by Richard Pipes

97   THE EIGHTEENTH CENTURY CONFRONTS THE GODS *by Frank E. Manuel*

103   JACOBEAN PAGEANT *by G. P. V. Akrigg*

104   THE MAKING OF VICTORIAN ENGLAND *by G. Kitson Clark*

107   RUSSIA LEAVES THE WAR *by George F. Kennan*

108   THE DECISION TO INTERVENE *by George F. Kennan*

121   DRIVING FORCES IN HISTORY *by Halvdan Koht*

124   THE FORMATION OF THE SOVIET UNION *by Richard Pipes*

127   THE THREE LIVES OF CHARLES DE GAULLE *by David Schoenbrun*

128   AS FRANCE GOES *by David Schoenbrun*

141   SERGEI WITTE AND THE INDUSTRIALIZATION OF RUSSIA
      by Theodore Von Laue

152   A HISTORY OF THE WEIMAR REPUBLIC *by Erich Eyck,*
A&B *2 vols.*

161   QUANTIFICATION IN AMERICAN HISTORY *by Robert P. Swierenga*

HISTORY—ASIA

44   CHINA'S RESPONSE TO THE WEST *by Ssu-Yü Teng and John K. Fairbank*

63   THE SINO-SOVIET CONFLICT 1956–1961 *by Donald S. Zagoria*

70   THE CHINA TANGLE *by Herbert Feis*

87   A DOCUMENTARY HISTORY OF CHINESE COMMUNISM
      by Conrad Brandt, Benjamin Schwartz and John K. Fairbank

92   THE LAST STAND OF CHINESE CONSERVATISM *by Mary Clabaugh Wright*

93   THE TRAGEDY OF THE CHINESE REVOLUTION *by Harold R. Isaacs*

147   AFTER IMPERIALSM *by Akira Iriye*

153   CHINA'S EARLY INDUSTRIALIZATION *by Albert Feuerwerker*

154   LI TA-CHAO AND THE ORIGINS OF CHINESE MARXISM *by Maurice Meisner*

164   COMMUNISM AND CHINA: IDEOLOGY IN FLUX *by Benjamin I. Schwartz*

168   LITERARY DISSENT IN COMMUNIST CHINA *by Merle Goldman*

Atheneum Paperbacks

HISTORY—AMERICAN

2   POWER AND DIPLOMACY *by Dean Acheson*

6   ROGER WILLIAMS *by Perry Miller*

7   THE REPUBLICAN ROOSEVELT *by John Morton Blum*

17   MYTHS AND REALITIES *by Carl Bridenbaugh*

32   STRANGERS IN THE LAND *by John Higham*

40   THE UNITED STATES AND MEXICO *by Howard F. Cline*

43   HOLMES-LASKI LETTERS: THE CORRESPONDENCE OF JUSTICE OLIVER

A&B   WENDELL HOLMES AND HAROLD J. LASKI *1916—1935 edited by Mark De Wolfe Howe, abridged by Alger Hiss, 2 vols.*

51   TURMOIL AND TRADITION *by Elting E. Morison*

70   THE CHINA TANGLE *by Herbert Feis*

84   THE DIMENSIONS OF LIBERTY *by Oscar and Mary Handlin*

86   THE CORPORATION IN MODERN SOCIETY *edited by Edward S. Mason*

110   DRED SCOTT'S CASE *by Vincent C. Hopkins, S.J.*

111   THE DECLINE OF AMERICAN LIBERALISM *by Arthur A. Ekirch, Jr.*

113   HARVARD GUIDE TO AMERICAN HISTORY *edited by Oscar Handlin, Arthur Meier Schlesinger, Samuel Eliot Morison, Frederick Merk, Arthur Meier Schlesinger, Jr., Paul Herman Buck*

115   THE ROOTS OF AMERICAN LOYALTY *by Merle Curti*

116   THE POLITICS OF PREJUDICE *by Roger Daniels*

117   CENTURY OF STRUGGLE *by Eleanor Flexner*

118   BOSTON'S IMMIGRANTS *by Oscar Handlin*

123   THE AMERICAN APPROACH TO FOREIGN POLICY *by Dexter Perkins*

125   THE EIGHTEENTH-CENTURY COMMONWEALTHMAN *by Caroline Robbins*

126   THE AMERICAN AS REFORMER *by Arthur M. Schlesinger*

129   THE LEGEND OF HENRY FORD *by Keith Sward*

132   ASA GRAY *by A. Hunter Dupree*

134   THE COLONIAL MERCHANTS AND THE AMERICAN REVOLUTION— *1763—1776 by Arthur M. Schlesinger*

136   THE ROAD TO APPOMATTOX *by Bell Irvin Wiley*

137   FREE SPEECH IN THE UNITED STATES *by Zechariah Chafee, Jr.*

139   CONSERVATION AND THE GOSPEL OF EFFICIENCY *by Samuel P. Hays*

140   MASSACHUSETTS PEOPLE AND POLITICS, 1919—1933 *by J. Joseph Huthmacher*

142   THE PROFESSIONAL ALTRUIST *by Roy Lubove*

144   POVERTY AND PROGRESS *by Stephan Thernstrom*

145   STREETCAR SUBURBS *by Sam B. Warner*

149   THE COMMUNIST CONTROVERSY IN WASHINGTON *by Earl Latham*

150   THE DECLINE OF AGRARIAN DEMOCRACY *by Grant McConnell*

151   POLITICS AND POWER *by David J. Rothman*

160   UP AGAINST THE IVY WALL *by Jerry Avorn and members of the staff of the* Columbia Daily Spectator

161   QUANTIFICATION IN AMERICAN HISTORY *by Robert P. Swierenga*

162   PROHIBITION AND THE PROGRESSIVE MOVEMENT *by James H. Timberlake*

163   FARM POLICIES AND POLITICS IN THE TRUMAN YEARS *by Allen J. Matusow*

166   THE CATTLE TOWNS *by Robert R. Dykstra*

167   SENATOR ROBERT F. WAGNER AND THE RISE OF URBAN LIBERALISM *by J. Joseph Huthmacher*

169   POLICING THE CITY: BOSTON: 1822-1885 *by Roger Lane*

Atheneum Paperbacks

STUDIES IN AMERICAN NEGRO LIFE

NL1   THE NEGRO IN COLONIAL NEW ENGLAND *by Lorenzo Johnston Greene*

NL2   SEPARATE AND UNEQUAL *by Louis R. Harlan*

NL3   AFTER FREEDOM *by Hortense Powdermaker*

NL4   FREDERICK DOUGLASS *by Benjamin Quarles*

NL5   PREFACE TO PEASANTRY *by Arthur F. Raper*

NL6   W. E. B. DU BOIS: PROPAGANDIST OF THE NEGRO PROTEST
     by Elliott Rudwick

NL7   THE BLACK WORKER *by Sterling D. Spero and Abram L. Harris*

NL8   THE MAKING OF BLACK AMERICA *edited*
A&B   *by August Meier and Elliott Rudwick, 2 vols.*

NL9   BLACK MANHATTAN *by James Weldon Johnson*

NL10 THE NEW NEGRO *edited by Alain Locke*

NL11 THE NEGRO'S GOD AS REFLECTED IN HIS LITERATURE
     by Benjamin Mays

NL12 NEGRO POETRY AND DRAMA AND THE NEGRO IN AMERICAN FICTION
     by Sterling Brown

NL13 WHEN NEGROES MARCH *by Harbert Garfinkel*

NL14 PHILOSOPHY AND OPINIONS OF MARCUS GARVEY *by Marcus Garvey,*
     edited by Amy Jacques-Garvey

NL15 FREE NEGRO LABOR AND PROPERTY HOLDING IN VIRGINIA, 1830–1860
     by Luther Porter Jackson

NL16 SEA ISLAND TO CITY *by Clyde Vernon Kiser*

NL17 NEGRO EDUCATION IN ALABAMA *by Horace Mann Bond*

NL18 POLITICS, PRINCIPLE AND PREJUDICE, 1865–1866
     by LaWanda and John H. Cox

NL19 NEGRO POLITICAL LEADERSHIP IN THE SOUTH *by Everett Carll Ladd, Jr.*

NL20 BLACK RECONSTRUCTION IN AMERICA, 1860–1880 *by W. E. B. Du Bois*

NL21 NEGROES IN CITIES *by Karl E. and Alma F. Taeuber*

NL22 TWO JAMAICAS *by Philip De Armond Curtin*

NL23 VASSOURASS: A BRAZILIAN COFFEE COUNTY, 1850–1900 *by Stanley J. Stein*

NL24 THE ROYAL AFRICAN COMPANY *by K. G. Davies*

NL25 STRANGE ENTHUSIASM: A LIFE OF THOMAS WENTWORTH HIGGINSON
     by Tilden G. Edelstein

NL26 THE *Guardian* OF BOSTON: WILLIAM MONROE TROTTER
     by Stephen R. Fox

NL27 LEWIS TAPPAN AND THE EVANGELICAL WAR AGAINST SLAVERY
     by Bertram Wyatt-Brown

NL28 THE NEGRO IN BRAZILIAN SOCIETY *by Florestan Fernandes*

Atheneum Paperbacks

LAW AND GOVERNMENT

20 DOCUMENTS ON FUNDAMENTAL HUMAN RIGHTS *edited by Zechariah*
A&B *Chafee, Jr., 2 vols.*
23 THE CONSTITUTION AND WHAT IT MEANS TODAY *by Edward S. Corwin*
27 COURTS ON TRIAL *by Jerome Frank*
30 GHANA IN TRANSITION *by David E. Apter*
46 THE FUTURE OF FEDERALISM *by Nelson A. Rockefeller*
53 THE BILL OF RIGHTS *by Learned Hand*
72 MR. JUSTICE HOLMES AND THE SUPREME COURT *by Felix Frankfurter*
84 THE DIMENSIONS OF LIBERTY *by Oscar and Mary Handlin*
89 MAKERS OF MODERN STRATEGY *edited by Edward M. Earle*
105 DILEMMAS OF URBAN AMERICA *by Robert C. Weaver*
110 DRED SCOTT'S CASE *by Vincent C. Hopkins, S.J.*
130 THE REVOLUTION OF THE SAINTS *by Michael Walzer*
138 OF LAW AND LIFE AND OTHER THINGS THAT MATTER *by Felix
    Frankfurter, edited by Philip B. Kurland*
148 POLITICAL CHANGE IN A WEST AFRICAN STATE *by Martin Kilson*
149 THE COMMUNIST CONTROVERSY IN WASHINGTON *by Earl Latham*
150 THE DECLINE OF AGRARIAN DEMOCRACY *by Grant McConnell*
156 VARIETIES OF POLICE BEHAVIOR *by James Q. Wilson*
157 AFRICA: FROM INDEPENDENCE TO TOMORROW *by David Hapgood*
160 UP AGAINST THE IVY WALL *by Jerry Avorn and members of the staff of
    the* Columbia Daily Spectator

DIPLOMACY AND INTERNATIONAL RELATIONS

2 POWER AND DIPLOMACY *by Dean Acheson*
4 THE ROAD TO PEARL HARBOR *by Herbert Feis*
15 CALL TO GREATNESS *by Adlai E. Stevenson*
34 THE DIPLOMACY OF ECONOMIC DEVELOPMENT *by Eugene B. Black*
40 THE UNITED STATES AND MEXICO *by Howard F. Cline*
41 THE DIPLOMATS 1919–1939 *by Gordon A. Craig and*
A&B *Felix Gilbert*
44 CHINA'S RESPONSE TO THE WEST *by Ssu-Yü Teng and John K. Fairbank*
54 STRATEGIC SURRENDER *by Paul Kecskemeti*
63 THE SINO-SOVIET CONFLICT 1956–1961 *by Donald S. Zagoria*
70 THE CHINA TANGLE *by Herbert Feis*
74 STALIN'S FOREIGN POLICY REAPPRAISED *by Marshall Shulman*
89 MAKERS OF MODERN STRATEGY *edited by Edward M. Earle*
107 RUSSIA LEAVES THE WAR *by George F. Kennan*
108 THE DECISION TO INTERVENE *by George F. Kennan*